Creativity & Innovation

Theory, Research, and Practice

Creativity

& Innovation

Theory, Research, and Practice

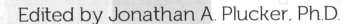

Edited by Jonathan A. Plucker, Ph.D.

PRUFROCK PRESS INC.
WACO, TEXAS

Prufrock Press Inc.
P.O. Box 8813
Waco, TX 76714-8813
Phone: (800) 998-2208
Fax: (800) 240-0333
http://www.prufrock.com

Table of Contents

Dedication

To my parents, who encouraged us to work hard
and be creative in everything we did.

Foreword

David Neustadter

In 2003, I was struggling with my "quarter-life crisis." This was right around the time they decided to hand a clever moniker to what had up until then just been known as "being clueless like everyone else when you graduate college." I was quickly losing interest in a graduate program that didn't feel like the right fit to me. I had made the ill-thought-out decision to obtain my master's at the same school I received my undergraduate degree, which only heightened my unease with the constant feeling that I was a glorified super senior whose friends had all gone off to have jobs and families while I was still getting excited about half-priced wing Wednesdays and nickel beer night. I had always been a massive movie nerd and desperately wanted to find a way to work in movies. After my first semester, my level of unhappiness began to motivate my courage to take some not-so-calculated risks. Chiefly, dropping out of a master's program and moving to Los Angeles to work in movies doing . . . movie things, I guess.

I hadn't yet told anyone about this genius plan. Not even my family or my girlfriend. But I had taken this fascinating class on creativity my senior year and the professor was always supportive of me during all of my weird "creative" presentations (I delivered my final paper orally, dressed up like a superhero, tights and all). So for some strange reason, he felt like the one guy who just might understand a rash, somewhat vague, and not all that well-thought-out life change.

We met at a deli that was synonymous with those German-beer-garden-sized steins, and I proceeded to down two-thirds of one to build up my confidence to finally come clean to someone about this crazy idea I had brewing. But instead of "talking some sense" into me as I thought he might, Dr. Jonathan Plucker listened to this incredibly rough draft of my genius future intentions, looked at me across the table, took a sip from his own liter mug of flat keg ale, and said the following: "Dave, you're 23 years old. If you go out there and it doesn't work, you'll come back and figure out something else. But that's what you're supposed to do when you're 23. And it sounds awesome by the way."

Here was an incredibly well-respected professor telling me to quit school, a master's program within his same department at that. To pursue a crazy dream that lacked any specifics. But his unexpected (yet very welcome) enthusiasm was exactly what I needed. I dropped out the next day, packed all my belongings into a very trusty Toyota Camry and drove out to California about 3 months later. And I have lived in L.A. ever since.

What does any of this have to do with creativity? For me, just about everything. Fear is the chief prohibitor of creativity. (That's not a researched statement incidentally, and I have absolutely no proof to back it up. But it sounds very elegant, so if you believe it, awesome.) There's that kid in middle school who never wants to share his short story, but when the teacher finally forces her to do so it's a revelation, the best one in class. Or the guy who waits 25 years to sing in front of an audience and it turns out he has the voice of an angel. And in my case, the kid who was terrified to work in the movie industry because he didn't know one person who did and had zero idea how the movie industry worked. But once I got past my biggest fears of moving out and being squashed by film school geniuses or the grandchildren of Hollywood moguls, I was able to enter into a field that excited me more than any other, and my mind was able to think freely and more creatively than ever before.

I always loved that in *Dead Poets Society*, John Keating (played by Robin Williams) is not trying to turn all of his students into English teachers or authors like himself, he's just motivating all of them to "make your lives extraordinary." Doctor, lawyer, bricklayer, or barista, doesn't matter the profession. As long as it's something that continuously motivates you personally to think in new and unique ways. And that's what I learned about creativity from the class I took with Dr. Plucker and the friendship I am very fortunate to still have with him today. Although necessity may be the mother of all invention, passion and enthusiasm could very well be the doting parents to creativity.

Is everyone creative or capable of being creative? That was the big question in the creativity course I took with Dr. Plucker years ago. And although many people in the class claimed to not be creative (hence why they were taking the class), my opinion has never wavered. Everyone is creative and has the capability of being creative, they just have to guide themselves into the profession or subject where their brain is hungry and excited to learn and create. I was sleep-walking through my graduate classes, but as soon as I got in the car to drive west, I began writing stories and coming up with ideas for future screenplays.

I've lived in L.A. for 13 years now and I've probably told the Dr. Plucker/beer mug story to about 250 young professionals or college students debating the move to Los Angeles. His lessons on creativity and his enthusiasm and knowledge of the subject challenged and motivated me to find the medium that would satiate my creative appetite. No one on the planet understands the subject matter better, so congrats on choosing the right creativity book to read. The topics are impressively comprehensive in their exploration of the many facets of creativity and innovation, and you'll be reading the work of the world's top scholars in each chapter.

And Dr. Plucker, thanks again for the beer and the life-changing advice. The next round is on me.

David Neustadter
Senior Vice President, Production
New Line Cinemas

Creativity

It's Not Just for Hippies Anymore

Jonathan A. Plucker

When I started graduate school, I thought my classmates' passion for creativity was bizarre. In fact, "passion" doesn't begin to describe how much they loved talking about creativity—it came up almost every day and several times a day at that. I'd sit in class or at my desk and listen to creativity this, creativity that, creativity everything all the time! It drove me to distraction, in part because the word *creativity* immediately made me visualize hippies running barefoot through a field of daisies, probably rubbing crystals on their foreheads and singing "Age of Aquarius" (rather like the last scene of *The 40-Year Old Virgin*, now that I think about it, but with the hippies being hairier and a little rougher around the edges).

Then a funny thing happened: After about a year of listening to these conversations and reading some of the research on creativity, it didn't seem so wacky. The conversations about creativity started to make sense, leading me to reflect on my own creativity and problem solving. Then I read a little more and, gasp!, jumped into a few of the creativity conversations. Once I made that commitment, it became clear that much of what I had dismissed as endless blathering about creativity was, more often than not, *debate* about creativity: Is this thing creative? How should someone solve this particular problem? How would you evaluate the creativity of a particular product in this context? And perhaps most importantly, how can we teach this aspect of creativity to students? Over the past 25 years, these and similar questions have guided my work in the study of creativity.

However, I was hardly alone in my initial negative reactions to creativity. I still frequently encounter people who won't utter the word *creativity* for a million dollars, but who will throw themselves enthusiastically into a conversation about innovation or entrepreneurialism. Creativity is surrounded with such deep and all-encompassing myths that it is hard to break through the stereotypes and discover all we know about this fascinating construct.

But over the past quarter century, our understanding of creativity has advanced significantly—we know more about what it is (and isn't), we better understand how to foster it, and we have deeper, more complex knowledge about how it relates to intelligence, leadership, personality, and other constructs.

And that's where this book comes in, as it is meant to be an introduction to the science of creativity. There are many comprehensive volumes on this research (see Kaufman & Sternberg, 2010; Runco & Pritzker, 2011), but this book is designed to focus on topics that are important to anyone who wants to help increase creativity in themselves or others.

Organization of the Book

In putting this book together, I reflected on what tends to interest people about creativity and innovation. The foundation of the book is formed by 14 chapters on major topics, ranging from definitions and theories to fostering creativity to the role of technology. You will also find seven Hot Topics covering important issues and debates within the field of creativity that don't require full chapters in an introduction to the field. This is admittedly a unique structure . . . hey, if you can't experiment in a creativity book, when can you?

In inviting authors, I conducted a thought exercise: If I had a question about the research on creativity and personality, for example, who would I ask? That was an easy one, because it's a no-brainer that I'd ask Greg Feist. What about leadership and creativity? Definitely Roni Reiter-Palmon. Developmental trends? Dean Simonton, of course. I went through the topic list in this way, then invited the authors, all of whom graciously accepted. So when you read the Hot Topic on creativity and mental illness by James Kaufman, or the chapter on creativity and play by Sandra Russ, or the chapter on creative products by David Cropley, rest assured that you are reading cutting-edge material by the world's experts on that particular topic.

Enjoy the book, and please contact me with feedback, positive or otherwise! This book has basically been 20 years in the making, and I appreciate the support of our colleagues at Prufrock Press, especially Joel McIntosh for making the book happen and Lacy Compton for her amazing work as the book's managing editor, and the contributions of the many authors, who in addition to being top scholars and educators are wonderful people.

References

Kaufman, J. C., & Sternberg, R. J. (Eds.). (2010). *The Cambridge handbook of creativity*. New York, NY: Cambridge University Press.

Runco, M. A., & Pritzker, S. R. (Eds.). (2011). *Encyclopedia of creativity*. San Diego, CA: Academic Press/Elsevier.

CHAPTER 1

Defining Creativity

Gayle T. Dow

Key Take-Aways

- It is a common misconception to believe creativity is notoriously difficult to define. In truth, many researchers, over several hundreds of years, have given extensive thought to the key components of a creative idea or product.
- Historically, these components include:
  1. **Novelty:** The idea or product must be original, rare, or statistically infrequent.
  2. **Usefulness or appropriateness:** The idea or product must have value to either meet a need or be the solution to a problem.
  3. **Social context or environment:** The novelty and usefulness of the idea or product is established by the surrounding social context. Therefore, the degree of creativity is dictated by the environment.

- This leads to a consensus that creativity is defined as a product or idea that is ***novel*** *(or original, unique, or unusual) and* ***useful*** *(or has value, or fits, or is appropriate), within a specific* ***social context.***

> We are living in a time
> When the plural is killing the singular
> Nothing has real value
> When everything comes in thousands
> —Jean Cocteau

Defining Creativity

What is creativity? Everyone implicitly *knows* what creativity is and most people can provide an example of a creative idea or invention. Nearly everyone also recognizes that creativity is a worthwhile attribute to be welcomed, encouraged, and respected. In fact, the promotion of creativity and the term *creative* is found in many diverse contexts from classrooms to advertisements to the backs of cereal boxes and even on restaurant menus. Creativity, it seems, falls into every possible domain, which may explain why philosophers and psychologists have devoted much of their time to the theoretical and empirical study of creativity.

Beginning several hundreds of years ago, early Greek philosophers including Socrates, Plato, and Aristotle viewed creativity as a *period of spiritual enlightenment that led to intellectual pursuit resulting in inspired poetry, art, and music* (Sternberg & Lubart, 1999). While Socrates and Plato favored the idea that the muses were the inspiration behind the creative product, Aristotle opted for a pragmatic approach that believed creators engaged in goal-directed methods when engaged in writing or musical composition (Paul & Kaufman, 2014).

The viewpoint that creativity is primarily associated with the fields of art and music still remains strong today, and as a result, we often witness this within the educational curriculum. The development of creative skills is typically viewed as the responsibility of the classroom teachers but restricted to the limited topics of creative writing, art, and music (Belden, Russonello, & Stewart, 2005). This perspective was recently witnessed in the proceeding from a conference on education focused on promoting creativity in school.

> The creative skills children develop through the arts carry them toward new ideas, new experiences and new challenges, as well as offering personal satisfaction . . . Schools and society must develop our children to become happy, well-adjusted citizens, rather than pupils who can just pass a test and get through school. We must ensure that our children can think creatively, skillfully, and "outside the box." (Nunan & Craith, 2009, p. 3)

And although it is certainly true that creativity can be developed within the art curriculum, it is vital to understand how that development occurs (Runco, 1996). Furthermore, it is important to understand how creativity impacts and is impacted by a much larger scope of disciplines. But to truly understand the development of creativity, what impacts creativity, and how to promote creativity, we must first start at the beginning and determine an explicit, conceptual definition of creativity. So in this chapter we begin with the basic question, "What is creativity?"

Attention to the methodological inquiry into the study of creativity most notably started with Gestalt psychologists Kohler (1925) and Wallas (1926) as they focused on creative problem solving. Empirical work then continued to midcentury psychometric approaches spearheaded by Guilford (1950) and Torrance (1974). Afterward, it expanded to theoretical models generated by Gardner (1985), Runco (1985), Amabile (1996), and Sternberg (1999). Today, we find contemporary views that define creativity in the work of Plucker, Beghetto, and Dow (2004), Beghetto and Kaufman (2007), and Simonton (2012).

Wolfgang Kohler (1925) assessed creative problem-solving strategies in primates during World War I. After observing apes' problem-solving strategies to reach bananas suspended above their heads in a cage, Kohler noted that after regular approaches to reach the bananas had failed, one by one the apes would often lapse into a period of inactivity (including sitting on an empty crate), which was then followed by a sudden rush to rearrange crates to stand upon. He noted the consistent sudden rush to solve the problem and concluded that creative thinking was defined as *the reorganization of elements resulting in a shift of perspective to form new associations or reach a novel solution to new problems.* This shift in perception is followed by a sudden flash of insight or knowledge of the correct solution (Dow & Mayer, 2004; Kohler, 1929).

As a result of this definition of creativity, insight problems, such as the nine-dot problem, seen in Figure 1.1, were often employed as a creativity assessment. In this, and other insight problems, the solution requires a shift in perspective that the dots are not final end points and the solver must pass through several dots on the periphery[1]. It is this sudden shift in perspective that characterizes insight problems from typical routine problems (Davidson, 1995; Metcalf, 1986; Sternberg, 1999).

Elaborating on the period of intense thinking and originality speculated by Kohler, Graham Wallas (1926) developed a Four-Stage Model to define creativity that included: preparation, incubation, illumination, and verification. During preparation, Wallas adopted an approach similar to Aristotle, suggesting we apply goal-directed methods to the creative task, such as determining

---

1   See solution on final page of this chapter.

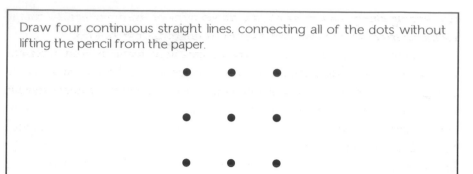

Draw four continuous straight lines, connecting all of the dots without lifting the pencil from the paper.

Figure 1.1. Nine-dot problem.

the goals, defining the problem, and establishing a criterion for verifying the solution's acceptability. During Stage 2, incubation, direct conscious efforts to solve the problem should be abandoned in favor of contemplation at an unconscious level. During this stage, creative problem solving still continues but occurs below conscious awareness. During Stage 3, illumination, the sudden realization of the solution results from the unconscious mind's successful problem solving. Unlike the other stages, illumination is often very brief, involving a tremendous rush of insight within a few seconds. In the final stage of verification, the conscious mind evaluates and refines ideas and solutions that have emerged during the stage of illumination and these ideas are assessed by the criteria defined in the preparation stage. From Wallas's view, creativity would be defined as *the process of thinking through preparation, incubation, illumination, and verification that results in creative insight.*

Borrowing from the ideas of Socrates and Plato, another view that incorporated conscious and unconscious thinking in the creative process was the Primary-Secondary Process continuum proposed by Kris (1950). Primary processing is the unconscious state of creativity often evoked through lucid dreams, imagery, and fantasy. It is characterized by subsequent elaborate thoughts of concrete images that are typically associated with creative ideas. He viewed creativity *as forming new combinations or discovering new associations as a result of primary processing.*

It was around this time that interest in creativity, as a topic for scientific study, greatly increased, and was further inspired after Guilford gave his seminal conference address entitled "Creativity" to the American Psychological Association (APA) in 1950. Guilford's previous work on intelligence had sparked his interest in the scientific study of creativity. In his address, he accused the psychological community of neglecting creativity, which he initially defined as *"sensitivity to problems, ideational fluency, flexibility of set, ideational novelty, synthesizing ability, analyzing ability, reorganizing or redefining ability, span of ideational structure, and evaluating ability"* (Guilford, 1950, p. 453).

Consequently, there was a flurry of creativity research, and researchers no longer associated creativity with only the arts and music, but instead shifted their attention to understanding its value in effective problem solving. Creativity was most likely viewed as playing a pivotal role in successful problem solving due to the need for novel and productive thinking (Barron, 1955; Stein, 1953; Thurstone, 1952). Thurstone, similarly to Guilford, originally focused his efforts to understanding intelligence and believed that creativity *was any solution that was unique from the perspective of the creator regardless of whether it has actually been created before by another individual.* Stein (1953) also recognized the need to include novelty but added that the value is not limited to the individual, thus defining creativity as a *"process which results in a novel work that is accepted as tenable or useful or satisfying by a group at some point in time"* (p. 172). The novel work could be a creative solution or an idea or a tangible item such as a painting, poem, or a mathematical formula. The creative product could be generated by an individual or a group as pointed out by Barron (1955), who included the key concept of originality when he referred to it as *"uncommonness in the particular group being studied"* (p. 478). Osborn (1953) outlined logical stages in the creative problem solving process, reminiscent of Plato's and Wallas's initial view of goal-directed activity, to include fact-finding, idea-finding, and solution-implementing.

Even after Guilford had roused interest in the scientific study of creativity, there was still not a consensus answer to the "What is creativity?" question. However, there was some agreement that the concept of novelty (e.g., originality or uniqueness) must be included in the definition of creativity. Thus, **novelty** began to emerge as a key feature in defining creativity. So at this point in time, we could summarize the various viewpoints to generate a somewhat vague definition that creativity must involve *the ability to generate novel ideas and solutions to everyday problems and challenges.* Although most scholars agreed that the creative idea or product must be novel or original, other concepts were beginning to emerge as vital in the definition of creativity, such as the viewpoint that the idea or product should also be useful (Stein, 1953) and perhaps include an element of surprise (Bruner, 1962).

Subsequently, many researchers (Guilford, 1967; Mednick, 1962; Runco & Albert, 1985; Torrance, 1976, 1989) were unsatisfied with the proposed role of the unconscious in creativity and creative problem solving, reflecting increasing dissatisfaction with the role of the unconscious within psychology in general. They instead turned their attention to the psychometric properties used to define creativity and focused on test construction. Based on the Gestaltian concept of productive thinking (Kohler, 1929; Stein, 1953), and including the agreed upon concept of novelty, Mednick (1962) proposed that creativity *is the process of forming new associations or ideas by creating novel combinations of elements.* His test, the Remote Associations Test (RAT; Mednick & Mednick, 1967), was based on the idea that creativity is a result of forming associations, therefore he presented participants with a triad of verbal elements (see Figure 1.2)[2] and instructed them to formulate the remote word to associate these three elements.

This view of creativity allows for a combination of both divergent thinking and convergent thinking. First, the respondent must engage in divergent thinking by generating a schema containing multiple ideas for each single word presented word in the triad. For example the word *heart* may activate thoughts of lungs, love, Valentine, or sweet. Once three schemas have been formed, the respondent must engage in convergent thinking, by narrowing in on the one idea that appears in each of the activated schemas. In Figure 1.3, the term *sweet* has been activated by all three schemas.

Continuing the idea that creativity is a result of generating new associations, Guilford (1967) expanded on the work of Osborn (1953) and Mednick and Mednick (1967) and viewed the creative process as generating many possible solutions to a given problem. This led him to return from his initial call for creativity research presented at the 1950 APA address with renewed efforts devoted to measuring creativity though divergent thinking tasks. Guilford (1967) described divergent thinking as the production of consciously generating new ideas that branch out to many possible solutions for a given problem. Divergent thinking is also referred to as the intellectual ability to think of many novel, diverse, and elaborate ideas. Using this approach, he developed one of the leading measures of creativity, which is still a popular assessment used today. In Guilford's (1967) Alternative Uses Task, participants are asked to generate as many substitute uses as possible for common items such as a brick, a tin can, or an empty bottle. In Figure 1.4, a participant has responded to "Name all of the uses for a brick."

Instead of providing a single correct response, the respondent is free to generate as many responses as desired. Creativity is determined through four features of the responses: fluency, originality, flexibility, and elaboration. Fluency refers to the sheer quantity of responses. In this example, tallying up the responses yields a fluency score of eight. Originality refers to those responses that are given by very few respondents. For example, "a mock coffin at a Barbie funeral" is a very original response, where as a "wall" is very common. Flexibility refers to responses that come from different categories. For example, "a wall" and "a walkway" are from a similar building category, whereas "paperweight" is from a different category. Elaboration refers to the amount

Figure 1.4

---

2   See correct solution on final page of this chapter.

Triad			Solutions
1. COOKIES	SIXTEEN	HEART	_____
2. RAT	BLUE	COTTAGE	_____
3. WIDOW	BITE	MONKEY	_____

Figure 1.2. Remote Association Task (Mednick & Mednick, 1967).

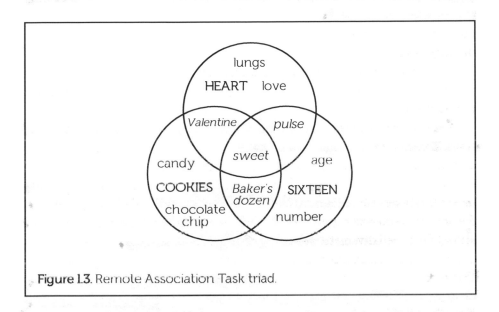

Figure 1.3. Remote Association Task triad.

Name all of the uses for a brick. Try to think of things no one else would come up with

wall	walkway
paperweight	door stop
hammer	to hit my brother over the head with
weapon	mock coffin at a Barbie funeral

Figure 1.4. Uses for a brick (Guilford, 1967).

of detail in a response. For example, stating "a weapon" is not very detailed whereas stating "to hit my brother over the head with" contains significantly more detail (including a victim of the act of aggression!).

Another leading contributor to the assessment of creativity, Torrance (1976) focused on scientific creativity and defined creativity to accommodate both the layperson and scientist. He defined creativity as "*the process of becoming sensitive to problems, deficiencies, gaps in knowledge, missing elements, disharmonies, and so on; identifying the difficult; searching for solutions, making guesses, or formulating hypotheses and possibly modifying them and retesting them; and finally communicating the results*" (p. 35). Following Guilford, Torrance developed a quantitative assessment that included a measure of divergent thinking but also a figural drawing task and a series of verbal tasks such as a "Just suppose task" and a "Product improvement task," in which participants are asked to imagine consequences to hypothetical imaginary situations and to improve a product to increase sales.

After the surge of midcentury creativity research, a second aspect emerged in definitions of creativity: **usefulness** (Cropley, 1967). Although novelty seems to be fairly straightforward to determine, the concept of usefulness is much more complicated. The usefulness of a problem solving task is more explicit: it involves reaching a solution, but the usefulness when generating a creative product, particularly one that engages a personal aesthetic appeal, is more subjective and could shift from one context to another.

Reflecting on the role that context has on determining the creative value, Amabile (1982), like Wallas (1926), mapped out a multiple-step process that began with identifying the problem, then preparing elements in the problem, moving to ultimately generating creative responses. These responses were then evaluated for usefulness or value. In her Consensual Assessment Technique (CAT; Amabile, 1982), the creative solution or product is evaluated by a team of judges who have content experience in the same domain of the product. For example, artists would evaluate a creative drawing, whereas writers would evaluate a creative story. A new aspect included in the CAT is the inclusion of the subject evaluation from experts within the domain. This allows the degree of usefulness from the creativity product to shift from one context to another. Additionally, in her componential model (1983, 1996), Amabile addressed the role that society has on influencing the views of what is useful, thus impacting the value of the creative product. In keeping with other researchers' views of creativity, Amabile included both novelty and usefulness with her definition of creativity that was *the process of generating an idea that is both original and appropriate to achieve a goal* (Amabile, 1983). To include external elements that often impact the usefulness, she added *internal elements of personality such as a mentality to take risks, have a difference perspective, and intrinsic motivation and domain relevant skills such as ability and experience* (Amabile, 1996).

Looking back at the 50-year period of creativity research from the 1950s to the end of the century, **novelty and usefulness** had been established as the two key features in defining creativity. As the consensus that usefulness is required when defining creativity began to take root, the logical conclusion that follows would be that society impacts the value placed on the creative product. Around the end of the century, this relationship between creativity and society became a focus among researchers. In fact, several reasoned that this relationship is recursive such that as society influences the merit and value of the creativity product, the creative product must also have an impact on shifting the views of society (Feldman, Csikszentmihalyi, & Gardner, 1994; Gardner, 1993; Runco & Dow, 1999; Sternberg, 1999, Sternberg, Kaufman, & Pretz, 2002). Gardner (1993) explained this distinction as Big-C and little-c creativity. Big-C creativity has global significance and is useful to society as a whole. Examples of Big-C creativity include the invention of the personal computer, a Picasso painting, the design of the Sydney Opera house, or the vision of Disneyland. This Big-C creativity is often defined as "*the achievement of something remarkable and new, something which transforms and changes a field of endeavor in a significant way*" (Feldman et al., 1994, p. 1). Little-c creativity, on the other hand, has personal value and is limited in usefulness to a specific individual or only a few others. Examples of Little-c creativity include a child's kindergarten painting, your high school poem that was never published, or the novel way you convince your 8-year-old to eat broccoli ("I hear that, if you eat it all, it can make your teeth turn green."). Although usefulness does not have a large-scale value, other little-c activities such as problem discovery, problem identification, and problem posing are important operations in the creative problem-solving process (Runco & Chand, 1994; Runco & Dow, 1999). Thus, little-c creativity could evolve into Big-C creativity so its merit is not undeserved. Interestingly, the concept of little-c was not a completely new idea. It had been originally been introduced by Thurstone (1952) 40 years earlier, when he noted that novelty of the creative product was determined by the creator at the moment and not society.

The importance that society and the environment has on the creative process was becoming more apparent in the research on creativity. Sternberg (1999) theorized about this topic as he explained the idea that creativity must propel a field forward, either through an incremental push to move the field a small amount to a new direction or by changing the whole field in its entirety. Partly as a result of this, we began to witness the start of societal context and environment being incorporated into the definition of creativity, as witnessed with Sternberg, Kaufman, and Pretz's (2002) definition that creativity is the "*ability to produce work that that is novel (i.e., original, unexpected), high in quality, and appropriate (i.e., useful, meets task constraints) taking place in the interactions between persons and their environment*" (p. 1).

Delving further into the role that environment plays on creativity, Csikszentmihalyi (1996, 1999) focused his attention at the microdomain level of environment and delineated between a society that participates and serves as a filter in a specific field of creativity from the culture within a specific domain of creativity. The "field is related to the person [the gatekeeper who] operates the social organization in the world. A field is necessary to determine whether the innovation is worth making a fuss about" (Csikszentmihalyi, 1996, p. 41). He therefore defined creativity *as an interactive system of the creative person with the field of society, and the domain of the culture. This interaction must cause a change within an existing domain or causes an existing disciplinary context to change into a new domain* (see Figure 1.5).

Amabile (1996) embraced the interrelated relationship between the creative person and societal context by concluding that creativity can only occur within a supportive environment. According to her componential model seen in Figure 1.6, creativity is defined as *a strong degree of intrinsic motivation and content knowledge along with a propensity for flexible, imaginative, and original thinking all occurring within an environment that supports creativity.*

Although we have outlined many diverse theoretical orientations, researchers appear to have reached an implicit consensus on the basic components of creativity: **novelty** (or original, unique, or unusual) and **usefulness** (or have value, or fit, or be appropriate), and the **social context**. *Novelty* refers to uniqueness or originality typically measured by statistical infrequency. *Usefulness* refers to the solution to the proposed problem or the value of the product. Creativity is, of course, multifaceted and involves distinct concepts within each domain of *social context*.

Moreover, the social context is inherently linked to the merit of creative product.

Additionally, the importance of the environmental setting with which creative thought on creativity occurs is also important. Original ideas and problem solving must be encouraged and respected in order for it to flourish. Such a setting requires that individuals are allotted the time to engage in creative thinking to produce divergent ideas, rather than only be given limited time to generate quick single-answer responses, solutions, or explanations. This narrowly promotes convergent patterns of thought thereby not encouraging flexibility of thought or open mindedness to produce several potential responses.

Even though there are several well-thought-out definitions of creativity presented from a variety of researchers, the omission of a single standard definition might explain why some still believe the "concept of creativity has

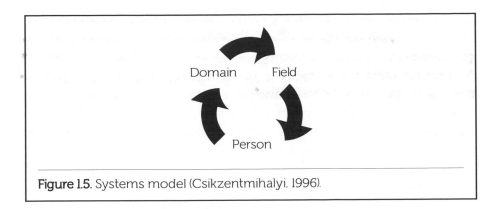

Figure 1.5. Systems model (Csikzentmihalyi, 1996).

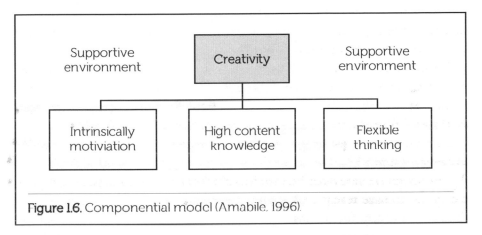

Figure 1.6. Componential model (Amabile, 1996).

traditionally proved an elusive one to pin down" (Craft, 2001, p. 13) and others to conclude there is not agreement among researchers as witnessed by the concern that "If the lack of definitional consensus and clarity of measurement methods has obfuscated and hampered creativity research, it may be that the new heuristic framework for creativity measurement can help structure this important field of research" (Batey, 2012, p. 63).

In truth, several researchers have reviewed the creative literature to form a definitional consensus and have always noted **novelty** and **usefulness** or appropriateness of ideas are included (Runco, 2004). A thorough review of creativity research was conducted by Plucker, Beghetto, and Dow (2004) to determine the most common definitions in the scientific literature. They reviewed a sample of nearly 100 peer-reviewed published articles with the terms *creativity* or *creative* in the title from the *Journal of Creativity Research*, *Journal of Creative Behavior*, and representative articles from the fields of general psychology, business, and education journals. They found that only one-third of the researchers provided an explicit definition of creativity, with another one-third including an implicit definition. After reviewing the creativity definitions from these publications and the overall historic concepts of creativity over centuries, they returned to the question, "What is creativity?", and generated an explicit answer. Creativity is "**the interaction among** *aptitude, process,* **and** *environment* **by which an individual or group produces a** *perceptible product* **that is both** *novel* **and** *useful* **as defined within a** *social context*" *(italics in original,* Plucker et al., 2004, p. 90). In the 10 years following the publication of this explicit definition, this paper was cited in subsequent publications more than 450 times, evidence that it provided one of the most accepted definitions of creativity.

As we witness the continuing empirical investigation into creativity in contemporary times, many researchers have begun synthesizing their work with that of previous researchers to develop more sophisticated theories of creativity based on new concepts and synthesized theories. For example, Beghetto and Kaufman (2007), who defined creativity as "*the ability to produce work that is novel (i.e., original, unexpected), high in quality, and appropriate*" (p. 73) further elaborated on the concept of Gardner's (1993) Big-C/little-c distinction by including a precursor of mini-c to little-c and a precursor of Pro-c (Kaufman & Beghetto, 2009) to Big-C. They defined mini-c as *the first attempt to be creative in a particular domain often through play or learning a new task* (Beghetto & Kaufman, 2007). If this creative act is valued or deemed useful and then accompanied with appropriate feedback, then it will evolve into little-c. Pro-c often precedes Big-C because it is *the professional level of a creative product that is a result of sustained effort and deliberate practice.*

Subsequently, researchers have continued to define creativity based on similar constructs addressed in Plucker, Beghetto, and Dow's (2004) definition. For example, in blending Bruner's (1962) idea that the creative product must be surprising with Gardner's (1993) personally meaningful little-c, Simonton (2012, 2013), who based his definition on United States Patent and Trademark Office guidelines, defined creativity as *a concept that is original, useful, and surprising in either a personal manner or a societal one.* Thus, the viewpoint that creativity should be defined parsimoniously (Runco & Jaeger, 2012) and involving three distinct concepts continues. First, creativity must include a **novel** idea of product. Second, the idea or product must be **useful** or appropriate to meet a need or solve a problem. Third, the novel and useful idea must form the ideal as defined within the **social context.** The degree of creativity of the idea or product depends on the environment with which the idea or product is embedded.

For more than two centuries, philosophers and psychologists have diligently worked to define creativity. As highlighted in Table 1.1 and outlined throughout this chapter, defining the construct of creativity has been a topic of critical importance historically. This importance is partly due to the diversity of contexts and fields in which creativity resides (e.g., art, business, cognitive science, economics, education, linguistics, philosophy, psychology, music, neuro-

Table 1.1
The Evolution of Definitions of Creativity

Creativity is …	Author	Year
a period of spiritual enlightenment that led to intellectual pursuit resulting in inspired poetry, art, and music	Socrates, Plato, and Aristotle	450–300 BCE
the process of thinking through preparation, incubation, illumination and verification that results	Wallas	1926
the reorganization of elements resulting in the sudden insight of knowledge or the correct solution	Kohler	1929
the process of moving from the primary processing of dreams, imagery, and fantasy to secondary processing of new ideas	Kris	1950
is comprised of ideas that are high on fluency, flexibility, and novelty	Guilford	1950
is a unique solution from the perspective of the solver	Thurstone	1952
is a novel idea or product that is useful to society	Stein	1953
an original product that is generated by an individual or a group	Barron	1955
an idea that surprises	Bruner	1962
the formation of new associations or a novel combinations of ideas	Mednick	1962
novel and useful ideas or products	Cropley	1967
being sensitive the problems and then searching for solutions	Torrance	1976
producing ideas that are original and appropriate to achieve a goal	Amabile	1983
a novel idea that transforms the field	Feldman, Csikszentmihalyi & Gardner	1994
novel and useful ideas from people who are intrinsically motivated and have expertise in their field	Amabile	1996
the interaction of the person, the field and culture to produce a new domain	Csikszentmihalyi	1996
flexible, imaginative, and original thinking from an intrinsically motivated person with a high degree of content knowledge	Amabile	1996
novel and useful ideas that occur in specific environments	Sternberg, Kaufman, & Pretz	2002
a novel and useful idea or product resulting from the interaction of ability, process, and environment	Plucker, Beghetto, & Dow	2004
high-quality, novel, and useful ideas or products	Beghetto & Kaufman	2007
original, useful, and surprising to either the individual or society	Simonton	2013

science, etc.). With such a diverse array of fields, a consistent definition is vital for effective communication and collaboration. It is also important due to the need to develop clear explicit operational definitions, which form the foundation of reliable and valid psychometric measures. And lastly, it is important due to the need to identify and target components of creativity in order to develop educational programs that foster creativity. As previously stated, nearly everyone recognizes that creativity is a worthwhile construct (one to be encouraged) and now hopefully, we can move toward nearly everyone recognizing and understanding the main components of creativity, so they are able to answer the basic question: What is creativity?

Recommended Readings

Kaufman, J. C., & Beghetto, R. A. (2009). Beyond big and little: The Four C model of creativity. *Review of General Psychology, 13,* 1–12.

Plucker, J. A., Beghetto, R. A., & Dow, G. T. (2004). Why isn't creativity more important to educational psychologists? Potentials, pitfalls, and future directions in creativity research. *Educational Psychologist, 39,* 83–96.

Runco, M. A., & Jaeger, G., J. (2012) The standard definition of creativity. *Creativity Research Journal, 24,* 92–96. doi:10.1080/10400419.2012.6500 92

Simonton, D. K. (2013). What is a creative idea? Little-c versus Big-C creativity. In K. Thomas & J. Chan (Eds.), *Handbook of research on creativity* (pp. 69–83). Cheltenham, England: Edward Elgar.

Sternberg, R. J. (Ed.). (1999). *Handbook of creativity.* Cambridge, England: Cambridge University Press.

References

Amabile, T. M. (1982). Social psychology of creativity: A consensual assessment technique. *Journal of Personality and Social Psychology, 43,* 997–1013.

Amabile, T. M. (1983). The social psychology of creativity: A componential conceptualization. *Journal of Personality and Social Psychology, 45,* 357–376. doi:10.1037/0022-3514.45.2.357.

Amabile, T. M. (1996). *Creativity in context: Update to "The Social Psychology of Creativity."* Boulder, CO: Westview Press.

Barron, F. (1955). The disposition towards originality. *Journal of Abnormal and Social Psychology, 51,* 478–485.

Batey, M. (2012). The measurement of creativity: From definitional consensus to the introduction of a new heuristic framework. *Creativity Research Journal, 24,* 55–65. doi:10.1080/10400419.2012.649181

Beghetto, R. A., & Kaufman, J. C. (2007). Toward a broader conception of creativity: A case for mini-c creativity. *Psychology of Aesthetics, Creativity, and the Arts, 1,* 73–79.

Belden, N., Russonello, J., & Stewart, N. (2005). *Integrating the arts: Reports on focus groups among parents, teachers and school administrators in Baltimore, Northern California, Dallas, and Washington DC: Arts & Economic Prosperity III.* Retrieved from http://www.brspoll.com/reports/

Bruner, J. S. (1962). The conditions of creativity. In H. Gruber, G. Terrell, & M. Wertheimer (Eds.), *Contemporary approaches to creative thinking* (pp. 1–30). New York, NY: Atherton.

Craft, A. (2001). *An analysis of research and literature on creativity in education.* Retrieved from http://www.creativetallis.com/uploads/2/2/8/7/2287089/creativity_in_education_report.pdf

Cropley, A. J. (1967). *Creativity.* London, England: Longmans, Green.

Csikszentmihalyi, M. (1996). *Creativity: Flow and the psychology of discovery and invention.* New York, NY: HarperCollins.

Csikszentmihalyi, M. (1999). Implications of a systems perspective for the study of creativity. In R. Sternberg (Ed.), *Handbook of creativity* (pp. 313–338). Cambridge, England: Cambridge University Press.

Davidson, J. E. (1995). The suddenness of insight. In R. J. Sternberg & J. E. Davidson (Eds.), *The nature of insight* (pp. 125–155). Cambridge, MA: MIT Press.

Dow, G. T., & Mayer, R. E. (2004). Teaching students to solve insight problems: Evidence for domain specificity in creativity training. *Creativity Research Journal, 16,* 389–402.

Feldman, D., Csikszentmihalyi, M., & Gardner, H. (1994). *Changing the world: A framework for the study of creativity.* Westport, CT: Praeger.

Gardner, H. (1985). *The mind's new science.* New York, NY: Basic Books.

Gardner, H. (1993). *Creating minds.* New York, NY: Basic Books.

Guilford, J. P. (1950). Creativity. *American Psychologist, 5,* 444–454.

Guilford, J. P. (1967). *The nature of human intelligence.* New York, NY: McGraw-Hill.

Kaufman, J. C., & Beghetto, R. A. (2009). Beyond big and little: The Four C model of creativity. *Review of General Psychology, 13*(1), 1–12.

Kohler, W. (1925). *The mentality of apes* (E. Winter, Trans.). London, England: Kegan, Trench.

Kohler, W. (1929). *Gestalt psychology.* New York, NY: Liveright.

Kris, E. (1950). Psychoanalysis and developmental psychology. *Bulletin of the American Psychoanalytic Association, 6,* 48–58.

Mednick, S. A. (1962). The associative basis of the creative process. *Psychological Review, 69,* 220–232.

Mednick, S. A., & Mednick, M. T. (1967). *Examiner's manual, Remote Associates Test.* Boston, MA: Houghton Mifflin.

Metcalf, J. (1986). Premonitions of insight predict impending error. *Journal of Experimental Psychology: Learning Memory, and Cognition, 12,* 623–634.

Nunan, S., & Craith, D. (2009). *Proceedings from Creativity and the Arts in the Primary School.* Irish National Teachers Organization. Retrieved from https://www.into.ie/ROI/Publications/CreativityArtsinthePS.pdf

Osborn, A. (1953). *Applied imagination.* New York, NY: Charles Scribner.

Paul, E. S., & Kaufman, S. B. (2014). Introducing the philosophy of creativity. In E. S. Paul & S. B. Kaufman (Eds.), *The philosophy of creativity: New essays* (pp. 3–16). Oxford, England: Oxford University Press.

Plucker, J. A., Beghetto, R. A., & Dow, G. T. (2004). Why isn't creativity more important to educational psychologists? Potentials, pitfalls, and future directions in creativity research. *Educational Psychologist, 39,* 83–96.

Runco, M. A. (1985). Reliability and convergent validity of ideational flexibility as a function of academic achievement. *Perceptual and Motor Skills, 61,* 1075–1081.

Runco, M. A. (1996). Personal creativity: Definition and developmental issues. *New Directions for Child and Adolescent Development, 72,* 3–30.

Runco, M. A. (2004). Creativity. *Annual Review of Psychology, 55,* 657–687.

Runco, M. A., & Albert, R. S. (1985). The reliability and validity of ideational originality in the divergent thinking of academically gifted and nongifted children. *Educational and Psychological Measurement, 45,* 483–501.

Runco, M. A., & Chand, I. (1994). Problem finding, evaluative thinking, and creativity. In M. A. Runco (Ed.), *Problem finding, problem solving and creativity* (pp. 40–76). Norwood, NJ: Ablex.

Runco, M. A., & Dow, G. T. (1999). Problem finding and creativity. In M. Runco & S. Pritzker (Eds.), *Encyclopedia of creativity* (pp. 433–435). San Diego, CA: Academic Press.

Runco, M., A., & Jaeger, G., J. (2012). The standard definition of creativity. *Creativity Research Journal, 24,* 92–96. doi:10.1080/10400419.2012.650092

Simonton, D. K. (2012). *Assessing scientific creativity: Conceptual analyses of assessment complexities.* Commissioned paper for The Science of Science and Innovation Policy Conference, National Academy of Sciences.

Simonton, D. K. (2013). What is a creative idea? Little-c versus Big-C creativity. In K. Thomas & J. Chan (Eds.), *Handbook of research on creativity* (pp. 69–83). Cheltenham, England: Edward Elgar.

Stein, M. I. (1953). Creativity and culture. *Journal of Psychology, 36,* 31–32.

Sternberg, R. J. (Ed.). (1999). *Handbook of creativity.* Cambridge, England: Cambridge University Press.

Sternberg, R. J., Kaufman, J. C., & Pretz, J. E. (2002). *The creativity conundrum: A propulsion model of kinds of creative contributions.* New York, NY: Psychology Press.

Sternberg, R. J., & Lubart, T. I. (1999). The concept of creativity: Prospects and paradigms. In R. Sternberg (Ed.), *Handbook of creativity* (pp. 3–15). Cambridge, England: Cambridge University Press.

Thurstone, L. L. (1952). Creative talent. In L. L. Thurstone (Ed.), *Applications of psychology (pp. 18–37).* New York, NY: Harper & Row.

Torrance, E. P. (1974). *The Torrance Tests of Creative Thinking.* Princeton, NJ: Personnel Press.

Torrance, E. P. (1976). *Creativity in the classroom.* Washington, DC: National Education Association, University Press.

Torrance, E. P. (1989). Scientific views of creativity and factors affecting its growth. In J. Kagan (Ed.), *Creativity and learning* (pp. 73–91). Boston, MA: Houghton Mifflin.

Wallas, G. (1926). *The art of thought.* New York, NY: Harcourt Brace.

Solution #1:

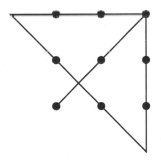

Solution #2: In this example, the link words are "sweet," "cheese," and "spider."

Connected but Different

Comparing and Contrasting Creativity, Innovation, and Entrepreneurship

Richard N. Dino

Key Take-Aways

- Research in creativity, innovation, and entrepreneurship generally occurs separately from one another, with little interaction and fertilization across these three areas. This is not the case in practice.
- Practice has demonstrated that there are inextricable, self-reinforcing linkages between the three.
- Outcome-oriented Experiential Learning Programs integrate creativity, innovation, and entrepreneurship in practice.
- Conceptualizing creativity, innovation, and entrepreneurship as related constructs has significant theoretical and practical advantages as we seek to solve society's problems.

This Hot Topic seeks to provide clarity with respect to the differences between creativity, innovation, and entrepreneurship. These three constructs are often used as synonyms, and while they are connected, they are not the same. Creativity differs from innovation, and innovation from entrepreneurship.

The Contextual Importance of Creativity, Innovation, and Entrepreneurship

The ability to produce and implement new, useful ideas is rapidly becoming the critical attribute for leveraging knowledge and increasing the quality of life, whether that ability is used to create works of art, find ways to provide inexpensive and abundant sources of water or energy, develop noninvasive surgical devices, eradicate the scourge of cancer, or improve urban infrastructure. Hence, today, a societal premium is placed on creative, innovative, and entrepreneurial thinking and abilities. Unfortunately, for scholars trying to understand these phenomena, creativity, innovation, and entrepreneurship appear inextricably connected yet conceptually distinct. Simply put, creativity focuses on the *generation* of new or novel ideas or associations between existing concepts; innovation focuses on the *implementation* of these ideas or concepts in some specific context, with an eye toward producing outcomes that are original, useful, appropriate, and actionable; and entrepreneurship focuses on the *identification and capture* of opportunities for useful and actionable outcomes in which a need could be satisfied, value could be created, or a solution could be found for an intractable problem.

Although economic growth has its roots in knowledge-based economies, new knowledge now diffuses across the globe instantaneously with the subsequent life cycle of its competitive advantage being short-lived. Consequently, there is a well-documented, shifting global paradigm from knowledge-based economies to creative, innovative, and entrepreneurial-based economies.[3] Essentially, in an age in which much of the world's information and knowledge base can be quickly accessed on handheld devices, a premium is currently placed on the ability to use that knowledge in creative, innovative, and entrepreneurial ways to produce valuable outcomes, as well as solve the many complex problems facing humanity. The creative ideas and innovative solutions that enable these outcomes are wide-ranging and multidisciplinary in that they are not limited to a particular domain.

Thus, it is no surprise that creativity, innovation, and entrepreneurship have become a focus of national economic development and education policies in many countries (e.g., Pang & Plucker, 2012),[4] and many are advocating for

---

3   See, for example, Richard Florida's essay on this shift (http://www.cato-unbound.org/2006/06/04/richard-florida/future-american-workforce-global-creative-economy), the website of the British effort to support the transition to a creativity economy (http://creativeconomy.britishcouncil.org), and a recent *Forbes* article on the implications of the innovation economy (http://www.forbes.com/sites/stevedenning/2012/01/31/is-the-us-in-a-phase-change-to-the-creative-economy).

4   The OECD maintains a database of national innovation policies at http://www.oecd.org/sti/inno/oecd reviewsofinnovationpolicy.htm.

a similar emphasis in the United States.[5] The demand for a creative, innovative, entrepreneurial, and critical thinking workforce is projected to increase and intensify in coming years, providing a tremendous opportunity for individuals, organizations, and governments that seek to obtain sustainable competitive advantage and broad-based economic development.

But how are these three constructs related? This Hot Topic begins with a separate examination of each construct, followed by a synthesis that allows us to view them holistically.

Creativity Research

The most commonly used and accepted definition positions creativity as "the development of ideas about products, practices, services or procedures that are (a) novel or original and (b) potentially useful . . . (see Amabile, 1996; Zhou & Shalley, 2003" (Shalley, Zhou, & Oldham, 2004, p. 934). Similarly, it is defined as "the interaction among *aptitude, process, and environment* by which an individual or group produces a *perceptible product* that is both novel and useful as defined within a *social context*" (Plucker, Beghetto, & Dow, 2004, p. 90).

Used overwhelmingly as a dependent variable in studies that focus on the individual, group, and organization, creativity has taken on many quantitative and qualitative forms. For example, using a framework supported by cognitive and expertise theories, Mitchell, Smith, Stamp, and Carlson (2015) reviewed an extensive assortment of creativity definitions/descriptions going back almost 50 years and classified them within a taxonomy of three conceptual levels of analysis (individual, organizational, or level-neutral) and two different foci (outcome or process). Of particular interest is their concept of level-neutral because it captures more theoretically abstract notions of creativity. For example, a *level-neutral outcome* is represented by Ford and Gioia's (2000) definition that views creativity as "publicly visible attributes of a product presented by an actor to a field" (p. 707). On the other hand, a *level-neutral process* can be seen in Drazin, Glynn, and Kazanjian's (1999) example of

> engineers working on a project . . . attempt[ing] to design an apparatus that is creative; they may collect data, consult past solutions, contemplate alternatives, propose inventive ideas, and become emotionally invested in their work. Their ideas

---

5   For example, recent reports and op-eds, such as http://www.forbes.com/sites/elainepofeldt/2013/05/27/u-s-entrepreneurship-hits-record-high, http://mag.newsweek.com/2010/07/10/the-creativity-crisis.html, *Rising to the Challenge: U.S. Innovation Policy for Global Economy* (available at http://www.nap.edu/catalog.php?record_id=13386), and http://www.usinnovation.org.

may or may not be considered by others as creative, but the process of generating those ideas logically can be called 'creativity;' in effect, creativity as a process is a necessary, but not sufficient, condition for creative outcomes. (p. 290)

Innovation Research

Like creativity, innovation is studied on the person and organization levels with an emphasis on processes, outcomes, and the context/environment. Couger, Higgins, and McIntyre (1990) argued that the many definitions of innovation are (even) less uniform in meaning than those of creativity. This, also, is largely due to the plentiful theoretic lenses and approaches used in studying the phenomenon. Arguing for the need of a multidisciplinary definition "adaptable to different disciplines and covering different aspects of innovation," Baregheh, Rowley, and Sambrook (2009) stated that, "a general definition . . . would be beneficial [/insightful]" as "the term 'innovation' is notoriously ambiguous and lacks either a single definition or measure" (p. 1324; also see Adams, Bessant, & Phelps, 2006).

Interestingly, innovation has some definitional overlap with creativity, as both have been defined using the attributes of novelty (originality) and usefulness (Amabile, 1996; Glynn, 1996). That said, there is common agreement on a broader definition of innovation that has provided some general unanimity; specifically, whereas creativity is the *successful generation* of an original and potentially useful idea, innovation is the *successful implementation* of such an idea. Couger et al. (1990) delineated the differences between creativity and innovation by using an insightful, comparative analogy of the relationship between discovery and invention. In particular, they suggested that "where invention is concerned with implementation of discovery, innovation is concerned with implementation of inventive [creative] ideas" (p. 372). Thus, innovation can be viewed as a proximal link in the chain of a larger interconnected process to capture value or benefit an individual or organization from the creative idea.

Entrepreneurship Research

Entrepreneurship is the youngest research domain compared to either creativity or innovation. Interestingly, Bygrave and Hofer (1991) reasoned that as late as the early 1980s, entrepreneurship was, "at best, a potentially promising field of scholarly inquiry" (p. 13). They argued that, "by the end of that decade [the 1980s], due primarily to impressive advances in its body of empirical knowledge, entrepreneurship could claim to be a legitimate field of academic inquiry *in all respects except one*: it lack[ed] a substantial theoretical foundation" (p. 13; italics added).

This missing link was a gaping hole in entrepreneurship's intellectual legitimacy that needed to be filled, in large part to show that it, indeed, had a "distinctive domain," where interesting research questions could be answered by using "a conceptual framework that explains and predicts a set of empirical phenomena not explained or predicted by conceptual frameworks already in existence in other fields" (Shane & Venkataraman, 2000, p. 217). Entrepreneurship scholars were sensitized to this issue and worked diligently to better frame and define the field. A seminal study by Venkataraman (1997) attempted to define such a "distinctive domain" with this baseline framework:

> At its core, the field is concerned with (1) why, when, and how opportunities for the creation of goods and services in the future arise in an economy; (2) why, when, and how some are able to discover and exploit these opportunities while others cannot or do not; and, finally, (3) what are the economic, psychological, and social consequences of this pursuit of a future market not only for the pursuer, but also for the other stakeholders and for society as a whole. (p. 4)

Similar to research in creativity and innovation, entrepreneurship is studied at the person and organization levels with an emphasis on processes, outcomes, and the context/environment.

Commonalities Across Research Domains

In sum, there are four macro level commonalities across the research domains of creativity, innovation, and entrepreneurship. These include: (1) the numerous theoretical frameworks used in studying each; (2) the resulting variance in and variety of definitions utilized; (3) the multiple levels (person and organization) and foci (processes, outcomes, and the context/environment) of research studies; and (4) the principal use of each centerpiece concept as the dependent/deterministic variable. Given these four commonalities in toto, one could readily conclude a fifth (i.e., that these have led each set of scholars to work diligently and independently to address conceptual issues with relatively common theories, definitions, and measures in each domain). Interestingly, despite the conceptual proximity of these research domains, there is little else in common.

In their historical considerations of creativity, Ryhammar and Brolin (1999) stated that

> creativity research will continue along many paths, both wide and narrow, but there are already a fair number of studies on different levels, with different perspectives and different methods. Nevertheless, it seems reasonable to say, with some exceptions, that there is still a general lack, or failure, *when it comes to relating the various results to one another*. The research has been extremely fragmentary and its conceptual apparatus extremely varied and *has chiefly been pursued as if every particular part of the phenomenon of creativity could be understood in isolation from every other part*. (p. 270; italics added)

Evidence of siloed behavior within the innovation research domain can be found in Hauser, Tellis, and Griffin (2006), where they argued that "research on innovation has proceeded in many academic fields *with incomplete links across those fields. For example, research on market pioneering typically does not connect with that on diffusion of innovations or the creative design of new products*" (p. 1; italics added). And in their interdisciplinary perspective on entrepreneurship research, Herron, Sapienza, and Smith-Cook (1991) maintained that

> one interesting observation that emerged . . . is that *each discipline has its own unique way of viewing entrepreneurship which remains relatively unaffected by the perspectives of other disciplines*. In other words, *we see evidence that many 'uni-' rather than one or more 'multi-' disciplinary views of our field currently exist*. (p. 7; italics added)

Despite any logical and reasoned argument, should we expect integrated behavior *across* creativity, innovation, and entrepreneurship domains, when, in fact, it is not practiced *within* these domains? Whatever the reason, in any combination, creativity, innovation, and entrepreneurship researchers have little communication outside their boundaries. In this regard, clearly theory may well be different than practice. Perhaps the time has come for researchers to stop viewing these as separate domains, but rather subdomains in a larger value-adding ecosystem?

Which Came First, the Chicken or the Egg?

Researchers have attempted to answer this interesting question and causality dilemma for thousands of years. Not unlike interesting research questions in creativity, innovation, and entrepreneurship, answers to this question, too, have been developed using multiple lenses and frameworks such as philosophy, genetics, chemistry, physics, physiology, and cognitive science. And although a search for a definitive answer might matter to researchers, practitioners would likely argue the contrary—that, in fact, it does not. From a practitioner's viewpoint, the egg is needed to hatch a chicken and a chicken is needed to lay an egg; thus, they are inextricably linked and these links reinforce the vital relationship between the two.

The relationships among creativity, innovation, and entrepreneurship echo those of the chicken and the egg. Creativity, innovation, and entrepreneurship, too, are connected and these connections reinforce their vital relationships. As well, these links are crucial to the development of value-laden outcomes. Just as we need an egg to hatch a chicken, the generation of a creative (novel/original and potentially useful) idea/solution that is implementable (innovation) is necessary to capture an identified opportunity or solve a complex problem (entrepreneurship). The entrepreneurship component of the ecosystem is where the potential usefulness or value is determined. And just as the chicken is needed to lay an egg, an identified opportunity/complex problem needs a creative and innovative solution. Extending this line of reasoning, we can ask another interesting and related question, specifically, "which comes first (or, put differently, is more important), creativity, innovation, or entrepreneurship?" Notwithstanding any theoretical argument, the practitioner would likely say that they are of equal importance in a larger ecosystem of relationships. Creativity without innovation generates just another idea. Innovation without a potentially useful and novel idea supporting it will likely be unsustainable and creates no value (has little or no usefulness) unless a market need or problem is identified and solved. Like the chicken and the egg, in practice, creativity, innovation, and entrepreneurship need each other. Figure HT1.1 illustrates the linkages and flows among the three.

Innovation Quest

In stark contrast to the siloed research domains of creativity, innovation, and entrepreneurship, in which researchers in each area have little to no cross-communication, many practitioners believe in, focus on, and utilize the

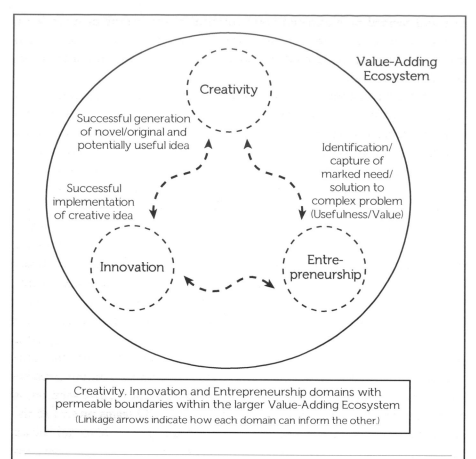

Creativity, Innovation and Entrepreneurship domains with permeable boundaries within the larger Value-Adding Ecosystem
(Linkage arrows indicate how each domain can inform the other.)

Figure HT1.1. The Reinforcing Linkages of Creativity, Innovation and Entrepreneurship. From "Crossing boundaries: Toward integrating creativity, innovation, and entrepreneurship research through practice" (p. 143) by R. N. Dino, 2015, *Psychology of Aesthetics, Creativity, and the Arts, 9*(2). Copyright 2015 by American Psychological Association. Reprinted with permission.

inextricable, reinforcing linkages among the three in their attempt to produce valuable solutions to both market needs and complex problems. With such efforts, practitioners are able to synthesize and utilize knowledge developed in each research domain for the benefit of education and practice. An example that illustrates this point is the Innovation Quest (iQ) Program at both the California Polytechnic State University (CalPoly) and the University of Connecticut (UConn). A brief description follows, and readers are directed to Dino (2015) for additional information about the program.

Innovation Quest is a university-wide innovation competition and startup incubator, designed specifically to help students with great ideas solve business and societal problems and build companies. The mantra of iQ is "idea, prototype, company," with each element mapping directly to the research and knowledge domains of creativity (idea), innovation (prototype), and entrepreneurship (company).

There are two components to the program: The first is the "Innovation Phase," during which student teams generate and sharpen their creative ideas and build prototypes (apply those ideas) that are linked to what is oftentimes an evolving initial/perceived market need. An expert evaluation is conducted assessing each idea with the intention of identifying the most promising with the highest probabilities of success. A summer incubator begins the "Entrepreneurship Phase" of the program where working teams acquire a "best practices" knowledge base and skill set that help them better identify and evaluate associated market opportunities and choose whether or not they would like to pursue them (see also Brown & Kuratko, 2015; Goldsby, Kuratko, & Nelson, 2014). Although the program treats the creativity, innovation, and entrepreneurship domains as inextricably linked components of a larger ecosystem, time is spent within each domain acquiring capabilities and capacities that are designed to benefit the outcome of the whole. For example, participating teams are taught how to identify and evaluate market needs/opportunities (entrepreneurship domain) that are aligned with their novel/original solutions (creativity domain) using innovation, the actual application of the creative solution, as a constraining function. At the end of the Incubator, iQ teams present to the financial community (another market test; see Goldsby et al., 2014 and Brown & Kuratko, 2015). The relationships and network connections that have been established during the formal aspects of the program continually develop and expand for years to come as the students turn into entrepreneurs and work tirelessly to build their businesses.

Conclusion

In this Hot Topic, five commonalities among creativity, innovation, and entrepreneurship have been identified: (1) the numerous theoretical frameworks used in studying the three constructs; (2) the resulting variance in definitions; (3) the multiple levels (person and organization) and foci (processes, outcomes, and the context/environment) of research; (4) the principal use of each concept as the dependent/deterministic variable; and (5) the previous four leading scholars to work diligently and independently to address relevant conceptual issues with somewhat common theories, definitions, and measures in each domain. Researchers in these domains have little else in common and, quite frankly, have little to no integrative conversations.

This Hot Topic proposes the notion that there is a significant difference between theory and practice when it comes to creativity, innovation, and entrepreneurship, and this difference is not beneficial. By approaching their research in silos, creativity, innovation, and entrepreneurship scholars fail to integrate the new knowledge generated by their individual domain inquiries in ways that would be productive and insightful for the entire creativity, innovation, and entrepreneurship research ecosystem. By failing to focus on the inextricable and reinforcing linkages that exist between creativity, innovation, and entrepreneurship, scholars are missing out on at least two opportunities: (1) the ability to ask even more interesting research questions; and (2) the chance to leverage knowledge discovery from each domain into beneficial insights across them. To the contrary, by focusing on these linkages, practitioners significantly benefit outcomes by producing results from the alignments of market needs/opportunities, the generation of creative solutions, and their innovative implementation.

Creativity, innovation, and entrepreneurship scholars can learn from practice. By integrating the three domains, practitioners are able to "connect the dots" and produce outcomes that occur due to their leveraging of knowledge that emanates from the larger integrated value-adding ecosystem. The successful synthesis of creativity, innovation, and entrepreneurship in education and practice, as exemplified through programs such as Innovation Quest, should serve as a catalyst to encourage researchers and practitioners to step forward and break down their disciplinary barriers and, as a result, work together, with the potential for considerable growth in both the quantity and quality of creativity, innovation, and entrepreneurship research and its resulting flow to education, implementation, and practice. Then, perhaps, we will experience the full benefits of theory informing practice.

Recommended Readings

Baregheh, A., Rowley, J., & Sambrook, S. (2009). Towards a multidisciplinary definition of innovation. *Management Decision, 47,* 1323–1339.

Dino, R. N. (2015). Crossing boundaries: Toward integrating creativity, innovation, and entrepreneurship research through practice. *Psychology of Aesthetics, Creativity, and the Arts, 9,* 139–146.

Mitchell, R. K., Smith, J. B., Stamp, J. A., & Carlson, J. (2015). Organizing creativity: Lessons from the Eureka! Ranch experience. In C. E. Shalley, M. A. Hitt, & J. Zhou (Eds.), *The Oxford handbook of creativity, innovation, and entrepreneurship* (pp. 301–337). Oxford, England: Oxford University Press.

Shane, S., & Venkataraman, S. (2000). The promise of entrepreneurship as a field of research. *Academy of Management Review, 25,* 217–226.

References

Adams, R., Bessant, J., & Phelps, R. (2006). Innovation management measurement: A review. *International Journal of Management Reviews, 8*(1), 21–47.

Amabile, T. M. (1996). *Creativity in context.* Boulder, CO: Westview Press.

Baregheh, A., Rowley, J., & Sambrook, S. (2009). Towards a multidisciplinary definition of innovation. *Management Decision, 47,* 1323–1339.

Brown, T. J., & Kuratko, D. F. (2015). The impact of design and innovation on the future of education. *Psychology of Aesthetics, Creativity, and the Arts, 9,* 147–151.

Bygrave, W. D., & Hofer, C. W. (1991). Theorizing about entrepreneurship. *Entrepreneurship Theory and Practice, 16*(2), 13–22.

Couger, J. D., Higgins, L. F., & McIntyre, S. C. (1990, January). Differentiating creativity, innovation, entrepreneurship, intrapreneurship, copyright and patenting of IS products/processes. In *System Sciences, 1990, Proceedings of the Twenty-Third Annual Hawaii International Conference on Systems Sciences* (Vol. 4, pp. 370–379). Kailua, HI: IEEE.

Dino, R. N. (2015). Crossing boundaries: Toward integrating creativity, innovation, and entrepreneurship research through practice. *Psychology of Aesthetics, Creativity, and the Arts, 9,* 139–146.

Drazin, R., Glynn, M. A., & Kazanjian, R. K. (1999). Multilevel theorizing about creativity in organizations: A sensemaking perspective. *Academy of Management Review, 24,* 286–307.

Ford, C. M., & Gioia, D. A. (2000). Factors influencing creativity in the domain of managerial decision making. *Journal of Management, 26,* 705–732.

Goldsby, M. G., Kuratko, D. F., & Nelson, T. E. (2014). Design centered entrepreneurship: A process for designing opportunities. In M. H. Morris (Ed.), *Annals of Entrepreneurship Education and Pedagogy* (pp. 200–217). Northampton, MA: Edward Elgar Publishing.

Glynn, M. A. (1996). Innovative genius: A framework for relating individual and organizational intelligences to innovation. *Academy of Management Review, 21,* 1081–1111.

Hauser, J., Tellis, G. J., & Griffin, A. (2006). Research on innovation: A review and agenda for marketing science. *Marketing Science, 25,* 687–717.

Herron, L., Sapienza, H. J., & Smith-Cook, D. (1991). Entrepreneurship theory from an interdisciplinary perspective: Volume I. *Entrepreneurship Theory and Practice, 16*(2), 7–12.

Mitchell, R. K., Smith, J. B., Stamp, J. A., & Carlson, J. (2015). Organizing creativity: Lessons from the Eureka! Ranch experience. In C. E. Shalley, M. A. Hitt, & J. Zhou (Eds.), *The Oxford handbook of creativity, innovation, and entrepreneurship* (pp. 301–337). Oxford, England: Oxford University Press.

Pang, W., & Plucker, J. A. (2012). Recent transformations in China's economic, social, and education policies for promoting innovation and creativity. *The Journal of Creative Behavior, 46*, 247–273.

Plucker, J. A., Beghetto, R. A., & Dow, G. T. (2004). Why isn't creativity more important to educational psychologists? Potentials, pitfalls, and future directions in creativity research. *Educational Psychologist, 39*, 83–96.

Ryhammar, L., & Brolin, C. (1999). Creativity research: Historical considerations and main lines of development. *Scandinavian Journal of Educational Research, 43*, 259–273.

Shalley, C. E., Zhou, J., & Oldham, G. R. (2004). The effects of personal and contextual characteristics on creativity: Where should we go from here? *Journal of Management, 30*, 933–958.

Shane, S., & Venkataraman, S. (2000). The promise of entrepreneurship as a field of research. *Academy of Management Review, 25*, 217–226.

Venkataraman, S. (1997). The distinctive domain of entrepreneurship research. *Advances in Entrepreneurship, Firm Emergence and Growth, 3*, 119–138.

Zhou, J., & Shalley, C. E. (2003). Research on employee creativity: A critical review and directions for future research. *Research in Personnel and Human Resources Management, 22*, 165–217.

CHAPTER 2

Theories of Creativity

Ronald A. Beghetto and James C. Kaufman

Key Take-Aways

- There are a number of thoughtful, well-developed theories of creativity.
- These theories can be categorized in several ways, and we use the following four categories in this chapter:
  - Who is creative: Theories that clarify what it takes to be creative as well as the developmental trajectory of creativity.
  - How we're creative: Theories that describe the factors and processes that lead to creative outcomes.
  - Why we're creative: Theories that explain reasons why people engage in creative thinking and action.
  - What is creative: Theories that describe different types of creativity and what counts as creative in and across different domains.

Theories are like containers. They help us organize the way we think about complex topics, like creativity. Some theories of creativity provide a very broad overview of creativity (e.g., Rhodes, 1962; Glăveanu, 2013). Many theories try to answer core questions about creativity.

These questions can be very broad (such as "How do we conceptualize creativity as a research topic?") or more focused. Examples of focused questions include "Who is creative?", "How are we creative?", "Why are we creative?", and "What is creative?" In this chapter, although we will briefly touch on the broader theories, we are interested in theories that help clarify these more specific questions. In what follows, we briefly highlight a few key theories that can help address these questions (also summarized in Table 2.1). We close with a brief discussion of how these theories can be helpful in thinking about creativity as well as potential pitfalls in rigidly relying on any one theory.

How Do We Conceptualize Creativity as a Research Topic?

The foremost example of a theory that highlights how we might begin the study of creativity is the Four P's (Rhodes, 1962), which provides an overview of various features of creativity. The Four P's stand for person, product, process, and press; this structure has launched several hundred introduction sections. Specifically, they represent the creative *person* (e.g., openness to experience, sensible risk taking), the creative *process* (e.g., steps in generating, developing, and selecting ideas), the creative *product* (e.g., ideas, behaviors, artifacts), and creative *press* (e.g., the motivational influence of the environment on people). A new take on the 4 P's that is becoming more and more popular is the 5 A's (Glăveanu, 2013), which transforms the 4 P's and helps to further clarify key features of creativity. The 5 A's are the actor, action, artifact, audience, and affordances. Roughly speaking, the first three A's map onto person, process, and product; audience and affordances are two aspects of creative press (audience is the group who receives the creative work, and affordances are the resources the creator has available). These broad theories help provide a framework for how we can even begin to answer the more specific questions below.

Who Is Creative?

The first question that theories of creativity can help us address is "Who is creative?" Specifically, these theories clarify what it takes to be creative as well

Table 2.1
Summary of Key Theoretical Questions About Creativity

Question Addressed	How Creativity Theories Address This Question	Example Theories	Example Theorists
Who is creative?	Helps clarify what it takes to be creative as well as the developmental trajectory of creativity	• Componential Model • Investment Theory • 4-C Model	• T. Amabile • R. J. Sternberg, T. Lubart • J. C. Kaufman, R. A. Beghetto
How are we creative?	Describes the factors and processes that lead to creative outcomes	• Creative Process Models • Geneplore • Blind Variation and Selective Retention • Janusian Thinking	• G. Wallas • T. B. Ward, S. M. Smith, R. A. Finke • D. K. Simonton, D. T. Campbell • A. Rothenberg
Why are we creative?	Helps explain reason why people engage in creative thinking and action	• Intrinsic/Extrinsic • 4-G Growth, Gain, Guidance, and Giving • Matrix Model • Creative Learning	• E. Deci, R. Ryan, T. Amabile, B. Hennessey • M. Forgeard, A. C. Mecklenburg • K. L. Unsworth • R. A. Beghetto
What is creative?	Describes different types of creativity and what counts as creative in and across different domains	• Propulsion Theory of Creative Contributions • Systems Model • Amusement Park Theoretical Model	• R. J. Sternberg, J. C. Kaufman, J. E. Pretz • M. Csikszentmihalyi • J. Baer, J. C. Kaufman

as the developmental trajectory of creativity. In this section, we highlight three such theories: 4-C Model of Creativity, Componential Model of Creativity, and Investment Theory.

4-C Model of Creativity

When we think of creative people, it is instinctive to split them into two categories: everyday (little-c creativity) or legendary (Big-C creativity). This split has long held sway in the creativity research literature and has produced useful insights, including the idea that everyone can be creative (i.e., everyday creativity) and what it takes to be a creative legend (e.g., some blend of necessary expertise, time, opportunities, and the right sociocultural and historical circumstances). Although helpful, such dichotomies are limited. The

4-C Model (Beghetto & Kaufman, 2007; Kaufman & Beghetto, 2009) was introduced to address these limitations and provide a broader, developmental perspective on who can be creative and how one develops their creativity. The 4-C model introduced two additional categories ("mini-c" and "Pro-c") and explained how each of the 4-Cs are connected along a developmental trajectory. Mini-c creativity refers to the subjective experience of creativity any time you learn something new or have an original and personally meaningful idea, insight, or interpretation of an experience. Mini-c is part of the learning process and serves as the basis for all higher forms of creativity. Pro-c refers to professional-level or highly accomplished creativity. It is the kind of creativity that comes from having spent many years of intense, deliberate practice in a domain.

Componential Model of Creativity

Amabile (1996) proposed the Componential Model of Creativity. This theory suggests that three factors are needed for creativity to occur: domain-relevant skills, creativity-relevant skills, and task motivation. Domain-relevant skills refer to personal attributes such as content knowledge, specific skills related to the domain, and specialized talent in the area. A creative physicist would, for instance, need to have a deep understanding of physics, know how to develop and test models, and be able to apply this specialized knowledge and skills in new and meaningful ways. Creativity-relevant skills are more general characteristics that a person needs to be creative, such as taking sensible risks, being open to new experiences, or looking at a problem from multiple perspectives. The creative physicist would be able to look at a long-standing problem in a new way. The final element of Amabile's theory is task motivation. An accomplished creative scientist likely would be motivated by intrinsic factors (the passion and challenge of solving a longstanding problem in physics) as opposed to working for some more extrinsic reasons (such as making money).

Investment Theory

Sternberg and Lubart's (1995) Investment Theory of creativity made the argument that people who are creative are like investment bankers, except with ideas instead of money. Good creators "invest" in ideas that are promising but not fully developed, work with them and convince the world of their value, and then move on to new ideas. A creative person initiates the bandwagon instead of simply riding on it. Sternberg and Lubart further posited that the six components a creative person needs to possess are ideal levels of motivation, intelligence, knowledge, personality, and thinking style, as well as a nurturing environment.

How Are We Creative?

The second question theories of creativity can help us address is: "How are we creative?" Specifically, these theories help clarify the factors and processes that lead to creative outcomes. In this section, we highlight three such theories: Creative Problem Solving, Geneplore, and Blind Variation and Selective Retention (BVSR).

Creative Process Models

Theories that attempt to explain the creative process represent one of the oldest and most active areas of study for creativity researchers. Graham Wallas (1926) described four stages of the creative process: *preparation*, *incubation*, *illumination*, and *verification*. Preparation refers to clarifying or defining the problem through gathering relevant information. Incubation is the next stage and refers to stepping away from a problem, which is thought to help generate different ideas and perspectives (rather than stay too focused on the problem at hand). Next comes illumination, where solutions are generated. Verification is the final stage wherein the idea or solution is tested out. This can result in verifying the solution, refining the solution, or restarting the process in search of a more effective solution.

In the years following Wallas's description of the model, several models have been proposed that have added, elaborated on, and even contested some of the stages. The incubation stage, for instance, has been criticized as implying a passive or even magical process in which ideas or solutions "spring forth fully formed" (Cropley & Cropley, 2010, p. 311), rather than requiring deliberate effort. Contemporary models and descriptions have also highlighted that the creative process doesn't always follow a strictly linear or step-like fashion, but can cycle backward and forward through different stages. Still, even with the critiques and elaborations, it is difficult to deny the impact that the stages proposed by Wallas have had on helping to explain the creative process (see Kozbelt, Beghetto, & Runco, 2010; Sawyer, 2012 for discussion of these stages and more contemporary perspectives on the creative process).

Geneplore

Comparable to Guilford's (1967) distinction between divergent and convergent thinking, the Geneplore model (Finke, Ward, & Smith, 1992), has two broad phases: Generation and Exploration. In the generative phase, the creative person develops an idea of how a problem might be solved. There are many different visual images and ideas that may pop into the creator's head throughout the phase; only some of these ideas will even be articulated into words. Once there are many possible ideas, the exploration phase begins. Ideas are developed, tested against the constraints of the desired goal, and then chosen for implementation. Sometimes an idea works; other times, an idea doesn't succeed, and the process begins again. You may need to go through many different cycles before hitting on the best answer for a dilemma.

Blind Variation and Selective Retention (BVSR)

Blind Variation and Selective Retention (BVSR) theory is an evolutionary approach to how people create. Campbell (1960) first outlined the BVSR theory, which has been subsequently developed by Simonton (2009, 2011). BVSR proposes that creative ideas are blind—namely, they are generated in an unplanned way without a necessary emphasis on eventual success or implementation. As our species evolves over time, ideas are selectively retained such that the creative ideas that are passed along over generations are (ideally) the best possible ones.

Why Are We Creative?

The third question theories of creativity can help us address is "Why are we creative?" Specifically, these theories help explain the reasons why people engage in creative thinking and action. In this section, we highlight three such theories: 4-G, Creative Learning, and the Matrix Model.

4-G Theory

In the 4-G theory, Forgeard and Mecklenburg (2013) integrated the concept of intrinsic versus extrinsic motivation with the intended audience. Intrinsic motivation is doing something because it is enjoyable and personally meaningful, whereas extrinsic motivation is performing an activity for an outside reward, such as money, grades, or praise (Deci & Ryan, 2010). Intrinsic motivation has traditionally been linked to creativity (Amabile, 1996; Hennessey, 2010; Hennessey & Amabile, 2010). In their 4-G theory, Forgeard and Mecklenburg (2013) argued that *growth*, *gain*, *guidance*, and *giving* each represent a reason for being creative. If the intended audience is one's self, then the motivations mirror intrinsic and extrinsic motivation. Growth is being creative for one's self because it is enjoyable; gain is being creative for a reward. Guidance is when someone uses his or her creative abilities to mentor someone else and help that person develop and be creative. Giving is the act of using one's creativity to help other people in a tangible way (such as by helping to design a building that can house many people in need).

Creative Learning Model

Beghetto's (2016) model of creative learning introduces a new way of thinking about the interdependent relationship between creativity and learning. It provides an explanation of the role that creativity plays in individual learning (*creativity-in-learning*) and the role that sharing personal learning plays in making creative contributions to others (*learning-in-creativity*). More specifically, the model explains how new understanding results from a creative process of combining new information and experiences with one's previous understanding. This internal combinatorial process—creativity-in-learning—is consistent with the concept of mini-c creativity (Beghetto & Kaufman, 2007) and explains how creativity supports the individual learning process. The model also explains how sharing new and personally meaningful learning can result in creative contributions to others (e.g., the learning and understanding of peers and teachers). This externalized process—learning-in-creativity—describes the sociocultural and situational factors necessary for the expression of learning to result in creative contributions. In sum, this model helps explain how creative learning is both an intrapsychological (individual) and interpsychological (sociocultural) process.

Matrix Model

Unsworth (2001) proposed a theoretical matrix model that emphasizes a person's reason and context for being creative. She explored the interaction between whether a creative problem is open or closed and whether a person's reason for being creative is rooted in internal or external engagement. She thus proposed a matrix of four types of creativity. *Responsive creativity* is handling a specific problem for an external reason—such as discovering a novel way to plug a stopped-up toilet. *Expected creativity* is when someone is asked to produce something creative, often to a particular prompt or circumstance. For example, a student writing an essay to a topic may be creative, but for a specific purpose and assignment. *Contributory creativity* occurs when a person is engaged for his or her own reasons, but it's to a specific circumstance. For example, someone who enjoys tinkering with autos might be asked to help fix a friend's car. It's a task that person enjoys, but it is creative work done for a reason and within a more narrow context. Finally, *proactive creativity* is a person engaged in creative activity for his or her own reasons and in a broad, open context.

What's Creative?

The fourth question that theories of creativity can help us address is "What's creative?" Specifically, these theories help clarify different types of creativity and what counts as creative in and across different domains. In this section, we highlight three such theories: Propulsion Theory of Creative Contributions, Systems Theory, and the Amusement Park Theoretical Model.

Propulsion Theory of Creative Contributions

The Propulsion Theory of Creative Contributions (Sternberg & Kaufman, 2012; Sternberg, Kaufman, & Pretz, 2002) helps clarify eight different types of creative contributions. The first four refer to work that makes contributions in existing directions of the field. These four types have been labeled *replication, redefinition, forward incrementation,* and *advanced forward incrementation.* Replications reproduce past works—movie sequels would be an example. Redefinitions, on the other hand, instead approach the domain as it exists from a different angle. Podcasts redefined the format of talk shows by hosting them on the Internet to be streamed on demand (instead of live broadcasting them from radio or television). The third type of contribution, forward incrementation, moves the field forward through small-scale developments. The different generations of the iPhone would be an example. Similarly, advance forward incrementation goes even further and some might say goes even too far by being ahead of its time. Self-driving cars are an example of advanced forward incrementation.

The remaining four types of creative contribution go beyond building on an existing direction and, instead, provide new alternatives. Those four types include *redirection, reconstruction, reinitiation,* and *initiation.* Redirection, as its name suggests, seeks to alter the direction of something. Netflix streaming service is an example of creating a new direction for how people watch movies and television shows. Reconstruction contributions try to take the field back to a point in its past and progress from that point in a different direction from what has already been explored. An example would be a contemporary "remake" or "reboot" of a movie from the past. Reinitiations, which are more radical, seek to advance the field to an unreached point and begin their work from this new starting point. The Segway personal transportation device is an example of reinitiating. Initiation, lastly, seeks to take two different domains and blend them in order to create something new. The development of smartphones, for instance, integrated cellphones and portable computing devices.

Systems Theory

Csikszentmihalyi's (1999) systems model looks at how creative contributions represent a systemic interaction among *domain*, *field*, and *person*. Domain refers to the area of study. It can be broad, like "writing," or more specific, such as "epic poetry." The concept of the field is defined as the "gatekeepers" who decide what counts as creative. These are individuals and groups such as critics, scholars, editors, and professional peers. Finally, the concept of person is simply the creator (e.g., the artist, the dancer, the writer). This theory tends to focus on more accomplished creators at the Pro-C and Big-C level (see description of the 4-C model), however it does have implications for people who have creative aspirations. Specifically, it helps clarify that higher levels of creativity are not simply a matter of individual achievement, but result from the interaction of various individual, sociocultural, and historical factors (many of which are out of the hands of individual creators). This helps explain why some people whose accomplishments received little or no attention during their life can later be "discovered" and acclaimed by critics and historians of a field (e.g., art critics and historians) as revolutionary and others who achieved fame in their day are now long forgotten.

Amusement Park Theoretical Model

The Amusement Park Theoretical (APT) Model of creativity (Baer & Kaufman, 2005; Kaufman & Baer, 2004) integrates both generalist and domain-specific views of creativity (see also the hybrid view proposed by Plucker & Beghetto, 2004). The APT model uses the metaphor of an amusement park to outline how creative people get more and more specific and specialized in their work. The initial requirements to be creative are a certain level of intelligence, motivation, and a supportive environment (just as to go to an amusement park you need a ticket, a ride, and transportation). Broadly, there are General Thematic Areas for creativity, such as everyday, scholarly, performance, science, and art (Kaufman, 2012), just as there are broad categories of amusement parks (roller coasters vs. animal themes). Next come Domains; within science, for example, there might be biology, physics, chemistry, and so on; similarly, there are specific parks (such as Disneyland). Finally, there are Microdomains within Domains; for example, biology encompasses many subfields such as genetics and evolutionary biology (just as each park has individual rides).

Conclusion

Creativity is a complex concept. There are so many facets to cover and questions surrounding the topic that it can quickly become overwhelming. In this chapter, we have provided a brief overview of several major questions that creativity theories can help address, including "Who is creative?", "How are we creative?", "Why are we creative?", and "What is creative?" We covered a lot of ground in a brief amount of space. Still, we hope that this chapter provides a general introduction to how theories can help organize and clarify a topic as complex as creativity.

Who is creative? The theories we reviewed in this chapter help explain that everyone has the capacity to be creative. There are, however, different levels of creative accomplishment (4-C Model of Creativity). Higher levels of creative accomplishment develop from a combination of domain-relevant skills, creative-relevant skills, and task motivation (Componential Model of Creativity). Moreover, highly accomplished creators know how to invest in promising ideas and convince others of the value of those ideas (Investment Theory).

How are we creative? Theorists have highlighted several different ways that people can be creative. This includes theories that help explain the steps of the creative process (Creative Process Models), how ideas are developed and chosen for implementation (Geneplore), and how that process resembles an evolutionary approach of Blind Variation and Selective Retention (BVSR).

Why are we creative? The third group of theories we covered help explain what motivates creative thinking and action. One reason people are creative is because it supports their learning process (Creative Learning). There are numerous other reasons including intrinsic reasons (e.g., enjoyment and personal meaning) and extrinsic reasons (e.g., money and praise) for engaging in creative work (4-Gs of creativity). Moreover, depending on the type of problem people are trying to solve (open or closed) their reasons for being creative can be classified into four different types: responsive, expected, contributory, and proactive creativity (Matrix Model).

What is creative? The final group of theories we covered in this chapter help explains what counts as creativity and how creators. Creativity can range from slight changes in past works to somewhat radical transformations (Propulsion Theory of Creative Contribution). Creativity tends to be domain specific and creative people get more and more specialized in their creative contributions (Amusement Park Theoretical Model). Finally, creativity represents a systemic interaction among the area of study, the gatekeepers who decide what counts as creativity, and the creator (Systems Theory).

Recommended Readings

Forgeard, M. J. C., & Kaufman, J. C. (in press). Who cares about imagination, creativity, and innovation, and why? A review. *Psychology of Aesthetics, Creativity, and the Arts.*

Glaveanu, V. P., Gillespie, A., & Valsiner, J. (2015). *Rethinking creativity: Contributions from social and cultural psychology.* New York, NY: Guilford Press.

Hennessey, B. A., & Amabile, T. M. (2010). Creativity. *Annual Review of Psychology, 61,* 569–598.

Kaufman, J. C. (2016). *Creativity 101* (2nd ed.). New York, NY: Springer.

Kharkhurin, A. V. (2014). Creativity.4in1: Four-criterion construct of creativity. *Creativity Research Journal, 26,* 338–352.

Kozbelt, A., Beghetto, R. A., & Runco, M. A. (2010). *Theories of creativity.* In J. C. Kaufman & R. J. Sternberg (Eds.), *Cambridge handbook of creativity* (pp. 20–47). New York, NY: Cambridge University Press.

Runco, M. A. (2014). *Creativity: Theories and themes: Research, development, and practice* (2nd ed.). San Diego, CA: Academic Press

Sawyer, R. K. (2012). *Explaining creativity: The science of human innovation* (2nd ed.). New York, NY: Oxford University Press.

Sternberg, R. J. (2006). Creating a vision of creativity: The first 25 years. *Psychology of Aesthetics, Creativity, and the Arts, S,* 2–12.

References

Amabile, T. M. (1996). *Creativity in context: Update to "The Social Psychology of Creativity."* Boulder, CO: Westview Press.

Baer, J., & Kaufman, J. C. (2005). Bridging generality and specificity: The Amusement Park Theoretical (APT) Model of creativity. *Roeper Review, 27,* 158–163.

Beghetto, R. A. (2016). Creative learning: A fresh look. *Journal of Cognitive Education and Psychology, 1,* 6–21.

Beghetto, R. A., & Kaufman, J. C. (2007). Toward a broader conception of creativity: A case for "mini-c" creativity. *Psychology of Aesthetics, Creativity, and the Arts, 1,* 73–79.

Campbell, D. T. (1960). Blind variation and selective retentions in creative thought as in other knowledge processes. *Psychological Review, 67,* 380–400.

Cropley, D., & Cropley, A. (2010). Functional creativity: "Products" and the generation of effective novelty. In J. C. Kaufman & R. J. Sternberg (Eds.),

Handbook of creativity (pp. 301–320). Cambridge, England: Cambridge University Press.

Csikszentmihalyi, M. (1999). Implications of a systems perspective for the study of creativity. In R. J. Sternberg (Ed.), *Handbook of creativity* (pp. 313–335). Cambridge, England: Cambridge University Press.

Deci, E. L., & Ryan, R. M. (2010). *Self-determination.* New York, NY: Wiley.

Finke, R. A., Ward, T. B., & Smith, S. M. (1992). *Creative cognition: Theory, research, and applications.* Cambridge, MA: MIT Press.

Forgeard, M. J. C., & Mecklenburg, A. C. (2013). The two dimensions of motivation and a reciprocal model of the creative process. *Review of General Psychology, 17,* 255–266.

Guilford, J. P. (1967). *The nature of human intelligence.* New York, NY: McGraw-Hill.

Glăveanu, V. P. (2013). Rewriting the language of creativity: The Five A's framework. *Review of General Psychology, 17,* 69–81.

Hennessey, B. A. (2010). Intrinsic motivation and creativity in the classroom: Have we come full circle? In R. A. Beghetto & J. C. Kaufman (Eds.), *Nurturing creativity in the classroom* (pp. 329–361). New York, NY: Cambridge University Press.

Hennessey, B. A., & Amabile, T. M. (2010). Creativity. *Annual Review of Psychology, 61,* 569–598.

Kaufman, J. C. (2012). Counting the muses: Development of the Kaufman-Domains of Creativity Scale (K-DOCS). *Psychology of Aesthetics, Creativity, and the Arts, 6,* 298–308.

Kaufman, J. C., & Baer, J. (2004). Sure, I'm creative—but not in mathematics!: Self-reported creativity in diverse domains. *Empirical Studies of the Arts, 22,* 143–155.

Kaufman, J. C., & Beghetto, R. A. (2009). Beyond big and little: The Four C Model of Creativity. *Review of General Psychology, 13,* 1–12.

Kozbelt, A., Beghetto, R. A., & Runco, M. A. (2010). Theories of creativity. In J. C. Kaufman & R. J. Sternberg (Eds.). *Cambridge handbook of creativity* (pp. 20–47). New York, NY: Cambridge University Press.

Plucker, J. A., & Beghetto, R. A. (2004). Why creativity is domain general, why it looks domain specific, and why the distinction does not matter. In R. J. Sternberg, E. L. Grigorenko, & J. L. Singer (Eds.), *Creativity: From potential to realization* (pp. 153–167). Washington, DC: American Psychological Association.

Rhodes, M. (1962). An analysis of creativity. *Phi Delta Kappan, 42,* 305–311.

Sawyer, R. K. (2012). *Explaining creativity: The science of human innovation* (2nd ed.). New York, NY: Oxford University Press.

Simonton, D. K. (2009). *Genius 101.* New York, NY: Springer

Simonton, D. K. (2011). Creativity and discovery as blind variation and selective retention: Multiple-variant definitions and blind-sighted integration. *Psychology of Aesthetics, Creativity, and the Arts, 5,* 222–228.

Sternberg, R. J., & Kaufman, J. C. (2012). When your race is almost run, but you feel you're not yet done: Application of the Propulsion Theory of Creative Contributions to late-career challenges. *Journal of Creative Behavior, 46,* 66–76.

Sternberg, R. J., Kaufman, J. C., & Pretz, J. E. (2002). *The creativity conundrum.* Philadelphia, PA: Psychology Press.

Sternberg, R. J., & Lubart, T. I. (1995). *Defying the crowd.* New York, NY: Free Press.

Unsworth, K. (2001). Unpacking creativity. *Academy of Management Review, 26,* 289–297.

Wallas, G. (1926). *The art of thought.* New York, NY: Harcourt Brace and World.

The Dark Side of Creativity

Potential Better Left Unfulfilled

Mark A. Runco

Key Take-Aways

- Creativity contributes hugely to progress but is sometimes used for immoral and unethical ends.
- Immoral creativity ("the dark side") has now been studied for 30 years. Four strands of thought stimulated an interest in "the dark side."
- These four strands of thought parallel the personality, product, process, and place approaches to creativity and are explored in this Hot Topic.
- The immoral or dark side of creativity is only indicative of creative products and is extricable from creative personality, process, and place.
- Creative potentials can be fulfilled in different ways, some moral, some immoral, and some neither moral nor immoral.
- The most useful way to view the dark side of creativity is that it is a kind of creative potential that is best left unfulfilled.

Are creative people always good? This may sound like an odd question when you think about the fact that creative efforts are responsible for technological advance, cultural evolution, innovation, design, and invention. The contribution of creativity to the arts, including painting, sculpting, music, writing, and drama is obvious. Look around you right now and you will probably see a computer or cell phone; some attractive, functional, and comfortable clothing; and perhaps walls covered with art. Very likely an attentive glance around your immediate surroundings will show you hundreds of things that resulted from creative efforts.

The question about creative people being good people will not be as surprising if you consider the weaponry and computer viruses that have also resulted from creative efforts, or lies and crimes intended to cheat and steal. These can each be original and effective, which means that they fit the standard definition of creativity (Runco & Jaeger, 2012). No wonder morals and ethics have become key issues in the current creativity research. This Hot Topic reviews the research and theory that helps to understand the relationship between creativity and morality. It addresses the question, "Are creative people always good?"

Perspectives on Creativity

The concept of a "dark side" to creativity was introduced by McLaren (1993) in a special issue of the *Creativity Research Journal* devoted entirely to "creativity in the moral domain." Thus you might think that the question posed above, "Are creative people always good?" has only been discussed in the last 20–25 years. Actually, the sentiment behind it has a long history. Indeed, four strands of thought have led up to the question of creativity and morality. One of these is apparent in the personality approach to creativity. The personality approach represents what is probably the oldest approach used by researchers to empirically investigate creativity. Early research did not predict immoral or unethical tendencies being tied to creativity, but instead, various traits indicative of a dark side were included in the investigations because standard personality inventories throw a wide net and include a very wide range of dimensions. They assess both socially desirable and socially undesirable traits. The best-known studies of personality and creativity, and some of the best early research on creativity, was conducted at the Institute for Personality Assessment and Research in Berkeley, CA (Barron, 1955, 1963, 1995; MacKinnon, 1965; for a history see Helson, 1999).

A bit more about the personality research: Although no one was predicting evil to be correlated with creativity, there was an expectation of psychopathology. This followed from the very long-standing interest in the "mad genius," which has roots going back literally hundreds or thousands of years. Recent data on the correlation between psychopathology and creativity were presented by Ludwig (1998) and Richards (1990), to name just two of many examples. The interest in a mad genius and the connection of creativity with psychopathology is relevant because, if creativity was always associated with psychopathology, and psychopathology includes narcissism, the questioning of norms, and antisocial behavior, there would be good reason to expect at least some creative individuals to have socially undesirable or even immoral tendencies.

There is fair agreement about the so-called core personality traits for creativity. The typical traits uncovered include openness, autonomy, intrinsic motivation, flexibility, and playfulness. These do seem to vary from domain to domain, and thus it is not surprising that some traits may be vital specifically for moral creativity. Richards (1993) pointed specifically to courage (cf. May, 1975) as the key trait for moral creativity. Others have attempted to identify the traits associated with immoral creativity. Kapoor (2015), for example, pointed to the "subclinical dark triad (DT) of personality—narcissism, psychopathy, and Machiavellianism" (p. 58). Furnham (2015) pointed to a different set of traits (schizotypal, histrionic, obsessive compulsive, and paranoia), but he relied on divergent thinking as his criterion and worked specifically with managers. Lee and Dow (2011) also used tests of divergent thinking (but didn't study managers), and they found correlations with (low) conscientiousness and aggression—as well as gender. Values, honesty, conscientiousness, and responsibility have also been studied in the research on benevolent and malevolent creativity (Eisenman, 2008; Family, 1993; Gruber, 1993; Rappaport & Kren, 1993).

The second line of thought that led up to the current interest in the dark side approaches creativity quite differently. This approach focuses on creative products. Works of art are often studied in the research on creativity (Amabile, 1982; Dudek, 1993; Runco, 1989; Schwebel, 1993), as are publications, patents, and a wide range of other products (Huber, 1998; Simonton, 1999). Products have an advantage in that they can be counted and thus objectively studied. There are of course different kinds and levels of products (Ghiselin, 1963). Ultimate creative products are those that represent expert efforts and are professional, if not world-class (e.g., paintings in a museum). There are also intermediate products that may be professional, but may not win awards and influence large groups of people (e.g., a book with only a moderate readership and no awards). Then there are immediate products, which include ideas and solutions. The weaponry mentioned above would be an example of a dark side creative product, as would a computer virus.

A third line of thought that led up to questions of the dark side focuses on the process approach to creativity. To explain this, it is useful to consider the theory of divergent thinking. This is the cognition that often leads to original ideas. There are tests of divergent thinking, for example, which present open-ended tasks to a respondent and ask for "as many solutions and ideas as you can think of." This kind of task is very different from most academic tests that tend to assess convergent thinking, which is the cognition involved in finding the one correct or conventional solution to a problem (e.g., Who was the first President of the United States?). Divergent thinking allows the respondent to produce a large number of ideas and provides scores for fluency (the number of ideas given), originality (the number of unique or unusual ideas given), and flexibility (the number of conceptual categories in the ideas). Tests of divergent thinking have reasonable correlations with real-world creative activities and achievements (Plucker, 1999; Runco, Millar, Acar, & Cramond, 2011), though of course there is more to creativity than just divergent thinking. Tests of divergent thinking are best viewed as estimates of the potential for creative problem solving.

This is all relevant to the dark side and the underlying process because immoral ideas are in some ways divergent. Associative theory predicts that when generating ideas and solutions, people first think of common and conventional options and only when those are exhausted are less conventional ideas found. It is as if there is a small universe of conventional options that easily come to mind, but outside of that are more remote ideas that are unconventional and original. Think for a moment about immoral ideas. They are immoral precisely because they are inconsistent with societal morals and conventions. Thus it follows that the capacity to think divergently and to find remote ideas probably contributes to the capacity to think in an immoral fashion. This logic is supported by reports by Rothenberg (1990) and Walczyk, Runco, Tripp, and Smith (2008).

A related line of research also used tests of divergent thinking and found evidence of the capacity to think in unconventional and sometimes immoral ways. This investigation administered six tests of divergent thinking, but then evaluated the resulting ideas using 13 dimensions identified *a priori* to represent what Acar and Runco (2015) called *ideational hyperspace.* That label was chosen because the overarching interest was in assessing divergent thinking in a literal fashion. As Acar and Runco noted, previous testing of divergent thinking gave credit to ideas that were remote and original, but not literally divergent (as in moving in different conceptual directions). Acar and Runco found that the scoring of ideas using the *a priori* dimensions of thought was reliable. They also reported a significant correlation between the number of categories used by any one individual and that same individual's originality and fluency scores. In addition, they found the use of the conceptual categories was correlated with a measure of creative attitudes and values. All of this is pertinent because each conceptual category was in fact a dimension with a range of options and two polarities. One of these dimensions captured ideation that was either taboo or not taboo. A second dimension captured ideation that was amoral, unethical, illegal, and malevolent or, at the other extreme, moral, ethical, legal, and benevolent. Clearly the first polarities in each of those two dimensions (i.e., taboo and amoral) relates to the question of a dark side of creativity. In this research paradigm, the dark side was apparent in that some individuals did in fact produce solutions to problems that were identified as taboo and amoral.

The fourth line of thought that led to the recent interest in the dark side of creativity (and, using the terminology from the research just reviewed, *malevolent creativity*) can be aligned with yet another of the alliterative Four P's approaches to creativity. The personality, product, and process approaches have already been mentioned in this chapter, and the fourth and last approach focuses on "places" that influence the development or expression of creativity. The place approach, or what was originally labeled the "press" approach (from the word "pressure"), focuses on contextual influences on creativity. Organizational settings can, for example, influence employees' creative tendencies (Amabile & Gryskiewicz, 1989; Runco, 1995), just as educational settings (i.e., the classroom) can influence students' creative tendencies. The broadest place or contextual influence on creativity is culture (Kharkhurin, 2014; Runco, 2010; Tan, 2016). Culture determines what is appropriate. This in turn determines which domains of activity are valued or ignored. Gardner's (1983) detailed discussion of domains suggests that different domains are valued by different cultures, and at different points in history. At present, the mathematical and verbal domains are highly valued, especially in Western culture (and schools). Some attention is also given to bodily-kinesthetic performances, as is evidenced by the fact that someone can make a career out of dancing or athletics, and to musical talents and performances. Gardner also identified interpersonal, intrapersonal, spatial, and naturalistic domains.

These domain differences are sometimes debated. Two questions in this debate have led to additional research on the dark side of creativity (as well as to humane and benevolent creativity). One question is "why these domains," and another is "why isn't society supporting performances in the moral domain?" It is quite clear that people can be exceptional in their moral and benevolent creativity, as is evidenced by the actions and methods of Gandhi, Jesus, Henry David Thoreau, and Martin Luther King, Jr. To be even more concrete, consider Gandhi's method of *satyagraha*, or passive resistance (Gardner, 1993). The two words *passive* and *resistance* sound oxymoronic, but it was a creative insight to find a way to resist, but in a pacifistic and nonviolent fashion. (The fact that passive resistance seems to be oxymoronic implies that it may have resulted from the literally divergent thinking described above. Oxymorons can be considered when thinking creatively, at least if divergent, paradoxical, diametric ideas can be brought together into a creative solution.)

Perhaps the time is right and moral creativity will be given more respect. As a matter of fact, that may be why the topic of a dark side has become a popular one! You might say that we are now in a place where moral creativity is more important than ever before. Something like this was suggested by McLaren (1993) and the other contributors to the special issue of the *Creativity Research Journal*. They pointed to the number and magnitude of the environmental, social, and moral problems now facing humanity. Gruber (1993) put it this way:

> The relations between creativity and morality require fresh attention in a time of rapid social and technological change and multiple global crises. World civilization as presently constituted is committed to policies entailing exponential growth, which in the long run, unfortunately, will be impossible to maintain. . . . Such conditions affect moral issues of fairness, justice, caring for others, and even truth. As a result, we witness a growing awareness of moral diversity and the slow— too slow?—emergence of new moral orientations, not least of which is planetary morality. (p. 1)

There Is No Dark Side

One additional perspective on the dark side must be noted. It suggests that the dark side of creativity is either exaggerated by the research or even nonexistent. Consider the other undesirable tendencies that are sometimes correlated with creativity, but are not truly vital parts of creativity. This happens because, as the cognitive sciences have repeatedly demonstrated, humans are often less than logical. We sometimes make guesses or estimate, even if we could invest the energy and time into absolutely correct calculations. To use the terms from cognitive psychology, people often use *heuristics* when thinking (and thus merely estimate), rather than *algorithms* for perfectly accurate solutions. People also have some predictable biases, as indicated by our tendency to remember interesting or surprising things, even if those things are uncommon and what we really should remember are the more common and representative events. Think back to the discussion of the "mad genius." There are an enormous number of creative people in the world who show no signs of psychopathology, but they may attract very little attention. Creators who stand out attract attention, and one way to do this is to act a little crazy. In some domains, the stereotype of a highly creative individual includes madness, or at least eccentricities. Think here of the talented scientists you see in the movies, such as Dr. Emmett Brown in the *Back to the Future* movies. How about a creative writer? The stereotype there is F. Scott Fitzgerald, with a martini, a cigarette, and an ongoing party. Crazy creators are salient and as such attract attention, are in the news, and are easy to remember. The media and biographers love crazy creators. People generally have no interest in spending their hard-earned money to watch a movie about creative people who love their job, get along well with everyone around them, and have no crises or drama. So the dark side of creativity can be salient and yet not indicative of real creativity.

Then there is the complication that some malevolence is unintended. Nuclear weapons, for example, were developed when the implications of splitting the atom, for the sake of clean energy, was deemed possible. There are, in fact, theories of creativity that include intentions in order to exclude accidental originality. Cropley, Kaufman, and Cropley (2008), for example, felt that benevolent and malevolent creativity can only be distinguished from one another by their intended purposes. Runco (1996) defined creativity such that it required (a) the construction of an original interpretation of experience, (b) intentions, and (c) discretion. The last of these is itself very relevant to a discussion of the dark side because it is possible that malevolent creative ideas are produced by a process that is neither moral nor immoral, but because the individual's decision making (which is a function of discretion) takes the idea in an immoral direction or uses it in an unethical matter. Admittedly the role of intentions is debated, with some holding that serendipity is a legitimate component of the creative process (Diaz de Chumaceiro, 1996, 1999).

Creative Potential

The theory presented here—there is no dark side of creativity—is just that, a theory. It is compelling but untested. Certainly there are creatively malevolent products, and perhaps even a dark side to personality, but the creative process itself is neither immoral nor moral. The creative process merely allows the individual to produce original and effective ideas. Sometimes effectiveness is obvious in that the new idea solves a socially meaningful or benevolent problem, but other times effectiveness is only apparent in some immoral use or application of the original idea.

This Hot Topic also suggested that this same theory (there is no dark side) fits well with the 4P framework that is so often cited in creativity research. In its original form, the 4P framework just had personality, product, process, and place (or press; Rhodes, 1961). The same alliterative framework has, however, been extended several times (Richards, 1999; Runco, 2007; Simonton, 1995). One of these was called the *hierarchical framework* because it identified two very broad categories, namely Creative Potential and Creative Performance, and then placed the original 4Ps underneath, thus forming a hierarchy. Simonton's (1995) idea about creative persuasion was also placed under the topic of Creative Performance. Simonton's position was that some creativity changes the way that people think—it is in that sense persuasive. This falls under the Creative Performance category because it refers to some socially observable act or an actual product. Similarly, the product approach is also under Creative Performance because products are manifest. Personality, process, and place are all under Creative Potential because none of them guarantees overt creative behavior or performance. They may contribute to creative performance, but a person can have the key personality traits for creativity, or some other facet of potential, but not actually perform in a creative fashion. The individual can even employ a creative process, perhaps thinking divergently, but not find any truly creative solutions. That person may find original ideas, for example, but they may only be original and not be effective, as is required by the standard definition of creativity (Runco & Jaeger, 2012). So again, the process used to produce those ideas is not malevolent. It is neither moral nor immoral. Creativity is just a cognitive process that leads in varied and sometimes original directions (Runco, 2010). The dark side of creativity is, in this sense, just one potential that humans have. And one that we can attempt to redirect, avoid, and minimize.

Recommended Readings

Gruber, H. E. (1993). Creativity in the moral domain: Ought implies can implies create. *Creativity Research Journal, 6,* 3–15.

McLaren, R. B. (1993). The dark side of creativity. *Creativity Research Journal, 6,* 137–144.

Runco, M. A. (1993). Moral creativity: Intentional and unconventional. *Creativity Research Journal, 6,* 17–28.

Runco, M. A. (2010). Creativity has no dark side. In D. H. Cropley, A. J. Cropley, J. C. Kaufman, & M. A. Runco (Eds.), *The dark side of creativity* (pp. 15–32). New York, NY: Cambridge University Press.

Runco, M. A., & Nemiro, J. (2003). Creativity in the moral domain: Integration and implications. *Creativity Research Journal, 15,* 91–105.

References

Acar, S., & Runco, M. A. (2015). Thinking in multiple directions: Hyperspace categories in divergent thinking. *Psychology of Art, Creativity, and Aesthetics, 9,* 41–53.

Amabile, T. M. (1982). Children's artistic creativity: Detrimental effects of competition in a field setting. *Personality & Social Psychology Bulletin, 8,* 573–578.

Amabile, T. M., & Gryskiewicz, N. D. (1989). The creative environment scales: Work environment inventory. *Creativity Research Journal, 2,* 231–253.

Barron, F. (1955). The disposition towards originality. *Journal of Abnormal and Social Psychology, 51,* 478–485.

Barron, F. (1963). *Creativity and psychological health.* Princeton, NJ: Van Nostrand.

Barron, F. (1995). *No rootless flower.* Cresskill, NJ: Hampton Press.

Cropley, D., Kaufman, J. C., & Cropley, A. J. (2008). Malevolent creativity: A functional model of creativity in terrorism and crime. *Creativity Research Journal, 20,* 105–115.

Diaz de Chumaceiro, C. L. (1996). Freud, poetry and serendipitous paradoxes. *Journal of Poetry Therapy, 9,* 227–234.

Diaz de Chumaceiro, C. L. (1999). Research on career paths: Serendipity and its analog. *Creativity Research Journal, 12,* 227–229.

Dudek, S. Z. (1993). The morality of 20th-century transgressive art. *Creativity Research Journal, 6,* 145–152.

Eisenman, R. (2008). Malevolent creativity in criminals. *Creativity Research Journal, 20,* 116–119.

Family, G. (1993). The moral responsibility of the artist. *Creativity Research Journal, 6,* 83–87.

Furnham, A. (2015). The bright and dark side correlates of creativity: Demographic, ability, personality traits and personality disorders associated with divergent thinking. *Creativity Research Journal, 27,* 39–46.

Gardner, H. (1983). *Frames of mind: The theory of multiple intelligences.* New York, NY: Basic Books.

Gardner, H. (1993). Mahatma Gandhi: A hold upon others. *Creativity Research Journal, 6,* 29–44.

Ghiselin, B. (1963). Ultimate criteria for two levels of creativity. In C. W. Taylor & F. Barron (Eds.), *Scientific creativity: Its recognition and development* (pp. 30–43). New York, NY: Wiley.

Gruber, H. E. (1993). Creativity in the moral domain: Ought implies can implies create. *Creativity Research Journal, 6,* 3–15.

Helson, R. (1999). Institute of Personality Assessment and Research. In M. A. Runco & S. Pritzker (Eds.), *Encyclopedia of creativity* (pp. 71–79). San Diego, CA: Elsevier.

Huber, J. C. (1998). Invention and inventivity is a random, Poisson process: A potential guide to analysis of general creativity. *Creativity Research Journal, 11,* 231–241.

Kapoor, H. (2015). The creative side of the dark triad. *Creativity Research Journal, 27,* 58–67.

Kharkhurin, A. V. (2014). Creativity.4in1: Four-criterion construct of creativity. *Creativity Research Journal, 26,* 338–352.

Lee, S., & Dow, G. (2011). Malevolent creativity: Does personality influence malicious divergent thinking? *Creativity Research Journal, 23,* 73–82.

Ludwig, A. (1998). Method and madness in the arts and sciences. *Creativity Research Journal, 11,* 93–101.

May, R. (1975). *The courage to create.* New York, NY: W. W. Norton.

MacKinnon, D. (1965). Personality and the realization of creative potential. *American Psychologist, 20,* 273–281.

McLaren, R. B. (1993). The dark side of creativity. *Creativity Research Journal, 6,* 137–144.

Plucker, J. A. (1999). Is the proof in the pudding? Reanalyses of Torrance's (1958 to present) longitudinal data. *Creativity Research Journal, 12,* 103–114.

Rappaport, L., & Kren, G. (1993). Amoral rescuers: The ambiguities of altruism. *Creativity Research Journal, 6,* 129–136.

Rhodes, M. (1961). An analysis of creativity. *Phi Delta Kappan, 42,* 305–310.

Richards, R. (1990). Everyday creativity, eminent creativity, and health: "Afterview" for *Creativity Research Journal* issues on creativity and health. *Creativity Research Journal, 3,* 300–326.

Richards, R. (1993). Seeing beyond: Issues of creative awareness and social responsibility. *Creativity Research Journal, 6,* 165–183.

Richards, R. (1999). Four Ps of creativity. In M. A. Runco & S. Pritzker (Eds.), *Encyclopedia of creativity* (Vol. 1, pp. 733–742). San Diego, CA: Elsevier.

Rothenberg, A. (1990). Creativity, mental health, and alcoholism. *Creativity Research Journal, 3,* 179–201.

Runco, M. A. (1989). The creativity of children's art. *Child Study Journal, 19,* 177–189.

Runco, M. A. (1995). The creativity and job satisfaction of artists in organizations. *Empirical Studies of the Arts, 13,* 39–45.

Runco, M. A. (1996). Personal creativity: Definition and developmental issues. *New Directions for Child Development, 72*(Summer), 3–30.

Runco, M. A. (2007). A hierarchical framework for the study of creativity. *New Horizons in Education, 55*(3), 1–9.

Runco, M. A. (2010). Creativity has no dark side. In D. H. Cropley, A. J. Cropley, J. C. Kaufman, & M. A. Runco (Eds.), *The dark side of creativity* (pp. 15–32). New York, NY: Cambridge University Press.

Runco, M. A., & Jaeger, G. (2012). The standard definition of creativity. *Creativity Research Journal, 24,* 92–96.

Runco, M. A., Millar, G., Acar, S., & Cramond, B. (2011). Torrance Tests of Creative Thinking as predictors of personal and public achievement: A 50 year follow-up. *Creativity Research Journal, 22,* 361–368.

Schwebel, M. (1993). Moral creativity as artistic transformation. *Creativity Research Journal, 6,* 65–81.

Simonton, D. K. (1995). Exceptional personal influence: An integrative paradigm. *Creativity Research Journal, 8,* 371–376.

Simonton, D. K. (1999). Historiometry. In M. A. Runco & S. Pritzker (Eds.), *Encyclopedia of creativity* (pp. 815–822). San Diego, CA: Academic.

Tan, C. (2016). Creativity and Confucius. *Journal of Genius and Eminence, 1,* 79–84.

Walczyk, J. J., Runco, M. A., Tripp, S. M., & Smith, C. E. (2008). The creativity of lying: Divergent thinking and ideational correlates of the resolution of social dilemmas. *Creativity Research Journal, 20,* 328–342.

CHAPTER 3

Creative Products

Defining and Measuring Novel Solutions

David H. Cropley

Key Take-Aways

- Change—climate, economic, social—creates *new* problems.
- Creativity is about finding *new solutions* to those new problems.
- Creative solutions—or *products*—can take many forms (e.g., artifacts or services).
- Product creativity can be *measured*, and what can be measured can be improved.
- Products give creativity its purpose.

Introduction

There are many different ways of looking at creativity. If you are a student of psychology, it would be surprising if you weren't interested in the role that personality plays in creativity: *Who* is creative—what personal properties favor creativity, what feelings are associated with it, and what factors motivate it? If your interests tend toward the cognitive and neuroscientific, you might also be concerned with the thinking processes behind creativity: *How* are we creative—what thinking styles, or processes, characterize creativity? If you are a student of sociology, with an interest in groups, or if you have a particular curiosity about organizations, you might be more interested in the places that creativity occurs: *Where* are we creative—what aspects of organizations, and the people within them, help or hinder creativity?

Regardless of the focus that you take, and that may include all of the above, you have probably also realized that creativity usually occurs for a reason, or in a particular context. In other words, we aren't creative simply for the sake of being creative. This begs one final question: *Why* are we creative? The answer to this question lies in the fact that creativity is, broadly speaking, a process of *generating an outcome*. A more concise way to say that is that creativity is concerned with generating *products*.

Focusing on the product probably sounds like it's less the business of social science majors, and more the concern of engineers, and if I tell you I'm a physicist/engineer, working in an engineering school, you may start to wonder why this chapter is in this book! The reasons are simple. First, although products are definitely at the applications end of creativity, we find creative products everywhere, not just in engineering. Second, the key characteristic of products, whether engineered or artistic, is creativity, and that comes from people, employing cognitive processes, within a given setting. In other words, creativity results from the *interaction* of *person*, *process*, *press* (the organizational climate), and *product*.

Having just made the case for a *systems model* of creativity, I am going to concentrate on the product, but I would like you to keep that big picture in mind—a creative product results from the interaction of the *who*, the *how*, and the *where*. However, before I start looking in a little more detail at exactly what we mean by a product, I want to address one other important question: *What* is creativity?

What Is Creativity?

In the discussion so far, I've avoided giving you a single, clear definition of creativity. I suggested that it results from the interaction of person, process, and press, and results in a product, but that still hasn't really pinned down the details. The risk of talking about creativity, without a clear definition of creativity, is that we drift into some common misconceptions, like the idea that creativity is synonymous only with artistic pursuits, or that creativity is some mystical quality that some people are lucky enough to be born with. Dispelling these myths is especially important in a discussion about products, because creative products play such a ubiquitous and important role across so many areas of modern life. I'll give you two definitions of creativity that say the same thing, but in different ways—one is more formal, one is more colloquial.

The first, formal, definition of creativity neatly captures the *systems* nature of interacting elements—the person, process, press, and product—and was spelled out by Plucker, Beghetto, and Dow (2004). It says that creativity is "the interaction among *aptitude* [i.e., person], *process and environment* [i.e., press] by which an individual or group produces a *perceptible product* that is both *novel and useful* as defined within a *social context*" (Plucker et al., 2004, p. 90). This definition highlights one element that we have not yet mentioned, but that is critical to the discussion of creative products. They note that products, in a discussion of creativity, must be both novel and useful. I said earlier that we aren't creative simply for the sake of being creative, and these qualities of a creative product help to explain why. If creativity was simply dreaming up crazy ideas, or scribbling on a notepad, then creativity might be an end in itself. But it isn't! Creativity is about solving problems and satisfying needs by developing novel and useful solutions—in other words, creativity is all about the aptitudes, processes, and environmental factors that help us to generate new and useful products—whether those products are pieces of music that satisfy an aesthetic need, or new electronic components that enable engineers to build new kinds of computers. The second, simple, definition of creativity is that creativity is concerned with the *generation of effective novelty* (Cropley & Cropley, 2012).

What Do We Mean by a Product?

Having explained that creativity is a systems phenomenon—the interaction of person, process, and press, resulting in novel and useful products—the next thing that we need to do is talk about what products are and where we find them. I alluded to this in the previous section when I talked about pieces or music and electronic components. Can we formalize what we mean by a *product* so that we can talk about creativity in any application domain, using a common language?

Creative—that is, novel and useful—products occur in every domain, from art and music to science and engineering. They *don't* have to be physical objects, but they do have to solve a problem or meet some sort of need (otherwise they wouldn't be useful), and they must be new, original, or surprising. I classify products as one of the following four options:

- **Artifacts:** These are tangible objects—things that you can touch—and include things like hammers, cell phones, and scissors;
- **Processes:** These are methods of doing or producing something. Processes include the production line used in a factory, or a sequence of actions that results in a particular outcome;
- **Systems:** These are complex combinations of interacting elements that form a unitary whole—things like a commercial airliner or a business information system; and
- **Services:** These are organized systems of labor and material aids used to satisfy defined needs—for example, bank accounts, retirement plans, or even home pizza delivery.

So you can see that a painting, for example, is a tangible artifact, and if it is novel and useful, then it can be regarded as a creative product, just the same as a new engineered product. These definitions are not limited by the domain of interest—art or engineering—because they focus on the same underpinning qualities of the product—novelty and usefulness. It's true that we might argue over exactly what makes something new and/or useful in a particular domain, but the underlying indicators are the same. Therefore, when we discuss creative products, in any domain, we are talking about novel and useful artifacts, processes, systems, and/or services.

Why Are Creative Products Important?

Creativity is a curious topic in that it crops up in a variety of different application domains, as I've already indicated. Not only that, but creativity also has a place in conversations about education, from early childhood learning right through to higher education, and indeed, as a component of lifelong learning. It is also a topic of discussion in business, and even, to the extent that creativity is a driver of innovation, in politics and discussions of national economic policy. This pervasive character of creativity is undoubtedly also tied to its systems nature and the fact that creativity involves the interaction of person, process, press, and product—the so-called Four P's (Rhodes, 1961).

One way to think of creativity, therefore, is as an *enabler*—it is a catalyst that helps other things to take place or to work more effectively. Although this might be reasonably self-evident in some areas of activity, like education, it is sometimes harder to identify the value or benefit that creativity brings in relation to products. In simple terms, why are creative products, in the sense already defined, important? What value do the components of a creative product—novelty and usefulness—bring to application domains? Why, for example, would a manufacturer of paperclips be interested in making her product more creative?

Creative products are important because they represent society's response to *change*. We see change occurring all around us in various forms:

- **Social change:** For example, people migrating away from politically or economically unstable countries;
- **Climate change:** Whether you believe it is caused by natural processes or human intervention, there seems little doubt that the Earth's climate is changing, leading to more frequent extreme weather events like droughts and hurricanes;
- **Economic change:** The global financial crisis of recent years is hard to overlook; and
- **Health change:** Epidemics of diseases such as Ebola, and the rise of conditions such as diabetes.

These changes are critical because they are the sources of *problems*. How we react to those problems—in broad terms, the solutions (i.e., the *products*) we develop—reveals the importance of creativity.

Every change results not just in a problem that needs to be solved, but a *new* problem. Even where a change resembles a previous change—for example, we might look at the financial crash of 2008 as similar to the crash of 1929—it is always unique in some respect. The particular set of conditions surrounding the outbreak of Ebola in West Africa in 2014–2015 is not the same as the set of conditions that surrounded the Spanish Flu pandemic of 1918–1920. Different populations were involved, with different preexisting characteristics. For this reason, the problems arising from change can never be solved simply by reapplying an old solution. Of course, there may be elements of an old solution that are relevant to the new problem situation, but each new problem will always have characteristics that are unique, unprecedented, and that therefore require . . . *new solutions*. This is why creativity is a vital, necessary component of products. Products—in the sense of artifacts, services, systems, and processes—represent society's reaction to change. Products are solutions to problems. If we hope to solve the constant stream of new problems that arise from change, then the products we create must be new—in other words, novel—as well as useful, otherwise they will fail to solve the problems that we face. Novel and useful mean that these solutions must therefore be creative.

There are, of course, situations—old problems—for which old solutions are perfectly adequate. These solutions must still be useful, but they do not require the novelty that is inherent in creative products. These tried-and-tested solutions fulfill an important role in society, and it is important to acknowledge that not everything has to be creative. However, for a great many problems—in particular, those stimulated by change—creativity offers the only viable pathway to tackling the problem. The solution to lowering emissions of greenhouse gases is *not*, for example, to build *more* coal-fired power stations! Trying to solve a new problem with an old solution is like trying to open a locked door with the wrong key. No matter how many times you try, that door isn't going to open!

Before I move on to discuss more about what it takes to generate the effective novelty that is a creative product, I want to return briefly to a question I posed at the start of this section—*Why would a manufacturer of paperclips be interested in making her product more creative?* It's tempting to think of this as an example of an old solution solving an old problem, and doing a serviceable job of meeting a need. Why would creativity be important in this example? Surely all that matters is that the paperclip does its job—is useful—and novelty isn't important? Surely the design of the basic paperclip was perfected decades ago? If I was to tell you that, even as recently as the 1990s, new paperclip patents were being filed in the U.S., you might begin to get a sense that there was still some room for novelty, even in the design of something as apparently simple as the humble paperclip.

Remember that it is change that drives creativity in products. The paperclip illustrates the fact that change can stimulate the need for *wholly new* solutions—a kind of *paradigm-breaking* change—but it can also stimulate the need for *incrementally new* solutions, in other words, making existing solutions better, faster, or cheaper. What might cause that sort of change? Competition! Our paperclip manufacturer may have been in the business for years, when suddenly a new player enters the market—one that makes existing paperclips a little cheaper than everyone else. This changed marketplace provides a stimulus to find ways to respond to that competition: Can we find a way to make our paperclips 10% cheaper? Or, can we improve our paperclip design, making it more effective, so that people will still buy it, even though there are cheaper alternatives? In both cases, novelty is required—new manufacturing methods, or new materials, or new ways to carry out the function of clipping paper—and this means that product creativity still plays a central role in how we respond to change[6].

What Do We Know About Producing Creative Products?

At the start of this chapter I noted that there are different ways to study creativity—the Four P's. The general thrust was that psychological elements of the person combine with the cognitive processes that they employ, under some set of environmental conditions, to produce an outcome—the product. That description, while entirely accurate, and the basis of modern definitions of creativity, masks the detail of *how* those elements actually come together in practice. The difference here is a matter of shifting from talking about creativity to talking about *creative problem solving*. How do people in the real world go about responding to change by developing novel and useful products?

The big change in thinking that we make in this section is to go from a *static* representation of creativity, to a *dynamic* representation of creative problem solving. Another good way to make this shift in thinking is to talk about *design*. When we produce a creative product (i.e., when we respond to the new problems stimulated by change), we are *designing* a solution. This concept has a long history in disciplines like engineering, which recognize that design requires us "to pull together something new or to arrange existing things in a new way to satisfy a recognized need of society" (Blumrich, 1970, in Dieter & Schmidt, 2012, p. 1), but may be less familiar in other application domains. However, the growth in popularity of Design Thinking (e.g., Puccio & Cabra, 2010) as a creative problem solving methodology demonstrates that this mental model resonates across a wide range of domains.

Perhaps the most important consequence of a dynamic view of creative problem solving is that it introduces the idea of stages, or steps, in the process of designing creative products. That also then suggests that there is an *interaction* between the Four P's and each stage in the design of a creative product. If person, process, and press interact to deliver the creative product, do they interact in the same way in each stage of design?

What we know about producing creative products—to answer the previous question—is that there are different requirements for person, process, and

6   In fact, there are at least six things about paperclips that are still open to improvement, and therefore creativity. Paperclips only go on one way, and sometimes have to be turned around before they can be used. They have to be spread apart a little in order to slide them on papers. They can get snagged on things and fall off. They can tear the paper they are holding. They twist or fall off if the stack of paper is too large. They bulk up the papers they are holding, taking up additional space. Each of these is an opportunity for creativity in paperclip design.

press depending on what stage of the design process we are currently engaged in. To illustrate this, let me pick out two key stages of the design process. Different models of design may call these stages by different names, so I'm going to go back to basics and use terminology that J. P. Guilford (1959) used. Why Guilford? He is the person whom we can probably regard as the father of the modern creativity era and his 1949 address to the American Psychological Association, in his capacity as president, is widely regarded as the stimulus for modern research into creativity (Guilford, 1950). He identified two key stages of creative problem solving (i.e., design), namely *idea generation* and *idea evaluation*.

In the first of these two stages—idea generation—we know that the key cognitive process is *divergent thinking*. This is such a key to creativity that it is the basis of many of the tests that are used to assess a person's creative thinking (e.g., the Torrance Tests of Creativity include activities such as the Alternate Uses Test, in which respondents generate as many different ideas as they can for using a given object). So it seems reasonable to say that if you want to produce creative products, what we know is that you need to be good at divergent thinking.

In the second of the two stages—idea evaluation—things are somewhat different. Here, we now have a set of alternative ideas, or solutions. The question now is not how do we generate these alternatives, but which one of them is the best solution? The key to this stage, therefore, is the ability to think analytically. We need to be able to formulate a set of evaluation criteria, and then examine each alternative against these, in order to find the single best solution to the problem. Not surprisingly, this kind of thinking is quite different from the thinking we employ to generate lots of ideas, and we refer to this as *convergent thinking*. The critical point is to recognize that producing a creative product is not simply a matter of generating ideas—divergent thinking—and it is not only a question of evaluating alternatives—convergent thinking. It is a combination of both!

It turns out that each of the core elements of creativity—person, process, press—needed to deliver a creative product is subject to the same paradox. At different stages of the creative problem solving process, the same parameter (e.g., a given cognitive process) can be either good for creativity or bad for creativity. When you are generating ideas, you need to be thinking divergently, and if you are thinking convergently, the process of producing a creative product will actually be impeded. Creativity is therefore a matter of doing the right things at the right time across elements of aptitude, process, and environmental factors.

How Do We Assess Creative Products?

We have seen that creative products are the outcome of a complex interaction between person, process, and press. We also noted that there are two key defining characteristics of creative products: novelty and usefulness. How do we measure these characteristics, and indeed, is that all that matters?

There are two issues to address in this section and they can be characterized in the following way. First, *what are the right things to measure* in assessing creative products, and second, *how do we measure things right?* The former is a matter of identifying the appropriate indicators of creativity in products[7], and the latter is a question of the methods we employ to express the creativity of a product in some more objective (usually numerical) form and their accuracy.

The definition I used earlier represents the general consensus in creativity research. The right things to measure in assessing creative products are, first and foremost, novelty and usefulness. *Novelty* because, without it, products remain shackled to old conditions and cannot address the new problems that are stimulated by change. *Usefulness* because any solution to a problem must, first and foremost, achieve a desired outcome. A product that is *novel, but useless* is regarded as an example of pseudocreativity. It may be unusual, or unconventional, and it may be very tempting to think of it as creative, but because it does not solve a problem, it cannot be regarded as a creative product. Similarly, a product that is *useful, but not novel,* is also not creative, even though it may serve an important purpose. To be regarded as creative, and to be capable of tackling the novel problems brought about by change, products must combine novelty and usefulness.

Creativity researchers have also proposed, and investigated, other qualities of products that may contribute to, or enhance, creativity. For example, the *elegance* of a product—how complete, well-made, and pleasing it is—may be important in characterizing the creativity. In engineering, we often say that a good solution usually *looks like* a good solution, capturing the notion that there is something inherently recognizable, and aesthetically pleasing, about useful (i.e., effective) solutions. Insofar as usefulness is a prerequisite for creativity, then anything that contributes to, and enhances, that usefulness must also play a role in creativity.

Along similar lines, *genesis* is a quality of creative products that captures what we can think of as higher order aspects of novelty. If novelty means that a product is new in the sense of solving the problem at hand, genesis examines the degree to which a solution may be transferable to other unforeseen situations. A simple example is the mousetrap—although invented for the purpose

---

7   Note that a more formal discussion of this issue concerns the validity of measuring instruments and spans content validity, criterion-related validity, and construct validity.

of catching mice, it can also be used to store energy (in the spring), which can then be used to power a toy car (by attaching a string to the spring and winding that around the car's axle). As a solution, the mousetrap offers a kind of two-for-one deal, and creative solutions often possess this quality of being able to solve more than just the *obvious* problem.

We assess creative products, therefore, by measuring their novelty and usefulness in the first instance, and, we may be able to enhance these measures by adding further criteria such as elegance and genesis. Although the first two indicators are widely recognized in creativity literature, the latter two are more *experimental* in nature, and have been the subject of studies seeking to improve the way the product creativity is measured (e.g., Cropley & Kaufman, 2012).

The second issue in assessing product creativity—*measuring things right*—concerns the methods and tools of measurement. How do we employ the indicators identified previously to deliver an accurate *measure* of product creativity? An important part of this question is the issue of *reliability* (i.e., accuracy). Regardless of the method used to assess product creativity, we want it to deliver values that properly reflect the *true* value of the creativity of the product. It goes without saying that like all measures used in research, we would like our assessments of product creativity to be *stable* over time and to be *consistent*. However, I'm going to treat that as a given, and focus here on two fundamentally different ways that we use the indicators to generate assessments of product creativity.

The first method that is frequently used to assess product creativity is founded on the simple principle that if you want to know how creative something is, then ask people who know! This is not as haphazard as it seems, and has a solid empirical foundation in the form of the Consensual Assessment Technique (CAT), first discussed by Amabile (1982). It has been used quite widely in creativity research, and is able to deliver assessments that seem to be stable and consistent, and reflect the thing we are interested in, namely creativity. In other words, at least when it comes to novelty and usefulness, domain experts—for example, art teachers—are able to form good judgments of the creativity of artistic products.

One weakness of the CAT, however, is the very fact that it relies on the judgments of experts. Imagine if, every time you wanted to know the temperature outside, you had to ring a meteorologist to find out! This very fact makes these assessments harder to access and may make them harder to explain. Although this may not be important in some situations—think of a competition in which "no further correspondence will be entered into"—it will be an issue in one very important, and common context where creativity is desired—namely, education. Part of the purpose in assessing product creativity is that it enables us to reflect on it, improve it, and do more of the things that enhance it.

If we can't explain *why* something is creative, in addition to simply saying how much creativity it has, then it is difficult to use measures of product creativity to educate and make decisions.

Imagine a teacher who is encouraging her class to come up with creative ideas for an essay. Each child gives her a draft of his or her essay, so that she can give them some feedback. If all that she did was to say, "no, this isn't creative" or "yes, this is creative," then there would be little for the child to learn and nothing he or she could do to change his or her creativity. Even giving feedback that the essay "lacks novelty" or is "very effective, but not very original" probably isn't enough to drive specific changes and actions that develop the student's creativity. What the teacher needs is a rating scale that addresses not only the indicators that we know are important—novelty, usefulness, and probably elegance and genesis—but also allows the teacher to rate these in such a way that the student can see the degree of novelty, or the degree of usefulness, and not just a binary, all-or-nothing indication of these qualities.

Rating scales for product creativity have a solid foundation in creativity research, starting with Taylor's (1975) Creative Product Inventory, and include more recent examples like the Creative Solution Diagnosis Scale (CSDS) developed by Cropley, Kaufman, and Cropley (2011). These, and others, share a common foundation around novelty and usefulness, and incorporate other criteria in varying levels of detail. All of them move the assessment of product creativity away from a reliance on the more subjective judgments of experts, to a more accessible, objective, and traceable quantification of specific indicators of product creativity. Not only that, but the detail and objectivity serve as a tool for explaining not only *how much* creativity a product has, but also *why* it is creative.

Can You Be Creative Without a Product?

I touched on this question earlier in the chapter when I suggested that we aren't creative simply for the sake of it. A systems model of creativity tells us that creativity emerges from the interaction of the 4Ps—the person, the process, and the press interact to deliver a product. It follows that if we remove any of these contributing elements, then we no longer have creativity. It stands to reason, therefore, that if there is no product, there is no creativity.

There is no doubt that a person who is open to experiences, flexible, and courageous can engage in divergent thinking and can do so most effectively in a setting that encourages this sort of activity. However, it is hard to see what purpose this would serve if no novel and useful *product* resulted from the effort. Divergent thinking, on its own, is fantasy. There's nothing wrong with that, but we recognize it for what it is, and label it accordingly. Personal qualities, like openness, are aptitudes, waiting to be employed to some end. A favorable press—an organizational or social climate that supports creativity—is a necessary, but not sufficient, condition for creativity. It's only when these elements interact as a system that the whole becomes greater than the sum of the parts. The act of *being creative* is the end result of the interaction of these four elements.

There is one obvious consequence of the preceding discussion for educators. If *no product means no creativity*, then it follows that if we wish to develop creativity in students—of whatever level—we must give them the opportunity to practice developing . . . creative products! I argued earlier that creativity arises in response to change, and creative solutions—novel and effective products—are how we solve the problems we face in society. Most of us would be reluctant to visit a dentist who had never actually filled a tooth before, no matter how good his or her rapport with patients or how deep his or her knowledge of anatomy and physiology. So it is with creativity. The best way to make a habit of finding and implementing novel solutions to problems is to practice finding and implementing novel solutions to problems! For this reason, and whatever the subject and level of education, students must be given appropriate and authentic opportunities to develop creative products in a setting that understands and values this problem-based approach to learning.

Conclusion

To close, I would like to leave you with some questions that are based on the material covered in the chapter. Creativity sometimes suffers from the fact that a number of common myths are repeated without question; for example, there is the myth that creativity is ill-defined and poorly understood. The more you think about these questions, challenge them, and look for solid answers, the more the myths are debunked, and that's how knowledge develops and expands.

I said that we aren't creative simply for the sake of being creative, but is that right? Why can't creativity be just fantasy? Most definitions of creativity seem to accept that usefulness is a key, but does usefulness mean only "solving a problem"? I like to think of products as one of four things: artifact, processes, systems, or services. Where does something like a piece of music fit in that scheme? Creativity is important because it helps us to generate new solutions to the new problems that arise from change. What happens when an old solution is applied to a new problem? The process of developing a creative product consists of more than one step. Is it sufficient to think of a step of idea generation, followed by a step of idea evaluation, or are there more steps surrounding these? There are a number of ways that have been devised to measure product creativity. But who, or what, decides on the *ground truth*? What do we compare these against to know if we are measuring the true value of the creativity of the product? Finally, systems models of creativity are based on the idea that a number of interacting elements combine to deliver something that the individual elements cannot deliver on their own. Is this valid for creativity? If we take away one of the 4Ps, can we still speak of creativity?

Recommended Readings

Cropley, D. H., & Cropley, A. J. (2015). *The psychology of innovation in organizations*. New York, NY: Cambridge University Press.

Cropley, D. H., & Kaufman, J. C. (2012). Measuring functional creativity: Non-expert raters and the creative solution diagnosis scale. *The Journal of Creative Behavior, 46,* 119–137.

Guilford, J. P. (1950). Creativity. *American Psychologist, 5,* 444–454.

Puccio, G. J., & Cabra, J. F. (2010). Organizational creativity: A systems approach. In J. C. Kaufman & R. J. Sternberg (Eds.), *The Cambridge handbook of creativity* (pp. 145–173). New York, NY: Cambridge University Press.

References

Amabile, T. M. (1982). Social psychology of creativity: A consensual assessment technique. *Journal of Personality and Social Psychology, 43,* 997–1013.

Blumrich, J. F. (1970). Design. *Science, 168,* 1551–1554.

Cropley, D. H., & Cropley, A. J. (2012). A psychological taxonomy of organizational innovation: resolving the paradoxes. *Creativity Research Journal, 24*(1), 29–40.

Cropley, D. H., & Kaufman, J. C. (2012). Measuring functional creativity: Non-expert raters and the creative solution diagnosis scale. *The Journal of Creative Behavior, 46,* 119–137.

Cropley, D. H., Kaufman, J. C., & Cropley, A. J. (2011). Measuring creativity for innovation management. *Journal of Technology Management & Innovation, 6*(3), 13–30.

Dieter, G. E., & Schmidt, L. C. (2012). *Engineering design* (5th ed.). New York, NY: McGraw-Hill.

Guilford, J. P. (1950). Creativity. *American Psychologist, 5,* 444–454.

Guilford, J. P. (1959). Traits of creativity. In H. H. Anderson (Ed.), *Creativity and its cultivation* (pp. 142–161). New York, NY: Harper.

Plucker, J. A., Beghetto, R. A., & Dow, G. T. (2004). Why isn't creativity more important to educational psychologists? Potentials, pitfalls, and future directions in creativity research. *Educational Psychologist, 39*(2), 83–96.

Puccio, G. J., & Cabra, J. F. (2010). Organizational creativity: A systems approach. In J. C. Kaufman & R. J. Sternberg (Eds.), *The Cambridge handbook of creativity* (pp. 145–173). New York, NY: Cambridge University Press.

Rhodes, M. (1961). An analysis of creativity. *The Phi Delta Kappan, 42,* 305–310.

Taylor, I. A. (1975). An emerging view of creative actions. In I. A. Taylor & J. W. Getzels (Eds.), *Perspectives in creativity* (pp. 297–325). Chicago, IL: Aldine.

High-Tech Innovation, Creativity, and Regional Development

Richard Florida

Key Take-Aways

- Regional innovation and economic growth are driven by creative people who are drawn to places that are diverse, tolerant, and open to new ideas.
- Places that are open to creativity—technical, cultural, economic—reflect an underlying environment that favors the kind of risk taking that stimulates entrepreneurship.
- Both entrepreneurship and creativity require diversity.
- Technological innovation, entrepreneurship, and regional growth stem from the 3Ts of economic development—technology, talent, and tolerance.
- The most successful places recognize the interdependence of the 3Ts.

Entrepreneurship, innovation, and creativity, both in the conventional wisdom and the academic view, have long been seen as the province of great individuals. Scores of books and articles have been written extolling the virtues of heroic creators and entrepreneurs. But this "great man" theory ignores the fundamental fact that innovation and entrepreneurship are collective processes.

Creativity is multifaceted and multidimensional (see also Dow and Beghetto and Kaufman, this volume). I identify three interrelated types of creativity: (1) technological creativity or innovation, (2) economic creativity or entrepreneurship, and (3) artistic and cultural creativity.

I argue that these three types of creativity are mutually dependent and reinforce one another. Entrepreneurship of the Schumpeterian sort—that is, the creation of innovative, high-growth firms, with which this volume as a whole is mainly concerned—is not simply the result of great inventors or entrepreneurs, but is instead embedded in places (Mokyr, 1990; Schumpeter, 1947). And both entrepreneurship and creativity require diversity. As the great urbanist Jane Jacobs (1961) observed some 40 years ago, creativity and innovation come from the clustering of diverse places in dense, open-minded urban environments.

This chapter provides an empirically based assessment of the relationships among high-tech innovation, creativity, and diversity at the regional level. The next section reviews prior work and introduces some of the central precepts of my creativity-based perspective. The third section presents the basic designs, methods, and indicators used in the research. I then examine the relationship between high-tech innovation, creativity, and diversity. The last section discusses the implications of these trends and findings for the emerging field of entrepreneurship policy.

Conceptual Frame

Economists and geographers have always accepted that economic growth is regional, that it is driven by and spreads from specific regions, cities, or even neighborhoods. Robert Park (Park, Burgess, & McKenzie, 1925), Jane Jacobs (1961, 1969, 1984), and Wilbur Thompson (1986), among others, long ago pointed to the role of places as incubators of creativity, innovation, and new firms and industries. The earliest explanation of this phenomenon was that places grow either because they are located on transportation routes or because they have endowments of natural resources that encourage firms to locate there. According to this conventional view, the economic importance of a place is tied to the efficiency with which one can make things and do business. Governments employ this theory when they use tax breaks and highway construction to attract business. But these cost-related factors are no longer key to success.

Another major theory of regional growth suggests that place remains important as a locus of economic activity because of the tendency of firms to cluster together. This view builds on the seminal insights of the economist Alfred Marshall. The contemporary variant of this view, advanced by Michael Porter (1998, 2000a, 2000b), has many proponents in academia and in the practice of economic development.

The question is not whether firms cluster, but why. Several answers have been offered. Some experts believe, as Marshall did, that "agglomerations" of similar firms capture efficiencies generated from tight linkages between the firms. Others say it has to do with the positive benefits of co-location, which are sometimes referred to as "spillovers." Still others claim agglomeration occurs because certain kinds of activity require face-to-face contact (Audretsch, 1998; Audretsch & Feldman, 1996; Feldman, 2000; Jaffe, 1989). But these are only partial answers.

Over the past decade or so, a more powerful theory to explain city and regional growth has emerged that identifies people as the motor for growth. Thus, its proponents refer to it as the "human capital" theory of regional development. They argue that the key to regional growth lies not in reducing the costs of doing business, nor in the clustering of firms, but in enhancing regional endowments of highly educated and productive people.

Human capital theory owes a particular debt to the work of Jane Jacobs. Decades ago, Jacobs (1984) noted the ability of cities to attract creative people and thus spur economic growth. For a long time, academic economists ignored her ideas, but in the past decade or two, they have been taken up with gusto. The Nobel-prize winning economist Robert Lucas, for instance, sees the productivity effect that comes from the clustering of human capital as the critical factor in regional economic growth, referring to it as a "Jane Jacobs externality." Building on Jacobs's seminal insight, Lucas (1988) contended that cities would be economically infeasible if not for the productivity effect associated with endowments of human capital:

> If we postulate only the usual list of economic forces, cities should fly apart. The theory of production contains nothing to hold a city together. A city is simply a collection of factors of production—capital, people and land—and land is always far cheaper outside cities than inside . . . It seems to me that the 'force' we need to postulate to account for the central role of cities in economic life is of exactly the same character as the 'external human capital' . . . What can people be paying

> Manhattan or downtown Chicago rents for, if not for being
> near other people? (pp. 59–60)

Studies of national growth find a clear connection between the economic success of nations and talent or human capital, as measured by the level of education. This connection has also been found in cities and regions. In a series of studies, Edward Glaeser and his collaborators (Glaeser, 1998, 2000; Mathur, 1999; Rauch, 1993; Simon, 1998; Simon & Nardinelli, 1996) found considerable empirical evidence that human capital is the central factor in regional growth. The clustering of talent and skill is the ultimate source of regional agglomerations of firms. Firms concentrate to reap the advantages that stem from common labor pools and not to tap the advantages from linked networks of customers and suppliers, as Porter (1998, 2000a) and others argued. Places with greater numbers of talented people grew faster and were better able to attract more talent. Places with high concentrations of talent both attract existing firms and provide the habitat required to create new innovation and entrepreneurial startup companies.

But why and how do talented, creative, and entrepreneurial people cluster in certain places? I offer three basic reasons.

- **Thick labor markets:** The presence not just of "a job," but of multiple job opportunities in a single place.
- **Diversity:** Visible signs of diversity, such as prevalence of various nationalities and ethnicities as well as a visible gay community, provide cues that a place is open to all and possesses "low entry barriers" to human capital.
- **Quality of place:** I define quality of place in terms of three attributes: what's there—the buildings, the neighborhoods, the physical design; who's there—the people, the diversity, the human energy; and what's going on—the vibrancy of street life, sidewalk cafes, restaurants and music venues, and active outdoor recreation.

I argue, then, that regional innovation and economic growth are driven by creative people who prefer and are drawn to places that are diverse, tolerant, and open to new ideas. This "creative capital" theory thus differs from human capital theory in two respects. First, it identifies a type of human capital—creative people—that is the key to economic growth. Second, it identifies the underlying factors that shape the location decisions of these people, instead of merely saying that regions are blessed with certain endowments of them. Furthermore, it suggests that creativity is linked to diversity. Diversity increases the odds that a place will attract different types of creative people with different skill sets and ideas. Places with diverse mixes of creative people are more likely to generate new and novel combinations. Diversity and concentration work together to speed the flow of knowledge. Greater and more diverse concentrations of creative capital in turn lead to higher rates of innovation, high-technology business formation, job generation, and economic growth. This theory suggests that places that are open to creativity of all sorts (technological and cultural as well as economic) reflect an underlying environment or habitat that favors risk taking and thus will stimulate entrepreneurship and new firm formation.

In more pragmatic terms, my creativity-based theory of regional growth says that technological innovation, entrepreneurship, and regional growth stem from what I call the "3Ts" of economic development: *technology*, *talent*, and *tolerance*. To spur innovation, economic growth, and other good things, a region must have all three of them. The 3Ts explain why regions like Baltimore, St. Louis, and Pittsburgh fail to stimulate innovation, entrepreneurship, and growth despite their deep reservoirs of technology and world-class universities: They are unwilling to be sufficiently tolerant and open to attract and retain top creative talent and stimulate risk-taking behavior. The interdependence of the 3Ts also explains why regions like Miami and New Orleans do not make the grade even though they are lifestyle meccas: They lack the required technology base.

The most successful places—Boulder, the San Francisco Bay Area, Greater Boston, Ann Arbor, Seattle, San Diego, Corvallis, and Durham—put all 3Ts together. They are truly creative places.

Research Design and Methods

To test this theory, my team and I (Florida, 2002, 2012) developed a series of new and unique indicators of the social and economic factors that are associated with innovation, entrepreneurship, and regional economic growth. Conventional studies of regional entrepreneurship have been plagued by an absence of reliable and systematic measures of new firm formation that are biased toward small service establishments and fail to get at the dynamic entrepreneurship of the Schumpeterian sort, which ultimately spurs economic growth. To remedy this, I employ a measure of high-tech innovation as a proxy for Schumpeterian creative destruction.

High-Tech Innovation

Instead of attempting to account for firm formation per se, I choose to focus instead on more robust measures of high-tech industry and innovation. I use the following index developed by Ross DeVol and a team of researchers at the Milken Institute (DeVol, Wong, Catapano, & Robitshek, 1999).

High-Tech Innovation Index. The High-Tech Innovation Index is a composite of three measures, including the Milken Institute's Tech-Pole Index, a measure of high-tech industry concentration, plus two measures of regional innovation: patents per capita and average annual patent growth. It is based on data from 2005–2009.

Creative Class

Creative Class Index. This is the share of the creative class as defined below (as per *The Rise of the Creative Class*; Florida, 2002). The rise of creativity as an economic force has registered itself in the rise of a new class. Some 50 million Americans, roughly one-third of all employed people, are members of the Creative Class, up from 15% in 1950 and less than 20% as recently as 1980. I define the core of the Creative Class to include people in science and engineering, architecture and design, education, arts, music, and entertainment whose economic function is to create new ideas, new technology, and new creative content. Around this core, the Creative Class also includes a broader group of creative professionals in business and finance, law, health care, and related fields. These people engage in complex problem solving that involves a great deal of independent judgment and requires high levels of education or human capital (Florida, 2012).

Bohemian Index. The Bohemian Index is our measure of cultural creativity. In their studies of Chicago, Richard Lloyd and Terry Clark (2001) dubbed revitalizing urban areas "entertainment machines." In a detailed statistical study, Glaeser (2001) and his collaborators found considerable support for this view, which they referred to as a shift from the producer to the "consumer city." The Bohemian Index is an improvement over the measures used by these scholars, because it directly counts the producers of cultural amenities using reliable U.S. Census data. The Bohemian Index is a measure of artistically creative people. It includes authors, designers, musicians, composers, actors, directors, painters, sculptors, printmakers, photographers, dancers, artists, and performers. It is based on the 2005–2009 U.S. Census American Community Survey.

Diversity

As Jacobs long professed, diversity of people is the catalyst for diversity of thought and innovation. In order to get at this phenomenon from a quantitative perspective, I use a variety of novel indicators to account for the social and economic factors that may condition or affect the process of high-tech entrepreneurship.

Gay-Lesbian Index. Drawing on original research by Gary Gates and others, the gay-lesbian index is a location quotient ranking of gay households per capita, based on the percentage of all U.S. gays and lesbians who live in the region divided by the percentage of the total U.S. population who live there (Black, Gates, Sanders, & Taylor, 2000).

Foreign-Born Index. This index measures the relative percentage of foreign-born people in a region, based on the 2005–2009 U.S. Census American Community Survey.

Tolerance Index. The Tolerance Index is a composite measure of the Gay-Lesbian Index, the Foreign-Born Index, and the Racial Integration Index, a measure of racial integration versus separation in a metro area.

Creativity Index. In order to get at the full magnitude of creativity and its link to entrepreneurship, I combined a number of different indices that are representative of a region's openness, tolerance, and innovation. The Creativity Index is a composite measure based on four indices for the most current year available: High-Tech Innovation Index, the Creative Class Index, Bohemian Index, and the Gay-Lesbian Index.

With the help of my colleague, Charlotta Mellander, I ran a basic correlation analysis between these variables. Of course, I point out that correlation cannot assess causality, but only accounts for associations between these variables. We ran the correlations for roughly 360 U.S. metros (the actual number varies per indicator) and for the 60 large metros with more than one million people. The appendix for this chapter provides the results of this correlation analysis.

The Creative Class and High-Tech Innovation

Table 4.1 shows how the top and bottom 10 metros on the High-Tech Innovation Index compare in terms of the Creative Class share of the workforce. Six of the top 10 Creative Class metros and 11 of the top 20 also rank among the leaders on the High-Tech Innovation Index.

The Creative Class Index is positively associated with the High-Tech Innovation Index with correlations of 0.622 for the 60 large metros and 0.648 for all 350 plus metros.

I now turn to the connection between the High-Tech Innovation Index and a measure of cultural creativity, the Bohemian Index. Table 4.2 shows how the leading and lagging Bohemian Index metros compare on the High-Tech Innovation Index. Ten of the 20 large metros on the Bohemian Index also rank among the top 20 on the High-Tech Innovation Index. Furthermore, the correlations between the High-Tech Innovation Index and the Bohemian Index

Table 4.1
The Creative Class and High-Tech Innovation Index

High-Tech Innovation Index Rank	Metro	Creative Class	
		Share	Rank
1	Seattle-Tacoma-Bellevue, WA	37.7 %	8
2	San Jose-Sunnyvale-Santa Clara, CA	46.9 %	1
3	San Francisco-Oakland-Fremont, CA	39.4 %	6
4	Portland-Vancouver-Beaverton, OR-WA	34.2 %	27
5	Austin-Round Rock, TX	34.4 %	24
6	Raleigh-Cary, NC	37.6 %	10
7	San Diego-Carlsbad-San Marcos, CA	35.6 %	17
8	Boston-Cambridge-Quincy, MA-NH	41.6 %	3
9	Tucson, AZ	33.9 %	30
10	Minneapolis-St. Paul-Bloomington, MN-WI	37.7 %	9
51	Honolulu, HI	32.4 %	42
52	Jacksonville, FL	30.4 %	54
53	Tulsa, OK	30.7 %	52
54	Birmingham-Hoover, AL	33.1 %	34
55	Dayton, OH	34.2 %	26
56	Buffalo-Cheektowaga-Tonawanda, NY	31.3 %	49
56	Louisville, KY-IN	29.5 %	56
58	Oklahoma City, OK	33.0 %	37
58	New Orleans-Metairie-Kenner, LA	30.9 %	51
60	Fresno, CA	28.3 %	58

are positive and significant—0.532 for the 60 large regions and 0.632 for the full set of 322 metros for which we have comparable data.

Diversity and High-Tech Innovation

From Andrew Carnegie in steel to Andy Grove in semiconductors, immigrants have been a powerful source of innovation and entrepreneurship. People who choose to leave their countries of origin are predisposed to take risks and can be thought of as "innovative outsiders." It seems obvious that people and groups facing obstacles in traditional organizations are more likely to start their own enterprises, and the facts bear this out. Between a third to half of Silicon Valley startups are reported to have a foreign-born person among their

Table 4.2

The Bohemian Index and High-Tech Innovation Index

High-Tech Innovation Index Rank	Metro	Bohemian Index Rank
1	Seattle-Tacoma-Bellevue, WA	8
2	San Jose-Sunnyvale-Santa Clara, CA	20
3	San Francisco-Oakland-Fremont, CA	7
4	Portland-Vancouver-Beaverton, OR-WA	12
5	Austin-Round Rock, TX	30
6	Raleigh-Cary, NC	41
7	San Diego-Carlsbad-San Marcos, CA	15
8	Boston-Cambridge-Quincy, MA-NH	NA
9	Tucson, AZ	33
10	Minneapolis-St Paul-Bloomington, MN-WI	4
51	Honolulu, HI	24
52	Jacksonville, FL	46
53	Tulsa, OK	NA
54	Birmingham-Hoover, AL	49
55	Dayton, OH	38
56	Buffalo-Cheektowaga-Tonawanda, NY	37
56	Louisville, KY-IN	46
58	Oklahoma City, OK	NA
58	New Orleans-Metairie-Kenner, LA	51
60	Fresno, CA	53

founding team (Saxenian, 1999, 2007; Wadhwa, Saxenian, Rissing, & Gereffi, 2008).

Table 4.3 shows how the leading and lagging metros on the Foreign-Born Index compare on the High-Tech Innovation Index. There is less overlap than for the Creative Class and Bohemian Indices. Ten out of the top large 20 metros on the Foreign-Born Index also rank in the top 20 on the High-Tech Innovation Index. More telling, however, the correlations between the High-Tech Innovation Index and the Foreign Born Index are positive and significant, though more modest than for the Creative Class or Bohemian Index—0.359 for the 60 large metros and 0.273 for all 350 plus metros.

I next turn to the Gay-Lesbian Index. My previous research with Gary Gates (Florida & Gates, 2002) has shown a significant association between the two. We argued that this is due to the fact that a place that is open to the gay and lesbian population will most likely have low barriers to human capital for

Table 4.3

The Foreign-Born Index and High-Tech Innovation Index

High-Tech Innovation Index Rank	Metro	Foreign Born Index Rank
1	Seattle-Tacoma-Bellevue, WA	20
2	San Jose-Sunnyvale-Santa Clara, CA	2
3	San Francisco-Oakland-Fremont, CA	4
4	Portland-Vancouver-Beaverton, OR-WA	26
5	Austin-Round Rock, TX	21
6	Raleigh-Cary, NC	32
7	San Diego-Carlsbad-San Marcos, CA	6
8	Boston-Cambridge-Quincy, MA-NH	18
9	Tucson, AZ	22
10	Minneapolis-St. Paul-Bloomington, MN-WI	35
51	Honolulu, HI	13
52	Jacksonville, FL	39
53	Tulsa, OK	51
54	Birmingham-Hoover, AL	57
55	Dayton, OH	60
56	Buffalo-Cheektowaga-Tonawanda, NY	51
56	Louisville, KY-IN	56
58	Oklahoma City, OK	40
58	New Orleans-Metairie-Kenner, LA	46
60	Fresno, CA	7

other populations as well. These low barriers to entry are critical for stimulating high-tech growth and innovation.

Table 4.4 shows how the leading and lagging Gay-Lesbian Index metros stack up on the High-Tech Innovation Index. Eleven of the top 20 large metros on the Gay-Lesbian Index also rank among the top 20 on the High-Tech Innovation Index.

The correlations between the Gay-Lesbian Index and the High-Tech Innovation Index are positive and significant, with correlations of 0.498 for the 60 large metros and 0.419 for the full set of 319 metros for which comparable data are available.

I next turn to our overall indicator of tolerance or diversity, the Tolerance Index, which combines the Gay-Lesbian, Foreign-Born, and Integration Indices. Table 4.5 shows how the leading and lagging metros on the High-Tech Innovation Index stack up on the Tolerance Index. Eleven of the top 20 large

Table 4.4
The Gay-Lesbian Index and High-Tech Innovation Index

High-Tech Innovation Index Rank	Metro	Gay-Lesbian Index Rank
1	Seattle-Tacoma-Bellevue, WA	2
2	San Jose-Sunnyvale-Santa Clara, CA	16
3	San Francisco-Oakland-Fremont, CA	1
4	Portland-Vancouver-Beaverton, OR-WA	7
5	Austin-Round Rock, TX	3
6	Raleigh-Cary, NC	34
7	San Diego-Carlsbad-San Marcos, CA	8
8	Boston-Cambridge-Quincy, MA-NH	NA
9	Tucson, AZ	19
10	Minneapolis-St. Paul-Bloomington, MN-WI	27
51	Honolulu, HI	38
52	Jacksonville, FL	33
53	Tulsa, OK	46
54	Birmingham-Hoover, AL	37
55	Dayton, OH	48
56	Buffalo-Cheektowaga-Tonawanda, NY	55
56	Louisville, KY-IN	43
58	Oklahoma City, OK	45
58	New Orleans-Metairie-Kenner, LA	15
60	Fresno, CA	26

metros on the Tolerance Index also rank among the top 20 on the High-Tech Innovation Index. The correlations between the High-Tech Innovation Index and the Tolerance Index are positive and significant, with correlations of 0.661 for the 60 large metros and 0.609 for all 350 plus metros.

The Creativity Index and High-Tech Innovation

The Creativity Index provides a single baseline indicator of a region's overall standing in the creative economy. Table 4.6 shows how the leading and lagging High-Tech Innovation metros stack up on the Creativity Index. Nine of the top 10 and 15 of the top 20 large metros on the Creativity Index are also among leaders on the High-Tech Innovation Index.

Table 4.5
The Tolerance Index and High-Tech Innovation Index

High-Tech Innovation Index Rank	Metro	Tolerance Index Rank
1	Seattle-Tacoma-Bellevue, WA	8
2	San Jose-Sunnyvale-Santa Clara, CA	27
3	San Francisco-Oakland-Fremont, CA	6
4	Portland-Vancouver-Beaverton, OR-WA	5
5	Austin-Round Rock, TX	16
6	Raleigh-Cary, NC	33
7	San Diego-Carlsbad-San Marcos, CA	1
8	Boston-Cambridge-Quincy, MA-NH	7
9	Tucson, AZ	11
10	Minneapolis-St Paul-Bloomington, MN-WI	23
51	Honolulu, HI	13
52	Jacksonville, FL	39
53	Tulsa, OK	53
54	Birmingham-Hoover, AL	60
55	Dayton, OH	58
56	Buffalo-Cheektowaga-Tonawanda, NY	57
56	Louisville, KY-IN	49
58	Oklahoma City, OK	43
58	New Orleans-Metairie-Kenner, LA	47
60	Fresno, CA	3

The correlations between the Creativity Index and the High-Tech Innovation Index are positive and significant, and among the highest of any in our analysis—0.854 for the 60 large metros and 0.872 for all 350 plus metros. Creativity and high-tech innovation go closely together.

Conclusion

Creativity, innovation, and entrepreneurship have become the driving force of wealth and growth in the advanced world. As this chapter has shown, all three are part of a collective process that comes together in places.

From a public policy perspective, that means setting in place the broad environment or *habitat* that can attract people, one where creativity and entrepreneurship can flourish. What it boils down to is moving beyond the notion of

Table 4.6
The Creativity Index and High-Tech Innovation Index

High-Tech Innovation Index Rank	Metro	Creativity Index	
		Index	Rank
1	Seattle-Tacoma-Bellevue. WA	0.96	3
2	San Jose-Sunnyvale-Santa Clara. CA	0.93	6
3	San Francisco-Oakland-Fremont. CA	0.97	1
4	Portland-Vancouver-Beaverton. OR-WA	0.93	7
5	Austin-Round Rock. TX	0.92	8
6	Raleigh-Cary. NC	0.89	16
7	San Diego-Carlsbad-San Marcos. CA	0.96	3
8	Boston-Cambridge-Quincy. MA-NH	0.97	2
9	Tucson. AZ	0.91	12
10	Minneapolis-St Paul-Bloomington MN-WI	0.92	10
51	Honolulu. HI	0.78	35
52	Jacksonville. FL	0.64	46
53	Tulsa. OK	0.54	56
54	Birmingham-Hoover. AL	0.52	59
55	Dayton. OH	0.54	55
56	Buffalo-Cheektowaga-Tonawanda. NY	0.50	60
56	Louisville. KY IN	0.54	57
58	Oklahoma City. OK	0.65	45
58	New Orleans-Metairie-Kenner. LA	0.55	54
60	Fresno CA	0.57	52

a business climate and supplementing or replacing that concept with a "people climate." And because people are different, this people climate must be broad enough to appeal to a wide range of them, regardless of age, gender, race, ethnicity, or marital status, and sexual orientation. This open-minded people climate is key to creating an innovative and entrepreneurial habitat or ecosystem.

When I originally advanced these ideas in the early 2000s, many were skeptical. They continued to argue that firms were the motor force of innovation and economic development and suggested I got it backward, saying that people go to jobs, not the other way around. There was particular criticism of my ideas that openness to diversity, as measured by the Gay Index or Bohemian Index, could play any role in innovation and economic development. The past decade has proven this conventional view pretty much dead wrong. Cities and metro regions like San Francisco, Boston, Seattle, Washington, DC, Austin, and others that scored highly on my 3Ts of economic development have, if

Chapter 4 Appendix
Correlation Analysis Results

	High-Tech Innovation Index	
	Large Metros	All Metros
Creative Class Index	.622★★	.648★★
	n = 60	N = 359
Bohemian Index	.532★★	.632★★
	n = 55	N = 322
Foreign-Born Index	.359★★	.273★★
	N = 60	N = 359
Gay-Lesbian Index	.498★★	.419★★
	N = 55	N = 319
Tolerance Index	.481★★	.518★★
	N = 60	N = 361
Creativity Index	.854★★	.872★★
	N = 60	N = 361

★ indicates significance at the 5 % level. ★★ at the 1 % level.

anything, expanded their lead in innovation, entrepreneurship, and economic growth (Florida, 2012). In fact, innovation and high-tech startup activity have shifted away from suburban office parks and so-called nerdistans into the dense urban neighborhoods of downtown San Francisco and New York City (Florida, 2014).

Recommended Reading

Jacobs, J. (1961). *The death and life of great American cities.* New York, NY: Random House.

Florida, R. (2012). *The rise of the creative class: Revisited.* New York, NY: Basic Books.

Porter, M. E. (1998). Clusters and the new economics of competition. *Harvard Business Review.* Retrieved from https://hbr.org/1998/11/clusters-and-the-new-economics-of-competition

Glaeser, E. (2011). *Triumph of the city: How our greatest invention makes us richer, smarter, greener, healthier, and happier.* New York, NY: Penguin.

References

Audretsch, D. (1998). Agglomeration and the location of innovative activity. *Oxford Review of Economic Policy, 14*(2), 18–30.

Audretsch, D., & Feldman, M. P. (1996). R&D spillovers and the geography of innovation and production. *American Economic Review, 86,* 630–640.

Black, D., Gates, G., Sanders, S., & Taylor, L. (2000). Demographics of the gay and lesbian population in the United States: Evidence from available systematic data sources. *Demography, 37,* 139–154.

DeVol, R., Wong, P., Catapano, J., & Robitshek, G. (1999). *America's high technology economy: Growth, development, and risks for metropolitan areas.* Santa Monica, CA: The Milken Institute.

Feldman, M. P. (2000). Location and innovation: The new economic geography of innovation, spillovers, and agglomeration. In G. L. Clark, M. P. Feldman, & M. S. Gertler (Eds.), *Oxford handbook of economic geography* (pp. 373–394). Oxford, England: Oxford University Press.

Florida, R. (2002). *The rise of the creative class: And how it's transforming work, leisure, community, and everyday life.* New York, NY: Basic Books.

Florida, R. (2012). *The rise of the creative class: Revisited.* New York, NY: Basic Books.

Florida, R. (2014). *Startup city: The urban shift in venture capital and high technology.* Toronto, Ontario: Martin Prosperity Institute. Retrieved from http://martinprosperity.org/media/Startup%20City_14-03-14.pdf

Florida, R., & Gates, G. (2002). Technology and tolerance. *The Brookings Review, 20,* 32–36.

Glaeser, E. L. (1998). Are cities dying? *Journal of Economic Perspectives, 12,* 139–160.

Glaeser, E. L. (2000). The new economics of urban and regional growth. In G. L. Clark, M. P. Feldman, & M. S. Gertler (Eds.), *Oxford handbook of economic geography* (pp. 83–98). Oxford, England: Oxford University Press.

Glaeser, E. L. (2001). Consumer city. *Journal of Economic Geography, 1*(1), 27–50.

Jacobs, J. (1961). *The death and life of great American cities.* New York, NY: Random House.

Jacobs, J. (1969). *The economy of cities.* New York, NY: Random House.

Jacobs, J. (1984). *Cities and the wealth of nations.* New York, NY: Random House.

Jaffe, A. B. (1989). Real effects of academic research. *The American Economic Review, 79,* 957–970.

Lloyd, R., & Clark, T. N. (2001). The city as an entertainment machine. In K. F. Gotham (Ed.), *Critical perspectives on urban redevelopment* (pp. 357–378). Oxford, England: JAI Press/Elsevier.

Lucas, R. E. (1988). On the mechanics of economic development. *Journal of Monetary Economics, 22,* 3–42.

Mathur, V. K. (1999). Human capital-based strategy for regional economic development. *Economic Development Quarterly, 13,* 203–216.

Mokyr, J. (1990). *The lever of riches: Technological creativity and economic progress.* New York, NY: Oxford University Press.

Park, R. E., Burgess, E., & McKenzie, R. D. (1925). *The city.* Chicago, IL: University of Chicago Press.

Porter, M. E. (1998). Clusters and the new economics of competition. *Harvard Business Review.* Retrieved from https://hbr.org/1998/11/clusters-and-the-new-economics-of-competition

Porter, M. E. (2000a). Location, clusters, and company strategy. In G. L. Clark, M. P. Feldman, & M. S. Gertler (Eds.), *Oxford handbook of economic geography* (pp. 253–274). Oxford, England: Oxford University Press.

Porter, M. E. (2000b). Location, competition, and economic development: Local clusters in a global economy. *Economic Development Quarterly, 14,* 15–34.

Rauch, J. E. (1993). Productivity gains from geographic concentrations of human capital: Evidence from cities. *Journal of Urban Economics, 34,* 380–400.

Saxenian, A. (1999). *Silicon Valley's new immigrant entrepreneurs.* San Francisco: Public Policy Institute of California.

Saxenian, A. (2007). *The new Argonauts: Regional advantage in a global economy.* Cambridge, MA: Harvard University Press.

Schumpeter, J. A. (1947). The creative response in economic history. *Journal of Economic History, 7,* 149–159.

Simon, C. J. (1998). Human capital and metropolitan employment growth. *Journal of Urban Economics, 43,* 223–243.

Simon, C. J., & Nardinelli, C. (1996). The talk of the town: Human capital, information and the growth of English cities, 1861–1961. *Explorations in Economic History, 33,* 384–413.

Thompson, W. R. (1986). Cities in transition. *The ANNALS of the American Academy of Political and Social Science, 488*(1), 18–34.

Wadhwa, V., Saxenian, A., Rissing, B. A., & Gereffi, G. (2008). Skilled immigration and economic growth. *Applied Research in Economic Development, 5,* 6–14.

CHAPTER 5

Cognition and Creative Thought

Cynthia Sifonis and Thomas B. Ward

Key Take-Aways

- The creative cognition approach assumes everyone has the ability to be creative, and that creativity involves applying normal cognitive processes to normal knowledge structures and occurs during problem solving.
- Creative imagery is often used during creative problem solving. Re-representing the problem as an image frees individuals from the constraints of the task, enabling insight.
- Mental set and design fixation can result from viewing flawed examples prior to generating ideas. This can be avoided by not viewing examples or by viewing examples with unusual features or correlations between features.
- Conceptual expansion involves basing new ideas on existing knowledge. Although ideas based on specific instances of a category may be practical, more creative solutions result from thinking abstractly rather than retrieving specific examples from memory.
- Combining existing ideas or concepts is a useful way to generate new ideas. It is possible to increase the creativity of such combinations by

combining dissimilar ideas/concepts, but it does make it more difficult to generate a workable combination.

- Many creative solutions have been attributed to modifying and applying a solution to a previous problem that is very different from the current problem being worked on.

The creative process has been of longstanding interest to psychologists and educators. Nearly 100 years ago, Graham Wallas (1926) described a model of creative thought that included stages of preparation, incubation, illumination, and verification. The model states that creative discoveries emerge from initially working consciously on a problem (preparation), temporarily withdrawing from those efforts on reaching an impasse (incubation), achieving an insight by noticing some clue (illumination), and returning to deliberate effort to confirm the validity of the insight (verification).

Wallas's model is well suited to anecdotal accounts of creative insights, such as Archimedes realizing he could determine if King Hiero's crown was pure gold by using displacement to measure its volume. Charged with the task of assessing its purity, and based on existing knowledge (preparation), Archimedes knew that the crown's weight would have to be appropriate to its volume, but he was at an impasse in knowing how to determine the volume of the irregularly shaped object. While bathing (incubating) and noticing water sloshing over the edge as he immersed himself, Archimedes had the insight (illumination) that the crown's volume could be measured by how much liquid it displaced.

Wallas's model has been an inspiration to generations of scholars who have sought to more clearly understand the nature of the creative process. A contemporary version is the cognitive approach to creativity—sometimes called the *creative cognition approach*. The modern cognitive approach to creativity extends Wallas's efforts in two important ways. First, because it is firmly rooted in experimental cognitive psychology, it bases conclusions on controlled laboratory studies rather than strictly on personal observation, anecdotes, and reasoning. It doesn't negate the value of anecdotes and reasoning, but claims that to advance our understanding, we need to empirically study phenomena under precisely controlled situations. In a related way, it seeks to more precisely define the processes involved, focusing on well-studied operations, such as memory retrieval, mental imagery, conceptual combination, and analogical transfer.

The creative cognition approach proposes that anybody has the ability to be creative. In fact, simply to function effectively in our world we are forced to be creative—often on a daily basis. Whenever our existing knowledge can't provide us with a plan of action for a situation, whenever we find ourselves in a problematic situation and have to go beyond what we already know—we have to be creative. The cognitive view of creativity further proposes that we can achieve creative outcomes by applying the "normal" types of cognitive processes mentioned above to "normal" knowledge structures such as schemas, categories, and episodic memory in order to generate novel products, ideas, or actions. So, in this sense, the cognitive view of creativity examines psychological creativity.

Another assumption of the cognitive view of creativity is that creativity occurs during problem solving. This may seem strange to some people because when we think of creative individuals, we think of artists, poets, and actors. What, then, does this type of creativity have to do with problem solving? Problem solving is essential to creativity because, in every case of creativity, the person being creative is solving some sort of problem. Poets need to solve the problems of expressing feeling and creating an image or scene in the mind of the viewer within the constraints of the poem. Painters are solving the problems of design, balance, and expression when painting. Similarly, actors need to choose the mannerisms, expressions, and behaviors that best convey their interpretation of the character they portray. In each of these cases, the creative individual (be it poet, actor, or painter) is developing creative solutions within a particular domain. When creativity is viewed as developing a creative solution to a particular problem, then we can see that scientists are also creative because they need to create experiments to test hypotheses or theories to explain the data.

The assumptions of the cognitive view of creativity lead to certain predictions. Creative problem solving should exhibit the same sorts of characteristics that are seen in normal problem solving. The cognitive processes that enable normal problem solving are also operating during creative problem solving. The knowledge structures used during creative problem solving should be the same as those used during normal problem solving, and this also applies to how those knowledge structures are applied to the problem.

The reason for this focus on problem solving is to illustrate how issues relevant to problem solving in general are applied to creative problem solving. The work discussed in this chapter will focus primarily on the creative cognition work first put forward by Finke, Ward, and Smith in their 1992 book *Creative Cognition: Theories, Research, and Applications*. The preceding discussion about the importance of problem solving for creative work should facilitate a better understanding of the manner in which the paradigms used to study issues in cognitive psychology are applied to studying creative cognition. This is seen primarily in the way in which the work of Finke et al. (1992) adapts and extends more traditional work in cognitive psychology. For example, Finke's cognitive psychology research focused on the characteristics of mental imagery (Finke, 1986), which he then adapted to study creative imagery. Smith's (1979) cognitive psychology research examined how recently encountered stimuli could adversely affect the ability to retrieve information from memory. This work was adapted to examine the processes underlying insight and fixation in creative problem solving (Smith & Blankenship, 1989). Ward's (1993; Ward & Becker, 1992) cognitive psychology research examined concept formation and how those concepts were represented in semantic memory, and this research was adapted to examine conceptual expansion (Ward, 1994). Other researchers examining creative cognition have done the same thing by adapting their more traditional creative cognition work to examine the manner in which normal cognitive processes and knowledge structures affect creative problem solving (Costello & Keane, 2000; Marsh, Landau, & Hicks, 1996; Sifonis, Chernoff, & Kolpasky, 2006; Wiley, 1998; Wilkenfeld & Ward, 2001)

Finke et al.'s (1992) application of cognitive paradigms to examine creative cognition was organized around the Geneplore Model of creativity. "Geneplore" stands for "generate and explore" and is a heuristic model of creative functioning. It is a broadly descriptive model rather than an explanatory theory and consists of two phases. In the initial phase, the inventor generates preinventive structures that are then explored and interpreted during the second phase. Any given creative product can be seen as the result of a cycling between the generation of ideas, modification of those starting points, and regeneration of new or altered ideas.

Idea generation is made possible through a variety of common generative processes including memory retrieval, mental imagery, and analogy. Exploratory processes include the search for novel or desired attributes in the ideas, metaphorical implications of the ideas, and the search for the proposed function of the ideas. Consequently, creative thinking can be characterized in terms of how generative and exploratory processes can be employed or combined.

These generation and exploratory processes operate on mental structures. The mental structures could include existing knowledge such as what we know about restaurants, previous solutions to problems, and what we ate at lunch today. These structures also include the preinventive structures formed during the generation stage that are explored during the exploration stage during creative cognition. Preinventive structures are generated in the first stage of creative thought. These structures are called *preinventive* because they are not complete ideas in their own right. However, they show some promise of yielding a solution to a problem and are then further explored in the second stage of the model. An example of Geneplore in action can be found in the reports of Kekule's insight into the molecular structure of benzene. Kekule reported that he was daydreaming in front of the fire after a long day working on the problem. As he was dreaming, he imagined strings of objects that looked like snakes swirling around each other (generative process). One of those "snakes" spun around and grabbed its own tail forming a circle (preinventive structure). This resulted in the creative insight that the molecular structure of benzene was a ring, which Kekule explored and verified the following day.

Because the same basic cognitive processes are involved in creative thinking as are involved in noncreative thinking, the creative cognition approach predicts that creative and noncreative thinking falls on a continuum. Where one falls on the continuum depends on the extent to which generative processes, exploratory processes, and preinventive structures are involved that give rise to emergent features. The more these types of experiences are involved in the creative process, the more creative the thinking.

Similarly, the creativity of the idea itself ranges on a continuum (Boden, 1991). At one extreme is psychological or P-creativity, in which the idea is creative to the individual but might actually be a common solution to that type of problem. At the other end is historical or H-creativity. Sometimes people generate psychologically creative ideas that are also historically creative. The creative cognition approach assumes the same types of processes give rise to both. Differences in creativity are a matter of the extent to which the Geneplore processes are engaged in. These creativity differences are also affected by a wide variety of noncognitive factors that also influence creativity such as motivation, experience, culture, and society.

Creative Imagery

Many creative individuals report using mental imagery as a basis for their ideas, including scientists, artists, musicians, and writers (see Finke, 1990; LeBoutillier & Marks, 2003; Roskos-Ewoldsen, Intons-Peterson, & Anderson, 1993; Shepard, 1978). A notable case is Albert Einstein, one of the greatest thinkers of the 20th century, who reportedly often thought in mental pictures rather than words and achieved insights by considering images such as an observer riding a light beam or alongside it.

The creative cognition approach seeks to use such anecdotal accounts and find ways to operationalize the processes describe in them so that the phenomena of interest can be studied in the laboratory. Ronald Finke extended cognitive psychology research to determine whether people could use visual imagery to combine and transform basic forms to generate useful insights, solutions, and innovations. As mentioned above, many eminent creators have attributed their creative insights to mental imagery by representing the problems they are working on visually (e.g., Kekule imagining molecular structure as a snake, Watson and Crick imagining different configurations of DNA). They often attribute the success of this technique to breaking the inherent constraints in the way they are thinking about the task by re-representing the problem visually (Shepard, 1978). Interestingly, Shepard (1978) justified the importance of studying mental imagery by noting the ubiquity of reports in which breakthrough thinking resulted from representing the problem visually. The research examining mental imagery that was spurred by this call to action resulted in our current understanding of the processes and representation of mental imagery in general. For example, Finke, Pinker, and Farah (1989) examined whether participants could "discover" novel patterns in mentally rotated or transformed images. This is essentially the process by which many creative insights are arrived at by creative individuals. Finke et al. (1989) demonstrated that participants given simple shapes to imagine (e.g., the letter D, the number 4) could perform mental transformations on those shapes to reveal a novel pattern. The transformations took the form of the following: "Imagine a capital D. Rotate it 90 degrees to the left so the straight line is on the bottom. Imagine the capital letter J and place it underneath the rotated D." If you performed these operations and "saw" an umbrella, your observation would have been counted as an accurate identification of the transformed images in their experiments. However, Finke noted that these experiments and others of a similar nature had one major flaw. Participants always made a series of transformations under the direction of the experimenter that were guaranteed to result in identifiable patterns. The retrospective reports of creative individuals suggest they perform transformations and rotations on mental images in the hopes of discovering novel, unexpected patterns that will help them to solve the problem they are working on. Thus, Finke and Slayton (1988) examined whether it was possible for "normal" individuals to discover novel patterns through mental transformation/rotation on their own.

Finke and Slayton (1988) adapted the mental transformation paradigm employed by Finke et al. (1989) by giving participants three simple forms (e.g., a circle, the letter J, a horizontal line) and having them mentally assemble the forms for 2 minutes as they tried to make a figure that could be easily recognized and named without a lengthy description. Once they did this, the figures were rated by judges in terms of creativity and the correspondence of the figure with the name it was given. If the drawn figure was creative and corresponded very well with the name given to it, that figure was rated as a "creative pattern."

The results of this study demonstrated that between 38.1% and 44.3% of the patterns participants generated were recognizable and 15% of those recognizable patterns were judged as being highly creative. Finke and Slayton (1988) also noted that the creative patterns arose from either the creative arrangement of the shapes used to make up the pattern or creative interpretations of the resulting combination. This is a good example of the interplay between generative and exploratory processes—an idea that Finke (1990) further examined by having participants arrange a set of complex shapes (e.g., wires, cones) and varying the number of constraints they had to work within. This research differed from the previous work in that the object participants created had to belong to one of eight categories—furniture, personal item, scientific instrument, appliance, transportation, utensil, toy, or weapon. The created objects were then rated on a 1–5 scale in terms of how practical and how original they were. In the one constraint condition, participants were allowed to pick three shapes but were provided the category of the invention *or* they were provided the three shapes and allowed to pick the category of invention. In the two-constraint condition, participants were provided the three shapes they were supposed to work with and told what category of item they had to create before they arranged the shapes. In these conditions, participants were mainly engaged in creatively *arranging* the shapes to generate their novel product. In the most restrictive three-constraint condition, participants were given the three shapes they were supposed to work with and told to create an object with those three shapes. After the invention had been created, *then* they were told the category of invention. Consequently, in this condition the creativity resulted from the creative *interpretation* of the object rather than the creative arrangement of the shapes. Even though the number of inventions rated as practical stayed the same across all three conditions, the originality of those products increased as the number of constraints increased. This could be interpreted as evidence that increasing the constraints of the task actually increases the creativity of a product. It could also be interpreted that the creative interpretation of a product (or task or problem) is at least as important to the perceived creativity of a product as the creative arrangement of elements in the product.

Mental Set and Design Fixation

We normally think that considering other people's ideas is useful for helping us to solve our own problems. If we can get an idea of how other people have accomplished some goal, it stands to reason that we might be better able to achieve our own goal. Interestingly though, exposing ourselves to examples of previous solutions to problems can backfire if there are flaws in those solutions. Consider work done by Jansson and Smith (1991). They had engineering students and design professionals develop ideas for practical products, such as spill-proof coffee cups and measuring devices for blind people after viewing examples of others' designs. The interesting result was that they tended to incorporate aspects of those other solutions into their own designs. Unfortunately, this included design flaws, such as straws incorporated into a spill-proof cup, which would not allow the passage of air over the beverage to cool it before the burning hot liquid reaches the unsuspecting consumer's tongue.

This type of fixation, the type that is caused by examples experienced immediately prior to a creativity task, is not limited to specialists in engineering design, but instead seems to be more general. Just like mental set in normal problem solving is believed to be caused by the context that the problem solving occurs in, the "conformity effect" of copying even inappropriate elements of a design into a novel product is caused by experiencing examples of potential solutions to a problem immediately before engaging in a creative generation task. When this happens, there is a strong tendency for people to conform to the examples by including features of those examples in their novel products (Smith, Ward, & Schumacher, 1993). A common paradigm used to examine how the conformity effect affects creative idea generation is to have participants create as many novel examples of a category of items (e.g., toys, animals) as possible. The instructions given to participants emphasize both novelty and quantity. For example, Smith et al. (1993) had participants generate novel examples of animals and toys. Then, before creating their examples, some participants were shown representative examples of those two categories. These examples all share three features such as the three example animals all having four legs, a tail, and antennae. Participants are told not to duplicate the examples or the features of examples. The other participants are not shown any examples. Participants then create novel category members that are then examined for the shared features of the examples. Despite these instructions, participants who saw examples, such as those in the Smith et al. (1993) study, are much more likely than participants who did not view examples to conform to the features they saw in the examples than participants who did not view those examples. This conformity effect is fairly robust, being demonstrated across a wide variety of categories including generating solutions to a problem (Bink, Marsh, Hicks, & Howard, 1999; Marsh, Landau, & Hicks, 1997) and creating novel nonwords (Landau & Lehr, 2004; Marsh, Ward, & Landau, 1999). Several factors have been shown to increase the conformity effect, including increasing the number of examples sharing the same feature and delaying the time between seeing examples and creating novel instances (Marsh et al., 1996). When designing new products, explicitly pointing out problematic elements of the design and telling participants why they are problematic still fails to prevent participants from incorporating those elements into their novel designs.

So how do we escape the effects of these examples? Simply educating people about the conformity effect, indicating the problematic features of design examples, and telling them not to use those features is not enough to eliminate this effect (Chrysikou & Weisburg, 2005). Neither is telling people to be more creative (Landau, Thomas, Thelen, & Chang, 2002). What does seem to help reduce, but not eliminate, the effect is providing detailed explanations about what the problematic elements of the examples are and exactly how participants are supposed to avoid incorporating them into their designs (Chrysikou & Weisburg, 2005). Telling them that their work will be checked by someone in authority to make sure they didn't copy the features also decreases conformity (Landau et al., 2002). However, the concern is that these authoritative approaches also run the risk of reducing creativity. Actually requiring the incorporation of a particular feature into the product (e.g., a shape into a drawing or a letter into a word) does reduce the conformity effect. So does the requirement to include an unusual feature into the product (Landau & Leynes, 2004).

Another method for dealing with the conformity effect is to make the effect work for you. Providing examples that have unusual features (e.g., words with numbers for letters) or unusual correlations between features (e.g., antennae and claws for animals) will result in products that conform to these unusual examples, but the perceived creativity of those examples will be increased (Landau & Lehr, 2004; Marsh et al., 1996). So seeking inspiration from others' ideas *can* be a valuable approach to boosting your own creativity as long as you carefully consider what might be flawed and what might be truly, originally useful about those ideas.

Conceptual Expansion

As we have shown, information can be activated when we see examples of previous problem solutions, but even without being primed that way, some parts of what we know are just more readily accessible than others. And those things that come to mind readily influence our creative thinking. This can be very helpful to give us a start on developing a new idea, but it can also constrain us. On the positive side, many inventions were made possible because inventors were able to build on their knowledge of the ideas of others who came before them, including Edison's light bulb and Eli Whitney's cotton gin (see, e.g., Basala, 1988; Friedel, Israel, & Finn, 1987). On the negative side, new products can include features of old ones that are harmful, such as the outside seating for conductors that was carried over from designers' knowledge of stagecoaches to the earliest railway passenger cars and may have contributed to some conductors' deaths (White, 1978).

Research examining conceptual expansion looks at how we use what we already know to come up with new examples of a category. If you were asked to design a new type of swing, you would probably use what you know about swings to generate the new example. If you had been asked to generate a new kind of alien animal, you would probably use what you know about Earth animals to do so. Just as inventors retrieve what they know about specific prior inventions, you would very likely pull from memory specific instances of things you already know as a starting point. This exemplifies the research conducted by Ward (1994) that demonstrates how our original ideas are constrained by our existing knowledge.

Before continuing reading, create a mental image of an alien animal. Draw it if you wish. Be as creative as you can be. Now examine your drawing. Is your alien bilaterally symmetric (the same on both sides)? Does it have legs and/or arms? Does your alien have senses such as eyes, ears, a nose, and a mouth? If so, are those senses in the head and are the eyes above the mouth? If the answer is "yes" to these questions, don't feel bad. It is only because your existing knowledge of animals on Earth constrained the features of the alien animal you imagined.

In a task similar to the one you engaged in, Ward (1994) asked participants to generate an animal from an alien planet. What he discovered was that 94% of those alien animals were bilaterally symmetric; 97% had standard senses such as eyes and ears and standard appendages such as legs and arms. More often than not, the alien animals also preserved the structural relationships between features such as the senses being placed in the head, which was above the body, and the eyes being above the nose, which was above the mouth. Just so you don't think that this is just because undergraduate college students are unoriginal, Ward (1994) found that science fiction authors also demonstrate this effect. An analysis of paintings of otherwise unusual science fiction creatures showed that the bulk of them were symmetric and had legs and eyes. Similarly, even a cursory look at science fiction movies reveals the tendency for exotic aliens to have many Earth animal features. Writers and movie producers are motivated to be creative, yet they, too, are constrained by their existing knowledge. This effect isn't just limited to aliens; we also conform to what we know when we create other novel members of a category, such as tools and fruits (Ward, Patterson, Sifonis, Dodds, & Saunders, 2002).

Ward's explanation for this phenomenon was that we tend to retrieve the first category member we think of when we are asked to create a new example of a category (e.g., we think of "dog" when asked to create a new type of animal). The category animal that first comes to mind is usually the most typical category member. Ward said that the reason we use this typical animal member is because generating new ideas is difficult. This causes many people to take the path of least resistance and use the first category example they can think of, because this is the easiest approach to take to a difficult task. There is a way around this though. If there was a way to get people to think about a category without thinking about specific examples of that category, their creations might be more creative. So Ward, Patterson, and Sifonis (2004) examined this hypothesis. They told half of the participants in their study to imagine an animal on a planet very different from our own. The other half of the participants they asked to think about the various functions an animal needs to survive such as protection, feeding, movement, and reproduction. What they found was that the participants who focused on function created more original aliens than those who were given just the category name.

This line of research also helps to show how memory retrieval can affect different aspects of creative outcomes, such as their novelty and usefulness. Ward (2008) had students develop ideas for new sports. As in studies using domains of animals, fruit, and tools, he found that those who retrieved abstract information developed sports that were higher in originality, but he also found that their sports were rated as less playable. So retrieving your knowledge at higher, more abstract levels can help you make ideas that are different than those that have come before, but it may come at a cost to their practicality. If the goal is to have a workable solution, retrieving more specific kinds of information (such as particular yet more uncommon sports) might be more helpful.

Conceptual Combination

Conceptual combination is also a very useful way to generate new ideas, in a variety of domains, including science, literature, and music (see, e.g., Rothenberg, 1979; Thagard, 1984; Ward, 2001). The information combined can be simple concepts, larger theories, and even artistic or musical genres. Consider for example, the interesting effects of combining electronic and folk music style, as in folktronica.

Traditional cognitive psychology research on conceptual combination focuses on the comprehension of novel noun-noun phrases (e.g., "game date"). This is actually a tricky research question because there is often more than one interpretation of the combination and that interpretation is often more than the intersection of the two nouns (e.g., a "game date" is more than the set of things "games" and "dates" have in common). It is also interesting because combinations with similar constituents ("computer dog" and "apartment dog") can have very different interpretations.

Hampton (1987) proposed that the conceptual combination takes the set of features of both nouns. The combination inherits the salient attributes of both sets subject to certain constraints. These constraints are (1) features that are *necessary*, for one of the constituents will be included in the combination and (2) features that are *impossible*, for one of the constituents will not be included in the combination. One of the interesting things that happens during conceptual combination, where creativity is concerned, is that it is possible for emergent features to become part of the interpretation. An emergent feature is one that is not (strongly) associated with either of the nouns in the combination. Work by Wilkenfeld and Ward (2001) indicated that emergent features are more likely when the nouns in a noun-noun combination are dissimilar from each other (motorcycle harp) rather than similar to each other (apple pear).

Perhaps the reason emergent features are more likely with dissimilar combinations is because one needs to engage in creative problem solving when trying to interpret the combinations involving dissimilar nouns/concepts. Perhaps it is this exact thing that results in added value when combining dissimilar things to create something new. It certainly is a technique suggested in many creativity enhancing techniques and put to use by creative individuals. Most of the time, these techniques use a random process to combine disparate elements. For example, some techniques suggest taking the idea you are working with and pairing it with the first object you see outside your window. The creativity often comes with the purposeful exploration of this combination.

As with what we discussed about the conformity effect, successfully combining concepts that are quite dissimilar to each other often results in creative products. However, it is quite difficult to combine disparate concepts. In fact, Poincare discussed conceptual combination and creativity. Poincare was a mathematician, a theoretical physicist, and a philosopher of science. He was deeply interested in the creative process and made detailed observations of his own creative processes. He believed that mathematical creation comes from useful combinations of elements and the way one can distinguish the useful combinations from the poor ones is through the use of analogy (to similar approaches or elements that have worked in the past). He noted that the greater the disparity between the elements in the combination, the more likely it was to be a more creative solution. However, the disparity between the elements also increased the likelihood that the combination would result in a totally unworkable solution.

Empirical research backs the idea that discrepancy of the items to be combined could pose problems for developing workable ideas. Mobley, Doares, and Mumford (1992) asked participants to come up with concepts that could explain grouping together exemplars from each of three distinct categories. For some problems, the three starting categories were closely related and in others they were not. When the component objects were more dissimilar, people generated more original outcomes, but the outcomes were also judged to be of lower quality. So, the need to integrate discrepant pieces of information provided a boost to originality, although not necessarily to overall quality. Just as with retrieval of category knowledge, then, the specifics of how the process is used can have different effects on the two key aspects of creative ideas: their originality and their usefulness.

Analogy and Creativity

Like conceptual combination, analogy is also frequently used by creative individuals (including Poincare) for creative problem solving. Analogy is interesting in that it is a very basic cognitive problem solving process that can result in some amazingly creative solutions. It is particularly useful for solving ill-defined problems—the types of problems that require creative problem solving methods. Innovators and scientists including Kepler (orbits of the planets), Henry Ford (assembly line), Darwin (evolution through natural selection), Hiram Maxim (silencer), and Philo Farnsworth (first working television system) have identified an analogy as the source of their breakthrough ideas or innovations.

Engaging in analogical problem solving involves two domains of knowledge and at least three analogical processes. The two domains of knowledge are referred to as the source and target domains. The *target domain* is the problem currently being worked on. For example, when motorcycles were first developed, it wasn't possible to travel far or to run errands on one because there was no way, short of a backpack, to carry items on the vehicle. In this example, the target domain is motorcycles. The *source domain* is the knowledge of some other domain—perhaps one in which a solution to a problem similar to the target problem has been reached. The three analogical problem-solving processes are retrieval, mapping, and transfer/inference.

The first step in using analogy for problem solving is to retrieve from memory information to use as the source domain. The information being retrieved from memory ranges on a continuum from being conceptually similar to the target domain to being conceptually distant (just like the conceptual combinations described in the previous section). Retrospective accounts by innovators suggest analogically driven solutions to their problem frequently involve source and target domains that are conceptually distant from each other.

The next process in analogical problem solving is to establish one-to-one correspondences between the source and target domains. This is known as mapping. When comparing a motorcycle to a horse, you would map the horse's front legs to the motorcycle's front tire; the horse's rear legs to the motorcycle's rear tire. You would note that the rider of the horse sits on a saddle, whereas the rider of the motorcycle sits on a seat. You would also notice that the saddle is between the front and rear legs of the horse just like the seat is between the front and rear motorcycle tires.

The final process is inference/transfer. Once you have established correspondences between the source and target domains, it is possible to identify differences between them. These differences can potentially suggest how to solve the problem in the target domain. This happens when you notice something in the source domain (the saddlebags behind the saddle for carrying things) that is missing in the target domain (motorcycle is missing the saddlebag). You transfer the knowledge from the source to the target and then adapt the solution to the specifics of the target domain (e.g., saddlebags could be hung across the motorcycle's rear fender to carry supplies!). It is the inference/transfer stage that is associated with creative insights during problem solving. Insight is often experienced as a sudden epiphany—an "AHA!" experience—and is believed to result from a sudden restructuring of the representation of the source domain that allows the solution to the target problem to be identified (Finke et al., 1992).

The first studies examining analogy in creative problem solving used ill-defined insight problems, such as Duncker's (1945) radiation problem. One of the functions of this initial research was to verify existing anecdotal evidence that analogy contributed significantly to scientific insight and problem solving through the use of distant analogies (Gick & Holyoak, 1980, 1983). Since then, much of analogy research focused more on the basic processes of analogy (especially retrieval) and less on how analogical problem solving enables highly creative solutions to problems. Consequently, little is known about the role these basic processes play in facilitating creativity. There are exceptions though. Dahl and Moreau (2002) empirically examined the use of analogy to aid in developing novel products. In their experiment, they had experienced product designers develop a system for eating food in an automobile. They recorded the designer's use of analogy in the development process. They found that the creativity of the product developed was positively correlated with the number and conceptual distance of analogies used during product development. The greater the number of analogies used by the designers, the more creative was the resulting product. The greater the conceptual distance between the source and target domains of the analogies used by the designers, the greater the creativity of the product they developed. The manner in which Dahl and Moreau (2002) examined the relationship between conceptual distance and creativity is typical for research of this nature. They examined the correlation between conceptual distance and creativity. In this and similar studies, the problem solver retrieved the source domain from memory to solve the problem. In comparison, Sifonis (2003) experimentally examined the relationship between the conceptual distance of the source and target domains and the creativity of the resulting solution to the problem. Rather than having participants retrieve the source domain from memory, Sifonis provided participants with a source domain. The target domain her participants were working with was solving the parking problem on campus. This problem was chosen because participants were familiar with the problem and deeply invested in generating solutions to the problem.

There has been some debate about the usefulness of near versus distant source domains (see, e.g., Christensen & Schunn, 2007; Dunbar, 1997), and the source domains Sifonis (2003) provided to participants differed in terms of the conceptual distance of the "parking on campus" target domain. Some were given the conceptually similar domain of parking at the mall. A second group was provided with a more distant domain that is still transportation oriented—that of parking downtown. The third group was told to use the source domain of an amusement park, and the fourth group was asked to use the most distant source domain of Darwin's Theory of Evolution. Participants mapped the source and target domains to each other to generate solutions that were then rated in terms of practicality and originality. The results showed that a source domain similar to the target domain (parking at the mall), led to the most practical solutions. The most original solutions were generated when using the moderately distant source domain of an amusement park. This supports the idea that more conceptually distant domains lead to more creative solutions . . . up to a point. Perhaps when the source domain is excessively distant from the target domain, creative and workable solutions are rare.

Perhaps an even more interesting component of this research involved the types of solutions generated by mapping the different source domains to the target domain. It appears that the specific source domain used to solve the target problem affected the types of solutions that were generated. For example, those using the mall as the source domain were more likely than those using other source domains to generate the parking solution of having the police enforce parking rules. Those working with the downtown parking source domain were more likely than the other participants to suggest solutions involving parking determined by need (e.g., more handicapped parking near the building; majors get to park closer to the department building). Those working with the amusement park source domain generate more solutions involving the addition of conveniences/safety (e.g., food vendors in the parking lot, protection from cars). Not surprisingly, participants working with Darwin's theory as their source domain were more likely to provide solutions that reduced the commuter population on campus.

These results suggest that the source domain constrains which aspects of the knowledge structure are explored to generate solutions to the target domain problem. This is consistent with prior analogical reasoning research (Keane, 1996; Spellman & Holyoak, 1996) and leads to an important takeaway message: There are many different solutions to a problem. When using analogy, the source domain exerts a strong influence on the target domain solution. This means that there are many different source domains that could be applied to a problem, leading to many potential solutions to that problem. However, it doesn't necessarily mean that solutions using one source domain are inherently better than those generated using a different source domain. As long as the mapping and transfer processes are engaged in thoroughly and methodically, it is possible for those different solutions to be equally effective and equally creative for solving the problem.

Conclusion

Creative cognition offers a way to understand creativity in terms of the nuts and bolts of creative thinking from which new and useful ideas originate. By considering basic mental operations we're all capable of, it also provides some guidance about how people can increase their chances of coming up with creative products. It is clear that it is not just the processes, but also the way they are implemented that matters. Generating mental images can spark new ideas, but it may be helpful to simply "mentally doodle" without a particular problem in mind and only then try to use knowledge to see how the result can be applied in a given domain. Exposure to examples of other solutions can help or hurt depending on whether those examples have flaws or unusual but useful characteristics. Retrieving from memory specific ideas can limit originality, but it can also help with the practicality of new ideas. Combinations of previous ideas can help, especially if those ideas are moderately discrepant. Analogies can help and the distance between the source and target domains can affect the outcome. So, in being creative, not only is it helpful to use ordinary processes, but it is important to be aware of how we're using those processes and capitalize on the strengths of those processes.

Recommended Readings

Christensen, B. T., & Schunn, C. D. (2007). The relationship of analogical distance to analogical function and pre-inventive structure: The case of engineering design. *Memory & Cognition, 35,* 29–38.

Costello, F. J., & Keane, M. T. (2000). Efficient creativity: Constraint-guided conceptual combination. *Cognitive Science, 24,* 299–349.

Dunbar, K. (1997). How scientists think: On-line creativity and conceptual change in science. In T. B. Ward, S. M. Smith, & J. Vaid (Eds.), *Creative thought: An investigation of conceptual structures and processes* (pp. 461–494). Washington, DC: American Psychological Association.

Finke, R. A., & Slayton, K. (1988). Explorations of creative visual synthesis in mental imagery. *Memory & Cognition, 16,* 252–257.

Sifonis, C. M., Chernoff, A., & Kolpasky, K. (2006). Analogy as a tool for communicating about innovation. *International Journal of Innovation and Technology Management, 3,* 1–19.

Smith, S. M., Ward, T. B., & Schumacher, J. S. (1993). Constraining effects of examples in a creative generation task. *Memory & Cognition, 19,* 168–176.

Ward, T. B. (1994). Structured imagination: The role of category structure in exemplar generation. *Cognitive Psychology, 27,* 1–40.

Wilkenfeld, M. J., & Ward, T. B. (2001). Similarity and emergence in conceptual combination. *Journal of Memory and Language, 45,* 21–38.

References

Basala, G. (1988). *The evolution of technology.* London, England: Cambridge University Press.

Bink, M. L., Marsh, R. L., Hicks, J. L. & Howard, J. D. (1999). The credibility of a source influences the rate of unconscious plagiarism. *Memory, 7,* 293–308.

Boden, M. (1991). *The creative mind: Myths and mechanisms.* New York, NY: Basic Books.

Christensen, B. T., & Schunn, C. D. (2007). The relationship of analogical distance to analogical function and pre-inventive structure: The case of engineering design. *Memory & Cognition, 35,* 29–38.

Chrysikou, E. G., & Weisburg, R. W. (2005). Following the wrong footsteps: Fixation effects of pictorial examples in a design problem-solving task. *Journal of Experimental Psychology: Learning, Memory, and Cognition, 31,* 1134–1148.

Costello, F. J., & Keane, M. T. (2000). Efficient creativity: Constraint-guided conceptual combination. *Cognitive Science, 24,* 299–349.

Dahl, D. W., & Moreau, P. (2002). The influence and value of analogical thinking during new product ideation. *Journal of Marketing Research, 39,* 47–60.

Dunbar, K. (1997). How scientists think: On-line creativity and conceptual change in science. In T. B. Ward, S. M. Smith, & J. Vaid (Eds.), *Creative thought: An investigation of conceptual structures and processes* (pp. 461–494). Washington, DC: American Psychological Association.

Duncker, K. (1945). On problem-solving (L. S. Lees, Trans). *Psychological Monographs, 58,* 1–113.

Finke, R. A. (1986). Mental imagery and the visual system. *Scientific American, 254*, 88–95

Finke, R. A. (1990). *Creative imagery: Discoveries and inventions in visualization.* Hillsdale, NJ: Lawrence Erlbaum.

Finke, R. A., Pinker, S., & Farah, M. J. (1989). Reinterpreting visual patterns in mental imagery. *Cognitive Science, 13*, 51–78.

Finke, R. A., & Slayton, K. (1988). Explorations of creative visual synthesis in mental imagery. *Memory & Cognition, 16*, 252–257.

Finke, R. A., Ward, T. B., & Smith, S. M. (1992). *Creative cognition: Theory, research, and applications.* Cambridge, MA: MIT Press.

Friedel, R. D., Israel, P., & Finn, B. S. (1987). *Edison's electric light: Biography of an invention.* New Brunswick, NJ: Rutgers University Press.

Gick, M. L., & Holyoak, K. J. (1980). Analogical problem solving. *Cognitive Psychology, 12*, 306–355.

Gick, M. L., & Holyoak, K. J. (1983). Schema induction and analogical transfer. *Cognitive Psychology, 15*, 1–38.

Hampton, J. A. (1987). Inheritance of attributes in natural concept conjunctions. *Memory & Cognition, 15*, 55–71.

Jansson, D. G., & Smith, S. M. (1991). Design fixation. *Design Studies, 12*(1), 3–11.

Keane, M. T. (1996). On adaptation in analogy: Tests of pragmatic importance and adaptability in analogical problem solving. *The Quarterly Journal of Experimental Psychology, 49*, 1062–1085.

Landau, J. D., & Lehr, D. P. (2004). Conformity to experimenter-provided examples: Will people use an unusual feature? *Journal of Creative Behavior, 38*, 180–191.

Landau, J. D., & Leynes, P. A. (2004). Manipulations that disrupt generative processes decrease conformity to examples: Evidence from two paradigms. *Memory, 12*, 90–103.

Landau, J. D., Thomas, D. M., Thelen, S. E., & Chang, P. (2002). Source monitoring in a generative task. *Memory, 10*, 187–197.

LeBoutillier, N., & Marks, D. F. (2003). Mental imagery and creativity: A meta-analytic review study. *British Journal of Psychology, 94*, 29–44.

Marsh, R. L., Landau, J. D., & Hicks, J. L. (1996). How examples may (and may not) constrain creativity. *Memory & Cognition, 24*, 669–680.

Marsh, R. L., Landau, J. D., & Hicks, J. L. (1997). Contributions of inadequate source monitoring to unconscious plagiarism during idea generation. *Journal of Experimental Psychology: Learning, Memory and Cognition, 23*, 886–897.

Marsh, R. L., Ward, T. B., & Landau, J. D. (1999). Implicit learning expressed in a generative cognitive task. *Memory & Cognition, 27*, 94–105.

Mobley, M. I., Doares, L. M., & Mumford, M. D. (1992). Process analytic models of creative capacities: Evidence for the combination and reorganization process. *Creativity Research Journal, 5,* 125–155.

Roskos-Ewoldsen, B., Intons-Peterson, M. J., & Anderson, R. E. (1993). *Imagery, creativity and discovery: A cognitive perspective.* Amsterdam, The Netherlands: North-Holland.

Rothenberg, A. (1979). *The emerging goddess.* Chicago, IL: University of Chicago Press.

Shepard, R. N. (1978). The mental image. *American Psychologist, 33,* 125–137.

Sifonis, C. M. (2003, November). *The effect of conceptual distance on analogical problem solving.* Paper presented at the annual meeting of the Psychonomic Society, Vancouver, BC.

Sifonis, C. M., Chernoff, A., & Kolpasky, K (2006). Analogy as a tool for communicating about innovation. *International Journal of Innovation and Technology Management, 3,* 1–19.

Smith, S. M. (1979). Remembering in and out of context. *Journal of Experimental Psychology: Human Learning & Memory, 5,* 460–471.

Smith, S. M., & Blankenship, S. E. (1989). Incubation effects. *Bulletin of the Psychonomic Society, 27,* 311–314.

Smith, S. M., Ward, T. B., & Schumacher, J. S. (1993). Constraining effects of examples in a creative generation task. *Memory & Cognition, 19,* 168–176.

Spellman, B. A., & Holyoak, K. J. (1996). Pragmatics in analogical mapping. *Cognitive Psychology, 31,* 307–346.

Thagard, P. (1984). Conceptual combination and scientific discovery. In P. Asquith & P. Kitcher (Eds.), *Proceedings of the biennial meeting of the Philosophy of Science Association* (Vol. 1, pp. 3–12). East Lansing, MI: Philosophy of Science Association.

Wallas, G. (1926). *The art of thought.* New York, NY: Harcourt, Brace and World.

Ward, T. B. (1993). Processing biases, knowledge, and context in category formation. In G. V. Nakamura, R. M. Taraban, & D. L. Medin (Eds.), *The psychology of learning and motivation: Categorization by humans and machines* (Vol. 2, pp. 257–282). Orlando, FL: Academic Press.

Ward, T. B. (1994). Structured imagination: The role of category structure in exemplar generation. *Cognitive Psychology, 27,* 1–40.

Ward, T. B. (2001). Creative cognition, conceptual combination and the creative writing of Stephen R. Donaldson. *American Psychologist, 56,* 350–354.

Ward, T. B. (2008). The role of domain knowledge in creative generation. *Learning and Individual Differences, 18,* 363–366.

Ward, T. B., & Becker, A. H. (1992). Learning categories with and without trying: Does it make a difference? In B. M. Burns (Ed.), *Percepts, concepts and categories: The representation and processing of information* (pp. 451–491). Amsterdam, The Netherlands: Elsevier Science Publishers.

Ward, T. B., Patterson, M. J., & Sifonis, C. M. (2004). The role of specificity and abstraction in creative idea generation. *Creativity Research Journal, 16,* 1–9.

Ward, T. B., Patterson, M. J., Sifonis, C. M., Dodds, R. A., & Saunders, K. N. (2002). The role of graded category structure in imaginative thought. *Memory & Cognition, 30,* 199–216.

Wiley, J. (1998). Expertise as mental set: The effects of domain knowledge in creative problem solving. *Memory & Cognition, 26,* 716–730.

White, J. H. (1978). *The American railroad passenger car.* Baltimore, MD: Johns Hopkins University Press.

Wilkenfeld, M. J., & Ward, T. B. (2001). Similarity and emergence in conceptual combination. *Journal of Memory and Language, 45,* 21–38.

Are Creativity and Intelligence Related?

Amber Esping

Key Take-Aways

- Researchers have different ways of defining concepts like intelligence and creativity.
- Many researchers believe that creativity is a part of a person's intelligence.
- Some researchers believe that intelligence is part of a person's creativity.
- Intelligence and creativity may be different constructs that overlap in important ways.

Before scholars can argue meaningfully about the best strategies for measuring or enhancing creativity, we need to be clear what it is they mean by the word *creativity*. The various authors represented in this book embrace several contrasting and complementary definitions, each well-reasoned and based on sound theoretical and empirical work. If you read Chapter 1, then you may have already formed some of your own opinions about what creativity is, and in what contexts it is appropriate to invoke the word. Before reading further, take a few minutes to think about what you've already learned about creativity, and jot down 5–10 words or phrases that come to mind as your working personal definition of "creativity."

A related psychological construct that requires the same careful consideration is human intelligence. What precisely do researchers mean when they say that word, *intelligence*? Based on what you've already learned about varying constructs of creativity, do you think there is scholarly consensus about what "intelligence" is? Perhaps more important at this point, what do *you* mean when you use that word? It might be helpful now to think about the most intelligent person you know (living or dead; friend, relative, or famous person), and write down a list of characteristics that make that person intelligent. When you group these words together, the list functions as your emerging personal definition of intelligence.[8]

Now, look at your two definitions. How are they different? In what ways are they similar? If you were to add to the lists, would you consider taking words from your creativity definition and adding them to your intelligence definition, or vice-versa? Are there concepts on your creativity definition that you absolutely would not include in your intelligence definition, or vice-versa? After doing this exercise, you probably see how difficult it has been for researchers to create unique constructs for these two concepts; intelligence and creativity seem to have a lot in common.

It is important from an ethical and practical standpoint that researchers attempt to differentiate these concepts where possible. One reason is this: In contemporary public schooling, greater value is placed on measuring and cultivating intelligence than creativity. (Case in point—think about the kinds of standardized testing you experienced prior to entering college. Were you rewarded for "creative" answers or "smart" ones?) However, in the so-called real world after schooling ends, both intelligence and creativity are valued. (The leaders of Microsoft and Apple are intelligent people, but their success also depends on their capacity to think creatively.) This disconnect has important implications for the success of schoolchildren and the adults they become (Sternberg & O'Hara, 1999; see also Kaufman & Plucker, 2011). Moreover, when researchers design intelligence or creativity studies, the ways in which

---

8   This is adapted from an activity described in Esping and Plucker (2011).

they collect and interpret the data will necessarily be informed by their beliefs about what these two constructs are and how they are related (Kaufman & Plucker, 2011). The remainder of this Hot Topic will address varying perspectives on the relationship between human intelligence and creativity.

Sternberg's Classifications of Creativity and Intelligence

In 1999, Robert Sternberg proposed a framework for organizing diverse perspectives on creativity and intelligence: Creativity as a subset of intelligence, intelligence as a subset of creativity, overlapping sets, coincident sets, and disjoint sets (Sternberg, 1999a). The first three perspectives have the strongest empirical and theoretical backing.

Creativity as a Subset of Intelligence

One way to conceptualize the relationship between creativity and intelligence is to think about creativity as being part of intelligence. One of the earliest theories to embrace this view was Guilford's Structure of Intellect (SOI) model, published in 1967. In this theory, divergent thinking was included as a cognitive operation that is part of intelligence. This has proven highly influential, forming the substrate for future tests of divergent thinking in creativity research (see Renzulli, 1973).

Creativity is also an implicit component of Howard Gardner's (1983) theory of multiple intelligences. He made this relationship explicit a decade later in his book, *Creating Minds* (Gardner, 1993). In this work, he used case studies of well-known creators like Picasso, Freud, and Einstein as evidence to support the existence of each of his proposed intelligences (e.g., spatial intelligence, intrapersonal intelligence, logical-mathematical intelligence, and so on). The creative output of these eminent individuals is seen as an indication of their high levels of these various intelligences. The experiential subtheory of Sternberg's (1997, 1999b) theory of successful intelligence also embraces creativity as a subset of intelligence by focusing on, among other things, behaviors that permit individuals to adjust to novelty.

The Cattell-Horn-Carroll (CHC) model, derived from the work of Horn and Cattell (1966, 1967) and Carroll (1993) also exemplifies the view that creativity is a subset of intelligence. In early forms of this theory, we find two distinct forms of intelligence: crystalized intelligence (Gc), which reflects accumulated knowledge and the ability to use that knowledge in problem solving; and fluid intelligence (Gf), which reflects the individual's ability to solve novel problems. Newer versions of the theory include other forms of *G*, including long-term storage and retrieval (*Glr*), of which one constituent is a person's originality and creativity (Flanagan, Ortiz, & Alfonso, 2007). Studies of *Glr* have found it to be important for fluency and originality in divergent thinking (Silvia, Beaty, & Nusbaum, 2013).

Intelligence as a Subset of Creativity

Another, less popular, perspective is the idea that intelligence is part of creativity. One example is Sternberg and Lubart's (1996) "investment" theory, which uses a metaphor of the stock market to explain creative achievement. The strategy is to buy low and sell high—not with money, but with ideas. Innovative ideas are often underappreciated or unpopular at first, but creators who persevere over the long term may be able to persuade others of their value. Besides being motivated enough to take on the challenge of convincing others that they ought to "buy into" the idea, the individual will need to possess other personal attributes, including adequate intelligence.

Amabile's (1982, 1996) componential theory of creativity also exemplifies the perspective that intelligence is a part of creativity. This view proposes that creativity depends on domain-relevant skills (like knowledge or technical skills), creativity-relevant skills (intrinsic factors like tolerance for ambiguity or the willingness to take risks), and task motivation (both intrinsic and extrinsic). Intelligence is a necessary developmental component of the hypothesized domain-relevant skill set.

Overlapping Sets

Some writers have proposed that intelligence and creativity are separate constructs that overlap considerably when conditions are right. A popular definition of creativity advanced by Plucker, Beghetto, and Dow (2004) illustrated the overlapping sets perspective. For these scholars, creativity is "the interaction among aptitude, process, and environment by which an individual or group produces a perceptual product that is both novel and useful as defined within a social context" (Plucker et al., 2004, p. 90). Here "aptitude" includes a constellation of dynamic characteristics, including intelligence. In another example, studies of the Planning, Attention, Simultaneous, and Successive (PASS) theory of intelligence proposed by Das, Naglieri, and Kirby (1994) revealed that the Planning component (which includes decision-making and self-monitoring) is related to creative output (see Kaufman & Plucker, 2011).

Researchers on the topic of giftedness and talent development have also articulated theories that can be categorized as coming from the overlapping sets perspective. One example is Renzulli's (1978) Three-Ring Conception of

Giftedness, which posits that giftedness results when high intellectual ability, creativity, and task commitment co-occur in the same individual. He differentiates between "schoolhouse" giftedness (that which is traditionally measured by academic achievement and test scores) and creative production, which encompasses openness to experience, aesthetic sensitivity, risk-taking, curiosity, and capacity for divergent thinking (see also Renzulli, 2002).

A final illustration of the overlapping sets perspective is the Threshold Theory, which maintains that a certain degree of intelligence is necessary for creativity (Barron, 1969; Yamamoto, 1964a, 1964b). Empirical evidence for this comes from older studies indicating that intelligence and creativity are moderately correlated up until an IQ of approximately 120. (The average IQ is 100. An IQ of 120 is one standard deviation above this.) Above 120, this correlation essentially disappeared (e.g., Fuchs-Beauchamp, Karnes, & Johnson, 1993; Getzels & Jackson, 1962). More recent research utilizing updated intelligence tests dispute the threshold theory, sometimes finding small or moderate positive correlations between measures of intelligence and creativity at all levels of intelligence (see Kim, 2005; Preckel, Holling, & Wiese, 2006), or significant correlations between intelligence and creative output among individuals with IQs above 120, thus pushing through any supposed threshold (see Sligh, Conners, and Roskos-Ewoldsen, 2005). This remains a fascinating area of inquiry.

Practical Considerations

It is rare to find scholars who maintain that intelligence and creativity are fundamentally unrelated (Plucker & Renzulli, 1999). However, some researchers have focused their attention on the external relationships between the two constructs. One such idea is certification theory, proposed by Hayes (1978). Certification theory posits that the role of intelligence in promoting creativity is a practical one. It has been long established that IQ scores are positively correlated with educational attainments; people with higher intelligence go further and are more successful in their formal education (see Deary & Johnson, 2010, for a review). Moreover, advanced education "certifies" people for high-status jobs, like college professor, scientist, or CEO, that both require and reward creative thinking. Conversely, low status jobs, such as grocery clerk or factory worker, do not require impressive educational attainments, nor do they require or reward creative thinking on the job. Therefore, it is possible that any empirical relationships found between creativity and IQ score reflect the fact that intelligence opens doors to careers that foster creativity. In essence, it's the person's job that matters in creativity, not the person's intelligence.

Conclusion

Both intelligence and creativity are dynamic and productive areas for research in the 21st century. These related constructs are inherently compelling for many scholars, but there are also practical problems to be solved that directly impact educational practice and postschooling career choices for graduates. It is clear that intelligence and creativity are related, but there are a variety of ways to look at this relationship. Most researchers believe that intelligence is a subset of creativity, creativity is a subset of intelligence, or creativity and intelligence are overlapping sets. Less popular are conceptualizations of creativity and intelligence as coincident or disjoint sets. It is essential that further research provide clarification regarding the nature of the relationship between these two constructs, as this has implications for the ways in which creativity and intelligence studies are designed and interpreted moving forward.

Recommended Readings

Kaufman, J. C., & Plucker, J. A. (2011). Intelligence and creativity. In R. J. Sternberg & S. B. Kaufman (Eds.), *Cambridge handbook of intelligence* (pp. 771–783). New York, NY: Cambridge University Press.

Plucker, J. A., & Esping, A. (2015). Intelligence and creativity: A complex but important relationship. *Asia Pacific Education Review, 16*, 153–159.

Plucker, J. A., Esping, A., Kaufman, J. C., & Avitia, M. J. (2015). Creativity and intelligence. In S. Goldstein & J. Naglieri (Eds.), *Handbook of intelligence: Evolutionary theory, historical perspectives, and current concepts* (pp. 283–291). New York, NY: Springer.

Plucker, J. A., Beghetto, R. A., & Dow, G. T. (2004). Why isn't creativity more important to educational psychologists? Potentials, pitfalls, and future directions in creativity research. *Educational Psychologist, 39*, 83–96.

Sternberg, R. J., & O'Hara, L. A. (1999). Creativity and intelligence. In R. J. Sternberg (Ed.), *Handbook of creativity* (pp. 251–272). Cambridge, England: Cambridge University Press.

References

Amabile, T. M. (1982). Social psychology of creativity: A consensual assessment technique. *Journal of Personality and Social Psychology, 43*, 997–1013.

Amabile, T. M. (1996). *Creativity in context.* Boulder, CO: Westview Press.

Barron, F. (1969). *Creative person and creative process.* New York, NY: Holt, Rinehart & Winston.

Carroll, J. B. (1993). *Human cognitive abilities: A survey of factor-analytic studies.* New York, NY: Cambridge University Press.

Das, J. P., Naglieri, J. A., & Kirby, J. R. (1994). *Assessment of cognitive processes: The PASS theory of intelligence.* Boston, MA: Allyn & Bacon.

Deary, I. J., & Johnson, W. (2010). Intelligence and education: Causal perceptions drive analytic processes and therefore conclusions. *International Journal of Epidemiology, 39,* 1362–1369.

Esping, A., & Plucker, J. A. (2011). Intelligence. In R. L. Miller (Ed.), *Promoting student engagement: Activities, exercises, and demonstrations for psychology courses* (Vol. 2, pp. 89–91). Washington, DC: American Psychological Association.

Flanagan, D. P., Ortiz, S., & Alfonso, V. C. (2007). *Essentials of cross-battery assessment* (2nd ed.). New York, NY: Wiley.

Fuchs-Beauchamp, K. D., Karnes, M. B., & Johnson, L. J. (1993). Creativity and intelligence in preschoolers. *Gifted Child Quarterly, 37,* 113–117.

Gardner, H. (1983). *Frames of mind: The theory of multiple intelligences.* New York, NY: Basic Books.

Gardner, H. (1993). *Creating minds.* New York, NY: Basic Books.

Getzels, J. W., & Jackson, P. W. (1962). *Creativity and intelligence: Explorations with gifted students.* New York, NY: Wiley.

Guilford, J. P. (1967). *The nature of human intelligence.* New York, NY: McGraw-Hill.

Hayes, J. R. (1978). *Cognitive psychology: Thinking and creating.* Homewood, IL: Dorsey Press.

Horn, J. L., & Cattell, R. B. (1966). Refinement and test of theory of fluid and crystallized intelligence. *Journal of Educational Psychology, 57,* 253–270.

Horn, J. L., & Cattell, R. B. (1967). Age differences in fluid and crystallized intelligence. *Acta Psychologica, 26,* 107–129.

Kaufman, J. C., & Plucker, J. A. (2011). Intelligence and creativity. In R. J. Sternberg & S. B. Kaufman (Eds.), *Cambridge handbook of intelligence* (pp. 771–783). New York, NY: Cambridge University Press.

Kim, K. H. (2005). Can only intelligent people be creative? *Journal of Secondary Gifted Education, 16,* 57–66.

Plucker, J. A., Beghetto, R. A., & Dow, G. T. (2004). Why isn't creativity more important to educational psychologists? Potentials, pitfalls, and future directions in creativity research. *Educational Psychologist, 39,* 83–96.

Plucker, J. P., & Renzulli, J. S. (1999). Psychometric approaches to the study of human creativity. In R. J. Sternberg (Ed.), *Handbook of creativity* (pp. 35–60). New York, NY: Cambridge University Press.

Preckel, F., Holling, H., & Wiese, M. (2006). Relationship of intelligence and creativity in gifted and non-gifted students: An investigation of threshold theory. *Personality and Individual Differences, 40,* 159–170.

Renzulli, J. S. (1973). *New directions in creativity.* New York, NY: Harper & Row.

Renzulli, J. S. (1978). What makes giftedness? Reexamining a definition. *Phi Delta Kappan, 60,* 180–184, 261.

Renzulli, J. S. (2002). Expanding the conception of giftedness to include co-cognitive traits and to promote social capital. *Phi Delta Kappan, 84,* 33–58.

Silvia, P. J., Beaty, R. E., & Nusbaum, E. C. (2013). Verbal fluency and creativity: General and specific contributions of broad retrieval ability (Gr) factors to divergent thinking. *Intelligence, 41,* 328–340.

Sligh, A. C., Conners, F. A., & Roskos-Ewoldsen, B. (2005). Relation of creativity to fluid and crystallized intelligence. *Journal of Creative Behavior, 39,* 123–136.

Sternberg, R. J. (1997). *Successful intelligence: How practical and creative intelligence determine success in life.* New York, NY: Plume.

Sternberg, R. J. (1999a). Intelligence. In M. A. Runco & S. R. Pritzker (Eds.), *Encyclopedia of creativity* (Vol. 2, pp. 81–88). San Diego, CA: Academic Press.

Sternberg, R. J. (1999b). The theory of successful intelligence. *Review of General Psychology, 3,* 292–316.

Sternberg, R. J., & Lubart, T. I. (1996). *Defying the crowd.* New York, NY: Free Press.

Sternberg, R. J., & O'Hara, L. A. (1999). Creativity and intelligence. In R. J. Sternberg (Ed.), *Handbook of creativity* (pp. 251–272). Cambridge, England: Cambridge University Press.

Yamamoto, K. (1964a). A further analysis of the role of creative thinking in high-school achievement. *The Journal of Psychology, 58,* 277–283.

Yamamoto, K. (1964b). Threshold of intelligence in academic achievement of highly creative students. *The Journal of Experimental Education, 32,* 401–405.

CHAPTER 6

Creative Productivity Across the Life Span

Dean Keith Simonton

Key Take-Aways

- Almost two centuries of empirical research has firmly established the relationship between age and creative productivity.
- Most typically, creative output first increases rapidly to a peak somewhere in the late 30s or early 40s, and thereafter slowly declines.
- However, the specific shape of this age curve depends on the specific domain of creativity. In some domains, the peak comes early, while in others the peak comes much later, with a much less drastic post-peak decline.
- Researchers must distinguish between quantity and quality of output, quantity representing pure productivity and quality representing actual creativity. This distinction is manifested in the location of a creator's three career landmarks: the first, best, and last major work.
- It is also important to recognize substantial individual differences in the career trajectory. The most highly creative persons produce their first major work at a younger age than most, maintain a high rate of output throughout their career, and produce their last major work at an older age than most—and thus exhibit much longer careers than "one-hit wonders."

When did the scientific study of creativity begin? What was the topic addressed by that very first investigation? A lot of people, even among creativity researchers, do not know the right answer. Many might guess Galton's (1869) *Hereditary Genius*. But that's more than three decades too late. And, besides, that book deals with the wrong topic. So what are the right answers to these two questions? First, the scientific study of creativity began with publication of Quételet's (1835/1968) *A Treatise on Man and the Development of His Faculties*. Although this mathematician was most concerned with establishing the normal (bell-shaped) distribution in the social sciences, he was also interested in intellectual development. Second, and in line with this latter interest, Quételet conducted the very first scientific study of how creative productivity changes across the life span—thus making the age-productivity relationship the oldest topic in creativity research!

I have a long-term affection for this topic as well. In fact, the first paper I had accepted for publication concerned this very same question (Simonton, 1975). And I have continued publishing on this issue for the past 40 years (e.g., Simonton, 2015b). Nor am I the only creativity researcher so engaged. Many other investigators have also tackled this topic (e.g., Beard, 1874; Dennis, 1966; Jones & Weinberg, 2011; Lehman, 1953; Raskin, 1936). This question has accumulated more than a century of empirical research (Simonton, 1988, 2012). Better yet, the empirical findings are actually cumulative! That is, certain central results have been replicated again and again. Hence, I can write this chapter knowing that the same findings will probably hold up for centuries to come. What was valid in 1835 remains valid today and will likely continue to be valid in 2935—at least if we continue to have productive creators who continue to get older with time! So what are these robust results?

Empirical Findings

Below I provide an overview of the following results: (a) the typical age curve, (b) interdisciplinary contrasts in that curve, (c) the distinction between quantity and quality, and (d) individual differences in the career trajectory.

The Typical Age Curve

Suppose we collect a sample of highly creative people in a given domain. Then we compile an inventory of all of the creative products and the ages at which they created those products. The products could be anything: scientific publications, patents, philosophical treatises, novels, plays, poems, paintings, sculptures, architectural designs, films, music compositions, etc. We then tabulate the number of products created in each age period. The result will come very close to the age-productivity curve shown in Figure 6.1. On average, the career will start in the 20s, exhibit a rapid rise to a peak where the output rate maximizes, and thereafter a gradual decline sets in. Happily, the decline doesn't usually go all the way to zero. Even an octogenarian creator can still be generating creative ideas—such as Giuseppe Verdi who composed his greatest comic opera, *Falstaff*, when he was 80 years old. In fact, the expectation is that the output rate at age 80 will still be about half that at age 40, where productivity maximizes. Older creators may be metaphorically "over the hill," but they haven't yet reached the bottom of the hill. Indeed, their creativity compares favorably with the young whippersnappers in the first decade of their own careers (Simonton, 2012).

It must be emphasized that the curve shown in Figure 6.1 represents only a statistical average, an average computed across multiple creators. Like all averages, any particular creative person may show exceptions on either side of the curve. For instance, a recent study of the patents of Thomas Edison—arguably the most prolific inventor who ever lived—showed that he almost ceased applying for patent protection in his mid-40s, when he should still have been going strong (Simonton, 2015b). The reason for this is that he ran into problems with the enforcement of his patent rights, which led him to stop applying for protection for an interval. He still was producing the inventions, but he was keeping them as trade secrets.

What happened to Edison was certainly idiosyncratic to him. Other inventors of his day did not respond the same way. Nonetheless, other departures from the typical curve shown in Figure 6.1 are more systematic—shared by many creators rather than just one. An important example follows next.

Interdisciplinary Contrasts

Creative disciplines can differ dramatically in the predicted age-productivity curve (Simonton, 2012). Some disciplines will tend to show a much earlier peak and a much more precipitous decline. Other disciplines are prone to display a much later peak followed by a decline so minimal that it is often difficult to speak of any age decrement at all. An example of the former are disciplines like lyric poets and pure mathematicians. It is no accident that one of the most prestigious awards that a mathematician can receive—the Fields Medal, which is often called the "Nobel of Mathematics"—cannot be bestowed upon anybody whose work appeared after age 40! Thus, poor Andrew Wiles, who was considered for the Fields because of his breakthrough proof of Fermat's Last Theorem, failed to receive the award. A flaw was found in his original demonstration that he was not able to correct before he turned 41! It was probably

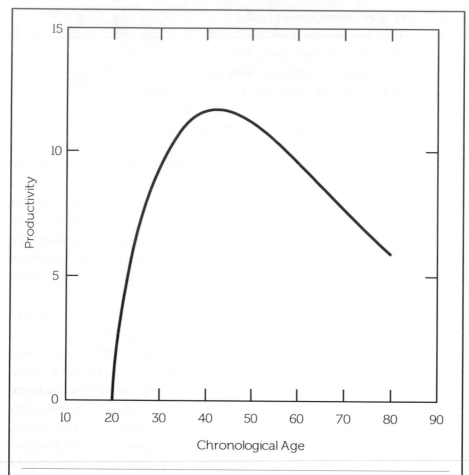

Figure 6.1 The typical relation between creative productivity and chronological age (Simonton, 2012).

disciplines like this one that inspired Oliver Wendell Holmes, Jr., to say "if you haven't cut your name on the door of fame by the time you've reached 40, you might just as well put up your jackknife" (quoted in Lehman, 1953, pp. 185–186).

Even so, sometimes 40 is yet too old! Theoretical physics underwent two major revolutions in the early part of the 20th century—the quantum and relativity theories. The physicists who participated in these developments were so young that their work was sometimes referred to as *Knabenphysiks*, which is German for "boys' physics." Thus Albert Einstein, a conspicuous participant in both revolutions, once said a "person who has not yet made his great contribution to science before the age of thirty will never do so" (quoted in Brodetsky, 1942, p. 699). Even more dramatic statement was advanced by Paul Dirac, who got the Nobel for his work in quantum theory:

> Age is, of course, a fever chill
> that every physicist must fear.
> He's better dead than living still
> when once he's past his thirtieth year.
> (quoted in Jungk, 1958, p. 27)

Naturally, Einstein and Dirac did their revolutionary work before reaching age 30: Both were 26 years old!

What about disciplines where the peak appears much later in life, and the decline more gentile if not absent altogether? The best examples are found in the humanistic disciplines, such as history, philosophy, and other scholarly domains (Simonton, 2012). Here a premium is placed on the accumulation of knowledge and even wisdom, which will likely take so much time that the peak cannot appear until much later. One of the greatest philosophers in the history of Western thought, Immanuel Kant, did not begin producing his most original ideas until he was in his late 50s!

An economist has recently proposed that the career trajectories of creators can be divided into two types (Galenson, 2005). On the one hand are the "young geniuses" (or "finders") who engage in *conceptual* creativity, arriving at bold concepts early, applying them quickly, and then fading out fast. On the other hand are the "old masters" (or "seekers") who engage in *experimental* creativity, learning gradually from experience, getting slowly better and better until they attain their acme toward the very end of their careers. Among artists, Pablo Picasso is said to be a conceptualist, Paul Cézanne an experimentalist. Similarly, just as poets may be either conceptual or experimental in orientation (e.g., T. S. Eliot vs. Robert Frost), so may novelists follow either path (e.g., F. Scott Fitzgerald vs. Mark Twain; see Simonton, 2007b).

The take-home message is that the curve shown in Figure 6.1 represents our best guess for the career trajectory. If we know about the discipline and the creator's approach to creativity in that discipline, the curve can be more precisely defined.

Quantity Versus Quality

We have so ignored a critical issue. Some early researchers obtained the age-productivity relation by tabulating every single work produced (e.g., Dennis, 1966), whereas others tended to count the truly great works (e.g., Lehman, 1953). Creative individuals will produce lots of creative products, but not all are equally creative, and some might not be creative at all. Charles Darwin put forward a theory of biological inheritance—his theory of pangenesis—that was an unmitigated disaster. His own cousin, Francis Galton, proved it wrong in a very simple experiment. Even a literary genius as great as William Shakespeare could create inferior plays and poems (Simonton, 2009). Among the plays, at the top stands *Hamlet*, at the low point is *Timon of Athens*, which was created only about 5 years later.

We might just pick quality over quantity. After all, if our interest is how creative productivity changes across the life span, why not focus on the creativity part rather than the productivity part? However, many researchers have been curious about the relation between the two (Simonton, 1988, 1997). Is quality (creativity) a positive function of quantity (productivity)? Or is the relation negative or zero? A related question is how the quality ratio—the proportion of the most creative works to total works—changes across the course of the career (Simonton, 2012). Does it increase, so that a larger proportion of the output is truly creative? Or does it decrease, so that by the end of the career productivity has completely replaced creativity? A third alternative is that the quality ratio might just fluctuate randomly over the career. Unfortunately, this question has received very mixed answers, definitely making it the most controversial subtopic (see, e.g., Hass & Weisberg, 2009; Kozbelt, 2008a). Rather than delve into all of the theoretical and empirical complexities, I'd rather touch upon a question that while closely related, enjoys less controversial answers (Simonton, 2012).

That question concerns what has been called *career landmarks* (Simonton, 1991a, 1991b, 1992, 1997; cf. Raskin, 1936; Zusne, 1976). These are major products that together define the beginning, peak, and termination of the most creative period of a creator's career. Thus, the first career landmark is the age at which creators produced their very first significant work—significant in the sense that the product continues to be considered a creative contribution to the discipline. The last career landmark is the age at which creators produced their very last significant work. Productivity may continue after that final work, but those later works contribute nothing to the creator's reputation. Between these two landmarks is the age at which creators produce their single best work—the creator's masterpiece that essentially anchors their posthumous reputation. For example, there can be no doubt whatsoever that the Fifth Symphony of Ludwig van Beethoven, the work that begins with the famous duh-duh-duh-dah theme indicating "fate knocking at the door," represents his single most high-impact work (Simonton, 2015a). Even people who have no interest whatsoever in classical music will recognize those four notes.

So our question now is how these three career landmarks relate to the curve shown in Figure 6.1, assuming that that curve represents total productivity (quantity) rather than creativity (quality). Empirical research shows the following (Simonton, 1991a, 1991b, 1997). First, and perhaps most obviously, the middle career landmark, the single best work, tends to appear very close to or a little after the peak for maximum output rate. Hence, given the curve in Figure 6.1, the optimal prediction is that the best work would emerge in the early 40s, on the average. For example, a study of 120 top classical composers found that the middle career landmark occurred at age 40, which was very close to the peak for maximum output, namely, 39 years old (Simonton, 2016). In line with these statistics, Beethoven's Fifth Symphony was completed when he was 38 years old.

What about the remaining two landmarks—the first and the last? Here the principle is not that different than what was said in the previous paragraph: productivity influences creativity. In the case of the first landmark, the faster creators accumulate products, regardless of quality, the sooner they will finally produce their first truly notable work. By the same token, the more prolific creators are toward the end of their careers, the later will emerge their last genuinely major work. Before the first landmark, creators will contribute juvenilia and other immature works, whereas after the last landmark, creators will produce works that add nothing to their lifetime achievement. Probably the last interval of the career is the most tragic. Einstein was selected "man of the century" by *TIME* magazine, yet people often forget that he devoted the last part of his career to devising a unified field theory that was an ultimate failure.

Earlier I pointed out that the curve in Figure 6.1 varies across disciplines. Sometimes, the acceleration to the peak is very fast and the post-peak decline very rapid. Other times, the peaks arrive much more slowly, and the age-decrement afterward is much more modest. Given what was just argued in the previous two paragraphs, the developmental location of the three career landmarks must reflect the underlying curve for total output. This implication has been verified in empirical research (Simonton, 1997). An excellent example is found in a study of more than 2,000 eminent scientists and inventors (Simonton, 1991a). The results are shown in Figure 6.2. No matter which career landmark we examine, substantial interdisciplinary contrasts are found. Hence, for mathematicians, the first major work tends to appear around age 27, whereas for medicine that career landmark does not emerge until around age 32, a 5-year difference. With respect to the second career landmark, the best work, the chemists come earliest, with an expected peak at 38, while for the geosciences this career landmark appears about 5 years later, at age 43. Lastly, in the case of the last career landmark, the chemists appear to run out of steam the earliest, with an average of 51 years of age, but in the geosciences, the last major work does not appear until around age 58, a 7-year difference.

All told, it is not even possible to make predictions about when creators will produce their first, best, and last major contribution without first knowing the discipline in which they are creating.

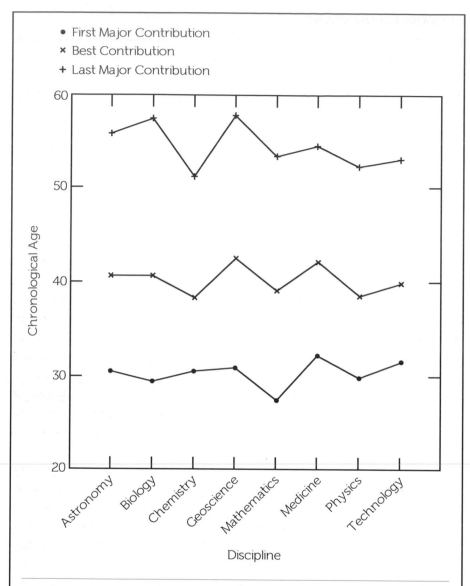

Figure 6.2. Mean chronological ages for the three career landmarks for eight disciplines of scientific and technological achievement. A contribution involved a discovery or invention that had a lasting impact on the history of the discipline. *Note.* From *Creativity in science: Chance, logic, genius, and zeitgeist* (p. 69) by D. K. Simonton, 2004, Cambridge, England: Cambridge University Press. Copyright D. K. Simonton. Reprinted with permission of the author. Based on data reported in Simonton (1991a).

Individual Differences

In the previous section, I introduced the concept of the three career landmarks and showed how the developmental placement of these landmarks is contingent on the creative discipline. It turns out that even more complications must be introduced. These complexities all result from individual differences among creators rather than interdisciplinary contrasts. Two are especially important (Simonton, 2012).

First, creative individuals vary immensely in lifetime creative productivity. The most prolific will produce dozens, even hundreds of works, over the course of their careers, a large number of these counting as masterpieces, whereas the least prolific will more often stake their fame on a single work. The latter are the so-called "one-hit wonders" (Kozbelt, 2008b). How does this variation in output affect the developmental location of the three career landmarks? In the case of the middle landmark, the age at best work, the response is easy: There's no substantial difference. On average, if the best work appears at 40 for the most prolific, it will most likely appear at 40 for the least prolific. Yet it gets more interesting for the first and last landmarks (Simonton, 1991a, 1991b, 1997). For the most prolific creators, the first career landmark occurs much earlier and the last career landmark occurs much later—lengthening the total time that they are making creative contributions. For the least productive creators, the first career landmark appears much later and the last career landmark appears much earlier. Indeed, in the extreme case of the one-hit wonders, the first, middle, and last major contribution are one and the same work! All three landmarks take place at the same age.

Second, creators can vary in the age at which they start producing works, whether creative or not (Simonton, 1991a, 1997). That is, some are early bloomers, who got an early start, and others are late bloomers, who got a late start. One of the main reasons for this variation is that creators differ regarding when they discover their creative domain. The composer Wolfgang Amadeus Mozart might have launched his career as a musical prodigy, already composing as a child, but other creators get a much later start. Grandma Moses, the famous folk artist, waited until her late 70s before she began her career as a serious painter. Happily for her, she lived until she was 101, so she could still have a career as long as Mozart's, who died in his mid-30s. Moreover, because the trajectory for creative productivity is actually a function of career age rather than chronological age, creators who get a late start will have the peak of their career shifted to later years. For example, the composer Anton Bruckner didn't dedicate himself to writing symphonies until he was in his 40s, which meant that his first career landmark did not emerge until his early 50s, and his greatest symphonies did not appear until he was in his 60s. Bruckner was still going strong when he died at age 72, leaving an unfinished Ninth Symphony that, by default, must be considered his last career landmark.

Significantly, the above pair of individual differences not only operate independently of each other, but also independently of the interdisciplinary contrasts discussed earlier. For instance, lyric poets generally start producing at a young age, but not all do, and, regardless of the age at career onset, some poets may be far more prolific than others who are closer to one-hit wonders. We are thus led to a highly differentiated picture of alternative career trajectories. To illustrate, Figure 6.3 shows the fourfold typology that results if we hold the discipline constant (i.e., all creators are active in the same discipline so that only the two individual difference variables operate).

On the left side of the figure appear two curves for highly prolific creators, the top graph showing the curve for early bloomers who start productivity at age 20, the bottom graph showing the curve for late bloomers who start productivity at age 30. Here the first (f), best (b), and last (l) career landmarks have about the same separation regardless of when creative productivity began. In either case, the best work appears about a decade after the first major work and the last major work appears more than two decades after the best work. On the right side, we again see two graphs representing early versus late bloomers, but this time the creators are assumed to be less prolific. As a consequence, the three landmarks are more scrunched together. As mentioned earlier, in the extreme case of the one-hit wonders, the three landmarks would collapse into a single developmental event.

It should be manifest by now that if the fourfold typology is combined with interdisciplinary contrasts, we obtain an even more refined conception of possible trajectories for creative productivity across the life span. Indeed, this framework has been converted into a complex mathematical model that makes specific predictions regarding the developmental placement of the three landmarks as a function of discipline, productivity, and age at career onset (Simonton, 1991a, 1997). These predictions have been confirmed for both artistic and scientific creators (Simonton, 1991a, 1991b, 1992, 2007a).

Conclusion

As might be expected for a topic that has attracted empirical research since 1835, we know a great deal about how creative productivity changes across the life span. Furthermore, this brief chapter could only touch upon the main points (cf. Simonton, 2012). Indeed, space limitations have obliged me to provide a general overview rather than detail some of the complexities unique to specific domains of creativity (see, e.g., Jones, Reedy, & Weinberg, 2014;

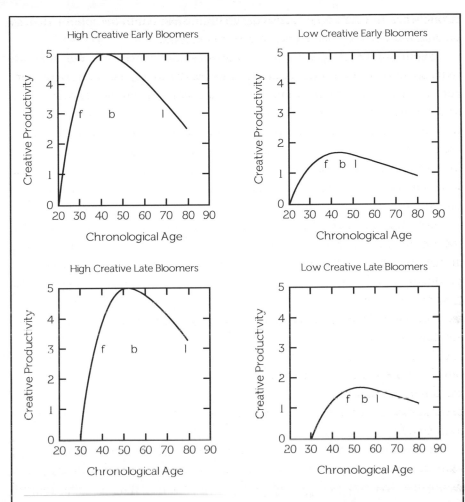

Figure 6.3. Fourfold typology of career trajectories and landmarks based on the distinctions between high and low creative and between early and late bloomers. The predicted location of the three career landmarks are indicated by letters, where f = first major contribution, b = best contribution, and l = last major contribution. *Note.* From *Great psychologists and their times: Scientific insights into psychology's history* (p. 94) by D. K. Simonton, 2002, Washington, DC: American Psychological Association. Copyright D. K. Simonton. Reprinted with permission of the author.

Kozbelt, 2014; McKay & Kaufman, 2014). For example, in some domains, such as writing novels or making movies, the creative products come in larger units with wider spacing between each work. How does this change what was said earlier? We have also ignored the research on how personal characteristics and sociocultural conditions might affect the expected developmental trajectories. For instance, what is the impact of gender or the influence of war? In truth, a whole book can be written solely on the subject of this chapter. Hence, you should consider this chapter a mere introduction to a topic enjoying great intrinsic interest and importance—particularly as you get older. If you become a creative individual, when can you expect to have your first success? At what age will you produce your best work? How old will you be when your creativity runs dry? For my part, I have found the research on this question ever more fascinating as I find myself slowly sliding down the post-peak portion of the age curve! Fortunately, I know I haven't yet hit the zero point!

Recommended Readings

Jones, B. F., Reedy, E. J., & Weinberg, B. A. (2014). Age and scientific genius. In D. K. Simonton (Ed.), *The Wiley handbook of genius* (pp. 422–450). Oxford, England: Wiley.

Kozbelt, A. (2014). Musical creativity over the lifespan. In D. K. Simonton (Ed.), *The Wiley handbook of genius* (pp. 451–472). Oxford, England: Wiley.

McKay, A. S., & Kaufman, J. C. (2014). Literary geniuses: Their life, work, and death. In D. K. Simonton (Ed.), *The Wiley handbook of genius* (pp. 473–487). Oxford, England: Wiley.

Simonton, D. K. (2012). Creative productivity and aging: An age decrement—or not? In S. K. Whitbourne & M. Sliwinski (Eds.), *The Wiley-Blackwell handbook of adult development and aging* (pp. 477–496). New York, NY: Wiley-Blackwell.

References

Beard, G. M. (1874). *Legal responsibility in old age.* New York, NY: Russell.

Brodetsky, S. (1942). Newton: Scientist and man. *Nature, 150,* 698–699.

Dennis, W. (1966). Creative productivity between the ages of 20 and 80 years. *Journal of Gerontology, 21,* 1–8.

Galenson, D. W. (2005). *Old masters and young geniuses: The two life cycles of artistic creativity.* Princeton, NJ: Princeton University Press.

Galton, F. (1869). *Hereditary genius: An inquiry into its laws and consequences.* London, England: Macmillan.

Hass, R. W., & Weisberg, R. W. (2009). Career development in two seminal American songwriters: A test of the equal odds rule. *Creativity Research Journal, 21*, 183–190.

Jones, B. F., Reedy, E. J., & Weinberg, B. A. (2014). Age and scientific genius. In D. K. Simonton (Ed.), *The Wiley handbook of genius* (pp. 422–450). Oxford, England: Wiley.

Jones, B. F., & Weinberg, B. A. (2011). Age dynamics in scientific creativity. *Proceedings of the National Academy of Sciences.* Retrieved from http://www.pnas.org/cgi/doi/10.1073/pnas.1102895108

Jungk, R. (1958). *Brighter than a thousand suns* (J. Cleugh, Trans.). New York, NY: Harcourt Brace.

Kozbelt, A. (2008a). Longitudinal hit ratios of classical composers: Reconciling "Darwinian" and expertise acquisition perspectives on lifespan creativity. *Psychology of Aesthetics, Creativity, and the Arts, 2*, 221–235.

Kozbelt, A. (2008b). One-hit wonders in classical music: Evidence and (partial) explanations for an early career peak. *Creativity Research Journal, 20*, 179–195.

Kozbelt, A. (2014). Musical creativity over the lifespan. In D. K. Simonton (Ed.), *The Wiley handbook of genius* (pp. 451–472). Oxford, England: Wiley.

Lehman, H. C. (1953). *Age and achievement.* Princeton, NJ: Princeton University Press.

McKay, A. S., & Kaufman, J. C. (2014). Literary geniuses: Their life, work, and death. In D. K. Simonton (Ed.), *The Wiley handbook of genius* (pp. 473–487). Oxford, England: Wiley.

Quételet, A. (1968). *A treatise on man and the development of his faculties.* New York, NY: Franklin. (Reprint of 1842 Edinburgh translation of 1835 French original)

Raskin, E. A. (1936). Comparison of scientific and literary ability: A biographical study of eminent scientists and men of letters of the nineteenth century. *Journal of Abnormal and Social Psychology, 31*, 20–35.

Simonton, D. K. (1975). Age and literary creativity: A cross-cultural and transhistorical survey. *Journal of Cross-Cultural Psychology, 6*, 259–277.

Simonton, D. K. (1988). Age and outstanding achievement: What do we know after a century of research? *Psychological Bulletin, 104*, 251–267.

Simonton, D. K. (1991a). Career landmarks in science: Individual differences and interdisciplinary contrasts. *Developmental Psychology, 27*, 119–130.

Simonton, D. K. (1991b). Emergence and realization of genius: The lives and works of 120 classical composers. *Journal of Personality and Social Psychology, 61*, 829–840.

Simonton, D. K. (1992). Leaders of American psychology, 1879–1967: Career development, creative output, and professional achievement. *Journal of Personality and Social Psychology, 62,* 5–17.

Simonton, D. K. (1997). Creative productivity: A predictive and explanatory model of career trajectories and landmarks. *Psychological Review, 104,* 66–89.

Simonton, D. K. (2002). *Great psychologists and their times: Scientific insights into psychology's history.* Washington, DC: American Psychological Association.

Simonton, D. K. (2004). *Creativity in science: Chance, logic, genius, and zeitgeist.* Cambridge, England: Cambridge University Press.

Simonton, D. K. (2007a). Cinema composers: Career trajectories for creative productivity in film music. *Psychology of Aesthetics, Creativity, and the Arts, 1,* 160–169.

Simonton, D. K. (2007b). Creative life cycles in literature: Poets versus novelists or conceptualists versus experimentalists? *Psychology of Aesthetics, Creativity, and the Arts, 1,* 133–139.

Simonton, D. K. (2009). The literary genius of William Shakespeare: Empirical lessons drawn from his dramatic and poetic creativity. In S. B. Kaufman & J. C. Kaufman (Eds.), *The psychology of creative writing* (pp. 131–145). New York, NY: Cambridge University Press.

Simonton, D. K. (2012). Creative productivity and aging: An age decrement—or not? In S. K. Whitbourne & M. Sliwinski (Eds.), *The Wiley-Blackwell handbook of adult development and aging* (pp. 477–496). New York, NY: Wiley-Blackwell.

Simonton, D. K. (2015a). Numerical odds and evens in Beethoven's nine symphonies: Can a computer really tell the difference? *Empirical Studies of the Arts, 33,* 18–35.

Simonton, D. K. (2015b). Thomas Alva Edison's creative career: The multi-layered trajectory of trials, errors, failures, and triumphs. *Psychology of Aesthetics, Creativity, and the Arts, 9,* 2–14.

Simonton, D. K. (2016). Early and late bloomers among classical composers: Were the greatest geniuses also prodigies? In G. McPherson (Ed.), *Musical prodigies: Interpretations from psychology, music education, musicology and ethnomusicology.* New York, NY: Oxford University Press.

Zusne, L. (1976). Age and achievement in psychology: The harmonic mean as a model. *American Psychologist, 31,* 805–807.

CHAPTER 7

Pretend Play and Creativity

Sandra W. Russ and Alexis W. Lee

Key Take-Aways

- Pretend play is a resource for children's adaptive development and should be encouraged by parents and teachers.
- There is substantial empirical support for the relationship between pretend play and various measures of creativity, such as divergent thinking and storytelling, and this relationship is stable over time.
- Children's play rating scales have been developed to objectively measure play skills, such as Russ's Affect in Play Scale (APS; Russ, 1993, 2014) that measures affect, imagination, organization in play, and enjoyment of play.
- There is some evidence that play intervention protocols increase children's play skills and divergent thinking. However, results of research studies are mixed, the stability of these findings is tenuous, and rigorous studies are needed.
- Engagement in elaborated role-play, such as play with imaginary friends, is associated with social perspective taking and creativity, assessed by picture drawing and story completion, although the direction of causality is not clearly defined.

- The association between pretend play and adult creative production needs to be addressed as the field moves closer to elucidating those aspects of play that contribute to creativity over time.
- Assessment of pretend play is one way to determine a child's creative potential.
- Educators should encourage pretend play in preschool and early elementary grades by providing appropriate toys, guidance, time, and space for play to occur.

What do you observe when you watch young children play? Usually, they are having fun and enjoying themselves. They are playing because they want to. They are making up stories, using LEGOs or blocks to represent all kinds of objects, role-playing different characters, and defying logic (flying on a magic carpet). They are also expressing lots of emotion, both positive (e.g., getting a present that they like) or negative (e.g., playing cops and robbers, sword fighting, being chased by a monster). Of course, in play, negative feelings like fear and anger are only pretend, so they are not really so negative. Children might be having a sword fight, but they are having a good time. Also, children can regulate feelings in pretend play by going at their own pace. By self-modulating feelings, they learn to regulate emotions.

There are many definitions of pretend play. Fein (1987) defined play as a symbolic behavior in which "one thing is treated 'as if' it were something else" (p. 282). For example, a block becomes a table or a stick becomes a sword. Fein also thought that the expression of feelings was an integral part of pretend play. This focus on emotion and pretend in play is important because it recognizes that both cognition and affect are involved in play, as they are in creativity. In fact, Fein thought that play is a natural form of creativity in children. Sawyer (1997) expanded on this idea and conceptualized pretend play as a form of improvisation for children in that it is unscripted, yet has loose outlines to be followed—like in jazz. Comparing pretend play to improvisation in jazz is a good analogy and captures the creativity in the play activity.

Krasnor and Pepler (1980) conceptualized play as involving nonliterality (not following rules of logic, time, and space), positive affect, intrinsic motivation, and flexibility. When children play, the story is often illogical, the children are having fun, and they are self-motivated to play. Krasnor and Pepler viewed play as reflecting the developmental level of the child and also as providing the child with an opportunity to practice skills. They also thought play was a causal agent in developmental change of many important cognitive, affective, and interpersonal processes.

What processes occur in pretend play? How can we measure pretend play? What kinds of creativity does play relate to? Does engaging in pretend play facilitate creativity? Are imaginary friends good or a problem for the child? How can we help children develop imagination in play? These are some of the questions that this chapter will address.

Purpose of Pretend Play

Play is a universal phenomena (Gaskins, Haight, & Lancy, 2007). Children in all cultures engage in play. Play also follows a developmental process. Before the age of 2, children play with objects similarly, no matter what their function. Around the age of 2, children begin to discover that objects have specific functions, and they begin to pretend (Hirsh-Pasek & Golinkoff, 2003). For example, a block becomes a table or a television. The child can engage in object transformation. As children get older, symbolism and narratives combine and become more complex. There are individual differences in how much imagination occurs in pretend play, but in most cultures, pretend play is part of childhood. Gaskins et al. (2007), after studying play in many cultures, concluded that the amount of pretend in the play depends upon how much it is valued in the culture. In complex societies, pretend play occurs more frequently in childhood than in simpler, work-oriented cultures where play may be a distraction and is curtailed.

Many animal researchers and evolutionary scholars have concluded that play is a form of practice for adult activities. Mitchell (2007) viewed animal play as practice for adult behavior. For example, play fighting is preparation for actual fighting in adulthood to establish dominance in the group or capture prey. For humans, childhood play can prepare for problem solving in adulthood. Boyd (2009) represents this view and stated that, "Play evolved through the advantages of flexibility; the amount of play in a species correlates with its flexibility of action" (p. 14). He thought that play facilitates a flexibility of mind that is facilitative of creativity, especially in the arts. On the other hand, Smith (2007) thought that play may be a facilitative experience for children, but did not hold a major adaptive role in child development.

A number of theorists view play as facilitative of child development and of creativity in particular. Piaget (1945/1967) thought that play was a part of assimilation and accommodation as the child interacted with the environment. He also thought that symbolic play helped the child differentiate reality from fantasy.

Vygotsky (1930/1967) theorized that imagination developed from children's play. Through play, children learn to combine elements of experience into new situations and behaviors. He referred to this ability as combinatory imagination. Combining different elements of thought is an important ingredient of creativity. Divergent thinking, the ability to generate a variety of ideas, is also important in creative production. Singer and Singer (1990) proposed that pretend play involves divergent thinking, the creation of new ideas, and is practice with creative thinking. Dansky (1980) thought that the free combination of objects and ideas that occur in play is similar to the process involved in creative thinking. These are just a few of the theorists who grappled with the association between play and creative problem solving. Often, their theories emerged from observations of individual children.

Pretend play also is a place for emotional expression and learning to process and modulate emotion (Freud, 1965). Children can think about and express both negative and positive feelings in a pretend situation and slowly gain access to and integrate uncomfortable ideation, memories, and associations. Fein (1987) introduced the concept of an affective symbol system that gets activated in pretend play and is important in creativity. An affective symbol system stores information about emotional events and affective relationships and is manipulated and recombined in pretend play. Russ (2014) has emphasized the importance of both affect themes and affect experiences in creative thinking, especially in the arts. For example, a fiction writer who has a rich store of emotional childhood memories to draw upon would have an advantage in creative writing.

Russ (1993, 2014) has identified cognitive and affective processes within the individual that are expressed and utilized in both pretend play and in creative activities. Table 7.1 summarizes these processes. For example, divergent thinking occurs in play when a child uses a block to represent many different objects or makes up different stories. Affect themes are expressed and manipulated when two dolls argue about what to do, get angry, make up, and decide to have fun on a swing. Fein (1987) would say the child is manipulating cognitive and affective representations that contribute to flexible thinking and to creative thinking.

From a variety of theoretical perspectives, pretend play is thought to not only reflect creative thinking, but also to help creative thinking develop. What does the research say?

What Does the Research Support?

In 1983, Nathan Kogan stated that the research on the link between play and creativity had resulted in the most promising set of findings in the children's creativity literature in the previous decade. The promise of that early research has been realized in that there is a robust set of findings that show that pretend play is associated with creativity in children, independent of intel-

Table 7.1
Model of Creativity and Pretend Play

Creative Processes in Pretend Play	Examples in Play
Divergent Thinking	Block transformations
	Different story ideas and elements
Broad Associations	Wide fantasy and remote images
Cognitive Flexibility/Recombining Ideas	Use toys in different ways
	Manipulating story elements
	Loosening of time and space
Insight and Problem Solving	Building novel objects
	Playing with mechanical objects
Perspective-Taking	Role playing
	Pretending to be different characters
Narrative Development	Story plots and sequences
Affect Themes and Symbols	Monsters; cops and robbers
	Yummy food
Emotional Expression	Dolls fighting; doll hugging
Joy in Pretending	Pleasure and absorption in the play
Integration of Affect/Affect Themes	Placing emotion in an appropriate narrative

Note. From *Pretend play in childhood: Foundation of adult creativity* (p. 25), by S. Russ, 2014, Washington, DC: American Psychological Association. Reprinted with permission of the author.

ligence. We know that intelligence is a resource for children. Pretend play can also be viewed as a resource for children, because it relates to creativity and other developmental correlates that are indicative of adaptive functioning in children.

Before we can study pretend play, we have to be able to measure it. How can we measure an activity that is spontaneous and hard to capture? Researchers have managed to develop reliable and valid measures of pretend play. Usually rating scales are used in which play segments are rated for imagination, use of fantasy, amount of pretend in the play, and amount of affect themes (see Gitlin-Weiner, Sandgrund, & Schaefer, 2000; Kaugars, 2011, for reviews of play measures). In the Russ research program, we developed a standardized task in which we ask the child to play with puppets and blocks for 5 minutes. Russ developed the Affect in Play Scale (APS; Russ, 1993, 2014), which measures imagination and organization of the narrative on a 1–5 scale. It also measures affect themes in the narrative with a frequency count. Examples of affect themes would be a puppet going down a slide and saying "Whee" or a puppet being chased by a monster and hiding. Finally, the APS measures enjoyment of and absorption in the play task. Children ages 6–10 are able to play with this task and there are many individual differences that emerge in the play, independent of intelligence. There is a preschool version of the task available for younger children. The cognitive and affective processes that are expressed in pretend play are different from those involved in intelligence tests. Measures of creativity are also generally independent of intelligence, so this is consistent with the play and creativity literature.

Most of the research on play and creativity in the literature has focused on play and divergent thinking. Some of the reasons for this are that divergent thinking is thought to be important in creativity, is relatively easy to assess in children, and has measures available that are valid. A typical item on a divergent thinking test is, "How many uses can you think of for a button?" There are a large number of studies that have found significant relationships between different measures of pretend play and divergent thinking (see Dansky, 1999; Russ, 2014, for reviews). For example, in one study, children who had more imagination and more affect themes in play could think of more uses for objects on a divergent thinking test than could children with less imagination (Russ & Grossman-McKee, 1990). These correlations were significant when intelligence was controlled for. Some of the play and divergent thinking studies have been criticized in a review by Lillard et al. (2013) for having the same individual administer the play task and the divergent thinking task, which raises the possibility of experimenter bias. However, there are studies that did use different examiners and found significant associations, as hypothesized, between the play measure and divergent thinking (Lieberman, 1977; Russ & Grossman-McKee, 1990; Russ, Robins, & Christiano, 1999; Singer & Rummo, 1973). For example, in the Russ, Robins, and Christiano (1999) longitudinal study, imagination and organization in early play (first and second grade) predicted divergent thinking 4 years later. Different examiners were used in the original and follow-up studies. In other studies with the APS that did use the same examiner for both, the APS was administered in a standard format and scoring was done at a later time. The divergent thinking task also was administered in a standard format with standard prompts and scoring was blind to APS performance. The APS has been found to relate to divergent thinking in five different studies with different school-aged child populations and different examiners (Hoffmann & Russ, 2012; Russ & Grossman-McKee, 1990; Russ et al., 1999; Russ & Schafer, 2006; Wallace & Russ, 2015). The preschool version of the APS related to divergent thinking in one study (Kaugars & Russ, 2009). In a recent longitudinal study that followed the children in the Hoffmann and Russ (2012) study, Wallace and Russ (2015) found that pretend play predicted divergent thinking over a 4-year period. This replicates the Russ, Robins, and Christiano (1999) findings. In addition, when baseline divergent thinking was controlled for, play continued to significantly predict divergent thinking. This suggests that components of play in addition to divergent thinking, such as affect expression or narrative organization, are associated with divergent thinking over time.

In most of the studies with the APS, both imagination and affect themes in fantasy play related to the divergent thinking measure. This is important because affect has been neglected in the play research area and yet is so important in creativity. The amount of affect expressed in play, positive and negative affect, related to divergent thinking.

Studies have found relationships between play and other measures of creativity as well. Kaugars and Russ (2009) found that pretend play in preschool children on the APS related to teacher ratings of make-believe in children's daily play behavior. Hoffmann and Russ (2012) found that pretend play related to creativity in storytelling, independent of verbal ability. Affect in the play also related to affect in stories. The stories were rated for creativity by independent raters. Given the number of studies in the literature in different research programs, with different child populations, and in different environments that have found significant relations between pretend play and creativity, with some studies using different examiners for the different tasks, our conclusion is that there is good evidence for the association between pretend play and creativity and that this association is relatively stable over time. Although there are no longitudinal studies that have followed children into adulthood to assess prediction of adult creativity from early play, there is research literature that has found that divergent thinking in children is predictive of adult creativity (Plucker, 1999).

Experimental Evidence

One of the key questions is whether there is a causal relationship between play and creativity. Does engaging in play have a facilitative effect on creativity? There is some evidence that play facilitates divergent thinking. In several well-done experimental studies, pretend play did facilitate divergent thinking in preschool children (Dansky, 1980; Dansky & Silverman, 1973). In the Dansky and Silverman study, it was found that children who played with objects during a play period gave significantly more uses for those objects than did a control group. Dansky (1980) refined the earlier study and found that play had a generalized effect on objects that were different from those in the play period.

A methodological criticism of the Dansky study was made by Smith and Whitney (1987) and, more recently, by Lillard, Lerner et al. (2013), who raised the issue of experimenter bias. The same experimenter who administered the play intervention also administered the divergent thinking task. Thus, unconscious experimenter bias could be a factor. Smith and Whitney (1987), in a carefully executed study, failed to confirm the hypothesis that play would enhance divergent thinking in preschool children. In their study, they had a different experimenter administer the divergent thinking task after the play task. There are different opinions about how the results of individual studies should be interpreted, but there is a consensus that methodologically rigorous studies with large samples, blinded experimenters, adequate control groups, and valid measures of play and creativity are needed (Lillard et al., 2013).

A carefully controlled study by Russ and Kaugars (2000–2001) did not find an effect of play on divergent thinking. This study was different from Dansky's study in that children did not play with objects. Rather, they played with puppets and blocks on the APS, making up stories. Also, the children were first- and second-grade children, rather than preschoolers. Eighty children were randomly assigned to one of four groups: a happy puppet playgroup, an angry puppet playgroup, a free playgroup, and a control puzzle group. Children were given different instructions about having the puppets play out a happy story, angry story, or neutral story. The Alternate Uses test (divergent thinking) was given immediately following the play, by the same examiner. There was no effect for any of the play conditions on divergent thinking. The experimental affect manipulation did work for the angry group (on a mood check) but not for the happy group. So, the hypothesis remains untested for the positive affect group. Perhaps a more appropriate outcome measure would have been a story-telling measure. This raises the methodological issue of choosing the outcome measure that makes the best conceptual sense in the study.

Another important factor is the "dose" of the intervention. How many play intervention sessions are needed to demonstrate an effect? Christie (1994) has cautioned against brief one-trial studies in the play intervention area. It may take time for the development of processes in pretend play that would, in turn, facilitate creativity tasks. There is evidence that when pretend play occurs in multiple sessions over time, increases in components of creativity occur. For example, Kasari, Freeman, and Paparella (2006), in a randomized controlled study with children with autism, found that a play intervention resulted in increased symbolic play. These were young children from 3–4 years of age. This was a rigorous study that began the intervention at the child's current developmental level. The training involved modeling and prompting. Children received 30 hours of intervention weekly for 6 weeks on a daily basis. This was a rather intensive intervention, but is necessary for children with autism. Children in the playgroup, compared with children in joint attention and control groups, had increased symbolic play that generalized to play with mothers.

There is a need for standardized play facilitation protocols that are easy to carry out in schools and homes and are empirically based. We have been developing a protocol that uses story stems and a variety of unstructured toys. In a pilot study by Russ, Moore, and Farber (2004), first- and second-grade children in an inner city school with a high degree of poverty received five individual 30-minute play sessions following a standard play intervention protocol. Different examiners blind to the group assignment assessed baseline play and outcome play on the APS. There were two playgroups (imagination and affect) and one control group (puzzles and coloring). The playgroups had a variety of toys available and played with the adult facilitator. They were asked to play out specific story themes that focused on imagination (have a boy go to the moon) or affect (have a girl be happy at a birthday party). The adult played with the child and followed the child's lead in the story, but also praised, modeled, and asked questions. We controlled for adult interaction in the control group as well (coloring sheets and puzzles).

The major result of this study was that the play interventions were effective in improving play skills on the APS. The affect play condition was most effective in that, after baseline play was controlled for, the affect playgroup had significantly higher play scores on all play processes. These children had more affect in their play (both positive affect and negative affect), a greater variety of affect content, and better imagination and organization of the story than did the control group. The imagination playgroup also had significantly more positive affect and variety of affect than the control group. Another major finding was that, on the outcome measure of divergent thinking, there were significant effects for the group. Although the individual contrast comparisons did not reach significance, inspection of the profile plots indicated that the playgroups (usually the affect playgroup) had higher scores on the divergent thinking test. However, one limitation of this study was that no baseline measure of divergent thinking was obtained.

In a follow-up study of these children 4–8 months later by Moore and Russ (2008), the imagination group had improved play skills over time. The affect group did not maintain the play changes over this period. It may be that an increase in affect expression from a play intervention is temporary, whereas an increase in imagination and pretend in play could be longer lasting. In the follow-up study, there no longer was a significant group effect for divergent thinking. In fact, the control group now had higher scores. Perhaps booster sessions would have been useful in maintaining the initial group effects.

In a group adaptation of the play intervention, Hoffmann and Russ (2016) found that small-group play sessions, when compared with a control group, did result in increased imagination and affective expression in play after 6 sessions. In addition, there was a transfer effect in that below-average players increased in play creativity and also increased on a divergent thinking task. In the Russ research program, we have been able to increase imagination and affective expression in pretend play with standardized play intervention sessions with elementary school children. There have been transfer effects to a divergent thinking measure in two studies.

Singer and Singer (1999) developed a video-based program for parents and other caregivers of preschool children that uses make-believe play to enhance literacy. The "My Magic Story Car" video program, in a nationally tested study, resulted in improved literacy skills. Many children continued to play the make-believe games on their own and taught the games to other children

Imaginary Friends and Role-Play

Many children have imaginary companions. Imaginary companions are pretend friends with whom children interact in pretend play or in daily life. Parents often worry that having an imaginary friend is indicative of psychopathology. The research indicates otherwise. Singer and Singer (1990) found that children with imaginary friends were more creative and smiled and laughed more when they played than children without imaginary friends. Marjorie Taylor (1999) has carried out extensive research in this area and concluded that having an imaginary companion was associated with creativity. She conceptualized that interacting with imaginary representations of people was practice with creative thought. She also found that many creative adults had imaginary friends in childhood. Hoff (2005) also found that the existence of imaginary friends was associated with creativity and that the depth of characterization of the pretend friend was associated with level of creativity.

Emotion is also involved in the imaginary friend phenomenon. Gleason (2013) proposed that interacting with pretend friends would help children process emotions. Because this type of pretend interaction is distanced from real interactions with people, children can practice with emotional expression in a safer place. This could be another form of the kind of emotional processing that occurs in pretend play.

Role-play is one kind of pretend play that children often engage in during the preschool and early elementary school years. Role-play can foster both cognitive and affective processes in play, as it provides a space for children to develop the cognitive skill of taking the perspective of another person, namely "theory of mind," and it allows the child a space to freely act out emotion-laden themes with other characters, perhaps to take the focus off the child by projecting behaviors and emotions onto another in order to make sense of the world.

Recent research on imaginary friends has begun to focus not exclusively on imaginary friends but on elaborated role-play more generally. Taylor, in particular, has published extensively in the area of elaborated role-play in the preschool and early school years period. Elaborated role-play is characterized by engagement in stable kinds of play involving imaginary friends, person-ified objects, and impersonation that children incorporate into regular play activities (Taylor, Sachet, Maring, & Mannering, 2013). There is some evi-dence that elaborated role-play may play a role in children's creative and social perspective-taking development independent of the benefits associated with typical developmental pretend play milestones (Mottweiler & Taylor, 2014; Taylor et al., 2013). Individual differences in role-play type seems to be related to gender and personality preferences rather than developmental differences, as no relation was found between type of play and the action pantomime task, which was used as a non-role-play control task involving symbolic use of tools (Taylor et al., 2013).

Three- to six-year-olds who engaged in any of the three types of role-play performed better on a task where they were asked to have a pretend phone conversation than young children who did not engage in any kind of role-play, even after controlling for shyness and extraversion (Taylor et al., 2013). In addition, contrary to pervading cultural beliefs that shy children have imagi-nary friends because they are less skilled interacting with peers, children who engaged in role-play were rated as less shy by their parents than those who did not (Taylor et al., 2013). There are many possible interpretations as to why young children who engage in role-play may be less shy than other children. Practicing social perspective taking with imaginary friends and personified objects may allow children to interact with peers more easily, for example (Taylor et al., 2013). It is possible that engagement in elaborated role-play provides children with an avenue to hone skills in the social domain of creativ-ity. According to a domain-specific framework, children may go on to develop creativity in one area, but not in another, as they enter adulthood (Kaufman, 2012). Perhaps children who practice with elaborated role-play in childhood develop a mastery over perspective taking that allows them to develop empathy and heightened emotional awareness.

Preschoolers who engaged in elaborated role-play performed better on measures of theory of mind, which assess the cognitive ability to under-stand mental representations and beliefs of another person external to the self (Taylor & Carlson, 1997). Three years later, the same children were asked about their role-play behaviors and completed emotion response predictions based on personality descriptions of hypothetical characters to assess theory of mind in school-age children (Taylor, Carlson, Maring, Gerow, & Charley, 2004). Although engagement in elaborated role-play in preschool did not predict emotional understanding scores 3 years later, school-age children who did not impersonate scored lower on the emotional understanding measure than those who did impersonate (Taylor et al., 2004). Again, many interpretations of this finding are possible, and it is important to keep in mind that one cannot infer the direction of causality of the relationship between the two variables. A better understanding of how children impersonate and for what purpose might help us better understand the relationship between emotion understanding and impersonation in young school-age children.

Mottweiler and Taylor (2014) investigated the relationship between elaborated role-play and creativity as measured by performance on two tasks they believed were appropriate for preschoolers. Preschoolers and their parents were interviewed about the child's engagement in role-play and asked follow-up questions to elicit elaborations of the made-up characters. To assess children's creativity, the children were asked to draw a picture of a real person and a made-up person and were prompted to complete a story-stem about a magic key. Raters scored creativity of the story-stem task and drawing task on a scale of 1–5 from Not Creative to Highly Creative based on subjective creativity definitions. Children who had imaginary friends and children who engaged in stable impersonation had more creative story-stem completions, and children with imaginary friends drew more creative pictures of made-up people (Mottweiler & Taylor, 2014). It may be inferred that children who are more socially creative have stronger proclivities toward engaging in elaborated role-play. Alternatively, practice with made-up characters and stories might facilitate the creative solutions children provide on tasks that have social components. A final alternative is that a third confounding variable may be promoting both children's engagement in role-play and their creative expression (Mottweiler & Taylor, 2014).

Research supports the assumption that pretend play in general, imaginary companions, and elaborated role-play in particular, are helpful in providing children with opportunities to think about the behaviors and emotions of others, which may place playful children in an advantageous position over their nonplayful peers. Playful children may prove more successful in relating to and engaging with others in social contexts, a skill that is beneficial throughout the lifetime.

Educational Implications

A major implication for educators is that pretend play, in all of its forms, should be taken seriously. Observing pretend play, either informally or with a standardized assessment of play, could help identify creative potential in children that other assessment measures may not identify. In pretend play, creative thinking can be observed in a way that intelligence tests do not measure. Pretend play is predictive of creativity over time, and would be a valuable addition to an assessment battery.

It is important that parents and teachers understand that aggression in pretend play is normal in children, especially in boys, and is related to creativity and prosocial behavior. If the aggression is pretend and well-integrated into the story, that bodes well for the child.

Finally, especially in preschool and early elementary years, time and space for pretend play to occur will help children engage in play, enjoy it, and develop their imagination. At times, some guidance from an adult, with modeling of pretend, could be helpful. It is important to have unstructured toys available that leave room for the child to use his or her imagination, such as blocks, LEGOs, dolls, action figures, plastic animals, a playhouse, etc. Ideally, program evaluation could determine whether and how pretend play time is facilitative of creativity and learning.

Future Directions

Researchers should continue to investigate how engaging in play in different ways affects creativity and child development in general. We need to learn how different processes in play relate to different kinds of creativity. Longitudinal studies that follow children into adulthood are needed to provide evidence that early pretend play skills are associated with creative productivity. One of the challenges in this research area is that so many variables determine creative achievement. Individual cognitive and affective processes are important, but so are motivation, opportunity, luck, and life events and circumstances. That is why looking at everyday examples of creativity (Richards, 2007) is important to consider in longitudinal studies as well.

Experimental research can answer questions about whether or not pretend play interventions actually facilitate creativity. Multisite studies and large samples are needed to enable more sophisticated statistical analyses to be carried out (Lillard, Russ, Hirsh-Pasek, & Golinkoff, 2013). Small sample sizes makes it difficult to find effects and to determine which children would benefit most from play interventions. Because this research is so time-consuming and labor-intensive, multisite studies with different child populations is important.

Finally, parents and educators need access to research findings, so that play protocols can be integrated into school and home settings. We, as a field, need to disseminate practical guidelines about how teachers and parents can facilitate play. Children need time, space, and encouragement to develop their play skills. Both solitary play and play with others is important. They need unstructured toys that can leave room for their imagination. Children need a society that values pretending, imagination, and creativity. We, as a society, need to recognize the importance of pretend play, so that parents, teachers, and all who interact with children make the time and the space for children to play.

Recommended Readings

Lillard, A., Lerner, M., Hopkins, E., Dore, R., Smith, E., & Palmquist, C. (2013). The impact of pretend play on children's development: A review of empirical evidence. *Psychological Bulletin, 139,* 1–34.

Smith, P. (2007). Evolutionary foundations and functions of play: An overview. In A. Goncu & S. Gaskins (Eds.), *Play and development* (pp. 21–49). New York, NY: Taylor & Francis.

References

Boyd, B. (2009). *On the origin of stories.* Cambridge, MA: Harvard University Press.

Christie, J. (1994). Academic play. In J. Hellendoorn, R. Van der Kooij, & B. Sutton-Smith (Eds.), *Play and intervention* (pp. 203–213). Albany: State University of New York Press.

Dansky, J. (1980). Make-believe: A mediator of the relationship between play and associative fluency. *Child Development, 51,* 576–579.

Dansky, J. (1999). Play. In M. Runco & S. Pritzker (Eds.), *Encyclopedia of creativity* (pp. 393–408). San Diego, CA: Academic Press.

Dansky, J., & Silverman, F. (1973). Effects of play on associative fluency in preschool-aged children. *Developmental Psychology, 9,* 38–43.

Fein, G. (1987). Pretend play: Creativity and consciousness. In P. Gorlitz & J. Wohlwill (Eds.), *Curiosity, imagination and play* (pp. 281–304). Hillsdale, NJ: Lawrence Erlbaum.

Freud, A. (1965). *Normality and pathology in childhood: Assessments of development.* New York, NY: International Universities Press.

Gaskins, S., Haight, W., & Lancy, D. (2007). The cultural construction of play. In A. Goncu & S. Gaskins (Eds.), *Play and development* (pp. 179–202). New York, NY: Taylor & Francis.

Gitlin-Weiner, K., Sandgrund, A., & Schaefer, C. (2000). *Play diagnosis and assessment* (2nd ed.). New York, NY: Wiley.

Gleason, T. (2013). Imaginary relationships. In M. Taylor (Ed.), *The Oxford handbook of the development of imagination* (pp. 251–271). New York, NY: Oxford University Press.

Hirsh-Pasek, K., & Golinkoff, R. (2003). *Einstein never used flash cards: How our children really learn—and why they need to play more and memorize less.* New York, NY: Rodale.

Hoff, E. V. (2005). Imaginary companions, creativity, and self-image in middle childhood. *Creativity Research Journal, 17,* 167–181.

Hoffmann, J., & Russ, S. (2012). Pretend play, creativity, and emotion regulation. *Psychology of Aesthetics, Creativity, and the Arts, 6,* 175–184.

Hoffmann, J., & Russ, S. (2016). Fostering pretend play skills and creativity in elementary school girls: A group play intervention. *Psychology of Aesthetics, Creativity, and the Arts, 10,* 114–125.

Kasari, C., Freeman, S., & Paparella, T. (2006). Joint attention and symbolic play in young children with autism: A randomized controlled intervention study. *Journal of Child Psychology and Psychiatry, 47,* 611–620.

Kaufman, J. C. (2012). Counting the muses: Development of the Kaufman Domains of Creativity Scale (K-DOCS). *Psychology of Aesthetics, Creativity, and the Arts, 6,* 298–308. doi:10.1037/a0029751

Kaugars, A. (2011). Assessment of pretend play. In S. Russ & L. Niec (Eds.), *Play in clinical practice: Evidence-based approaches* (pp. 51–82). New York, NY: Guilford Press.

Kaugars, A., & Russ, S. (2009). Assessing preschool children's pretend play: Preliminary validation of the Affect in Play Scale-Preschool Version. *Early Education and Development, 20,* 733–755.

Kogan, N. (1983). Stylistic variation in childhood and adolescence: Creativity, metaphor, and cognitive styles. In P. Mussen (Ed.), *Handbook of child psychology* (Vol. 3, pp. 631–706). New York, NY: Wiley.

Krasnor, L., & Pepler, D. (1980). The study of children's play: Some suggested future directions. *Child Development, 9,* 85–94.

Lieberman, J. N. (1977). *Playfulness: Its relationship to imagination and creativity.* New York, NY: Academic Press.

Lillard, A., Lerner, M., Hopkins, E., Dore, R., Smith, E., & Palmquist, C. (2013). The impact of pretend play on children's development: A review of empirical evidence. *Psychological Bulletin, 139,* 1–34.

Lillard, A., Russ, S., Hirsh-Pasek, K., & Golinkoff, R. (2013). Probing play: The research we need (Guest editors' afterword). *American Journal of Play, 6,* 161–165.

Mitchell, R. (2007). Pretense in animals: The continual relevance of children's pretense. In A. Goncu & S. Gaskins (Eds.), *Play and development: Evolutionary, sociocultural, and functional perspectives* (pp. 51–75). New York, NY: Taylor & Francis.

Moore, M., & Russ, S. (2008). Follow-up of a pretend play intervention: Effects on play, creativity and emotional processes in children. *Creativity Research Journal, 20,* 427–436.

Mottweiler, C. M., & Taylor, M. (2014). Elaborated role play and creativity in preschool age children. *Psychology of Aesthetics, Creativity, and the Arts, 8,* 277–286. doi:10.1037/a0036083

Piaget, J. (1967). *Play, dreams, and imitation in childhood.* New York, NY: Norton. (Original work published in 1945)

Plucker, J. (1999). Is the proof really in the pudding? Reanalysis of Torrance's longitudinal data. *Creativity Research Journal, 12,* 103–114.

Richards, R. (2007). *Everyday creativity.* Washington, DC: American Psychological Association.

Russ, S. (1993). *Affect and creativity: The role of affect and play in the creative process.* Hillsdale, NJ: Lawrence Erlbaum.

Russ, S. (2014). *Pretend play in childhood: Foundation of adult creativity.* Washington, DC: American Psychological Association Books.

Russ, S., & Grossman-McKee, A. (1990). Affective expression in children's fantasy play, primary process thinking on the Rorschach, and divergent thinking. *Journal of Personality Assessment, 54,* 756–771.

Russ, S., & Kaugars, A. S. (2000-2001). Emotion in children's play and creative problem solving. *Creativity Research Journal, 13,* 211–219.

Russ, S., Moore, M., & Farber, B. (2004, July). *Effects of play training on play, creativity and emotional well-being.* Poster presented at American Psychological Association, Honolulu.

Russ, S., Robins, D., & Christiano, B. (1999). Pretend play: Longitudinal prediction of creativity and affect in fantasy in children. *Creativity Research Journal, 12,* 129–139.

Russ, S., & Schafer, E. (2006). Affect in fantasy play, emotion in memories, and divergent thinking. *Creativity Research Journal, 18,* 347–354.

Sawyer, P. K. (1997). *Pretend play as improvisation.* Mahwah, NJ: Lawrence Erlbaum.

Singer, D. L., & Rummo, J. (1973). Ideational creativity and behavioral style in kindergarten-age children. *Developmental Psychology, 8,* 154–161.

Singer, D. G., & Singer, J. L. (1990). *The house of make-believe: Children's play and the developing imagination.* Cambridge, MA: Harvard University Press.

Singer, J. L., & Singer, D. G. (1999). *Learning through play* (Videotape). Instructional Media Institute, Connecticut.

Smith, P. (2007). Evolutionary foundations and functions of play: An overview. In A. Goncu & S. Gaskins (Eds.), *Play and development* (pp. 21–49). New York, NY: Taylor & Francis.

Smith, P. K., & Whitney, S. (1987). Play and associative fluency: Experimenter effects may be responsible for positive results. *Developmental Psychology, 23*, 49–53.

Taylor, M. (1999). *Imaginary companions and the children who create them.* New York, NY: Oxford University Press.

Taylor, M., & Carlson, S. M. (1997). The relation between individual differences in fantasy and theory of mind. *Child Development, 68*, 436–455. doi:10.1111/j.1467-8624.1997.tb01950.x

Taylor, M., Carlson, S. M., Maring, B. L., Gerow, L., & Charley, C. M. (2004). The characteristics and correlates of fantasy in school-age children: Imaginary companions, impersonation, and social understanding. *Developmental Psychology, 40*, 1173–1187. doi:10.1037/0012-1649.40.6.1173

Taylor, M., Sachet, A. B., Maring, B. L., & Mannering, A. M. (2013). The assessment of elaborated role-play in young children: Invisible friends, personified objects, and pretend identities. *Social Development, 22*, 75–93. doi:10.1111/sode.12011

Vygotsky, L. S. (1967). *Vaobraszeniye i tvorchestvov deskom voraste* [Imagination and creativity in childhood]. Moscow, Russia: Prosvescheniye. (Original work published in 1930)

Wallace, C., & Russ, S. (2015). Pretend play, divergent thinking, and math achievement in girls: A longitudinal study. *Psychology of Aesthetics, Creativity, and the Arts, 9*, 296–305.

CHAPTER 8

Creative Articulation

Jonathan A. Plucker

Key Take-Aways

- Creativity is becoming an increasingly popular student outcome in education systems around the world, both as an outcome in its own right and as part of broader models of 21st-century skills and learning.
- Our conceptual models of creativity have become more complex, in large part due to the acknowledgement of the role of social contexts and audience factors in judgments of creativity.
- Creative articulation is a concept designed to help explain how creators select potential audiences for their creative work and use communication and persuasion to maximize the value of their creative work in the eyes of those audiences.
- Creative articulation can and should be taught in a variety of educational settings.
- Most strategies for fostering articulation are straightforward and can be worked into many existing programs and units.

Most definitions of creativity include some combination of originality and usefulness (Dow, this volume). For example, Plucker, Beghetto, and Dow (2004) defined creativity as "the interaction among *aptitude, process, and environment* by which an individual or group produces a *perceptible product* that is both *novel and useful* as defined within a *social context*" (p. 90, emphases in original). But creativity scholars have yet to address comprehensively the question about how one's creativity is determined to be novel and useful within a given social context, and if an individual or group can influence the determination of whether the product is creative.

The topic of acceptance and communication of the creative product has received a considerable amount of study in sociology, marketing, management, communication science, and other fields as diffusion of innovation, diffusion of technology, and technology transfer (e.g., Kushner, Gibson, Gulick, Honigmann, & Nonas, 1962; Rogers, 2003), but little of this research and theory appears in the creativity literature. This lack of attention is surprising considering biographical and case study work suggesting that eminent creators engaged in considerable self-promotion and acceptance-gaining behaviors (Gardner, 1993; Robb, 1995). Furthermore, discussions of the educational and classroom implications of the communication and acceptance of creativity are rare and quite dated. Given recent advances in technology-aided communication, especially the use of social networks, the lack of recent conceptual work on the individual's role in gaining acceptance for his or her creative products is surprising and in need of attention.

This paper explores the complex dynamics of processes involved in the acceptance of creative products that an individual can influence; a fuller discussion, including the role of potential audiences and the environment is beyond the scope of this chapter. The process of attempting to gain acceptance for a creative product will be referred to as the *articulation of creative products* in this paper. The common usage of "articulation," the formation of vocal utterances as utilized in verbal communication (McKechnie, 1979), is broadened here to represent the processes through which an individual influences the numerous elements that interact to determine the acceptance or rejection of a creative product. This term is used instead of acceptance-gaining, because the attainment of acceptance involves many elements that are beyond an individual's control—those elements that an individual *can* influence are, therefore, referred to as articulation.

Treatment of Articulation in Classic
and Recent Models of Creativity

Despite advances in models and theories of creativity (Beghetto & Kaufman, this volume), psychological and educational theories that actually incorporate communication or articulation as vital constructs in the creative process are rare. Several theories—both older conceptualizations, such as the Creative Problem Solving (CPS) model (Parnes, 1981; Puccio, Firestien, Coyle, & Masucci, 2006) and Stein's (1974, 1975) three-stage process, and more recent models, such as the Investment Theory (Sternberg & Lubart, 1991, 1992), 4-C model (Kaufman & Beghetto, 2009), and 5A Framework (Glăveanu, 2013)—address aspects of articulation, but not yet in comprehensive ways that can help guide improvements in educational practice.

For example, the final step of the CPS model, *acceptance finding*, involves the implementation of an idea generated in order to solve a particular problem. A related model (Basadur, 1987) breaks the CPS stage of acceptance finding into planning and selling the idea. In a simplified version, these stages are combined with the action stage into "solution implementation." In both the CPS and Basadur models, the process of solution implementation involves a divergent thinking phase, during which numerous possibilities for implementation are created, and a convergent thinking phase, in which the most potentially useful idea is chosen and utilized (Basadur, 1987; Isaksen & Treffinger, 1985). Numerous suggestions are given to aid an individual during the convergent thinking phase, including techniques such as criterion listing, the use of evaluation matrices, and the identification of sources of assistance and resistance.

The role of society in the evaluation and adoption of creative products has been summarized by Csikszentmihalyi (1988) in his systems model of creativity. The interaction of three systems (person, domain, and field) yields a creative product. The *person* takes information from the culture (*domain*) in order to "produce some variation" (Csikszentmihalyi, 1988, p. 330). It is the role of the *field*, which includes those people and institutions that have an influence in a specific domain, to incorporate the most "promising variations" into that domain (Csikszentmihalyi, 1988, p. 330). Each field contains gatekeepers, those persons who exert some degree of control over the factual content of the domain. Csikszentmihalyi's model is similar to the work of Rank (1965), who felt that "only the community, one's contemporaries, or posterity" can declare one to be an "artist" (pp. 67–68). If accepted, the "variation" suggested by the individual's creative process may eventually be added to the information base of the domain. The person-domain-field interaction can then begin again, constantly building upon itself in an ascending spiral.

More recent conceptualizations of creativity, including Kaufman and Beghetto's (2009) 4-C model and Glăveanu's (2013) 5A framework, allow for the existence of creative articulation, but do not address it directly in their theories and models. For example, the well-regarded 4-C model proposes four distinct levels of creativity: mini-c, personally meaningful creative acts; little-c, everyday instances of creativity; Pro-c, creativity leading to and representing professional level expertise; and Big-C, unambiguously creative accomplishments with significant societal impact (Kaufman & Beghetto, 2009). The authors acknowledged that transitions occur between the various types of creativity, and they propose some initial mechanisms for those transitions; they do not, however, address the role of creators in advocating for their work and influencing others' decisions about how the creative value of that work is received. Glăveanu's (2013) 5A framework comes closest to addressing articulation directly, with its emphasis on actors interacting with their social context, and affordances facilitating interactions between actors and audiences. But again, the theory has not developed to the point where mechanisms for these interactions have been posited.

The purpose of the creative articulation model is not to replace these existing conceptualizations, but rather to build upon them, with the goals of providing insight into how these hypothesized processes can better model real-world creativity and be fostered in educational settings.

Components of Articulation

A review of the creativity literature reveals little as to how the acceptance of creative products is and can be influenced. Classic perspectives occasionally mention communication, but not the importance of or mechanisms for explaining individual-environment or individual-potential audience interactions. More recent perspectives have accentuated environmental, societal, and potential audience aspects, but a process through which an individual can affect the acceptance of a creative product is not given. Overall, creativity perspectives lack a potential mechanism through which the acceptance of creative products occurs, and when communication is mentioned, it is invariably presented as simple, direct, and either verbal or written. Variables such as enthusiasm, experience, and audience selection, all of which may influence the acceptance of creative products, are infrequently discussed. Too much responsibility for the acceptance of the product is put in the hands of potential audiences, and perspectives that include the role of the creative product's communicator deemphasize the positive influence that he or she may exert and/or stress the negative implications that may result from his or her involvement in the communication stage (Csikszentmihalyi, 1988; Stein, 1974, 1975; Sternberg & Lubart, 1991). Analysis of a product's attributes are suggested, but the benefits gained from an examination of the personal characteristics of the "acceptance-gainer" are rarely analyzed.

To formulate a list of the characteristics, processes, and abilities that constitute successful articulation, a three-stage process was used: First, historical cases of creative production from a wide range of domains were analyzed in order to find basic patterns and themes. Second, the experiences of contemporary individuals who have made outstanding creative contributions to their respective fields were used to create a hierarchy of processes and personality traits. Third, extensive observations of children showed which processes and characteristics were absent in individuals who have not yet learned to articulate.

The resulting hierarchy has two tiers. The general components that make up the first tier are: (a) communication, which involves putting the product in a form that is easily presented to and understood by the intended audience; (b) audience selection, or deciding which group or groups constitute an audience that is likely to accept the product; (c) selecting or creating the proper mood, or waiting until the atmosphere is "ripe for acceptance" for the creative product; and (d) alliance construction, which can be described as the process of finding advocates who are in a position to aid in the attainment of acceptance, be they peers, mentors, or gatekeepers.

Assuming that communication is strictly verbal or written would be ignoring the numerous ways that people transfer information. The communication component of articulation includes any process that transfers information pertaining to the creative product from the creator to the target audience. These processes attempt to transfer information through at least one of the five senses—for example, scratch and sniff ads in magazines, advertisements on television or social media, food samples at grocery stores, and music played on the Internet or satellite radio to help convince you to buy a certain album or product. In each of these examples, an articulator is utilizing a form of communication in an attempt to gain acceptance for a creative product.

Another aspect of communication of the creative product involves the construction of the message being transmitted to the audience. The study of communication and persuasion provide several suggestions: (a) avoid conflicting elements within a message or conflicting messages within a group of messages (Hovland, 1957), (b) the "content of the message" should include both the actual message and the influence of the product for which you are attempting to gain acceptance and (c) initially communicate items that the audience already favors or probably favors in order to get their attention and pique their interest (McGuire, 1957).

The concept of audience selection is an integral part of communication, persuasion, and business, where the "selection of markets to be served and the approach to be taken to those markets" is a core component of marketing strategy (Backman & Czepiel, 1977). Audience selection is critical for two reasons: First, approaching all potential audiences simultaneously is impossible; and, second, each audience's characteristics are unique. The variability of potential audiences and audience members is well documented with respect to order of presentation (Hovland, 1957; Janis & Feierabend, 1957), persuadability, rate of adoption or "innovativeness" (Rogers, 2003), prior knowledge and message comprehension, and many other traits. "Knowing your audience" may be a cliché, but it is pertinent to the articulation of creative products.

Audience selection can have a tremendous impact upon the articulation process; in marketing, distribution strategy is considered crucial because it involves "long term commitments with other firms and has a long-lasting effect on the firm's future range of alternatives" (Backman & Czepiel, 1977, p. 3). Due to the importance of audience selection, prearticulation studies that determine the needs and characteristics of the audience and the characteristics and resources of the articulator are commonplace in marketing and technological fields. A real-life example of the successful use of audience selection is that of American companies that sell sand to Saudi Arabia and other arid countries. By targeting certain manufacturers who require special grades of fine sand that cannot be found in otherwise sand-filled countries, American sand companies have been able to gain acceptance for their product.

Selecting or creating the proper mood would include the investment theory concept of choosing to develop the "undervalued" idea or product (Sternberg & Lubart, 1992), but would also include the individual's influence in convincing the potential audience that an idea was undervalued, actions of the individual that establish a more favorable or acceptable mood toward the product, and the influence of the environment upon the form of the articulator's message and how it is communicated. Beveridge (1957) felt that "discoveries made when the time is ripe for them are more readily accepted because they fit into and find support in prevailing concepts, or grow out of the present body of knowledge" (p. 146). However, these discoveries "often encounter some resistance before they are generally accepted" (p. 146). A common method of determining the mood of a potential audience is public opinion polling, although the mood can be ascertained in a number of ways.

However, Rogers (2003) believed that the awareness of an innovation may inspire a need, just as it may fill an existing need, and that "change agents" (i.e., articulators) are able to create the perception of a need. Although this topic will be addressed later, both researchers have too narrow of a focus, because the decision to adopt an innovation or accept a product is not based solely on need, but also on perceived risk and cost.

Alliance construction involves the targeting of individuals or groups of individuals who can help gain acceptance for the creative product. An example of alliance construction is a musician who comes up with a new song or style of music, which, because of its unique nature, does not gain the admiration of the rest of the band. By gaining the support of two other members of the band, the musician may eventually convince the entire group that they should accept and play the song or style (see Shenk, 2014).

Of course, individuals may also prove to be barriers to acceptance, so the identification and avoidance of potential roadblocks is also a function of alliance construction. Sigmund Freud was especially active in this regard (Gardner, 1993). He actively sought out individuals who he perceived to be threats to psychoanalysis and attempted to discredit and isolate them from the psychological community in Vienna.

Allies are usually members of the targeted, potential audience. For example, George Dantzig, a mathematician who pioneered the use of the linear programming model, met with the economist T. J. Koopmans in an effort to see if there was an economic application of the model. Koopmans became a very excited and enthusiastic supporter of the model, effectively making the transition from potential audience to ally (Albers, 1990).

Csikszentmihalyi (1988) described the gatekeepers in a field as those people who can exert some degree of control over the factual content of the domain. But diffusion research suggests that the concept of "allies" is more complex: Gatekeepers are individuals who tend to adopt innovation first within a given audience, thereby bringing the creative product into the audience's environment/social network. These gatekeepers are different from opinion leaders, who (in a society that favors change) are the most influential with respect to the acceptance of innovation (Bettinghaus, 1968; Rogers, 2003).

The role of experts can be overemphasized. Rogers (2003) mentioned the phenomenon of "overadoption," in which audiences adopt an innovation when experts recommend against it. With respect to the creative product, there are many examples of the experts being wrong: The early readers of Boccaccio's *Decameron* quickly distributed it to others, heavily promoting a book that academics chose to ignore for more than a generation. Recent research has also questioned the validity of expert evaluations of creativity, although no definitive conclusions have been reached on this point (e.g., Plucker, Holden, & Neustadter, 2008; Plucker, Kaufman, Temple, & Qian, 2009; Runco & Smith, 1992).

The supportive factors that constitute the second tier include personality factors, physical factors, motivation, thinking skills, image, communication skills, and other processes and traits that influence articulation less directly than the general components of the first tier. Many of these skills and factors have been mentioned in the literature, independently of articulation, with respect to creativity (e.g., personality factors by Woodman & Schoenfeldt, 1990; diplomacy by Beveridge, 1957), although most research that involves these characteristics and skills has occurred in the fields of communication and social psychology. The list of supportive factors is not meant to be comprehensive, because the study of compliance-gaining messages is still in the formative stages (Miller, 1987).

Taken separately, the elements of the tiers would seem to hold little importance for attempting to gain acceptance for creative products. But when viewed as a series of building blocks, with those abilities and characteristics of the third tier at the base, their collective effect is more substantial. Each of the supportive factors of the third tier influence the use of each of the general components that constitute the second tier, which then have a direct effect upon the articulation process. Using an analogy, an experienced chess player knows that the person who has the most pieces near the end of the match is not automatically expected to win; rather, the player who takes the remaining pieces and uses them in the most effective manner is most likely to achieve the desired outcome of winning the match. Correspondingly, the most proficient articulator of creative products would not have a complete hierarchy of favorable components, factors, and skills, but would instead be able to structure his or her abilities and attributes in a way that helps to articulate successfully, regardless of his or her deficiencies. Indeed, variability in message design and communication style necessitate flexible articulative strategies and processes (McCann & Higgins, 1984; O'Keefe, 1991).

For example, researchers investigating interpersonal communication found a considerable amount of variability in the general population with respect to sensitivity to nonverbal aspects of communication (Rosenthal, Hall, DiMatteo, Rogers, & Archer, 1979). Therefore, an articulator who finds nonverbal cues to be ineffective with a particular audience may wish to concentrate on other communication techniques and articulative strategies.

Theoretical Implications

A more comprehensive understanding of articulation will benefit a number of areas, including creativity theory and research, educational instruction and evaluation, social and emotional development of creative individuals, research dissemination, and management.

Rather than propose another theory of creativity, of which there are already fine examples, this chapter proposes a model of articulation, the first part of a model of acceptance of creative products. Articulation is compatible with many systems and economic views of creativity, yet it can exist and function independently from the creative process. With respect to Csikszentmihalyi's (1988) systems model, the individual would be responsible for producing variations *and* exerting influence on the field's evaluation process. The ever-spiraling and advancing nature of Csikszentmihalyi's model, as described above, could be modified to include *descending* arrows that represent rejection or suggestions for modification of a creative idea or product by the field. With respect to the articulation of Boccaccio's work, questions are raised about the necessity of gatekeepers for a domain—they may help gain acceptance, but other avenues exist as well. Another modification would be necessary if the articulator was not the person from whom the creative products originated, because Csikszentmihalyi designates some of the ownership of creativity to these articulation surrogates. These people may simply be articulating in a creative manner or redefining the product in order to articulate it more successfully.

Including articulation in systems theories (e.g., Sternberg & Lubart, 1992) allows the individual to "convince society" that his or her creative product was undervalued, effectively allowing the "salesperson" to employ articulative skill as it pertains to gaining acceptance for his or her creative product. This would allow the individual who is attempting articulation to influence the perceived supply and demand (or cost and risk) of an idea or other creative product. Each of these theories can incorporate articulation by the individual through expansion of the individual's role or a modification of the individual-potential audience/society interaction.

Educational Implications

Programs that attempt to increase personal creativity should include some instruction and practice in the articulation of creative products. How often are students required to present their work, receive constructive criticism, and incorporate that feedback into a revision of their work? Perhaps more importantly, how often are students taught how to provide constructive criticism, and how many opportunities are they provided to practice giving it? I would argue that a healthy chunk of the creative process in the real world involves giving and receiving feedback, yet we spend very little time teaching students how to do so successfully.

For example, Gorman and Plucker (2003) described a summer enrichment program for high school students focused on scientific creativity. For part of the experience, students designed and invented working telephones. The project of and by itself was interesting and challenging. But to help the students model real-world creativity more closely, the instructors embedded the work within a scenario in which the students pretended to be inventors in the late 1800s. They were given extensive documentation (e.g., copies of patents, notebooks, plans) from inventors who were pursuing voice communication at that time, such as Bell and Edison, along with ample supplies to build their prototypes. But what took the project to a highly realistic level was that each invention had to be presented to three scientists and inventors serving as a patent hearing panel. Therefore, students had to present their prototypes, show that they worked, and answer questions from both the panel and their peers. Adding the patent examination experience gave students experience with creative articulation that would not have been possible otherwise (see also Gorman, Plucker, & Callahan, 1998; Plucker & Gorman, 1999).

But articulation involves more than communication: Many students are deficient in certain skills (e.g., using tools, moving from two to three dimensions) that keep them from putting their ideas into a concrete, communicable form. Any situation in which students can develop and elaborate on their ideas, especially when coupled with opportunities to share their work persuasively with others, should foster articulation skills. Of course, time is a very limited resource in most educational settings, and allowing students to expand on, share, and revise their work is not feasible for every assignment and activity. But providing students with increased opportunities, even if only once or twice a month, will yield large, cumulative articulation benefits as students move through the education system.

Conclusion

Systems theories' inclusion of the influence of societal factors upon creativity is an improvement from previous work in creativity, diffusion of innovation, and technology transfer, but these theories and models are incomplete in two ways: First, many deal only with the role of societal factors as they influence the creative process, ignoring the societal factors' impact on the acceptance of creative products, and, second, those theories that consider the role of society in the acceptance of creative products fail to mention a mechanism through which individuals can directly influence that acceptance by exerting some control over the environment and potential audiences.

The articulation portion of this model involves the individual's role in gaining acceptance for a creative product in light of societal, audience, communication, and environmental variables. Although further extension and modification of the suggested hierarchy of components is necessary to better understand this process, an attempt has been made to represent more accurately the nature of the individual's role in gaining acceptance for a creative product. Coupled with the other aspects of the model of acceptance and rejection of creative products, a more comprehensive depiction of acceptance-gaining emerges.

Recommended Readings

Glăveanu, V. P. (2013). Rewriting the language of creativity: The Five A's framework. *Review of General Psychology, 17,* 69–81.

Rogers, E. M. (2003). *Diffusion of innovations* (5th ed.). New York, NY: Free Press.

Stein, M. I. (1974). *Stimulating creativity. Vol. 1. Individual procedures.* New York, NY: Academic Press.

Stein, M. I. (1975). *Stimulating creativity. Vol. 2. Group procedures.* New York, NY: Academic Press.

Sternberg, R. J., & Lubart, T. I. (1992). Buy low and sell high: An investment approach to creativity. *Current Directions in Psychological Science, 1,* 1–5.

References

Albers, D. J. (1990). George B. Dantzig. In D. J. Albers, G. L. Alexanderson, & C. Reid (Eds.), *More mathematical people: Contemporary conversations* (pp. 61–79). New York, NY: Harcourt Brace Jovanovich.

Backman, J., & Czepiel, J. (1977). Marketing strategies: Some basic considerations. In J. Backman & J. Czepiel (Eds.), *Changing marketing strategies in a new economy* (pp. 1–23). Indianapolis: Bobbs-Merrill.

Basadur, M. (1987). Needed research in creativity for business and industrial applications. In S. G. Isaksen (Ed.), *Frontiers of creativity research: Beyond the basics* (pp. 390–416). Buffalo, NY: Bearly Limited.

Bettinghaus, E. P. (1968). *Persuasive communication.* New York, NY: Holt, Rinehart and Winston.

Beveridge, W. I. B. (1957). *The art of scientific investigation* (3rd ed.). New York, NY: Vintage Books.

Csikszentmihalyi, M. (1988). Society, culture, and person: A systems view of creativity. In R. J. Sternberg (Ed.), *The nature of creativity* (pp. 325–339). New York, NY: Cambridge University Press.

Gardner, H. (1993). *Creating minds.* New York, NY: Basic Books.

Glăveanu, V. P. (2013). Rewriting the language of creativity: The Five A's framework. *Review of General Psychology, 17,* 69–81.

Gorman, M. E., & Plucker, J. A. (2003). Teaching invention as critical creative processes: A course on technoscientific creativity. In M. A. Runco (Ed.), *Critical creative processes* (pp. 275–302). Cresskill, NJ: Hampton Press.

Gorman, M. E., Plucker, J. A., & Callahan, C. M. (1998, March). Turning students into inventors: Active learning modules for secondary students. *Phi Delta Kappan,* 530–535.

Hovland, C. I. (1957). Summary and implications. In C. I. Hovland (Ed.), *Order of presentation* (pp. 129–157). New Haven, CT: Yale University Press.

Isaksen, S. G., & Treffinger, D. J. (1985). *Creative problem solving: The basic course.* Buffalo, NY: Bearly Ltd.

Janis, I. L., & Feierabend, R. L. (1957). Effects of alternative ways of ordering pro and con arguments in persuasive communications. In C. I. Hovland (Ed.), *Order of presentation* (pp. 115–128). New Haven, CT: Yale University Press.

Kaufman, J. C., & Beghetto, R. A. (2009). Beyond big and little: The Four C model of creativity. *Review of General Psychology, 13,* 1–12.

Kushner, G., Gibson, M., Gulick, J., Honigmann, J. J., & Nonas, R. (1962). *What accounts for sociocultural change? A propositional inventory.* Chapel Hill, NC: Institute for Research in Social Science.

McCann, C. D., & Higgins, E. T. (1984). Individual differences in communication: Social cognitive determinants and consequences. In H. E. Sypher & J. L. Applegate (Eds.), *Communication by children and adults: Social cognitive and strategic processes* (pp. 172–210). Beverly Hills, CA: Sage.

McGuire, W. J. (1957). Order of presentation as a factor in "conditioning" persuasiveness. In C. I. Hovland (Ed.), *Order of presentation* (pp. 98–114). New Haven, CT: Yale University Press.

McKechnie, J. L. (Ed.). (1979). *Webster's new twentieth century dictionary of the English language.* Tulsa, OK: World Publishing Company

Miller, G. R. (1987). Persuasion. In C. R. Berger & S. H. Chaffee (Eds.), *Handbook of communication science* (pp. 446–483). Newbury Park, CA: Sage.

O'Keefe, B. J. (1991). Message design logic and the management of multiple goals. In K. Tracy (Ed.), *Understanding face-to-face interaction: Issues linking goals and discourse* (pp. 131–150). Hillsdale, NJ: Lawrence Erlbaum.

Parnes, S. J. (1981). Guiding creative action. In J. C. Gowan, J. Khatena, & E. P. Torrance (Eds.), *Creativity: Its educational implications* (pp. 125–135). Dubuque, IA: Kendall Hunt.

Plucker, J. A., Beghetto, R. A., & Dow, G. (2004). Why isn't creativity more important to educational psychologists? Potential, pitfalls, and future directions in creativity research. *Educational Psychologist, 39,* 83–96.

Plucker, J. A., & Gorman, M. E. (1999). Invention is in the mind of the adolescent: Evaluation of a summer course one year later. *Creativity Research Journal, 12,* 141–150.

Plucker, J. A., Holden, J., & Neustadter, D. (2008). The criterion problem and creativity in film: Psychometric characteristics of various measures. *Psychology of Aesthetics, Creativity, and the Arts, 2,* 190–196.

Plucker, J. A., Kaufman, J. C., Temple, J. S., & Qian, M. (2009). Do experts and novices evaluate movies the same way? *Psychology & Marketing, 26,* 470–478.

Puccio, G. J., Firestien, R. L., Coyle, C., & Masucci, C. (2006). A review of the effectiveness of CPS training: A focus on workplace issues. *Creativity and Innovation Management, 15,* 19–33.

Rank, O. (1965). Life and creation. In H. M. Ruitenbeek (Ed.), *The creative imagination: Psychoanalysis and the genius of inspiration* (pp. 67–96). Chicago, IL: Quadrangle Books.

Robb, G. (1995). *Balzac.* New York, NY: W. W. Norton.

Rogers, E. M. (2003). *Diffusion of innovations* (5th ed.). New York, NY: Free Press.

Rosenthal, R., Hall, J. A., DiMatteo, M. R., Rogers, P. L., & Archer, D. (1979). *Sensitivity to nonverbal communication: The PONS test.* Baltimore, MD: Johns Hopkins.

Runco, M. A., & Smith, W. R. (1992). Interpersonal and intrapersonal evaluations of creative ideas *Personality and Individual Differences, 13,* 295–302.

Shenk, J. W. (2014). *Powers of two: Finding the essence of innovation in creative pairs.* New York, NY: Houghton Mifflin Harcourt.

Stein, M. I. (1974). *Stimulating creativity. Vol. 1. Individual procedures.* New York, NY: Academic Press.

Stein, M. I. (1975). *Stimulating creativity. Vol. 2. Group procedures.* New York, NY: Academic Press.

Sternberg, R. J., & Lubart, T. I. (1991). An investment theory of creativity and its development. *Human Development, 34,* 1–31.

Sternberg, R. J., & Lubart, T. I. (1992). Buy low and sell high: An investment approach to creativity. *Current Directions in Psychological Science, 1,* 1–5.

Woodman, R. W., & Schoenfeldt, L. F. (1990). An interactionist model of creative behavior. *Journal of Creative Behavior, 24,* 10–20.

CHAPTER 9

Why Do We Create?

The Roles of Motivation, Mindset, and Passion in Human Creativity

Magdalena G. Grohman and Heather T. Snyder

Key Take-Aways

- Being creative requires long periods of tedious hard work.
- Research suggests that why we create is important for our outcomes.
- Creativity is more likely when people have intrinsic motivation, a growth mindset, and passion for the task.
- Findings from research can be applied so people can be more creative.

Why do we embark on the creative process? It requires hours, if not years, of preparation, it is demanding and often tedious. It takes our precious time away—time that could be spent with loved ones or on doing other more immediately satisfying activities, like watching our favorite television shows. The creative process leads to frustration, too: Even when we think we are moving forward with our best ideas, these ideas may not be perceived the same way by others—and they let us know it! There must be something that makes us want to be creative, that allows us to believe that we can be creative and that drives us toward being creative. In this chapter, we will discuss the roles of motivation, mindset, and passion in creativity.

Motivation

J. K. Rowling said that the character of Harry Potter came to her while she was stuck on a train, without any pens or pencils to take notes. The idea was "like meeting a new person and hitting it off right away; you knew you were going to like this person and wanted to know more about him" (Kirk, 2003, p. 66). She explored in her mind who the boy was and what happened to him, then she wrote notes when she got home hours later. Obviously, there was much work needed to go from having an idea for a character to writing a publishable book (then more work to find a publisher, and much more work to write and publish a series of six additional books). When Rowling created Harry Potter, she did not do it because she wanted to become a billionaire and create a merchandise empire (Jones, 2003). Indeed, she thought a few people would be interested in her story. She loved to write and wanted to write stories since she was a child. She wrote and illustrated her first book called "Rabbit and His Adventures" at age 6 (Vieira, 2007)!

What Is Motivation and How Does It Work?

We know that being creative requires hard work. Just because we *can* be creative at a task, does not mean we *will* be creative. Amabile (1996) argued that it is our motivation that determines whether we will be creative at any specific task. Our motivation is what causes us to act and is why we do what we do (Ryan & Deci, 2000). So why do we embark upon a creative task—whether to write a term paper or a song or create a new app?

The last 50 years of research provides evidence that motivation is multifaceted, contextual, and dynamic (Kaufman, 2013). This means that we can be motivated in multiple ways, depending on what we do or what we learn, and where the "doing" and "learning" takes place—at school, at home, while doing homework, or while engaging in a hobby. This also means that motivation is constantly changing. For example, even if we enjoyed writing a paper for a class last weekend, we may not be very motivated to write a different paper that is due tomorrow, even if it is on the same topic!

How does it work? Researchers in neuroscience discovered that dopamine—the chemical substance flowing through our brain—is largely responsible for motivated behavior. When dopamine flows through parts of our brains, it triggers emotions such as desire, excitement, and hope. It affects our behavior, thinking, and perception in such a way that we engage with things we want to do or have, for better or for worse. Dopamine triggers goal-oriented behavior (Broomberg-Martin, Matsumoto, & Hikosaka, 2010; Previc, 2011). Therefore, when you decide that you want to achieve the highest level in a videogame, dopamine likely plays a role in this desire, which keeps you working hard to achieve this goal!

The neuroscience evidence suggests that there are biological mechanisms for motivation. In order to understand motivation, we need to go beyond the dichotomy of whether we are motivated to complete a task or not. This is especially true regarding understanding the motivation to be creative. Two factors appear to influence whether we will be creative: whether our motivation comes from within us or outside of us and what type of goals we have.

Motivation From Within and Motivation From Outside: Intrinsic and Extrinsic Motivation

It is said that Michelangelo did not want to paint the Sistine Chapel. He considered himself a sculptor. He was asked to stop working on a sculpture project, for which he was passionate, in order to work on the Sistine Chapel. He did it after some convincing by the Pope (Michelangelo initially refused, but his rivals convinced the Pope he should do it because they expected Michelangelo to fail, so the Pope persisted). Michelangelo worked on the Sistine Chapel because he was commissioned to do it, for "fame," and to show his rivals that he could do it (Vasari, 1912/1915). Michelangelo's portrayal of Adam was novel and inventive for the time (Sperling, 2003). So can anyone be creative even if it is for a paycheck, fame, or to protect their reputation, and not because of interest?

One of the most influential social psychologists who studied creativity, Teresa Amabile (1996), proposed that our motivation to engage in creative activity comes from two different sources. The first source comes from within us. We engage in the creative process because it is a rewarding experience; we enjoy it and want more of it. This type of motivation is called *intrinsic* motivation. The second source of motivation comes from outside; it is an external—

or *extrinsic*—factor that is often related to how well we do, and what we get in return for doing something. It can be a grade, praise, or money. Amabile's (1996) theory suggests that intrinsic task motivation is what is essential for creativity.

Ryan and Deci (2000) discussed two factors that are necessary for us to experience intrinsic motivation. These factors are autonomy and competence. Autonomy refers to how much control we feel we have over an activity. We are more likely to experience intrinsic motivation toward a task or activity if we have freedom to do it because we want to and in the way we want to do it. However, if we feel we do not have control and therefore must complete a task because someone else requires us to do so, or feel like we are being micromanaged, we are less likely to be intrinsically motivated. For example, we, the authors, teach a Psychology of Creativity course to undergraduate students at our respective universities. We enjoy teaching! Our supervisors support our teaching of this course (including our lectures and assignments) in ways we think best meet our course objectives, which promotes our autonomy. If our supervisors were to tell us what to do and how to do it, we are sure we would enjoy it much less! The next factor—competence—has to do with our desire to feel capable of accomplishment and mastery of the task. If a task or activity is too easy, we will likely feel no intrinsic motivation to engage in it and we may feel bored; similarly, if a task is way too difficult, we may feel anxious (Csikszentmihalyi, 1990). But if an activity has the optimal level of difficulty, we will perceive it as a thrilling challenge, which will motivate us to stay on that task. We, the authors, also feel this about our teaching. Developing course content that engages our students and promotes learning is a thrilling challenge to which we apply our decades of teaching experience and training. Csikszentmihalyi (1990) noted that when the skills and challenge meet, we are more likely to experience flow, which he defined as a "state in which people are so involved in an activity that nothing else seems to matter" (p. 4). When experiencing flow, we are likely to lose track of time, concentrate intensely, not realize that there are people around, and feel intense enjoyment of what we are doing. We have certainly spent hours preparing lectures only to discover that time passed without notice and we forgot to eat!

Amabile's research suggested that it is intrinsic motivation that leads to increased creativity. For example, Amabile (1996) and her colleagues conducted a series of studies that found that when participants expected that their work would be evaluated, creativity scores were lower. Other studies showed that those reporting enjoyment or other intrinsic motivation for a task received higher creativity scores (e.g., Amabile, Hill, Hennessey, & Tighe, 1994). Although Amabile's original theory was that intrinsic motivation increases and extrinsic motivation decreases creativity, current research and her current theory suggest that it is more complex because extrinsic motivation can actually contribute to creative work (Amabile, 1996). For example, in a meta-analysis of research on creativity and motivation, Byron and Khazanchi (2012) found that when rewards were directly connected to creative performance, creativity increased as compared to the situation in which rewards were not connected to creative performance or were connected to other performance, like finishing quickly. This was especially true when participants had more choice (such as a choice of rewards or tasks to complete) and when participants were provided with useful feedback regarding their creative performance. This suggests that factors that promote intrinsic motivation may also make extrinsic motivation more conducive to creativity. Although we, the authors, get paid for our work as teachers, we do consider ourselves creative teachers. For example, Dr. Snyder developed creative assignments for the Psychology of Creativity course (see Snyder, 2013) that students typically enjoy and find not only creative, but that also contribute to their own creativity (as they write in course evaluations). Dr. Grohman creatively adapted her Creative Problem Solving workshop for the Psychology of Creativity course. This adapted workshop allows students to practice their creativity skills while working on the course's creative project.

The type of motivation we have helps to determine our goals (Amabile, 1996). Intrinsic motivation is associated with the *process* of making or doing something. It turns out that if we like the process, we no longer pay too much attention to the outcome of that process. It means, that if we are motivated to teach, because we enjoy the process of teaching, students' evaluations at the end of the semester will not be our primary goal. Rather, our goal will be to help students learn psychology, so we will work hard to develop our teaching skills to better help our students learn. Such goals centered on learning and mastering a skill are called *learning goals*; they are typically associated with intrinsic motivation.

Contrary to intrinsic motivation, extrinsic motivation is tied to "the pay" we get for what we do. It entails pursuit of *performance goals*. If our motivation to teach comes from external factors, such as students' evaluations, our goal will not necessarily be to master our teaching, but to please students, and avoid any situations that may affect their perceptions of us as teachers. And we all know what that can look like! Easy lectures, homework that is not challenging enough, routine teaching practices, no venturing out of the safety zone, etc. And although students, at least some, may be pleased with such teaching, chances are that neither they nor we would grow and develop.

Performance Goals and Mastery Goals

Carol Dweck—one of the most renowned researchers in psychology—wondered how different types of goals motivate us, and how they affect our achievements (Dweck & Elliot, 1983; Dweck & Leggett, 1988; Smiley & Dweck, 1994). In one study (Dweck & Elliot, 1983), fifth graders were divided into two groups. Both groups had easy and difficult tasks to solve. Fifth graders in one group were told that their performance on these tasks would be later evaluated, and the other group was told that they would learn something valuable while solving the problems. When the fifth graders were solving easy tasks, she didn't see any differences. Can you guess what happened when the groups were solving difficult tasks? Well, it turned out that those students who focused on performance goals ("I have to do it in a perfect way") solved the least number of tasks, growing more and more helpless with each task. Those, however, who focused on learning goals ("I am learning more with each task I've attempted to solve, whether I fail or not"), in the end had much higher performance. In a similar study, Cain and Dweck (1995) investigated the connection between elementary students' beliefs about their academic success and their motivation to persevere in the face of failure. Specifically, the researchers were interested in how children explained their academic success, and whether they—like in our previous example—attributed success to the process of learning or to the outcome (performance). Cain and Dweck were also interested in how the students approached solving challenging, unsolvable puzzles. Based on the approach demonstrated by the children (for instance, "I want to solve just easy puzzles; I'm not good at it" or "I will try the difficult puzzle again"), the researchers divided 139 first, third, and fifth graders into two groups: those displaying helplessness and those displaying mastery orientation. One of the findings of this study was that those students who showed mastery orientation were less likely to quit solving puzzles, and they were less likely to predict their failure in solving difficult puzzles in the future. Another important finding, which will become more clear in the next section of our chapter, was that students, especially fifth graders, who felt helpless and focused on performance goals saw their abilities as fixed, while the students who showed mastery orientation understood their abilities as malleable—that is, changeable (Cain & Dweck, 1995).

When our goal is a perfect performance, intrinsic motivation does not play such a great role. What "kicks in" is our extrinsic motivation. We will continue striving toward our performance goal only if positive outcomes are expected, but when we don't expect that positive reward, we tend to drop the activity/learning altogether, especially when faced with failure. We suspect that this is what's going on with many of our students who get not-so-good grades during the first test, make a quick calculation of their GPA, and decide to drop the class. Those who stay give themselves chances to improve, just like the students in Cain and Dweck's (1995) study who kept working on challenging puzzles despite the initial failure to solve them.

Our Mindsets: Rising From Failure

In our Psychology of Creativity courses, we require our students to complete a creative project. Students have a choice of different types of projects, including completing a children's book, comic, poem, or creative essay. Some students immediately tell us that they cannot complete the project, because they are not creative and some students drop the class. Other students say that while they are not good at drawing, they will try to complete the illustrated task anyway (but it will not be good). Still others share with us that although their drawing skills are not up to par, they will search for a way to complete the illustrations that do not rely on their drawing skills. All of these students approach the creative project with different mindsets. It turns out that students' mindsets influence how creative they can be.

Different Types of Mindset and Their Modus Operandi

Carol Dweck and her colleagues show in their research that the beliefs about our abilities (they are innate and fixed or we can develop them) create different patterns of response to the challenges and failures we experience in our everyday lives (Blackwell, Trzesniewski, & Dweck, 2007; Dweck, 1999; Henderson & Dweck, 1990). They dictate if we will continue striving toward our goal or if we will quit.

Fixed Mindset and How It Creates Setbacks

Researchers found that we look at the nature of our abilities, motivations, and personality traits from two different perspectives: our abilities as fixed or stable entities or our abilities as malleable characteristics (Blackwell et al., 2007; Karwowski, 2014). If we believe that our abilities are fixed and think "Only Big-C creators can be creative," "I don't have what they have," or "I am not as intelligent or creative," then we are less likely to change anything about those abilities. Blackwell and her collaborators (2007) showed that we are more likely to be motivated by our expectations about our performance, and when we fail we are more likely to attribute the failure to lack of ability. In other words, having such a belief may often prevent us from even trying new things! This is how it works. For example, imagine a student who is taking one of our creativity courses and needs to do a creative project. Her initial responses could be "But I cannot draw!" or "I need an A in this!" or "I don't have a talent to do it!" If such thinking is initiated, then she may try to do something she has done before that she knows she can do, such as write a poem that does not require illustrations. She deeply believes that trying and learning to draw will not change the fact that she doesn't have the talent, so why even bother? At the first curveball, she is likely to quit or she will avoid engaging in the activity altogether.

Growth Mindset and How It Helps to Rise From Failure

In another study conducted by Blackwell (Blackwell et al., 2007), junior high students who believed that abilities can be changed and developed (growth mindset), also believed that putting effort into changing those abilities makes sense; they were less likely to show any signs of helplessness and did not give up in the face of challenge or failure. Those beliefs were then translated into using effective learning strategies, which in turn led to higher achievements in math. And it makes perfect sense! If we believe that our ability can change and grow, then we are more likely to use strategies and put more effort into things. On the other hand, when we believe that our abilities are fixed, we may not use any productive strategies, because no matter what we do, our intelligence or creativity, or math scores, or drawings or whatever, can never change. We are not even considering giving ourselves a chance. Therefore, if faced with the creative project with a growth mindset, the student may decide to try the children's book and do something different from what she has done before. She may search for YouTube videos for how to draw a character, or search for ways to do the illustrations that do not require drawing.

Research suggests that we differ in our mindsets regarding creativity and that these mindsets may influence whether we are indeed creative (e.g., Karwowski, 2014; O'Connor, Nemeth, & Akutsu, 2013). There is still limited research applying the mindset literature to creativity, but the evidence so far suggests that the growth mindset is more related to creative achievement, creative problem solving, whether we think we can be creative, and whether we think of ourselves as being creative people.

Passion

J. K. Rowling had said that although she had creative story ideas before, there was something special about Harry: "I had this, 'God, I'd love to write that!'" moment (Vieira, 2007, para. 31). She reported that she "went home and started writing" (Vieira, 2007, para. 31). It took her 5 years, living through her mother's death, multiple moves, a marriage, giving birth to her daughter, divorce, raising her daughter as a single mother, finding jobs where she could, and time on welfare, to write her story. She persisted. Not only was Rowling passionate about writing her story, she was even described as "passionately" protective of Harry (Jones, 2003).

You have probably heard the term *passion* fairly often lately. CEOs call for more passion in their employers, teachers want passionate students, and life coaches urge us to find passion in our lives. So, what is a passion? Robert Vallerand (Vallerand et al., 2003) described passion as a "strong inclination towards an activity that a person likes, finds important, and invests time and energy" (p. 756). Julia Moeller (2013) wrote that passion used to be understood as intense affect (feeling) and desire to do something, and it was attributed to intense negative feelings, like suffering and loss of control. Recently, however, scholars have reconceptualized passion as being a positive and desirable virtue (Moeller, 2013; Vallerand et al., 2003; see also Moeller, Keiner, & Grassinger, 2015), understood as something more than just an intense negative or positive feeling toward an activity. Passion produces flow, feelings of pleasure, and sometimes it is seen as romance with a topic or discipline (Renzulli, Koehler, & Fogarty, 2006), which includes elements such as intense emotions coupled with future and long-term commitment.

Different Elements of Passion

According to Moeller (2013) and her colleagues (Moeller et al., 2015), passion includes elements of commitment, intense approach motivation, persistence, and identity. She argued that passion is linked to the type of practice we engage in when we want to know our area of interest inside out or when we want to master a skill. It turns out that just having intrinsic motivation and the right mindset may not be enough for the deliberate practice over a long period of time needed to master the skill. This very strong inclination—stronger than mere joy from the activity—will help us to stay on track. Moeller called this strong inclination a commitment, and proposed that passion is seen as co-occurrence of high commitment and intense approach motivation. When we commit to engage in an activity or hobby, we are likely to set long-term goals and we also are likely to have the intention to persist in realizing those goals. The role of intense approach motivation is that it makes us desire and want to engage in the activity or hobby. So, these ingredients are needed for the passion to develop (Moeller, 2013; Moeller et al., 2015). And as Robert Vallerand and his colleagues (2003) noted, often the activity we commit to and have desire to engage in satisfies our need for autonomy and competence (as we discussed earlier). If we find ourselves interested in such an activity over and over again, such that it becomes a part of us, the interest may change into passion. We no longer say, "I like writing;" we are more likely to say, "I am a writer" (Vallerand et al., 2003; see also Fredricks, Alfeld, & Eccles, 2010). We, the authors, are passionate about teaching! We love what we do, have committed long years of study to our discipline, and willingly work hard on our teaching. When people ask what we do, we answer, "we are teachers."

Of course, passion is not just a flame that burns quickly. To be passionate about something means to commit, with all of our might, intrinsic motivation, and mindset, to our goal; it means that we intend to engage in our pursuit, we prioritize our other goals such that they help us stay engaged, we feel an intense urge or desire to meet our goal, and we identify with our activity (Moeller, 2013; Moeller et al., 2015). In short, we are passionate if we love what we do, we are committed to doing it, we set goals that help us stay engaged, we have a strong motivation and desire to continue, and we identify with it.

Different Types of Passion

Vallerand and his colleagues (2003; see also St-Louis & Vallerand, 2015) focused on different types of passion: harmonious passion and obsessive passion. They proposed the distinction based on different concepts of passion in psychological literature (passion as intense positive or intense negative motivational state), and then planned and carried out a study to see if this theoretical distinction makes sense in the real world. They asked 539 college students to think about an activity that was "dear to their heart." The students reported various activities like physical activities (swimming or jogging), passive leisure (listening to music, watching movies), music (playing instruments), reading, the arts, work/education, and even interpersonal relationships. And they were quite committed to them because they spent an average of 8.5 hours per week on the activity for at least 6 years! To the majority of students, the activity they reported was indeed their passion, highly valued and a part of their identity. The results of the study confirmed the theoretical distinction between the two types of passion.

How can we distinguish the two types of passion? Take for example, jogging. A person with a passion for jogging may identify herself as a jogger. If this is a harmonious passion, she does not lose her autonomy (choice to engage in jogging) because of that activity. In other words, she may be passionate about jogging, but she knows that she shouldn't do that when the conditions on the road or trail are questionable or her significant other wants her to come to an important family event. She can stop at will. This allows for harmonious coexistence of the passion and other important aspects of her life. This also applies to creativity. For example, a scientist may be passionate about her research and may identify herself as a scientist. She commits long hours in her lab, but can stop at will to go home to her family at night for dinner. Moreover, Vallerand and his collaborators discovered that harmonious passion correlated most with positive emotions and lack of negative emotions after the engagement; there were no negative feelings when prevented from engagement with passion (St-Louis & Vallerand, 2015). If the jogger were to be obsessively passionate about an activity, the activity would start to control her behavior and choices, and in general—well-being. In other words, she may feel compelled to jog even if the visibility is poor and trail surface uneven, but she cannot help it. She may even cancel plans with her significant other, jeopardizing their relationship. There are stories of creative people showing obsessive passion. For example, Steve Jobs was said to push himself and his staff to work exceptionally hard and long hours, and pushed for perfection in their products. He even required his iPhone design team staff to work nights and weekends to start over after 9 months of hard work on the iPhone because after a sleepless night, he realized that he didn't "love it" (e.g., Isaacson, 2012). Not all of his staff and family appreciated his passion at all times.

Moeller, in her most recent research (Moeller et al., 2015), discovered that people who are very much passionate about an activity can be at times harmoniously and at times obsessively passionate about it. She said, "the general degree of passion, rather than the distinction between harmonious and obsessive individuals, accounted for the inter-individual differences in passion" (Moeller et al., 2015, p. 131). Therefore, finding the activity for which you are passionate, and recognizing when you exhibit harmonious and obsessive passion, will lead to better outcomes, such as creativity (and a healthy body and relationships).

Educational Implications

In the previous paragraphs, we discussed factors that research shows impact creativity: motivation, mindset, and passion. There are educational implications of this research for teachers and for students. In other words, what can be done to balance students' intrinsic and extrinsic motivation, promote their growth mindsets, and balance harmonious and obsessive passions in order to develop and enhance their creativity? Although there is an entire literature devoted to enhancing creativity (for example, see Scott, Leritz, & Mumford, 2004, and Sawyer, 2013), there are several suggestions that emerge from the literature summarized earlier in this chapter.

First, let's consider the motivation research. Intrinsic motivation is increased with autonomy. Therefore, creativity may be more likely when students have choices and can include their own interests and preferences in assignments. Students can select topics that relate to their hobbies or career goals. We offer our students choices in two ways for the creative project assignment: (1) They can choose to write a poem or song lyrics, write a children's book or comic strip, or they can try a creative essay, and (2) they can select any influential artist, scientist, or inventor to include in the course project (many students select someone who made a major contribution to their major domain of study).

A second suggestion is based on the research on learning goals and growth mindset. This research suggests that teachers could show students examples of term projects, break them down into manageable parts, and provide feedback after each part. Our students complete multiple preparation tasks with feedback, before working on the final project. By doing so, we help our students to feel more competent at each step, and increase the likelihood that they feel that the challenge matches their skills, which makes them considerably less overwhelmed (or bored). The feedback also helps students to recognize that the task is not restricted by current ability. Students could develop their skills and try new approaches for the project. For example, we remind our students that there are multiple ways to illustrate children's books, and these do not have to be drawings. Students should note whether they are thinking about a course/skill with a fixed or growth mindset, and if fixed, try to change their mindset by changing their thinking and study approach to the topic.

Finally, the passion research also offers suggestions to teachers and students. Teachers should show their passion! Many of our students write in our evaluations that they become more interested in learning and practicing creativity when we share our passion. College is an exceptional opportunity to explore and pursue passions. Students should take the time to explore their interests and identify their passions by taking different courses, even courses outside their majors and in subjects that they have no previous experience learning about. Students should also take time to recognize their priorities; for example, although it is important to pursue passions, it is also important to take care of health and relationships.

Conclusion

Let's summarize what we know from research regarding the role of motivation, mindset, and passion. Intrinsic motivation is important for creativity, and it requires feeling autonomous and competent. Extrinsic factors can be helpful when they provide feedback regarding performance and actually reward creative work. Taking a growth mindset, wherein we seek to learn and develop our creativity skills, is important toward taking risks in creativity and being more creative. And finally, finding our passion, committing to it, and recognizing when we are showing harmonious and obsessive passion can help us to be willing to spend the hours/years of hard work to be creative in healthy ways.

Recommended Readings

Amabile, T. M. (1996). *Creativity in context.* Boulder, CO: Westview Press.

Csikszentmihalyi, M. (1990). *Flow: The psychology of optimal experience.* New York, NY: Harper Perennial.

Dweck, C. (2006). *Mindset: The new psychology of success.* New York, NY: Ballantine Books.

Kaufman, S. B. (2013). *Ungifted: Intelligence redefined.* New York, NY: Basic Books.

Sawyer, K. (2013). *Zig zag: The surprising path to greater creativity.* San Francisco, CA: Jossey-Bass.

Vallerand, R. J. (2007). On the psychology of passion: In search of what makes people's lives most worth living. *Canadian Psychology, 49*(1), 1–13.

References

Amabile, T. M. (1996). *Creativity in context.* Boulder, CO: Westview Press.

Amabile, T. M., Hill, K. G., Hennessey, B. A., & Tighe, E. M. (1994). The Work Preference Inventory: Assessing intrinsic and extrinsic motivational orientations. *Journal of Personality and Social Psychology, 66,* 950–967.

Blackwell, L. S., Trzesniewski, K. H., & Dweck, C. S. (2007). Implicit theories of intelligence predict achievement across an adolescent transition: A longitudinal study and an intervention. *Child Development, 78,* 246–263.

Broomberg-Martin, E. S., Matsumoto, M. & Hikosaka, O. (2010). Dopamine in motivational control: Rewarding, aversive, and alerting. *Neuron, 68,* 815–834.

Byron, K., & Khazanchi, S. (2012). Rewards and creative performance: A meta-analytic test of theoretically derived hypotheses. *Psychological Bulletin, 138,* 809–830.

Cain, K. M., & Dweck, C. S. (1995). The relation between motivational patterns and achievement cognitions through the elementary school years. *Merrill-Palmer Quarterly, 41,* 25–52.

Csikszentmihalyi, M. (1990). *Flow: The psychology of optimal experience.* New York, NY: Harper Perennial.

Dweck, C. S. (1999). *Self-theories: Their role in motivation, personality, and development.* Philadelphia, PA: Psychology Press.

Dweck, C. S., & Elliot, E. S. (1983). Achievement motivation. In P. Mussen & E. M. Hetherington (Eds.), *Handbook of child psychology* (pp. 634–692). New York, NY: Wiley.

Dweck, C. S., & Leggett, E. L. (1988). A social-cognitive approach to motivation and personality. *Psychological Review, 95,* 256–273.

Fredricks, J. A., Alfeld, C., & Eccles, J. S. (2010). Developing and fostering passions in academic and nonacademic domains. *Gifted Child Quarterly, 54,* 18–30. doi:10.1177/0016986209352683

Henderson, V. L., & Dweck, C. S. (1990). Achievement and motivation in adolescence: A new model and data. In S. Feldman & G. Elliott (Eds.), *At the threshold: The developing adolescent* (pp. 308–329). Cambridge, MA: Harvard University Press.

Isaacson, W. (2012, April). The real leadership lessons of Steve Jobs. *Harvard Business Review.* Retrieved from https://hbr.org/2012/04/the-real-leadership-lessons-of-steve-jobs

Jones, M. (2003). Her magic moment: J. K. Rowling has a new husband, a new baby—and a great new 'Harry Potter.' A rare, candid interview in Edinburgh. *Newsweek.* Retrieved from https://www.highbeam.com/doc/1G1-104573209.html

Karwowski, M. (2014). Creative mindsets: Measurement, correlates, consequences. *Psychology of Aesthetics, Creativity and the Arts, 8,* 62–70.

Kaufman, S. B. (2013). *Ungifted: Intelligence redefined.* New York, NY: Basic Books.

Kirk, C. A. (2003). *J. K. Rowling: A biography.* Westport, CT: Greenwood Press.

Moeller, J. (2013). *Passion as concept of the psychology of motivation. Conceptualization, assessment, inter-individual variability and long-term stability* (Doctoral dissertation, University of Erfurt, Germany). Retrieved from http://www.db-thueringen.de/servlets/DerivateServlet/Derivate-29036/DissJuliaMoeller.pdf

Moeller, J., Keiner, M., & Grassinger, R. (2015). Two sides of the same coin: Do the dual "types" of passion describe distinct subgroups of individuals? *Journal for Person-Oriented Research, 1,* 131–150.

O'Connor, A. J., Nemeth, C. J., & Akutsu, S. (2013). Consequences of beliefs about the malleability of creativity. *Creativity Research Journal, 25,* 155–162.

Previc, F. H. (2011). *The dopaminergic mind in human evolution history.* New York, NY: Cambridge University Press.

Renzulli, J. S., Koehler, J. L., & Fogarty, E. A. (2006). Operation Houndstooth intervention theory: Social capital in today's schools. *Gifted Child Today, 29,* 14–24.

Ryan, R. M., & Deci, E. L. (2000). Self-determination theory and the facilitation of intrinsic motivation, social development, and well-being. *American Psychologist, 55*(1), 68–78.

Sawyer, R. K. (2013). *Zig zag: The surprising path to greater creativity.* San Francisco, CA: Jossey-Bass.

Scott, G., Leritz, L. E., & Mumford, M. D. (2004). The effectiveness of creativity training: A quantitative review. *Creativity Research Journal, 16,* 361–388.

Smiley, P. A., & Dweck, C. S. (1994). Individual differences in achievement goals among young children. *Child Development, 65,* 1723–1743.

Snyder, H. T. (2013). Designing creative assignments: Example of journal assignments and a creative project. In M. B. Gregerson, H. T. Snyder, & J. C. Kaufman (Eds.), *Teaching creatively and teaching creativity* (pp. 163–173). New York, NY: Springer Science + Business Media.

Sperling, J. (2003). *Famous works of art in popular culture: A reference guide.* Westport, CT: Greenwood Press.

St-Louis, A. C., & Vallerand, R. J. (2015). A successful creative process: The role of passion and emotions. *Creativity Research Journal, 27,* 175–187. doi:10.1080/10400419.2015.1030314

Vallerand, R. J., Mageau, G. A., Ratelle, C., Leonard, M., Blanchard, C., Koestner, R., . . . Marsolais, J. (2003). Les passions de l'âme: On obsessive and harmonious passion. *Journal of Personality and Social Psychology, 85,* 756–767.

Vasari, G. (1912/1915). *Lives of the artists* (G. C. Devere, Trans.). Retrieved from http://members.efn.org/~acd/vite/VasariLives.html

Vieira, M. (2007). *Harry Potter: The final chapter.* Retrieved from http://www.nbcnews.com/id/20001720/ns/dateline_nbc-harry_potter/t/harry-potter-final-chapter

CHAPTER 10

The Creative Personality

Current Understandings and Debates

Gregory J. Feist

Key Take-Aways

- There are certain neurological and neurochemical conditions that make particular personality traits more likely.
- These personality traits cluster into cognitive, social, motivational-affective, and clinical groups.
- Being high in certain personality dispositions (e.g., being open to experience, driven, norm-doubting, and autonomous, and having unusual and even bizarre associations) function to make creative thought and behavior more likely.

For psychologists who study it, personality is an important influence on our behavior. Traits make certain behaviors more likely and others less likely. But what about creative thought and achievement? Do particular personality traits make creative behavior more likely? That is the fundamental question I will address in this chapter. After reviewing the current literature and proposing a model on the topic, I will end the chapter with some thought questions that these findings bring up.

Personality Defined

Before delving into the connection between personality and creativity, however, let me first briefly define what I mean by each term. How do psychologists define *personality*? When psychologists use the term, they are referring to the unique and relatively enduring set of behaviors, feelings, thoughts, and motives that characterize an individual. There are two key components to this definition. First, personality is what distinguishes us from one another and makes us unique. Second, personality is relatively enduring, or consistent. In sum, personality represents the relatively enduring unique ways that individuals think, act, and feel. As it turns out, recent research has begun to demonstrate that unique and consistent different styles of behaving (i.e., personalities) are found within many different species of animal, from octopus and mice to birds and horses. Personality is not just a trait of humans, but of most mammals and some birds, reptiles, and fish (Gosling & John, 1999).

The most common model of personality currently used is the so-called "Big Five" model. It argues that human personality consists of five major dimensions or traits that exist on a continuum from really low to really high: openness to experience, conscientiousness, extraversion, agreeableness, and neuroticism (O-C-E-A-N; John & Srivastava, 1999; McCrae & Costa, 1999). Briefly, *openness* is the tendency to use your imagination and to seek out novel situations, experiences, and ideas, and *conscientiousness* is the disposition to be organized, orderly, punctual, and detail oriented. *Extraversion* is the tendency to seek out social situations, thrilling experiences, and to be generally happy. *Agreeableness* is the disposition to be warm, friendly, and trusting, whereas *neuroticism* is the tendency to experience negative emotions, such as anxiety, fear, sadness, and depression. Each of these personality dimensions exists on a continuum from low to high and so they each have an opposite pole (such as closed, disorganized, introverted, hostile, and calm and stable).

Creativity Defined

Many people assume, especially artists, that creativity is inherently unknowable, mysterious, and immeasurable. Hence, the argument continues, researchers can't agree even on what creativity means. It may be true that creativity is difficult to measure and to quantify, but it's not impossible and it is false to say no consensual definition has emerged on how to define it. In fact, creativity researchers have for the last 60 years been nearly unanimous in their definition of the concept: Creative thought or behavior must be both novel/original and meaningful. It is easy to see why originality per se is not sufficient—there would be no way to distinguish eccentric or schizophrenic from creative thought. Both are original. But to be classified as creative, thought or behavior must also have meaning to other people. Being weird or different just to be weird or different is not creative (see Dow, this volume, for additional discussion of these points).

Functional Model of Personality and Creativity

Since the 1950s and 1960s, creativity researchers have examined empirically the association between creative thought and behavior and personality traits (Barron, 1955, 1963; MacKinnon, 1962). By the 1990s, enough literature on the topic had accumulated for the first meta-analysis to be conducted (Feist, 1998). The current chapter is an expanded and updated review of the literature on personality and creativity.

As I first proposed in the late 1990s, personality facilitates creativity by lowering behavioral thresholds (Feist, 1998, 1999b, 2010). In this model, genetic differences influence brain structures and temperamental differences, which lead to personality variability (social, cognitive, and motivational-affective, and now clinical traits), which finally affect creative thought and behavior. The idea was and still is that a particular constellation of personality traits function to lower the thresholds of creative behavior, making it more rather than less likely. The part of the model that has been most intensively investigated over the last decade since the model was first proposed is biological foundations component, especially genetic and neuroscientific. However, one component of the model is completely new, reflecting even greater growth in research, namely the clinical personality traits of psychoticism, schizotypal personality, latent inhibition, and negative priming. Hence, this review will give more weight to these components than the others.

My functional model builds ties between biology and personality and argues for the causal primacy of biological factors in personality in general and the creative personality in particular (Feist, 2010). To be clear, the updated model of the creative personality includes six main latent variables, in order of causal priority (see Figure 10.1):

- genetic and epigenetic influences on personality,
- brain qualities,
- cognitive personality traits,
- social personality traits,
- motivational-affective personality traits, and
- clinical personality traits.

By combining the biological and the function of traits arguments, in Figure 10.1, I propose a model for the paths from specific biological processes and mechanisms to psychological dispositions to creative thought and behavior. The basic idea is that causal influence flows generally from left to right, with genetic and epigenetic influences having a causal effect on brain influences. Brain-based influences in turn causally influence the four categories of personality influence: cognitive, social, motivational, and clinical. These traits individually and collectively lower thresholds for creative thought and behavior, making each more likely in those individuals who possess that cluster of traits. For example, the trait of being open to new and varied experiences, ideas, and values seems to make having novel and meaningful ideas more likely.

It is important to point out, however, that the causal direction is not always unidirectional, but in fact also could be bidirectional. Creative thought and behavior can also influence personality, and personality traits—in so far that they shape experience—can even affect gene expression through the process of epigenetics. It's best to see this model as being somewhat simplistic, but a first step toward a model of how personality and creativity affect each other.

Evolutionary and Genetic Influences on Personality and Creativity

How does creativity come about, both at an individual level, but also at a species level? Creativity is one of the, if not *the*, trademark traits of the human species. Darwin and Wallace's idea of natural selection is well-known: Traits that serve some adaptive purpose for survival get selected over the generations and become more common in a species, and sometimes even create new species. Less well-known, but also very important, is Darwin's idea of sexual-selection:

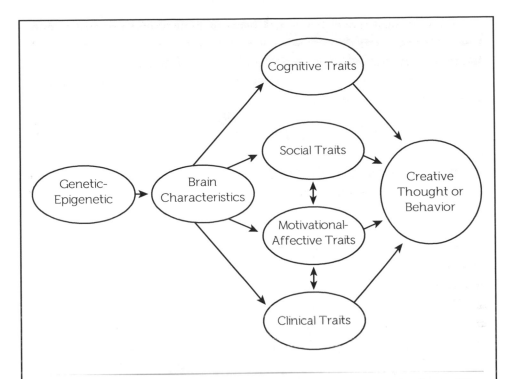

Figure 10.1. Functional model of the creative personality. *Note.* From "The function of personality in creativity: The nature and nurture of the creative personality" (p. 115), by G. J. Feist, 2010, in J. C. Kaufman & R. J. Sternberg (Eds.), *Cambridge handbook of creativity* (pp. 113-130), New York, NY: Cambridge University Press. Copyright 2010 Cambridge University Press. Reprinted with permission.

Members of the same sex compete for mating opportunities and the opposite sex finds particular competitively successful traits and qualities attractive. Over generations, these attractive traits also become more common and characteristic of the species.

Some have argued that sexual-selection is most relevant for explaining species-wide traits like intelligence and creativity. Geoffrey Miller (2000) put forth the most comprehensive theory that sexual-selection processes are behind the evolution of human creativity, because wit, intelligence, charm, and creativity are attractive qualities in a potential mate, especially in men (Beaussart, Kaufman, & Kaufman, 2012; Haselton & Miller, 2006). Furthermore, twin-adoption research has revealed creativity to be a sexually selected trait (Verweij, Burri, & Zietsch, 2014).

Feist (2001), however, argued for a finer distinction: Natural selection pressures have shaped applied forms of creativity (technology, science, engineering), whereas sexual selection pressures have shaped ornamental forms of creativity (art, music, dance, writing). Recent empirical evidence has supported Feist's argument in that ornamental-aesthetic behaviors were rated as more sexually appealing than applied-technical creative behaviors (Kaufman et al., 2014). Additional support for this view comes from findings showing that successful male creative artists have more sexual partners than less successful ones (Clegg, Nettle, & Miell, 2011). Moreover, the personality trait of openness to experience was the strongest predictor of those who found aesthetic creative behaviors sexually attractive (Kaufman et al., 2014).

Twin-adoption research into the heritability of creative behavior has found that creative achievement, especially artistic, has a sizable genetic component (Barron & Parisi, 1976; Hur, Jeong, & Piffer, 2014; Nichols, 1978; Piffer & Hur, 2014; Velázquez, Segal, & Horowitz, 2015). For instance, in a study of more than 160 pairs of twins, more than 50% of artistic creative achievement and nearly 40% of scientific creative achievement could be explained by genetic influence (Hur et al., 2014).

Brain Structures and Processes Involved in Creativity

As is true in most every domain of psychology, the neuroscience of creativity has witnessed an explosion of research over the last 15–20 years. A full treatment of this literature is beyond the scope of the current chapter, but some general trends can be outlined.

One general conclusion from this literature is there is no one brain region where creative activity occurs. But as way of introduction to the neuroscience of creativity, let us first review the basics of the creative process. The creative process really has two major phases: generation of novel ideas and evaluation and selection of the most meaningful and useful ones (Simonton, 2013). Idea generation involves wider, more defocused, disinhibitory, divergent cognitive processes, whereas the evaluation and selection of those ideas involves more cognitive control and focused attention. This two-phase model of the creative process is also consistent with the dual-processing model that integrates more automatic cognitive flexibility with more deliberative cognitive processes of creative thinking (Baas, Roskes, Sligte, Nijstad, & De Dreu, 2013; Chen et al., 2014; Li et al., 2015; Zabelina & Robinson, 2010).

Classic and recent research into the neural substrates of creative thought generally supports this two-phase model of creative thought (Chen et al. 2014; Jung, Mead, Carrasco, & Flores, 2013; Martindale, 1999; Park, Kirk, & Waldie, 2015). Jung and colleagues (2013), for example, argued that idea generation involves the Default Network (DN), which is a disinhibitory network of brain regions that interact and are involved when people are not responding to stimuli from the outside world, that is, they are just daydreaming or engaged in "mind-wandering." Some refer to this spontaneous and self-generated thought as "defocused attention," and more colloquially we might say, "not paying attention." These networks have hubs in the frontal, parietal, and temporal lobes, and much neuroimaging and lesion evidence suggests integrated activity between these networks during creative thought. Moreover, it appears that higher levels of neural integration in these regions are associated with creative thought (Jung et al., 2013; Takeuchi et al., 2010).

The second phase of evaluation and selection of novel ideas involves brain regions known as the cognitive control network (CCN), which is an excitatory network of brain regions in the prefrontal cortex and the anterior cingulate (which, among other things, is involved in error detection and attention; Jung et al., 2013). The CCN is activated when we are focused on stimuli from the outside world. Jung and colleagues reviewed neuroscientific evidence that the CCN is mostly involved in the second—idea evaluation—phase of the creative process.

Some of the first theory and research on the brain structures and processes involved in creative thought and behavior came from Hans Eysenck. Eysenck's (1967, 1995) theory of introversion and extraversion argues for low cortical arousal in extraverts compared to introverts. Research into the association between cortical arousal, extraversion, and creative thought generally supports the view that extraverted and original people show the lowest levels of cortical arousal while solving creative problems (Fink & Neubauer, 2008).

Other classic lines of neuroscientific research into the brain bases of creative thinking reveal important and telling differences between right and left hemisphere functioning (Kuonios & Beeman, 2014, 2015). Neural networks in the left hemisphere (especially near the language centers) are activated in smaller and tighter brain regions, whereas in the right hemisphere the networks are weakly activated in a broader and wider region. The left hemisphere, therefore, is more likely to make narrower and more converging associations, whereas the right is more likely to make broader, wider, and more diverging associations. Insights, solutions, and inferences are outcomes of these wider and more diffuse neural networks of the right hemisphere (more specifically the right anterior region of the temporal lobe). Moreover, directly stimulating—with transcranial direct current stimulation (tDCS)—the right frontal-temporal cortex while simultaneously inhibiting left frontal-temporal cortical activity enhances the odds of insight solutions (Kuonios & Beeman, 2014).

Finally, there is some research that examines the interplay between brain, personality, and creativity (Jauk, Neubauer, Dunst, Fink, & Benedek, 2015;

Passamonti et al., 2015). Beaty et al. (2015), for example, examined the association between the brain's default mode (its efficiency) and the personality trait of openness to experience (the most consistent personality correlate of creative behavior). In two separate studies, they found a positive association—the more efficient the default mode was, the higher the participants were in openness to experience. This line of research suggests a biological foundation of openness to experience.

The causal nature of brain influences is precisely what the model of creativity (Figure 10.1) assumes. These brain differences make creative traits more or less likely, which in turn make creative thought and behavior more or less likely. So personality traits mediate the relationship between the brain and creative thought and behavior. By having genetic dispositions that create CNS differences that facilitate creative thinking, highly creative people also develop a set of personality traits consistent with their biological dispositions.

Personality Influences on Creativity

As put forth in Figure 10.1, evolutionary, genetic, and brain processes are causally prior to and influence personality traits. Building upon the qualitative and quantitative reviews of the personality and creativity literature from 10 to 15 years ago, the personality traits most consistently connected to creativity are clustered into cognitive, social, motivational-affective, and clinical categories.

Cognitive Personality Traits

Feist (1998) classified particular traits as "cognitive" because they deal with how people habitually process information, solve problems, and respond to new situations. Chief among the cognitive personality traits connected to creative thought and behavior is "openness to experience." Open people tend to be imaginative and curious and so it is not surprising that open people are more creative. This is not just a theoretical connection, but an empirical one (Agnoli, Franchin, Rubaltelli, & Corazza, 2015; Chang, Wang, Liang, & Liang, 2014; Dollinger, Urban, & James, 2004; Feist, 1998; Ivcevic & Brackett, 2015; Karwowski & Lebuda, 2015; Kaufman, 2013; Kaufman et al., 2015; van Tilburg, Sedikides, & Wildschut, 2015). Recent research suggests that the openness component is most strongly associated with artistic creativity, whereas the intellect component is more associated with scientific creativity (Kaufman et al., 2015). Moreover, the openness-creativity relationship is moderated by breadth of attention, as measured by the tendency to look at less relevant stimuli (Angoli et al., 2015). That is, the relationship was only significantly positive for people who looked longest at irrelevant visual stimuli. Similar to its relation to creativity, openness also predicts the tendency to be more moved by aesthetic experiences and to more readily experience awe (Silvia, Fayn, Nusbaum, & Beaty, 2015).

Cognitive flexibility is another trademark of creative thought and achievement. Flexibility involves fluidly switching and moving between different categories of ideas or coming up with many ideas from distinct categories (Guilford, 1968). Although a cognitive ability, flexibility is also part of the personality constellation of openness to experience. In alignment with the classic view of Frank Barron (1963) that creative people have the ability to traverse a wide latitude of cognitive and personality states, recent research suggests that creative individuals are both more controlled and flexible in their cognitive processing (Baas et al., 2013; Zabelina & Robinson, 2010).

Social Personality Traits

Social traits of personality involve first and foremost behaviors and attitudes that concern one's relationships to other people, such as questioning or accepting what authority figures say, being comfortable or uncomfortable around strangers and large groups of people, being warm or hostile toward others, and believing one is better or worse than others. The trait terms that summarize these tendencies are norm-doubting, nonconformity, independence, extraversion-introversion, aloofness, hostility, coldness, and dominance/self-confidence/arrogance. Recent research suggests an inverse-U relationship between agreeableness and imagination, with imaginative ability in designers peaking with moderate levels of agreeableness (Chang, Peng, Lin, & Liang, 2015; Kaufman et al. 2015).

After openness, extraversion is the personality trait with the strongest and most robust association with creativity (Chiang, Hsu, & Shih, 2015; Feist, 1998; Furnham, Batey, Anand, & Manfield, 2008; Karwowski & Leduba, 2015). As Feist (1998) argued, however, the general factor of extraversion does not quite reflect its accurate relationship with creativity. When one splits extraversion into two of its main components, sociability-gregariousness and confidence-assertiveness, a clearer association emerges. Highly creative people are generally not more sociable and outgoing, but they are more independent, confident, and assertive. In fact, there is some evidence that in many domains (e.g., science, literature, art, poetry, and musical composition) creative people are more introverted, autonomous, and socially withdrawn than sociable and outgoing (Feist, 1999a).

Autonomy and independence are the opposite of conformity and conservatism. Creative people tend to doubt and buck social norms and question tradition and authority. Rubinstein (2003), for instance, examined authoritarianism and creativity in Israeli college students (design, behavioral science, and law). Rubinstein found strong negative relationships between creativity and authoritarianism as well as a linear relationship between career choice (major) and authoritarianism. Highly creative people doubt, question, and often reject norms, traditions, and conservative ideology. Indeed, one could argue these findings validate both constructs, for creativity concerns producing novel and unusual ideas and conservatism/authoritarianism values tradition.

Motivational-Affective Personality Traits

Motivational traits are defined by a person's desire to persist in activities and to be successful in his or her activities. Trait terms characteristic of motivation are *persistent, driven, ambitious,* and *impulsive.* That some people are driven to be creative is both undeniable and perplexing. Why do people want to create? Some people are willing to forgo social relationships and economic well-being to create lasting works.

If those who have a desire to produce works that leave a mark on the world are to succeed, they also need to be driven, focused, and ambitious. They are not the kind of person who gives up easily in the face of hindrances and roadblocks. And that is generally what the research on drive and creativity continues to show: Creative artists, businesspeople, and scientists are driven, ambitious, and persistent (Amabile, 1996; Batey & Furnham, 2006; Ceci & Kumar, 2015).

But what kinds of things motivate them? Need to know? Self-expression? Success? Recognition? Money? Joy from the process? It could be each of these depending on the nature of the creative task. Scientists are probably driven more by the need to know and artists more by the need for self-expression. And both are often driven by the pleasure the process of discovery or expression brings, otherwise known as intrinsic motivation. Indeed, intrinsic motivation is often associated with highly creative thought or behavior and quite a body of research supports this idea (e.g., Amabile, 1996; Hannam & Narayan, 2015). That is, when the drive and energy for carrying out a task is pleasure and excitement, then the end product often is more creative than if the drive is lacking or extrinsic. Amabile's classic work on motivation and creativity has reported that often extrinsic motivation (reward, surveillance, or recognition) has a detrimental effect on creative achievement.

In addition to motivation, both trait- and state-level positive affect can broaden one's cognitive processes and associations and under some circumstances be positively correlated with creative thought and problem solving (Feist, 2012; Fredrickson, 2001; Rogaten & Moneta, 2015). Similarly, milder degrees of mania (hypomania and/or cyclothymia) are also associated with creative thought (Jamison, 1993; Ludwig, 1995; Zabelina, Condon, & Beeman, 2014). The theory is that the increased fluency of thought during hypomania makes original and even meaningful associations more likely.

Clinical Traits

Not only affect, but also certain affective disorders do appear to be consistently connected to high levels of creative achievement, especially in the arts (Ludwig, 1995). Bipolar disorder, for instance, is found in many highly creative writers, musicians, artists, and poets (Andreasen & Glick, 1988; Bowden, 1994; Jamison, 1993; Johnson, Tharp, & Holmes, 2015; Johnson et al., 2015; Richards & Kinney, 1990)

Researchers have long demonstrated a link between psychoticism and creativity, especially in artists and the general population (Eysenck, 1995; Feist, 1998; Ludwig, 1995). Results, however, have been mixed and have led some researchers to propose that psychoticism is too broad and general a construct and, in fact, its relationship to creativity would be better understood if broken down into specific components, such as latent inhibition and schizotypy (Batey & Furnham, 2008; Mason, Claridge, & Jackson, 1995). Rado (1953) first abbreviated the phrase "schizophrenic genotype" to "schizotype" and described it as the eccentric behaviors that predispose a person to schizophrenia. Current conceptualizations consider schizotypy to exist on a continuum in the general population and define it as consisting of the following core traits: unusual experiences (i.e., hallucinatory and/or magical thinking), cognitive disorganization (i.e., difficulty concentrating, feelings of worthlessness, and social anxiety), introvertive anhedonia (i.e., lack of enjoyment), and impulsive nonconformity (i.e., violent and self-abusive behaviors; Mason et al., 1995). Indeed, a growing body of literature reveals a positive connection between schizotypy and creativity (Acar & Sen, 2013; Batey & Furnham, 2008; Claridge & McDonald, 2009; Claridge, Pryor, & Watkins, 1990; Nettle, 2006).

Conclusions

The research and theory on the connection between personality and creativity remains a vital topic of investigation for psychological scientists. The basic conclusions from 15 years still hold. The largest change over that time period has been the explosion of research on the genetics and function and structure of brain processes, and their impact on creative thought and behavior. In addition, there is even some recent research on the evolutionary basis of sexual selection and why certain traits such as artistic creativity, in particular, are so sexually appealing.

Although the model proposes that epigenetic factors may also play an important role in creative thought and behavior, as of today, the empirical evidence for this claim is lacking. Epigenetics involves changes in gene expression after the genome has been established during fertilization. That is, environmental events postconception tag DNA sequences and turn on or off the genes. These events can be diet, exercise, exposure to chemicals, or a whole host of experiences. In short, genetic influence is a changing and dynamic process rather than a static one. It is left to future creativity and behavioral genetics researchers to unpack the epigenetic influences of creative thought.

At this point, however, we can safely conclude that there are certain neurological and neurochemical conditions that make particular personality traits more likely. These personality traits cluster into cognitive, social, motivational-affective, and clinical groups. Being high or low in certain personality dispositions functions to make creative thought and behavior more or less likely.

As is true for the scientific process in general, these answers raise more questions. Here are a few thought questions that are raised by the findings reviewed in this chapter:

- Why do rock stars have groupies (i.e., are often sexually attractive to large numbers of people)? Why don't creative computer scientists or mathematicians have groupies?
- Given the modest genetic component to creative ability, what does that suggest about how teachable creative thought is? Could anyone be taught to be a creative genius?
- If the default mode in the brain involves daydreaming and mind-wandering and is also associated with creativity, could being alone, bored, or taking a shower facilitate the creative process?
- Are personality traits causes or effects of creative thinking? Don't high levels of creativity also change one's personality? That is, couldn't the arrows in Figure 10.1 also point back from creative thought to personality?

There are still many unanswered questions about the role and function of personality in creative thought and behavior. Patterns have emerged and personality does seem to consistently lower thresholds for thinking and behaving in an original and meaningful way—that is creatively. If the next 30 years are like the last 30, then the future of the field is just starting.

Recommended Readings

Barron, F. X. (1963). *Creativity and psychological health*. Oxford, England: Van Nostrand.

Clegg, H., Nettle, D., & Miell, D. (2011). Status and mating success amongst visual artists. *Frontiers in Psychology, 2,* 1–4.

Eysenck, H. J. (1995). *Genius: The natural history of creativity*. New York, NY: Cambridge University Press.

Feist, G. J. (1998). A meta-analysis of the impact of personality on scientific and artistic creativity. *Personality and Social Psychological Review, 2,* 290–309.

Jung, R. E., Mead, B. S., Carrasco, J., & Flores, R. A. (2013). The structure of creative cognition in the human brain. *Frontiers in Neuroscience, 7,* 1–13. doi:10.3389/fnhum.2013.00330

Kaufman, S. B., Kozbelt, A., Silvia, P., Kaufman, J. C., Ramesh, S., & Feist, G. J. (2014). Who finds Bill Gates sexy? Creative mate preferences as function of cognitive ability, personality, and creative achievement. *Journal of Creative Behavior, 48,* 1–19. doi:10.1002/jocb.78

Ludwig, A. M. (1995). *The price of greatness*. New York, NY: Guilford Press.

Silvia, P. J., Fayn, K., Nusbaum, E. C., & Beaty, R. E. (2015). Openness to experience and awe in response to nature and music: Personality and profound aesthetic experiences. *Psychology of Aesthetics, Creativity, and the Arts, 9,* 376–384. doi:10.1037/aca0000028

References

Acar, S., & Sen, S. (2013). A multilevel meta-analysis of the relationship between creativity and schizotypy. *Psychology of Aesthetics, Creativity, and the Arts, 7,* 214–228. doi:10.1037/a0031975

Agnoli, S., Franchin, L., Rubaltelli, E., & Corazza, G. E. (2015). An eye-tracking analysis of irrelevance processing as moderator of openness and creative performance. *Creativity Research Journal, 27,* 125–132. doi:10.1080/1040 0419.2015.1030304

Amabile, T. (1996). *Creativity in context*. Boulder, CO: Westview.

Andreasen, N. C., & Glick, I. D. (1988). Bipolar affective disorder and creativity: Implications and clinical management. *Comprehensive Psychiatry, 29,* 207–216.

Baas, M., Roskes, M., Sligte, D., Nijstad, B. A., & De Dreu, C. W. (2013). Personality and creativity: The dual pathway to creativity model and a research agenda. *Social & Personality Psychology Compass, 7,* 732–748. doi: 10.1111/spc3.12062.

Barron, F. X. (1955). The disposition toward originality. *Journal of Abnormal Social Psychology, 51*, 478–485.

Barron, F. X. (1963). *Creativity and psychological health.* Oxford, England: Van Nostrand.

Barron, F. X., & Parisi, P. (1976). Twin resemblances in creativity and in esthetic and emotional expression. *Acta Geneticae Medicae et Gemellologiae, 25*, 213–217.

Batey, M., & Furnham, A. (2006). Creativity, intelligence, and personality: A critical review of the scattered literature. *Genetic, Social and General Psychology Monographs, 132*, 355–429.

Batey, M., & Furnham, A. (2008). The relationship between measures of creativity and schizotypy. *Personality and Individual Differences, 45*, 816–821.

Beaty, R. E., Kaufman, S. B., Benedek, M., Jung, R. E., Kenett, Y. N., Jauk, E., . . . Silvia, P. J. (2015). Personality and complex brain networks: The role of openness to experience in default network efficiency. *Human Brain Mapping.* Advance online publication. doi:10.1002/hbm.23065

Beaussart, M. L., Kaufman, S. B., & Kaufman, J. C. (2012). Creative activity, personality, mental illness, and short-term mating success. *Journal of Creative Behavior, 46*, 151–167.

Bowden, C. L. (1994). Bipolar disorder and creativity. In M. P. Shaw & M. A. Runco (Eds.), *Creativity and affect* (pp. 73–86). Norwood, NJ: Ablex.

Ceci, M. W., & Kumar, V. K. (2015). A correlational study of creativity, happiness, motivation, and stress from creative pursuits. *Journal of Happiness Studies.* Advance online publication. doi:10.1007/s10902-015-9615-y

Chang, C., Peng, L., Lin, J., & Liang, C. (2015). Predicting the creativity of design majors based on the interaction of diverse personality traits. *Innovations in Education and Teaching International, 52*, 371–382. doi:10.1 080/14703297.2014.999697

Chang, C., Wang, J., Liang, C.-T., & Liang, C. (2014). Curvilinear effects of openness and agreeableness on the imaginative capability of student designers. *Thinking Skills and Creativity, 14*, 68–75. doi:10.1016/j. tsc.2014.09.001

Chen, Q., Yang, W., Li, W., Wei, D., Li, H., Lei, Q., & . . . Qiu, J. (2014). Association of creative achievement with cognitive flexibility by a combined voxel-based morphometry and resting-state functional connectivity study. *Neuroimage, 102*(Part 2), 474–483. doi:10.1016/j.neuroimage.2014.08.008

Chiang, Y., Hsu, C., & Shih, H. (2015). Experienced high performance work system, extroversion personality, and creativity performance. *Asia Pacific Journal of Management, 32*, 531–549. doi:10.1007/s10490-014-9403-y

Claridge, G., & McDonald, A. (2009). An investigation into the relationships between convergent and divergent thinking, schizotypy, and autistic traits. *Personality and Individual Differences, 46,* 794–799. doi:10.1016/j. paid.2009.01.018

Claridge, G., Pryor, R., & Watkins, G. (1990). *Sounds from the bell jar: Ten psychotic authors.* London, UK: Macmillan Press.

Clegg, H., Nettle, D., & Miell, D. (2011). Status and mating success amongst visual artists. *Frontiers in Psychology, 2,* 1–4.

Dollinger, S. J., Urban, K. K., & James, T. A. (2004). Creativity and openness: Further validation of two creative product measures. *Creativity Research Journal, 16,* 35–47.

Eysenck, H. J. (1967). *The biological basis of personality.* Springfield, IL: Charles C. Thomas.

Eysenck, H. J. (1995). *Genius: The natural history of creativity.* New York, NY: Cambridge University Press.

Feist, G. J. (1998). A meta-analysis of the impact of personality on scientific and artistic creativity. *Personality and Social Psychological Review, 2,* 290–309.

Feist, G. J. (1999a). Autonomy and independence. In M. A. Runco & S. R. Pritzker (Eds.), *Encyclopedia of creativity* (Vol. 1, pp. 157–163). San Diego, CA: Academic Press.

Feist, G. J. (1999b). Personality in scientific and artistic creativity. In R. J. Sternberg (Ed.). *Handbook of human creativity* (pp. 273–296). Cambridge, England: Cambridge University Press.

Feist, G. J. (2001). Natural and sexual selection in the evolution of creativity. *Bulletin of Psychology and the Arts, 2,* 11–16.

Feist, G. J. (2010). The function of personality in creativity: The nature and nurture of the creative personality. In J. C. Kaufman & R. J. Sternberg (Eds.), *Cambridge handbook of creativity* (pp. 113–130). New York, NY: Cambridge University Press.

Feist, G. J. (2012). Affective states and traits in creativity. In M. Runco (Ed.), *The creativity research handbook* (Vol. 3, pp. 61–102). New York, NY: Hampton Press.

Fink, A., & Neubauer, A. C. (2008). Eysenck meets Martindale: The relationship between extraversion and originality from the neuroscientific perspective. *Personality and Individual Differences, 44,* 299–310. doi:10.1016/j. paid.08.010

Fredrickson, B. L. (2001). The role of positive emotions in positive psychology: The broaden-and-build theory of positive emotions. *American Psychologist, 56,* 218–226.

Furnham, A., Batey, M., Anand, K., & Manfield, J. (2008). Personality, hypomania, intelligence, and creativity. *Personality and Individual Differences, 44,* 1060–1069.

Gosling, S., & John, O. P. (1999). Personality dimensions in nonhuman animals. A cross-species review. *Current Directions in Psychological Science, 8,* 69–75.

Guilford, J. P. (1968). *Intelligence, creativity and their educational implications.* New York, NY: Robert R. Knapp.

Hannam, K., & Narayan, A. (2015). Intrinsic motivation, organizational justice, and creativity. *Creativity Research Journal, 27,* 214–224. doi:10.1080/10400419.2015.1030307

Haselton, M. G., & Miller, G. F. (2006). Women's fertility across the cycle increases the short term attractiveness of creative intelligence. *Human Nature, 17*(1), 50–73. doi:10.1007/s12110-006-1020-0

Hur, Y., Jeong, H., & Piffer, D. (2014). Shared genetic and environmental influences on self-reported creative achievement in art and science. *Personality and Individual Differences, 68,* 18–22. doi:10.1016/j.paid.2014.03.041

Ivcevic, Z., & Brackett, M. A. (2015). Predicting creativity: Interactive effects of openness to experience and emotion regulation ability. *Psychology of Aesthetics, Creativity, and the Arts, 9,* 480–487. doi:10.1037/a0039826

Jamison, K. R. (1993). *Touched with fire: Manic-depressive illness and the artistic temperament.* New York, NY: Free Press.

Jauk, E., Neubauer, A. C., Dunst, B., Fink, A., & Benedek, M. (2015). Gray matter correlates of creative potential: A latent variable voxel-based morphometry study. *Neuroimage, 111,* 312–320. doi:10.1016/j.neuroimage.2015.02.002

John, O. P., & Srivastava, S. (1999). The Big Five taxonomy: History, measurement, and theoretical perspectives. In L. A. Pervin & O. P. John (Eds.), *Handbook of personality: Theory and research* (pp. 102–138). New York, NY: Guilford Press.

Johnson, S. L., Tharp, J. A., & Holmes, M. K. (2015). Understanding creativity in bipolar I disorder. *Psychology of Aesthetics, Creativity, and the Arts, 9,* 319–327. doi:10.1037/a0038852

Johnson, S. L., Murray, G., Hou, S., Staudenmaier, P. J., Freeman, M. A., & Michalak, E. E. (2015). Creativity is linked to ambition across the bipolar spectrum. *Journal of Affective Disorders, 178,* 160–164. doi:10.1016/j.jad.2015.02.021

Jung, R. E., Mead, B. S., Carrasco, J., & Flores, R. A. (2013). The structure of creative cognition in the human brain. *Frontiers in Neuroscience, 7,* 1–13. doi:10.3389/fnhum.2013.00330

Karwowski, M., & Lebuda, I. (2015). The Big Five, the Huge Two, and creative self-beliefs: A meta-analysis. *Psychology of Aesthetics, Creativity, and the Arts.* Advance online publication. doi:10.1037/aca0000035

Kaufman, S. B. (2013). Opening up openness to experience: A four-factor model and relations to creative achievement in the arts and sciences. *Journal of Creative Behavior, 47,* 233–255. doi:10.1002/jocb.33

Kaufman, S. B., Kozbelt, A., Silvia, P., Kaufman, J. C., Ramesh, S., & Feist, G. J. (2014). Who finds Bill Gates sexy? Creative mate preferences as function of cognitive ability, personality, and creative achievement. *Journal of Creative Behavior, 48,* 1–19. doi:10.1002/jocb.78

Kaufman, S. B., Quilty, L. C., Grazioplene, R. G., Hirsh, J. B., Gray, J. R., Peterson, J. B., & DeYoung, C. G. (2015). Openness to experience and intellect differentially predict creative achievement in the arts and sciences. *Journal of Personality.* Advance online publication. doi:10.1111/jopy.12156

Kounios, J., & Beeman, M. (2014). The cognitive neuroscience of insight. *Annual Review of Psychology, 65,* 71–93.

Kounios, J., & Beeman, M. (2015). *The eureka factor: Aha moments, creative insight, and the brain.* New York, NY: Random House.

Li, W., Li, X., Huang, L., Kong, X., Yang, W., Wei, D., & ... Liu, J. (2015). Brain structure links trait creativity to openness to experience. *Social Cognitive and Affective Neuroscience, 10,* 191–198. doi:10.1093/scan/nsu041

Ludwig, A. M. (1995). *The price of greatness.* New York, NY: Guilford Press.

MacKinnon, D. W. (1962). The nature and nurture of creative talent. *American Psychologist, 17,* 484–495.

Mason, O., Claridge, G., & Jackson, M. (1995). New scales for the assessment of schizotypy. *Personality and Individual Differences, 18,* 7–13.

Martindale, C. (1999). Biological bases of creativity. In R. Sternberg (Ed.), *Handbook of creativity* (pp. 137–152). Cambridge, England: Cambridge University Press.

McCrae, R. R., & Costa, P. T. (1999). A five-factor theory of personality. In L. A. Pervin & O. P. John (Eds.), *Personality theory and research* (pp. 139–153). New York, NY: Guilford Press.

Miller, G. F. (2000). *The mating mind: How sexual choice shaped the evolution of human nature.* New York, NY: Doubleday.

Nettle, D. (2006). Schizotypy and mental health amongst poets, visual artists, and mathematicians. *Journal of Research in Personality, 40,* 876–890.

Nichols, R. C. (1978). Twin studies of ability, personality, and interests. *Homo, 29,* 158–173.

Park, H. P., Kirk, I. J., & Waldie, K. E. (2015). Neural correlates of creative thinking and schizotypy. *Neuropsychologia, 73,* 94–107. doi:10.1016/j.neuropsychologia.2015.05.007

Passamonti, L., Terracciano, A., Riccelli, R., Donzuso, G., Cerasa, A., Vaccaro, M. G., . . . Quattrone, A. (2015). Increased functional connectivity within mesocortical networks in open people. *Neuroimage, 104,* 301–309. doi:10.1016/j.neuroimage.2014.09.017

Piffer, D., & Hur, Y. (2014). Heritability of creative achievement. *Creativity Research Journal, 26,* 151–157. doi:10.1080/10400419.2014.901068

Rado, S. (1953). Dynamics and classification of disordered behavior. *American Journal of Psychiatry, 110,* 406–416.

Richards, R. L., & Kinney, D. K. (1990). Mood swings and creativity. *Creativity Research Journal, 3,* 202–217.

Rogaten, J., & Moneta, G. B. (2015). Use of creative cognition and positive affect in studying: Evidence of a reciprocal relationship. *Creativity Research Journal, 27,* 225–231. doi:10.1080/10400419.2015.1030312

Rubinstein, G. (2003). Authoritarianism and its relation to creativity: A comparative study among students of design, behavioral sciences and law. *Personality and Individual Differences, 34,* 695–705.

Silvia, P. J., Fayn, K., Nusbaum, E. C., & Beaty, R. E. (2015). Openness to experience and awe in response to nature and music: Personality and profound aesthetic experiences. *Psychology of Aesthetics, Creativity, and the Arts, 9,* 376–384. doi:10.1037/aca0000028

Simonton, D. K. (2013). Creative thoughts as acts of free will: A two-stage formal integration. *Review of General Psychology, 17,* 374–383.

Takeuchi, H., Taki, Y., Sassa, Y., Hashizume, H., Sekiguchi, A., Fukushima, A., & Kawashima, R. (2010). White matter structures associated with creativity: Evidence from diffusion tensor imaging. *Neuroimage, 51,* 11–18. doi:10.1016/j.neuroimage.2010.02.035

van Tilburg, W. P., Sedikides, C., & Wildschut, T. (2015). The mnemonic muse: Nostalgia fosters creativity through openness to experience. *Journal of Experimental Social Psychology, 59,* 1–7. doi:10.1016/j.jesp.2015.02.002

Velázquez, J. A., Segal, N. L., & Horwitz, B. N. (2015). Genetic and environmental influences on applied creativity: A reared-apart twin study. *Personality and Individual Differences, 75,* 141–146. doi:10.1016/j.paid.2014.11.014

Verweij, K. H., Burri, A. V., & Zietsch, B. P. (2014). Testing the prediction from sexual selection of a positive genetic correlation between human mate preferences and corresponding traits. *Evolution and Human Behavior, 35,* 497–501. doi:10.1016/j.evolhumbehav.2014.06.009

Zabelina, D. L., Condon, D., & Beeman, M. (2014). Do dimensional psychopathology measures relate to creative achievement or divergent thinking? Advance online publication. *Frontiers in Psychology, 5.* doi:10.3389/fpsyg.2014.01029.

Zabelina, D. L., & Robinson, M. D. (2010). Creativity as flexible cognitive control. *Psychology of Aesthetics, Creativity, and the Arts, 4,* 136–143. doi:10.1037/a0017379

HOT TOPIC 4

Creativity and Mental Illness

So Many Studies, So Many Wrong Conclusions

James C. Kaufman

Key Take-Aways

- The relationship between creativity and mental illness is complex and nuanced.
- Although there is evidence from highly eminent populations that mental illness may be broadly associated with creative genius in specific domains (such as the arts), the studies looking at everyday populations are inconsistent.
- Some subclinical disorders are associated with some types of creativity (but not all); one possible reason is that creativity and mental illness share certain commonalities.
- Many studies suggest everyday creativity is connected to positive mental health.

Many debates or hot topics within creativity research may spur intense discussions in the field, but be of less interest to the general population. Whether creativity is more domain-specific or domain-general may spawn books (e.g., Kaufman & Baer, 2005), but may not necessarily inspire cocktail conversation. The relationship between creativity and mental illness, however, is a source of great interest both academically and casually. Creative people care a great deal (Kaufman, Bromley, & Cole, 2006).

It is unsurprising that the two concepts are connected. Think of how easy it is to conjure images of the mad genius, from the brooding poet to the demented artist to the cackling scientist. But popular conceptions can be wrong. John Kennedy never actually said he was a jelly donut, the Fiji mermaid wasn't real, and Paul McCartney is (as of this writing) still alive. The creativity-mental illness question isn't about disproving a myth or hoax, but rather trying to figure out exactly what question is being asked. Creativity is a multifaceted, enormous construct with countless ways of being measured. Mental illness is an even bigger variable, with volumes written simply to distinguish and label the thousands of possible diagnoses (Kaufman, 2014; Silvia & Kaufman, 2010).

Interpreting how to even conceptualize the relationship between creativity and mental illness can take many forms, yet most reviews tend to lump everything together. Consider five different studies. The first examines biographies of creative people and finds that those who are considered the most eminent are more likely to show symptoms of bipolar disorder than those who are merely good. The second gives divergent thinking tests and measures of depression to college students and finds a positive correlation. The third compares mental patients and random people on their ability to draw pictures and finds the patients' art is rated as more creative. The fourth has someone interview professional movie directors and clerks and finds that the directors are more likely to be diagnosed with schizotypy. The fifth asks children with and without behavioral disorders to rate themselves on their own creativity and finds the children with behavioral disorders think they are more creative.

I am purposely using mock studies instead of actual studies for the sake of argument, but there are 30 comparable studies for each of the five examples provided above. The problem is that these disparate research lines are too often combined and overextended to say that creativity is connected to mental illness. As I have noted before, collecting these types of studies together does not make much sense. It is comparable to reading that parrots can't eat avocado, dogs can't eat grapes, rats can't eat blue cheese, cats can't eat onions, and horses can't eat potatoes . . . and then concluding that giving any food to an animal is a bad idea (see Beaussart, White, Pullaro, & Kaufman, 2014; Kaufman, 2016).

So what do we know? The most cited studies on creativity and mental illness have countless flaws and fundamental errors (Schlesinger, 2009). Looking past this work, there are also numerous historiometric studies that use biographical information on historic people to assess both creativity and evidence of mental illness. It is difficult, if not impossible, to diagnose mental illness long after someone's death, but some basic indicators of illness can be determined through research. Quite extensive work (Ludwig, 1995; Simonton, 2014a) has established some connection between creative genius and higher levels of mental illness than in less-eminent populations. Further work has pointed broadly to the arts (Simonton, 2014b), more specifically writing (McKay & Kaufman, 2014), and even more specifically to female poets (Kaufman, 2001), as being more likely to show signs of mental illness than other creative geniuses.

Another (large) cluster of studies analyze creativity and subclinical disorders—in other words, people who have some traits associated with disorders but at a much lower level; they are also completely functional. It is common to find connections, but methodology and nuance play a large role in how to interpret these studies. For example, Zabelina, Condon, and Beeman (2014) studied divergent thinking and hypomania (in which people may have elevated moods but are not bipolar). They found that if divergent thinking was scored in a traditional way, with scores for fluency, flexibility, and elaboration, then creativity and hypomania were not related. When the same responses were scored using the Consensual Assessment Technique (which has raters assess creativity), the two constructs were related. Another example of the complexity of how creativity and mental illness are connected can be seen in Acar and Sen's (2013) meta-analysis on creativity and schizotypy (another subclinical disorder related to schizophrenia, but nowhere near as impactful). There are many types of schizotypy; positive schizotypy includes impulsive behavior, unusual experiences, and being a nonconformist, whereas negative schizotypy encompasses behaving withdrawn and not experiencing pleasure (anhedonia). In Acar and Sen's meta-analysis, the overall relationship between schizotypy and creativity was significant but very weak. Positive schizotypy showed a stronger relationship with creativity, but negative schizotypy was actually associated with lower levels of creativity.

What are some possible reasons that creativity and mental illness might be related? A popular theory is Carson's (2011, 2014) shared vulnerability model. She proposed three traits that creativity and mental illness share: latent inhibition (being unable to filter out irrelevant information), a preference for new things, and hyperconnectivity (when different areas in the brain not usually connected are linked, which can cause senses to overlap). What moderates these shared traits, influencing whether someone with this profile is more likely to be creative or have mental health issues? Carson argued that two protective factors are a strong working memory and high intelligence.

In discussing the creativity-mental illness question, it is also important to not overlook the opposite side—namely, that creativity can be a huge part of positive mental health. The benefits of creativity can be found in many areas. On a day-to-day level, creative people are more likely to be in better physical health (Stuckey & Nobel, 2010) and have less stress (Nicol & Long, 1996). Creativity can serve as a buffer when you feel exhausted from a long day's work (Eschleman, Madsen, Alarcon, & Barelka, 2014). In times of crisis, people can use creativity to build their resiliency and help recover from major trauma (Forgeard, 2013). Further, creativity can be part of meaningful therapy. Expressive writing (Pennebaker, 1997) and visual art (Drake & Winner, 2012) have both been empirically found to be helpful as a therapeutic process.

What is there to take away from the muddled research? There is enough evidence to believe there is some type of connection between creative *genius* and some aspect of mental health issues. There are also undoubtedly nuanced, domain-specific, and illness-specific connections that may become clearer in time. However, creativity also interacts in a positive way with mental health. From the current research, I would be hard-pressed to say anything more definitive, and you should be highly skeptical of anyone who claims the debate has been settled. Anything further would require extrapolating Big-C research to little-c populations or assuming one type of population, measure, or methodology is more generalizable than it actually is. Such speculation is ultimately dangerous. I am personally much more excited to follow research on how creativity can be used to help people (e.g., Forgeard & Kaufman, in press) than in trying to place negative labels on creators.

Recommended Readings

Carson, S. H. (2011). Creativity and psychopathology: A shared vulnerability model. *The Canadian Journal of Psychiatry/La Revue Canadienne De Psychiatrie, 56,* 144–153.

Kaufman, J. C. (2014). *Creativity and mental illness.* New York, NY: Cambridge University Press.

Schlesinger, J. (2009). Creative mythconceptions: A closer look at the evidence for "mad genius" hypothesis. *Psychology of Aesthetics, Creativity, and the Arts, 3,* 62–72.

Simonton, D. K. (2014). The mad-genius paradox: Can creative people be more mentally healthy but highly creative people more mentally ill? *Perspectives on Psychological Science, 9,* 470–480.

References

Acar, S., & Sen, S. (2013). A multilevel meta–analysis of the relationship between creativity and schizotypy. *Psychology of Aesthetics, Creativity, and the Arts, 7*, 214–228.

Beaussart, M. L., White, A. E., Pullaro, A., & Kaufman, J. C. (2014). Reviewing recent empirical findings on creativity and mental illness. In J. C. Kaufman (Ed.), *Creativity and mental illness* (pp. 42–59). New York, NY: Cambridge University Press.

Carson, S. H. (2011). Creativity and psychopathology: A shared vulnerability model. *The Canadian Journal of Psychiatry/La Revue Canadienne De Psychiatrie, 56*, 144–153.

Carson, S. H. (2014). The shared vulnerability model of creativity and psychopathology. In J. C. Kaufman (Ed.), *Creativity and mental illness* (pp. 253–280). New York, NY: Cambridge University Press.

Drake, J. E., & Winner, E. (2012). Confronting sadness through art-making: Distraction is more beneficial than venting. *Psychology of Aesthetics, Creativity, and the Arts, 6*, 251–266.

Eschleman, K. J., Madsen, J., Alarcon, G. M., & Barelka, A. (2014). Benefiting from creative activity: The positive relationships between creative activity, recovery experiences, and performance-related outcomes. *Journal Occupational and Organizational Psychology, 87*, 579–598.

Forgeard, M. J. (2013). Perceiving benefits after adversity: The relationship between self-reported posttraumatic growth and creativity. *Psychology of Aesthetics, Creativity, and the Arts, 7*, 245–264.

Forgeard, M. J. C., & Kaufman, J. C. (in press). Who cares about imagination, creativity, and innovation, and why? A review. *Psychology of Aesthetics, Creativity, and the Arts.*

Kaufman, J. C. (2001). The Sylvia Plath effect: Mental illness in eminent creative writers. *Journal of Creative Behavior, 35*, 37–50.

Kaufman, J. C. (2014). Creativity and mental illness: Reasons to care and beware. In J. C. Kaufman (Ed.), *Creativity and mental illness* (pp. 403–407). New York, NY: Cambridge University Press.

Kaufman, J. C. (2016). *Creativity 101* (2nd ed.). New York, NY: Springer.

Kaufman, J. C., & Baer, J. (Eds). (2005). *Creativity across domains: Faces of the muse.* Mahwah, NJ: Lawrence Erlbaum.

Kaufman, J. C., Bromley, M. L., & Cole, J. C. (2006). Insane, poetic, lovable: Creativity and endorsement of the "Mad Genius" stereotype. *Imagination, Cognition, and Personality, 26*, 149–161.

Ludwig, A. M. (1995). *The price of greatness.* New York, NY: Guilford Press.

McKay, A. S., & Kaufman, J. C. (2014). Literary geniuses: Their life, work, and death. In D. K. Simonton (Ed.), *Cambridge handbook of genius* (pp. 473–487). New York, NY: Cambridge University Press.

Nicol, J. J., & Long, B. C. (1996). Creativity and perceived stress of female music therapists and hobbyists. *Creativity Research Journal, 9*, 1–10.

Pennebaker, J. W. (1997). Writing about emotional experiences as a therapeutic process. *Psychological Science, 8*, 162–166.

Schlesinger, J. (2009). Creative mythconceptions: A closer look at the evidence for "mad genius" hypothesis. *Psychology of Aesthetics, Creativity, and the Arts, 3*, 62–72.

Silvia, P. J., & Kaufman, J. C. (2010). Creativity and mental illness. In J. C. Kaufman & R. J. Sternberg (Eds.), *Cambridge handbook of creativity* (pp. 381–394). New York, NY: Cambridge University Press.

Simonton, D. K. (2014a). The mad-genius paradox: Can creative people be more mentally healthy but highly creative people more mentally ill? *Perspectives on Psychological Science, 9*, 470–480.

Simonton, D. K. (2014b). More method in the mad-genius controversy: A historiometric study of 204 historic creators. *Psychology of Aesthetics, Creativity, and the Arts, 8*, 53–61.

Stuckey, H. L., & Nobel, J. (2010). The connection between art, healing, and public health: A review of current literature. *American Journal of Public Health, 100*, 254–263.

Zabelina, D. L., Condon, D., & Beeman, M. (2014). Do dimensional psychopathology measures relate to creative achievement or divergent thinking? *Frontiers in Psychology, 5*.

CHAPTER 11

Investing in Creativity in Students

The Long and Short (Term) of It

Stuart N. Omdal and Amy K. Graefe

Key Take-Aways

- Creativity can be developed.
- Teaching creative thinking strategies to students is a long-term investment upon which they will be able to draw throughout their lives.
- Though an element of the arts, creative thinking and action occur in all areas of human endeavor, including the everyday lives of all people.
- In the classroom, barriers to teaching creatively may be present, but they can be overcome through the application of creative thinking.
- When teachers develop an understanding of creativity, model creative thinking and behaviors, and teach creatively, a classroom climate can be established that enhances the teaching and learning experience for students.

Creativity, Teaching, and Learning

The relationship between creativity and learning is multifaceted: Teachers employ creative thinking to plan lessons, which can then be presented creatively to learners who utilize their creative abilities to integrate the new learning with previously learned content and skills and finally express what they have learned in a creative way that is meaningful to them. This method of instruction, with the concomitant goals of developing understanding and creating personal meaning, is poised to cause deep, long-lasting learning and knowing and the development of personal creativity. Attainment of this personal creativity has many potential, long-term benefits for the individual (Davies et al., 2013; Im, Hokanson, & Johnson, 2015). For example, adult creative achievement is more closely tied to creativity, measured by a test of divergent thinking, than to intelligence test scores in elementary students (Plucker, 1999), and Plucker, Beghetto, and Dow (2004) included creativity as a key component of "healthy social and emotional well-being and scholastic and adult success" (p. 83). The good news is that research in this area indicates that creativity can be systematically developed (Im et al., 2015).

The development of school environments that promote creative teaching and the nurturing of creative thinking and expression can, therefore, be considered to be a "long-term investment" in the lives of the students. This investment pays great dividends for the student by enhancing creative thinking abilities and creating cognitive connections and understanding, and for society by preparing citizens who will be better equipped to develop solutions for problems not yet imagined in this new century (Renzulli, 2012). This type of instruction is in contrast to the "short-term" investment that often takes place in school systems, where the focus and pragmatic necessity is to prepare students to take high-stakes tests and do well on them. With schools under the threat of reorganization or being taken over by the state department of education, with teachers operating under the weight of having the performance of their students determine part of their professional evaluation (and thus permanence of employment Saeki, Pendergast, Segool, & von der Embse, 2015), and with the general public voicing distrust of public schools while demanding accountability, it is of little surprise that creative teaching and learning are low priorities in many states, districts, and schools. This chapter explores barriers, addresses options, and helps teachers find opportunities to incorporate creativity in their classes for the development of creative thinking and expression in their students.

History of Creativity in Schools

The rise of interest in creativity in schools in the United States began with the growing interest in early childhood education in the 19th century and particularly with the work of several European educators. Friedrich Froebel of Germany maintained that education must nurture creativity. Swiss educator Johann Pestalozzi emphasized the value of play in the inner growth and development of a child. This type of play would have included concepts associated with creativity such as imagination, inventiveness, and improvisation. Similarly, American psychologist G. Stanley Hall also promoted the value of childhood play and its role in later adolescent development. John Dewey, a student of Hall and an educational reformer, promoted lessening the restrictive, rote learning style of teaching and replacing it with direct experience, inquiry, and play (Sawyer, 2011). Another student of G. Stanley Hall, Arnold Gesell, studied stages of child development and also promoted creative play in early childhood. His influence extended well into the mid-20th century (Feldman & Benjamin, 2006).

The focus on creativity within American schools became a priority with the Russian launching of Sputnik in October 1957. This event spurred the United States federal government to support new education programs in the sciences with the goal to exceed the space program of the Russians. Regarding this thrust, Cropley & Cropley (2000) stated, "This perceived failure of American science and engineering was attributed to lack of creativity, and judged to be the result of defects in education" (p. 208). Influential during this era was Jean Piaget's theory of cognitive development, which described how logico-mathematical thinking advanced across childhood and adolescence. His work greatly impacted the development of new methods of teaching math and science at this time as it reconsidered the capability of students to comprehend these topics at an earlier age than previously thought. Eleanor Duckworth, an American early childhood specialist, embraced Piaget's work, focusing on the creative and intellectual nature of the young child and his or her ability to develop understanding and create personal meaning within the context of his or her own environment (Feldman & Benjamin, 2006).

Throughout the 1960s, social and cultural change had an impact on many institutions. In education, a movement dissatisfied with the traditional, restrictive pedagogy and structure of schools adopted tenets from British Open Classroom schools. Larry Cuban (2004) compared it to the "pedagogical progressive" movement of the early 20th century and the "neoprogressives" of the late 1980s and early 1990s who favored integrated curriculum and forms of authentic assessment. The characteristics of Open Classroom (or Open Education) schools included learning by doing, inquiry-oriented methods, interest centers, and a student-centered/student-directed philosophy (Hennessey, 2015). They were open both in the philosophical sense and in the architectural; many schools had large open areas the size of several regular classrooms. The nurturing, development, and promotion of creativity was at the heart of the Open Classroom approach. Feldman and Benjamin (2006) stated that in these schools "creativity in the classroom was the order of the day" (p. 323). The implementation of the Open Classroom approach varied considerably among schools, and those whose faculties did not receive appropriate professional development ultimately failed, built walls between classrooms, and often went back to more traditional pedagogy. However, it did introduce a generation of teachers (including one of the authors) to new ways of considering what school could look like, how children could make choices about learning, and the role that creativity played in the larger picture of education.

Barriers to Creativity

Barriers to creativity can be either real or perceived. "Perceived" barriers may be attitudinal regarding the value or appropriate expression of creativity or the characteristics/behaviors commonly associated with creativity. "Real" barriers may come in the form of governmental or school district directives regarding curricular priorities that inhibit creative teaching or learning activities.

Perceived Barriers

Enhancing creativity. The question of whether creativity can be enhanced often arises and is based on the myth that people are born either creative or un-creative (Plucker & Dow, 2010). Within this (false) dichotomy, any creativity training or attempts at creativity development are seen as futile. However, the overwhelming response in the literature belies these notions (Aljughaiman & Mowrer-Reynolds, 2005; Piirto, 2011; Starko, 2013; Sternberg & Williams, 1996). Since J. P. Guilford's 1950 call for more "systematic, rigorous, experimental research" (Feldman & Benjamin, 2006, p. 325) on creativity, hundreds of such studies have been conducted with largely the same conclusion: Creativity can be enhanced with appropriate support, learning experiences, and opportunities to use the acquired skills in real-world settings.

One reason the question of creativity development continually surfaces is that a great many people equate creativity with artistic ability and/or with major inventions, literary works, and world-renowned discoveries (Newton & Newton, 2009; Runco & Johnson, 2002; Tan, 2000). Beghetto (2005) challenged this point of view, emphasizing the type of creativity anyone might exhibit on a daily basis:

> However, just because someone's creative contribution is not revolutionary doesn't mean it is not creative. Indeed, the novel and useful efforts of normal, everyday people are still, by definition, creative. This level of creativity, called "pedestrian or everyday creativity" (Plucker and Beghetto, 2004, p. 158), is important and representative of what often is hoped for in school settings. We want our students to be able and willing to solve problems, create products, and contribute ideas that are novel and useful in any given situation. (p. 255)

Researchers and writers in the area of creativity often refer to the distinction between different types of creativity as Big-C, which is associated with those who are legendary or revolutionary (e.g., Ghandi, Margaret Mead, John Lennon), and little-c, often described as "everyday" creativity (e.g., improvising when you don't have the right tool or ingredient, a parent making up a song to sing to his or her child, solving a problem when a change of plans occurs; see Beghetto, 2010; Kaufman & Beghetto, 2009). When one of the authors begins a class or professional development session for teachers on creativity, he always asks the attendees if they think they are creative. Usually only 20% or so of the hands go up; the other typically say, "I'm not artistic." He then talks to them about the concepts of Big-C and little-c creativity and shares quotations regarding creativity, including the quote from Abraham Maslow: "A first-rate soup is more creative than a second-rate painting."

Once the concept of little-c creativity sinks in, these teachers are ready to begin to form a conception of creativity broad enough for them to see how the aspects of their teaching (and their "everyday" personal lives) are, indeed, creative (Piirto, 2011). They are also ready to begin to recognize the many ways that their students are creative in their "everyday" school lives. This, coupled with the acquisition of information about characteristics and behaviors associated with creativity and how they may present in students in their classes, can help teachers reinterpret the behavior of students through the lens of creativity (particularly independence, nonconformity, and curiosity; Davis, 2004). However, for a teacher who is "creativity neutral" (neither promotes nor suppresses creativity) or who has a low tolerance for creative behavior, students in her class who exhibit the behaviors listed above and others associated with creativity (internally controlled, grand imagination, risk taker) may be seen as misbehaving rather than as a creative student (Beghetto, 2006). The manifestations of little-c creativity are not about changing the whole world, but if educators learn to understand and appropriate this type of creativity into daily classroom life, it *can* change the way creative students are considered in *their* worlds.

Real Barriers: Effects of Federal and State Legislation on Creativity

High-stakes testing. The No Child Left Behind Act (NCLB) was enacted in 2001 under the leadership of President George W. Bush (U.S. Department of Education, 2002). This act served to reauthorize the Elementary and Secondary Education Act and was ideally designed to provide

> increased accountability for States, school districts, and schools; greater choice for parents and students, particularly those attending low-performing schools; more flexibility for States and local educational agencies (LEAs) in the use of Federal Education dollars; and a stronger emphasis on reading, especially for our youngest children. (p. 1)

With the passage of this Congressional act, federal education funding was directly tied to high-stakes assessments designed to measure student achievement. In looking back, however, not only did the implementation of NCLB not have the intended effect of academic proficiency for all students, it also evidenced unintended negative consequences, maybe the most notably being that in high-stakes testing environments, curriculum tends to be narrowed to only what will be assessed on the tests (Berliner, 2011; Milner, 2014; Schul, 2011), often eliminating "art, music, and such skills as critical thinking, [and] creativity" (Hlebowitsh, 2007, para. 4).

Additionally, under the guidance of President Barack Obama, the Race to the Top (RTT) grant was created as part of the American Recovery and Reinvestment Act of 2009 (Lohman, 2010). Although similar in many respects to the NCLB requirements, one key difference in RTT was that in order for states to be eligible to apply for the monies, they must have devised a teacher evaluation system that directly linked students' standardized test scores to individual teachers. By 2013, 80% of states included student achievement and/ or growth as a significant factor in their teacher evaluation systems (Tooley, 2014). For example, the Colorado State Model Educator Evaluation System mandates that fully half of a teacher's evaluation be based on student performance (Colorado Department of Education, 2015). Certainly changes to the teacher evaluation systems have been undertaken with the best of intentions; however, in this movement toward greater educator accountability through the use of high-stakes assessments, teachers' desire to teach creatively is often trumped by the need to ensure that students are making adequate progress toward a testing goal.

Although this testing focus in K–12 schools has undoubtedly impacted the creative capabilities of a generation of youth leaving our public education system, the detriment may be perpetuated further by young teachers who were in elementary and secondary school during this era and who also experienced the focus on testing from the perspective of a student within a teacher-education program (Hanich & Bray, 2009; Sternberg, 2015; Ukpolo & Strauss, 2005). In other words, if it's true that we teach like we were taught, we may have unwittingly just produced a generation of future educators who can be predisposed to an approach to teaching that deemphasizes or even devalues creativity. As a case in point, universities during the NCLB period were encouraged to equip preservice teachers with the skills necessary to prepare their K–12 students for standardized testing (Ukpolo & Strauss, 2005), and these future teachers did indeed report that through their field experiences, they became familiar with "narrowing the curriculum, teaching to the test, and increased test preparation sessions" (Hanich & Bay, 2009, p. 33).

Not surprisingly, as this generation of future educators has matriculated into teacher education programs, professors have commented on the need of many of them for explicit instructions on what the professor wants on particular assignments: "Tell me exactly what you want." When one colleague told a student that what she wanted was for students to express what they had learned about the topic in a mode of their choice, the student responded, "Do we have to do this project? Can't we just take a test?" This attitude, while understandable based on past experiences where a single correct test answer was the expectation, is a barrier to creativity and indicates that the student has not had many, or many good, experiences with making choices about student products designed to nurture creativity (Batchelor, 2012; Shively & Yerrick, 2014). It is likely that many teachers who came of age in the NCLB era have not had to deeply process or synthesize what they have learned to attain understanding (Beghetto & Plucker, 2006) and have, instead, learned to be content with an external locus of control regarding learning.

Scripted curriculum. The NCLB legislation also required that schools and districts implement research-based instructional strategies within classrooms (U.S. Department of Education, 2002). This condition led to the adoption of many scripted curricula throughout the nation (Conrad, Moroye, & Uhrmacher, 2015; Duncan-Owens, 2009; Milner, 2014) and often to administrative directives that teachers adhere to a strict prescribed daily schedule in the name of fidelity of implementation. One first-grade teacher reported that her principal said that he wanted to be able to observe a lesson in the first classroom and, as he walked down the hall, hear the next teacher not only on the same lesson, but ideally at the same point in that lesson. Another teacher reported that she was told by her principal that he wanted curriculum so "foolproof" that he could "pull a bank teller walking the street," put him in a classroom with the scripted lessons, and he could successfully teach the class (Gerrard & Farrell, 2014).

Similarly, a young graduate student in a gifted education master's program, who had been teaching for about 5 years, was assigned to develop a unit of study on a topic of personal interest utilizing gifted education pedagogy. This assignment was important to her because she knew she would later teach this unit to a group of middle and high school students at a summer program for gifted, talented, and/or creative students. However, she did not know where to begin and told her professor, "I've never made up a lesson or unit before. They have always just been given to me to teach." Teachers who have had no opportunities for creative production on school assignments or opportunities to pursue personal in-depth studies often do not know how to facilitate these experiences for their students (Batchelor, 2012; Beghetto, 2006), another unintended consequence. The combination of going through a school system with a focus on high-stakes testing and then teaching in a school district with the same orientation establishes a strong likelihood that the succession of K–12 students who will not experience any manner of creativity in the school environment will be perpetuated. It is hoped that with the newest reauthorization of the Elementary and Secondary Education Act, which reduces the requirements for mandated testing, some of this pressure will be relieved and teachers will not only have the choice to use creative instructional strategies, but also to give students choices regarding the products they create to demonstrate their learning and understanding, thereby enhancing creativity within the classroom.

Supporting Creativity in the Classroom

Recommendations abound regarding methods and strategies for creative teaching and learning. We will address several that we believe are key for teachers in getting started in setting up a creative classroom or enhancing practices already in place. These are drawn from the literature and from the experiences of scores of teacher with whom we have worked.

Understanding Creativity

One can find hundreds of books of creativity enhancing activities for students. Many are very clever and focus on divergent thinking through brainstorming activities. Teachers can use them and see that the students are actively participating, thinking, and as a side benefit, having fun doing them. What is missing is the growth of teacher understanding of the larger domain of creativity outside of divergent thinking.

Jane Piirto writes extensively on creativity, creative processes, and creative individuals. She maintains that the study of creativity needs to go beyond the "learning about" level to a point where individuals really internalize the concepts and principles of creativity and contemplate the role of those concepts in their own lives. "I believe one cannot teach people to be creative without having experienced the creative process in a transformational way" (Piirto, 2011, p. xi). This "transformational way" would be a different experience for each individual. Davies and colleagues (2013) emphasized the importance of teachers' awareness of their personal conceptions of creativity, because of the impact that awareness has on the classroom. They also emphasized the importance of teachers "taking on the role of learners to develop their own creativity" (p. 88). Part of that creativity development includes learning about theories and definitions and exploring the biographical information of creative people. Through the acquisition of that information and the learning activities in which they participate, teachers are likely to experience a personal transformation regarding their creative self-efficacy (Piirto, 2011).

Modeling Creativity

The modeling of creative attitudes and behaviors by teachers is another area recommended in the literature (Davies et al., 2013; Yi, Plucker, & Guo, 2015). This includes demonstrating tasks or projects that require creative thinking, including the aspects of fluency, flexibility, originality, and elaboration. Modeling the "think aloud" approach (Hargrove, 2013) is a way to show students how to develop metacognitive skills through the teacher sharing his or her thinking process aloud. Teachers can also employ the method of "Artistic Modification" (Renzulli, Leppien, & Hays, 2000), whereby teachers enhance the curriculum by bringing in teaching resources, such as personal stories, hobby materials, collected documents, and other realia, to use in a creative way. This affords students the opportunity to see a creative aspect of their teachers' nonacademic lives in an academic context. This may enable the students to creatively connect the stories and objects of their own lives to the academic contexts they experience in school.

Climate

The classroom climate encompasses the balance between divergent and convergent questions and expectations, the number of choices students can make, and the openness of the teacher to a range of student responses (Davies et al., 2013; Plucker, Kaufman, & Beghetto, 2015). What would an observer see and feel in a creative classroom? When one of the authors was a doctoral student, he helped implement a thinking skills program that was part of a university study. As part of this process, he spent time observing a fourth-grade classroom in an urban elementary school. The veteran teacher he was observing was not comfortable having someone watch her teach and not comfortable with a productive thinking exercise at the beginning of a science unit on birds. She was doing a KWL chart (*What do you Know, What do you Want to learn, What have you Learned?*). She was hesitant because she realized she did not already know how the students would answer. She rarely asked *divergent* or open-ended questions preferring, instead, to ask questions that required *convergent* thinking—questions that had just one correct answer. She asked the students, "What do you already know about birds?" Hands went up and students told her fairly predictable facts about birds. Then she asked, "What do you want to learn about birds?" Several students had pretty ordinary questions, and then LeRoy raised his hand and was called upon. "I want to know why boy birds and girl birds are different." He was asking about why the feathers were different colors on male and female birds. The teacher's response was immediate and forceful, "That is no kind of question to ask, and you sit down and be quiet." There was definitely a climate in that room, and it was pretty stormy. No more hands went up. Nobody asked any more questions. Her response shut down any speculative thinking, and she was finished with questions that required divergent thinking.

Climate—it is the feeling tone of a classroom that is established by the teacher. It may be one like the one described above, or it may be one where open-ended questions are common and student responses are respectfully addressed. A positive climate is a safe environment to ask all kinds of questions and know that all answers will be thoughtfully considered and a safe place to take risks—academic, intellectual, creative, social, and personal (Claxton, Edwards, & Scale-Constantinou, 2006; Cullingford, 2007; Karwowski, 2011; Piirto, 2011).

One of the key factors in teachers successfully establishing a safe, creative environment is the questions they ask that reveal their personal perception of knowledge. If a teacher views his or her job as relaying information and particular skills to students (Beghetto & Kaufman, 2009), then he or she will be asking a majority of questions that only require convergent thinking. If a teacher views him- or herself as one who is learning with his or her students, using an inquiry approach to teaching, asking a majority of open-ended questions that require divergent thinking, and offering students some options in how they are assessed via student products, then that teacher will establish a classroom climate that fosters creativity and the creative growth of students (Beghetto, 2010). An example of one approach that utilizes questioning that leads to student understanding is Synectics (Aggarwal & Bhatia, 2011; Gordon, 1961). One of the many strategies in Synectics is metaphorical thinking. After introducing a new topic to students, the teacher asks, "What is this like?" (e.g., Photosynthesis—What is this like?). The students need to think about the attributes, characteristics, function, process, and outcomes of photosynthesis and look for relationships or similarities with other objects, ideas, or processes in science (or any other area for that matter). It is in this examination of the primary concept that the student uses both creative and evaluative thinking that can lead to deeper understanding.

Teaching Creatively

Another facet of creativity in classrooms is how the teacher teaches. The importance of the teaching strategies implemented are reflected in the previous section on "Climate," as it is the choice of teaching strategies that directly influences the climate of the classroom. The literature offers many potential teaching strategies associated with the development of student creativity. Schacter, Thum, and Zifkin (2006) listed practices that define teaching creatively:

1. Teaching creative thinking strategies including brainstorming, redefining a problem, or generating multiple ideas.
2. Providing opportunities for choice and discovery in content and mode of expression.
3. Reinforcing intrinsic motivation.
4. Encouraging students when they give answers that are nonconforming.
5. Developing an atmosphere supportive of inquiry, curiosity, and self-directed learning.
6. Engaging students in activities that use imagination and fantasy that address real-world issues and problems.

A set of strategies from the work of June Maker (Maker, Jo, & Muammar, 2008) incorporating the Discover curriculum model included several other features of teaching creatively: (a) active learning where students listen, ask questions, discuss, plan, express themselves, experiment, research, create, and/or compose; (b) access to varied materials (math manipulatives, art supplies, magazines) and a variety of ways to access information and to express what has been learned; (c) opportunities to explore topics of interest within the context of the curriculum or other topics of particular interest; (d) problem finding and problem solving; and (e) self-evaluation where students learn how to critique their own work based on self-determined criteria. The recommendations for developing a classroom "climate" that supports creative teaching and learning, questioning strategies for the development of understanding, and opportunities for choices in content and mode of expression, coupled with the strategies listed above, will support the goal of nurturing and enhancing creativity in students.

Conclusion

Every teacher has parameters within which he or she must operate as dictated by federal, state, and/or local school district directives. As we have pointed out, the level of imposed structure varies a great deal. For those with greater freedom to select content and instructional strategies, these recommendations may be implemented to a greater degree. For those who are in schools where all content and pedagogy is prescribed, on the surface these recommendations may appear untenable to even consider. When one of the authors was talking with a free-thinking friend who was in a very structured graduate program, the friend said that he was really going to have to think "outside the box" to survive. Then he paused and said, "No, I'm going to have to think harder *inside* the box."

For those in a more restrictive setting, the situation is similar. Sawyer (2011) offered the concept of looking for the "spaces" in between the elements of the structured curriculum and asking those open-ended questions, taking the opportunities to give students a choice in assignments, and/or conducting short creative thinking exercises. Sawyer called this "disciplined improvisation." By making an effort to gain more understanding of creativity, creating a favorable climate for students' creative expressions, and looking for opportunities to think harder *inside* the box for those spaces where creative thinking can be inserted, teachers communicate the value of creativity and how it can be part of everyday living. It is in these efforts that teachers make deposits in the long-term investments that will make a positive difference in the lives of their students.

Recommended Readings

Beghetto, R. A. (2010). Creativity in the classroom. In J. C. Kaufman & R. J. Sternberg (Eds.), *The Cambridge handbook of creativity* (pp. 447–463). New York, NY: Cambridge University Press.

Feldman, D. H., & Benjamin, A. C. (2006). Creativity and education: An American retrospective. *Cambridge Journal of Education, 36,* 319–336.

Hennessey, B. A. (2015). Assessing schools on creativity: A toolbox for U.S. teachers and policymakers and a to-do list for researchers worldwide. In A. G. Tan & C. Perleth (Eds.), *Creativity, culture, and development* (pp. 147–160). New York, NY: Springer.

Kaufman, J. C., & Beghetto, R. A. (2009). Beyond big and little: The Four C model of creativity. *Review of General Psychology, 13,* 1–12. doi:10.1037/a0013688

Maker, C. J., Jo, S., & Muammar, O. M. (2008). Development of creativity: The influence of varying levels of implementation of the DISCOVER curriculum model, a non-traditional pedagogical approach. *Learning and Individual Differences, 18,* 402–417.

Piirto, J. (2011). *Creativity for 21st century skills: How to embed creativity into the curriculum* (pp. 1–12). Rotterdam, The Netherlands: Sense Publishers.

Plucker, J. A., & Dow, G. T. (2010). Attitude change as the precursor to creativity enhancement. In R. Beghetto & J. Kaufman (Eds.), *Nurturing creativity in the classroom* (pp. 362–379). New York, NY: Cambridge University Press.

Plucker, J. A., Kaufman, J. C., & Beghetto, R. A. (2015). *What we know about creativity* [4Cs Research Series]. Washington, DC: Partnership for 21st Century Skills. Available at http://www.p21.org/our-work/4cs-research-series/creativity

Starko, A. J. (2013). *Creativity in the classroom: Schools of curious delight.* New York, NY: Routledge.

References

Aggarwal, M. Y., & Bhatia, M. N. (2011). Creativity and innovation in management. *International Journal of Multidisciplinary Research, 1,* 288–296.

Aljughaiman, A., & Mowrer-Reynolds, A. (2005). Teachers' conceptions of creativity and creative students. *The Journal of Creative Behavior, 39*(1), 17–34.

Batchelor, K. (2012). Pre-service teacher education methods courses: From discipline to democracy. *The Clearing House: A Journal of Educational Strategies, Issues and Ideas, 85,* 243–247.

Beghetto, R. A. (2005, September). Does assessment kill student creativity? *The Educational Forum, 69,* 254–263.

Beghetto, R. A. (2006). Creative justice? The relationship between prospective teachers' prior schooling experiences and perceived importance of promoting student creativity. *The Journal of Creative Behavior, 40,* 149–162.

Beghetto, R. A. (2010). Creativity in the classroom. In J. C. Kaufman & R. J. Sternberg (Eds.), *The Cambridge handbook of creativity* (pp. 447–463). New York, NY: Cambridge University Press.

Beghetto, R. A., & Plucker, J. A. (2006). The relationship among schooling, learning and creativity: "All roads lead to creativity" or "You can't get there from here"? In J. C. Kaufman & J. Baer (Eds.), *Creativity and reason in cognitive development* (pp. 316–332). New York, NY: Cambridge University Press.

Beghetto, R. A., & Kaufman, J. C. (2009). Intellectual estuaries: Connecting learning and creativity in programs of advanced academics. *Journal of Advanced Academics, 20,* 296–324.

Berliner, D. C. (2011). Foreword. In R. K. Sawyer (Ed.), *Structure and improvisation in creative teaching* (pp. xiii–xvi). New York, NY: Cambridge University Press.

Claxton, G., Edwards, L., & Scale-Constantinou, V. (2006). Cultivating creative mentalities: A framework for education. *Thinking skills and creativity, 1*(1), 57–61.

Colorado Department of Education. (2015). *Colorado state model educator evaluation system: 2015–2016 users guide.* Retrieved from https://www.cde.state.co.us/educatoreffectiveness/usersguide

Conrad, B., Moroye, C. M., & Uhrmacher, P. B. (2015). Curriculum disruption: A vision for new practices in teaching and learning. *Current Issues in Education, 18*(3), 1–19.

Cropley, D. H., & Cropley, A. J. (2000). Fostering creativity in engineering undergraduates. *High Ability Studies, 11,* 207–209. doi:10.1080/13598130020001223

Cuban, L. (2004). The open classroom: Schools without walls became all the rage during the early 1970s. Were they just another fad? *Education Next, 4*(2), 68.

Cullingford, C. (2007). Creativity and pupils' experience of school. *Education 3–13, 35,* 133–142.

Davis, G. A. (2004). *Creativity is forever.* Dubuque, IA: Kendall Hunt.

Davies, D., Jindal-Snape, D., Collier, C., Digby, R., Hay, P., & Howe, A. (2013). Creative learning environments in education—A systematic literature review. *Thinking Skills and Creativity, 8,* 80–91.

Duncan-Owens, D. (2009). Scripted reading programs: Fishing for success. *Principal, 88,* 26–29.

Feldman, D. H., & Benjamin, A. C. (2006). Creativity and education: An American retrospective. *Cambridge Journal of Education, 36,* 319–336.

Gerrard, J., & Farrell, L. (2014). Remaking the professional teacher: Authority and curriculum reform. *Journal of Curriculum Studies, 46,* 634–655.

Gordon, W. J. J. (1961). *Synectics: The development of creative capacity*. New York, NY: Harper & Row.

Hanich, L. B., & Bray, J. S. (2009). No Child Left Behind: An examination of preservice teachers' knowledge and preparation. *Pennsylvania Teacher Education, 8*, 27–37. Retrieved from https://www.pac-te.org/uploads/1443198775_Hanich%20and%20Bray%20-%202009.pdf

Hargrove, R. A. (2013). Assessing the long-term impact of a metacognitive approach to creative skill development. *International Journal of Technology and Design Education, 23*, 489–517.

Hennessey, B. A. (2015). Assessing schools on creativity: A toolbox for U.S. teachers and policymakers and a to-do list for researchers worldwide. In A. G. Tan & C. Perleth (Eds.), *Creativity, culture, and development* (pp. 147–160). New York, NY: Springer.

Hlebowtish, P. S. (2007, November 11). First, do no harm. *Education Week*. Retrieved from http://www.edweek.org/ew/articles/2007/11/07/11hlebowitsh.h27.html

Im, H., Hokanson, B., & Johnson, K. K. (2015). Teaching creative thinking skills: A longitudinal study. *Clothing and Textiles Research Journal, 33*, 129–142.

Kaufman, J. C., & Beghetto, R. A. (2009). Beyond big and little: The Four C model of creativity. *Review of General Psychology, 13*, 1–12. doi:10.1037/a0013688

Karwowski, M. (2011) Teacher personality as predictor of perceived climate for creativity. *IJCPS-International Journal of Creativity and Problem Solving, 21*(1), 37.

Lohman, J. S. (2010). *Comparing No Child Left Behind and Race to the Top*. Hartford: Connecticut General Assembly, Office of Legislative Research.

Maker, C. J., Jo, S., & Muammar, O. M. (2008). Development of creativity: The influence of varying levels of implementation of the DISCOVER curriculum model, a non-traditional pedagogical approach. *Learning and Individual Differences, 18*, 402–417.

Milner, H. R. (2014). Scripted and narrowed curriculum reform in urban schools. *Urban Education, 49*, 743–749.

Newton, D. P., & Newton, L. D. (2009). Some student teachers' conceptions of creativity in school science. *Research in science technological education, 27*(1), 45–60.

Piirto, J. (2011). *Creativity for 21st century skills: How to embed creativity into the curriculum* (pp. 1–12). Rotterdam, The Netherlands: Sense Publishers.

Plucker, J. A. (1999). Is the proof in the pudding? Reanalyses of Torrance's (1958 to present) longitudinal data. *Creativity Research Journal, 12*, 103–114.

Plucker, J. A., Beghetto, R. A., & Dow, G. T. (2004). Why isn't creativity more important to educational psychologists? Potentials, pitfalls, and future directions in creativity research. *Educational Psychologist, 39,* 83–96.

Plucker, J. A., & Dow, G. T. (2010). Attitude change as the precursor to creativity enhancement. In R. Beghetto & J. Kaufman (Eds.), *Nurturing creativity in the classroom* (pp. 362–379). New York, NY: Cambridge University Press.

Plucker, J. A., Kaufman, J. C., & Beghetto, R. A. (2015). *What we know about creativity* [4Cs Research Series]. Washington, DC: Partnership for 21st Century Skills. Available at http://www.p21.org/our-work/4cs-research-series/creativity

Renzulli, J. S. (2012). Reexamining the role of gifted education and talent development for the 21st century: A four-part theoretical approach. *Gifted Child Quarterly, 56,* 150–159.

Renzulli, J. S., Leppien, J. H., & Hays, T. S. (2000). *The Multiple Menu Model: A practical guide for developing differentiated curriculum.* Waco, TX: Prufrock Press.

Runco, M. A., & Johnson, D. J. (2002). Parents' and teachers' implicit theories of children's creativity: A cross-cultural perspective. *Creativity Research Journal, 14,* 427–438.

Saeki, E., Pendergast, L., Segool, N. K., & von der Embse, P. N. (2015). Potential psychosocial and instructional consequences of the common core state standards: Implications for research and practice. *Contemporary School Psychology, 19,* 89–97.

Sawyer, R. K. (2011). What makes good teachers great? The artful balance of structure and improvisation. *Structure and improvisation in creative teaching* (pp. 1–24). New York, NY: Cambridge University Press.

Schacter, J., Thum, Y. M., & Zifkin, D. (2006). How much does creative teaching enhance elementary school students' achievement? *Journal of Creative Behavior, 40,* 47–72. doi:10.1002/j.2162-6057.2006.tb01266.x

Schul, J. E. (2011). Unintended consequences: Fundamental flaws that plague the No Child Left Behind act. *JEP: EJournal of Education Policy.* Retrieved from http://nau.edu/uploadedFiles/Academic/COE/About/Projects/Unintended%20Consequences.pdf

Shively, C. T., & Yerrick, R. (2014). A case for examining pre-service teacher preparation for inquiry teaching science with technology. *Research in Learning Technology, 22.* Advance online publication. doi:10.3402/rlt.v22.21691

Starko, A. J. (2013). *Creativity in the classroom: Schools of curious delight.* New York, NY: Routledge.

Sternberg, R. J. (2015). Teaching for creativity: The sounds of silence. *Psychology of Aesthetics, Creativity, and the Arts, 9,* 115–117.

Sternberg, R. J., & Williams, W. M. (1996). *How to develop student creativity.* Alexandria, VA: ASCD.

Tan, A. (2000). A review on the study of creativity in Singapore. *Journal of Creative Behavior, 34,* 259–84.

Tooley, M. (2014). *A shifting landscape for state teacher evaluation policy.* Retrieved from http://www.edcentral.org/shifting-landscape-state-teacher-evaluation-policy

Ukpolo, F. T., & Strauss, J. E. (2005). No Child Left Behind and pre-service teachers. *Journal of Urban Education: Focus on Enrichment, 2*(1). Retrieved from http://web.calstatela.edu/faculty/jstraus/NCLB&Preservice.pdf

U.S. Department of Education. (2002). *The No Child Left Behind Act of 2001: Executive summary.* Retrieved from http://www2.ed.gov/nclb/overview/intro/execsumm.html

Yi, X., Plucker, J. A., & Guo, J. (2015). Modeling influences on divergent thinking and artistic creativity. *Thinking Skills and Creativity, 16,* 62–68.

HOT TOPIC 5

Creativity Assessment

Meihua Qian and Jonathan A. Plucker

Key Take-Aways

- Creativity can be assessed from four different perspectives—creative product, process, person, and environment.
- Popular methods of assessing creative products in education, psychology, and business range from rater-based techniques, such as the Consensual Assessment Technique, to self-reported measures, such as the Creative Behavior Inventory (Hocevar, 1979), the Creative Achievement Questionnaire (Carson, Peterson, & Higgins, 2005), and the Community Innovation Survey (Arundel & Smith, 2013).
- Little is known regarding creative process. But the Remote Associates Test (Mednick, 1962, 1968) has been used to test individuals' ability to build remote connections among seemingly unrelated items, and divergent thinking tests such as the Torrance Tests of Creative Thinking (Torrance, 2008) have been widely employed to examine individuals' divergent thinking ability.
- A number of creativity instruments concerning individual characteristics of creators have been developed. Among them, Gough (1979)'s Creative Personality Scale remains very popular.

- Both home and work environment influence creativity. Existing measures of creative work environment include KEYS to Creativity and Innovation (Amabile, Conti, Coon, Lazenby, & Herron, 1996) and the Creative Environment Perceptions scale (Mayfield & Mayfield, 2010).

Whenever people mention the word *creativity*, we tend to think creativity belongs to a group of geniuses like Albert Einstein. But according to the leading experts on creativity (e.g., Kaufman & Beghetto, 2009; Plucker & Beghetto, 2004), everyone can be creative. Creativity is generally defined as "the interaction among *aptitude*, *process*, and *environment* by which an individual or group produces a *perceptible product* that is both *novel* and *useful* as defined within a *social context*" (Plucker, Beghetto, & Dow, 2004, p. 90), and it plays an important role in many aspects of life. The following example will illustrate how closely creativity is related to our daily life and how creativity can be assessed.

Creative Product and Assessment

In the United States, at the beginning of each semester, undergraduate and graduate students always rush to the bookstore to buy the required textbooks or shop online in hopes of finding cheaper versions. Regardless, textbooks are expensive. Now technology is fundamentally changing the world, and people can't survive without access to Internet on a daily basis. It is extremely common for students to have computers, smartphones, and iPads. Considering these two factors, publishers have begun to create electronic versions of textbooks and enthusiastically persuade instructors to adopt the etexts. However, the etext is still not cheap.

Seeing this as an opportunity, two undergraduate students at Illinois State University, Kasey Gandham and Mike Shannon, started their own business, founding Packback in 2012. The essential idea is that students can rent a textbook for $5/day, as their research shows students rarely open their textbooks after buying them. But running a business is not easy and they needed investment to turn their creative idea into a creative product. In order to attract investors, Kasey Gandham and Mike Shannon appeared on ABC's *Shark Tank*, a TV program that allows creators to present their ideas or products to a panel of "shark" investors and seek investment. In the end, one of the judges, Mark Cuban, who is a graduate of Indiana University and now owns the NBA's Dallas Mavericks, Landmark Theatres, and Magnolia Pictures, was willing to invest $250,000 in Packback. A few months later, they raised additional

$750,000 in seed funding, and Packback had attracted thousands of users from 80 campuses in the U.S. (Kolodny, 2014).

This example clearly demonstrates how ordinary people without substantive expertise in a field can be creative, and how creativity is assessed. As long as an individual or group produces a tangible product that is considered *novel* and *useful* within a social context, then that is called creativity. Renting a textbook is not a new idea because several major companies such as Amazon's textbook rentals store and BookRenter offer textbook rental service. However, they only rent books or etexts by semester. Packback, instead, lets students rent an eBook for only 24 hours. In other words, Packback creatively meets college students' unique needs for easy access to a textbook when needed at a minimum cost.

The way that Packback was evaluated by a group of "shark" investors also reflects how creative products can be measured. It is called the consensual assessment technique (e.g., Amabile, 1982). The Consensual Assessment Technique (CAT) is a popular method in measuring creative products in which expert judges in the domain in question rate actual products (e.g., poems, collages, drawings, or musical compositions; e.g., Baer, 1998; Kaufman, Plucker, & Baer, 2008). In the example above, all of the "shark" investors are extremely successful entrepreneurs, and they were asked to rate a new business model as the experts in the domain of business.

A number of researchers (e.g., Baer & McKool, 2009; Kaufman, Baer, & Cole, 2009) have claimed that the CAT is a reliable and valid tool for measuring creativity, and it has even been called the "gold standard" of creativity assessment (Carson, 2006), because in the CAT, rather than try to measure some skills that are theoretically linked to creativity, the actual creative product participants have produced are assessed. However, one thing to keep in mind is that experts are people, and they have their own understandings of creativity. Their opinions probably change over time, and a different group of experts might rate a creative product very differently. This may partially explain why some famous artists such as Van Gogh were not recognized for their groundbreaking work until it was too late for them to continue their success.

Self-Reported Creativity Measures

Instead of gathering a group of experts in a domain to judge the creativity of a product, some researchers (Hocevar, 1981; Hocevar & Bachelor, 1989) have proposed another quick and effective way to measure creativity. They used creative behavior checklists to assess an individual's past or current creative accomplishments. This approach has become extremely popular due to its simplicity of administering and scoring. One example is the Creative Behavior Inventory (CBI; Hocevar, 1979) that has been very widely used (e.g.,

Kaufman et al., 2008; Plucker, 1999). The CBI was originally developed from the domain-specific perspective and intended to measure participants' creative behaviors in six different domains: literature, music, crafts, art, performing arts, and math/science (e.g., Kaufman et al., 2008). A few sample items are as follows:

1. Wrote and completed a novel.   Never   1–2 times   3–4 times   More than 5 times

2. Designed and made a piece of clothing.   Never   1–2 times   3–4 times   More than 5 times

3. Cooked an original dish.   Never   1–2 times   3–4 times   More than 5 times

4. Painted an original picture.   Never   1–2 times   3–4 times   More than 5 times

5. Performed a dance in a show or contest.   Never   1–2 times   3–4 times   More than 5 times

To answer these questions, individuals just need to indicate how many times they have participated in a list of activities that are considered to be creative. The more frequently they are engaged in these activities, the more creative they are.

Another similar measure is the Creative Achievement Questionnaire (CAQ; Carson et al., 2005), which assesses people's significant and observable creative accomplishments in 10 different domains: visual arts, music, dance, architectural design, creative writing, humor, inventions, scientific discovery, theater and film, and culinary arts. The following items are used to measure a person's creativity in the domain of music:

Music:

_____ 0. I have no training or recognized talent in this area (Skip to next section).

_____ 1. I play one or more musical instruments proficiently.

_____ 2. I have played with a recognized orchestra or band.

_____ 3. I have composed an original piece of music.

_____ 4. My musical talent has been critiqued in a local publication.

_____ 5. My composition has been recorded.

_____ 6. Recordings of my composition have been sold publicly.

*_____ 7. My compositions have been critiqued in a national publication.

Participants need to place a check mark beside each sentence that applies to them. For the sentence with an asterisk (*), they need to write the number of times that sentence applies to them. Scoring of the CAQ is fairly straightforward. A person will receive a score of zero if he or she checks the first sentence. Otherwise, the participant will receive the total number of points represented by the question numbers. For example, a person receives a domain (i.e., music) score of $[1+2+3+4+5+6+ (2)*7= 35]$ by endorsing items 1–7 and indicating his or her compositions have been critiqued in a national publication twice.

One concern regarding creative behavior checklists is that they are created from domain-specific perspectives, but empirical studies have supported the domain generality nature of these assessments (Plucker, 1998; Qian, 2014). Specifically, as far as everyday creativity (i.e., those creative actions that non-experts may participate in each day) is concerned, research findings have suggested an individual can be creative in multiple domains, although there is still no consensus as to what constitutes a domain and how many domains there are (Feist, 2005; Plucker, 1998; Plucker & Beghetto, 2004; Qian, 2014).

Another issue with regard to measuring creative product is that creativity is often referred to as innovation in industry, and it is typically achieved through research and development-related efforts (e.g., Lhuillery, Raffo, & Hamdan-Livramento, 2015). For example, research and development in industry are defined as "creative work undertaken on a systematic basis in order to increase the stock of knowledge, including knowledge of man, culture and society, and the use of this stock of knowledge to devise new applications" (OECD, 2002, p. 30). A number of national innovation surveys such as the Community Innovation Survey (CIS; Arundel & Smith, 2013) have been developed to measure creative outputs, such as new products produced by firms that are either new to the firm, new to the market, or new to the world; new or improved production processes; new ways of organizing firm resources; and new ways of commercializing products (Crespi & Peirano, 2007; Lhuillery et al., 2015). This has led to the creation of the Oslo Manual, which currently serves as the guidelines for collecting and interpreting innovation data in business (OECD, 1992, 1997, 2005).

Process

Csikszentmihalyi (1999) pointed out that, "If creativity is to have a useful meaning, it must refer to a process that results in an idea or product that is recognized and adopted by others" (p. 314). Hence, creative process and creative products are equally important. Creativity researchers in education and psychology have used a few tests to gain insights into creative process. For example, the Remote Associates Test (Mednick, 1962, 1968) is used to examine participants' ability to find similarities among seemingly disparate words (e.g., Kaufman et al., 2008). Here are two sample items:

> What word is related to these three words?
> *Item 1: Paint Doll Cat*   _____
> The answer is "house": house paint, dollhouse, and house cat.
> *Item 2: Rocking Wheel High*   _____
> The answer is "chair": Rocking chair, wheelchair, and high chair.

Another approach to process measures is represented by divergent thinking (DT) tests, such as the Torrance Tests of Creative Thinking (TTCT; Torrance, 2008) and the Wallach and Kogan (1965) tests. These tasks examine participants' divergent thinking skills by asking participants to provide as many responses as possible to verbal or figural prompts such as "List things that have wheels" (Plucker, Qian, & Wang, 2011). Individuals' responses are generally scored in terms of fluency (number of responses), originality (the rareness of responses), and flexibility (number of distinct categories of responses). DT tests are among the most popular techniques for measuring creativity in educational settings (Kaufman et al., 2008).

However, in business, innovation or creativity assessment is largely limited to creative product and creative environment approaches, with less work on creative process or creative people. But because the research and development department in a firm is solely committed to intentional innovative activities (Lhuillery et al., 2015), future research about their activities may provide great insights with regard to creative process.

Person

Because creativity involves the interaction among aptitude, process, and environment, it can be measured from other perspectives, too. Studies on the creative person often emphasize individual characteristics of the creator, including personality, motivation, intelligence, or knowledge (e.g., Collings & Mellahi, 2009; Lorenz & Lundvall, 2011; Sternberg & Lubart, 1995). Many creativity assessments concerning individual characteristics of creators have been developed. Among them, the Creative Personality Scale (CPS; Gough, 1979), which measures people's creative personality profile, is well-known, and has been very widely used (e.g., Hocevar & Bachelor, 1989; Oldham & Cummings, 1996). The CPS consists of 18 positive (see sample items 1–4) and 12 negative items (see sample items 5–8). Positive items represent creative personality traits, while negative items refer to noncreative personality traits. The test taker receives 1 point by endorsing a positive item and loses one point by checking one negative item. Higher scores suggest higher creativity. Sample CPS items include:

1. _____ Insightful
2. _____ Original
3. _____ Confident
4. _____ Humorous
5. _____ Conservative
6. _____ Narrow interests
7. _____ Submissive
8. _____ Commonplace

Environment

Researchers have found that both home and work environment have a significant impact on creativity (e.g., Amabile & Gryskiewicz, 1989; Greenan & Lorenz, 2013; Lorenz & Lundvall, 2011). Amabile and Gryskiewicz (1989) identified eight aspects of work environment that could stimulate creativity, including sufficient freedom, challenging tasks, appropriate resources, and so on. Meanwhile, factors like time pressure, frequent evaluation, and excessive organizational politics will harm creativity (Amabile & Gryskiewicz, 1989). With respect to the influence of home environment on creativity, studies have shown that the first-born child is more likely to acquire power and privilege, and later-born children are more likely to be open-minded, which is a key creative personality characteristic (Feist, 1998). Famous creators are also more likely to experience other kinds of life events, such as mental illness and parent loss before age 10 (e.g., Ludwig, 1995; Simonton, 1994). A recent study conducted in China suggested that internal migration from rural to urban areas could boost creativity because migration dramatically changed children's home and social environment (Shi, Qian, Lu, & Plucker, 2012).

As described before, Kasey Gandham and Mike Shannon successfully founded Packpack in the U.S. in 2012, but they can never do it in China because college students in China pay for their textbooks, but they do not buy them. The university decides which books to buy and how much students have to pay at the beginning of each semester. Hence, creativity only flourishes within a supportive social environment.

A few tools have been created by researchers to measure creative work environment. Amabile, Conti, Coon, Lazenby and Herron (1996) developed KEYS to Creativity and Innovation, a 78-item survey to assess the climate for creativity in an organization. It contains 10 subscales and targets many dimensions of the work environment such as the management practices, resources, pressure, freedom, and productivity. Several sample items are provided below:

1. I have the freedom to decide how I am going to Carry Out My Projects.
2. I feel little Pressure to meet someone else's specifications in how I do my work.
3. I have the freedom to Decide What Project(s) I am going to do.
4. In my daily work environment, I feel a Sense of Control over my own work and my own ideas.

Participants are asked to rate the items based on a four-point Likert scale (i.e., Never = 1, Sometimes = 2, Often = 3, Always = 4). Higher scores are correlated with higher levels of creativity.

Another similar measure is the Creative Environment Perceptions scale (Mayfield & Mayfield, 2010), which has nine items (see below) and can be used to measure three aspects of an organization' creative environment (i.e., creativity support, creativity blocks, and work characteristics).

1. My supervisor encourages me to be creative.
2. My work group is supportive of new ways of doing things.
3. My organization encourages me to work creatively.
4. I have the resources I need to do my job.
5. My work is challenging.
6. I have control over how I do my work.
7. My organization's politics make it difficult to be creative.
8. My organization's policies impede spontaneity in the workplace.
9. It is difficult to be creative with the work deadlines I have.

Respondents can answer the above questions by selecting one of the five options—strongly disagree, disagree, neutral, agree, and strongly agree. One concern about this instrument is that it is very short, and more solid evidence is needed to support its validity.

Conclusion

Conventional wisdom holds that creativity is difficult if not impossible to assess, and that existing measures are marked by low levels of reliability and validity. Unfortunately, these biases often find their way into the academic literature, which does a disservice to the many scholars and educators who have developed high-quality strategies for assessing several aspects of creativity. In this Hot Topic, we have provided a sample of creativity measures and resources for you to continue exploring this intriguing topic.

Recommended Readings

Kaufman, J. C., Plucker, J. A., & Baer, J. (2008). *Essentials of creativity assessment*. New York, NY: Wiley.

Plucker, J. A., & Makel, M. C. (2010). Assessment of creativity. In R. J. Sternberg & J. C. Kaufman (Eds.), *The Cambridge handbook of creativity* (pp. 48–73). New York, NY: Cambridge.

Carson, S. H., Peterson, J. B., & Higgins, D. M. (2005). Reliability, validity, and factor structure of the Creative Achievement Questionnaire. *Creativity Research Journal, 17*, 37–50.

Gough, H. G. (1979). A creative personality scale for the Adjective Check List. *Journal of Personality and Social Psychology, 37*, 1398–1405.

The Torrance Tests of Creative Thinking (appropriate for first graders through adults)— http://www.ststesting.com/2005giftttct.html

KEYS to Creativity and Innovation—http://www.ccl.org/Leadership/assessments/keysoverview.aspx

References

Amabile, T. M. (1982). The social psychology of creativity: A Consensual Assessment Technique. *Journal of Personality and Social Psychology, 43*, 997–1013.

Amabile, T. M., Conti, R., Coon, H., Lazenby, J., & Herron, M. (1996). Assessing the work environment for creativity. *The Academy of Management Journal, 39*, 1154–1184.

Amabile, T. M., & Gryskiewicz, N. (1989). The Creative Environment Scales: The Work Environment Inventory. *Creativity Research Journal, 2*, 231–254.

Arundel, A., & Smith, K. (2013). History of the Community Innovation Survey. In F. Gault (Ed.), *Handbook of innovation indicators and measurement* (pp. 60–87). Cheltenham, England: Edward Elgar.

Baer, J. (1998). The case for domain specificity of creativity. *Creativity Research Journal, 11*, 173–177.

Baer, J., & McKool, S. (2009). Asssessing creativity using the Consensual Assessment. In C. Schreiner (Ed.), *Handbook of assessment technologies, methods, and applications in higher education* (pp. 65–77). Hershey, PA: IGI Global.

Carson, S. (2006, April). *Creativity and mental illness.* Invitational panel discussion hosted by Mind Matters Consortium, Yale University, New Haven, CT.

Carson, S. H., Peterson, J. B., & Higgins, D. M. (2005). Reliability, validity, and factor structure of the Creative Achievement Questionnaire. *Creativity Research Journal, 17,* 37–50.

Collings, D. G., & Mellahi, K. (2009). Strategic talent management: A review and research agenda. *Human Resource Management Review, 19,* 304–313.

Crespi, G., & Peirano, F. (2007, May). *Measuring innovation in Latin America: What we did, where we are and what we want to do.* Paper presented at United Nations University and Maastricht Social and Economic Research and Training Institute on Innovation and Technology (UNU-MERIT) Conference on Micro Evidence on Innovation in Developing Countries, Maastricht.

Csikszentmihalyi, M. (1999). Implications of a systems perspective for the study of creativity. In R. J. Sternberg (Ed.), *Handbook of creativity* (pp. 313–335). Cambridge, England: Cambridge University Press.

Feist, G. J. (1998). A meta-analysis of personality in scientific and artistic creativity. *Personality and Social Psychology Review, 2,* 290–309.

Feist, G. J. (2005). Domain-specific creativity in the physical science. In J. C. Kaufman & J. Baer (Eds.), *Creativity across domains: Faces of the muse* (pp. 123–137). Mahwah, NJ: Lawrence Erlbaum.

Gough, H. G. (1979). A creative personality scale for the Adjective Check List. *Journal of Personality and Social Psychology, 37,* 1398–1405.

Greenan, N., & Lorenz, E. (2013). Developing harmonized measures of the dynamics of organizations and work. In F. Gault (Ed.), *Handbook of innovation indicators and measurement* (pp. 247–278). Cheltenham, England: Edward Elgar.

Hocevar, D. (1979, April). *The development of the Creative Behavior Inventory.* Paper presented at the annual meeting of the Rocky Mountain Psychological Association. (ERIC Document Reproduction Service No. ED170350)

Hocevar, D. (1981). Measurement of creativity: Review and critique. *Journal of Personality Assessment, 45,* 450–464.

Hocevar, D., & Bachelor, P. (1989). A taxonomy and critique of measurements used in the study of creativity. In J. A. Glover, R. R. Ronning, & C. R. Reynolds (Eds.), *Handbook of creativity* (pp. 53–75). New York, NY: Plenum Press.

Kaufman, J. C., Baer, J., & Cole, J. C. (2009). Expertise, domains, and the Consensual Assessment Technique. *Journal of Creative Behavior, 43*, 223–233.

Kaufman, J. C., & Beghetto, R. A. (2009). Beyond big and little: The Four C model of creativity. *Review of General Psychology, 13*, 1–12.

Kaufman, J. C., Plucker, J. A., & Baer, J. (2008). *Essentials of creativity assessment.* New York, NY: Wiley.

Kolodny, L. (2014, August 12). After *Shark Tank*, Packback seeded for 'pay-per-view' e-textbook rentals. *The Wall Street Journal.* Retrieved from http://blogs.wsj.com/venturecapital/2014/08/12/after-shark-tank-packback-seeded-for-pay-per-view-e-textbook-rentals

Lhuillery, S., Raffo, J., & Hamdan-Livramento, I. (2015). *Measurement of innovation.* Retrieved from http://www.researchgate.net/profile/Stephane_Lhuillery2/publication/283672126_Measurement_of_innovation/links/56433cab08ae451880a32703.pdf

Lorenz, E., & Lundvall, B. Å. (2011). Accounting for creativity in the European Union: A multi-level analysis of individual competence, labor market structure, and systems of education and training. *Cambridge Journal of Economics, 35*, 269–294.

Ludwig, A. M. (1995). *The price of greatness: Resolving the creativity and madness controversy.* New York, NY: Guilford Press.

Mayfield, M., & Mayfield, J. (2010). Developing a scale to measure the creative environments perceptions: A questionnaire for investigating garden variety creativity. *Creativity Research Journal, 22*, 162–169.

Mednick, S. A. (1962). The associative basis of the creative process. *Psychological Review, 69*, 220–232.

Mednick S. A. (1968). Remote Associates Test. *Journal of Creative Behavior, 2*, 213–214.

OECD. (1992). *Proposed guidelines for collecting and interpreting technological innovation data: Oslo manual.* Paris, France: OECD Publishing.

OECD. (1997). *Proposed guidelines for collecting and interpreting technological innovation data: Oslo manual.* Paris, France: OECD Publishing.

OECD. (2002). *The measurement of scientific and technical activities: Proposed standard practice for surveys of research and development.* Paris, France: OECD Publishing.

OECD. (2005). *Proposed guidelines for collecting and interpreting innovation data: Oslo manual.* Paris, France: OECD Publishing.

Oldham, G. R., & Cummings, A. (1996). Employee creativity: Personal and contextual factors at work. *The Academy of Management Journal, 39*, 607–634.

Plucker, J. A. (1998). Beware of simple conclusions: The case for content generality of creativity. *Creativity Research Journal, 11,* 179–182.

Plucker, J. A. (1999). Reanalyses of student responses to creativity checklists: Evidence of content generality. *The Journal of Creative Behavior, 33,* 126-137.

Plucker, J. A., & Beghetto, R. A. (2004). Why creativity is domain general, why it looks domain specific, and why the distinction doesn't matter. In R. J. Sternberg, E. L. Grigorenko, & J. L. Singer (Eds.), *Creativity: From potential to realization* (pp. 153–168). Washington, DC: American Psychological Association.

Plucker, J. A., Beghetto, R. A., & Dow, G. T. (2004). Why isn't creativity more important to educational psychologists? Potentials, pitfalls, and future directions in creativity research. *Educational Psychologist, 39,* 83–96.

Plucker, J. A., Qian, M., & Wang, S. (2011). Is originality in the eye of the beholder? Comparison of scoring techniques in the assessment of divergent thinking. *Journal of Creative Behavior, 45,* 1–22.

Qian, M. (2014). *Is creativity domain specific? Evidence from descriptive and explanatory item response theory models* (Doctoral dissertation). Retrieved from ProQuest Dissertations and Theses. (Accession Order No. 3612017)

Shi, B., Qian, M., Lu, Y., Plucker, J., & Lin, C. (2012). The relationship between migration and Chinese children's creative thinking. *Psychology of Aesthetics, Creativity, and the Arts, 6,* 106–111.

Simonton, D. K. (1994). *Greatness: Who makes history and why.* New York, NY: Guilford Press.

Sternberg, R. J., & Lubart, T. I. (1995). *Defying the crowd.* New York, NY: Free Press.

Torrance, E. P. (2008). *The Torrance Tests of Creative Thinking—Norms—Technical manual—Figural (streamlined) forms A and B.* Bensenville, IL: Scholastic Testing Service.

Wallach, M. A., & Kogan, N. (1965). *Modes of thinking in young children: A study of the creativity-intelligence distinction.* New York, NY: Holt, Rinehart and Winston.

CHAPTER 12

Creativity in Business

Richard Madden

Key Take-Aways

- Creativity is invaluable in business because it cuts through complexity, stimulates forward thinking, and drives differentiation in product and service design.
- Creativity is central to corporate and personal success because it is at the heart of storytelling, a talent that enables leaders to capture the imaginations and commitment of consumers and employees alike.
- Creativity is an intellectually and spiritually demanding discipline. Creative thinking can only be truly useful if it is pointed at a rigorously defined problem.
- Although they have their uses, brainstorms and workshops are not surefire ways to harness the creative energies of a diverse group of people.
- Physical environment is an important factor in harnessing a team's creative potential, as it encourages chance meetings and the sharing of insights and ideas.
- Educators can nurture the next generation of business leaders by teaching creativity as a core element of all subjects and encouraging their students to cultivate diverse interests, both inside and outside the classroom.

This chapter is a highly personal view of the importance of creativity in business, and of some of the practices that encourage it. It also touches on the role of educators in sowing the seeds of creativity in students who may soon be embarking on a career in business.

I add the huge caution that I am not a psychologist, I am a businessperson. And one who works in the only occasionally respectable field of advertising at that. In the process of assembling my thoughts, as in my professional life, I have plundered the work of academic psychologists whenever it might help me. Hopefully, I have not garbled their thinking too much in the process.

I begin by exploring the five reasons why I believe creativity is essential to the success of any modern commercial organization. I will then take a look at the ways in which I believe creativity can be encouraged in the workplace. I will close with a few observations about the implications of all this for educators.

Why Creativity Is Essential

The first and most important benefit that I believe creative thinking brings to business is its ability to cut through complexity. Deductive thinking is essential. But today there is so much material to absorb in order to reach a deduction that inductive thinking is more valuable than ever. As we are constantly told, we live in an age of "Big Data." Virtually every facet of human behavior is quantifiable. In fact, some observers have gone so far as to say that Big Data spells "the end of theory." Certainly, new statistical methods have an important role to play in pointing to unforeseen correlations between data items. However, almost invariably this only takes us to a "What." The really useful observation, the one from which value grows, is usually a "Why." That usually takes a degree of creative thinking.

Take the real example of a highly creative marketing analyst I had the pleasure of working with a few months ago. His client is a large, out-of-town hardware store. Their objective: sell more kitchen units. Our hero steeped himself in data from the store's loyalty card. This revealed some highly disparate patterns of customer behavior. Some shoppers would buy complete kitchens during a visit. Others would buy only a lightbulb or a small packet of birdseed.

Now why, he asked himself, would someone get in his or her car and drive 5 miles to buy a packet of birdseed? It's not as if it was some special kind of miracle birdseed. It was plain, simple, old-fashioned, run-of-the-mill birdseed. Then he had a creative insight. What if the birdseed buyers were visiting the store not to buy birdseed, but to browse the aisles for inspiration or seek information to inform a future, bigger purchase? What if they had just remembered on the spur of the moment that they were running low on birdseed and so grabbed some while they were there, perhaps even as a way to justify their trip?

The analyst went back to the data. Sure enough, people who only bought birdseed on one visit had a high propensity to purchase a kitchen on a subsequent occasion. Birdseed buyers were actually highly valuable future customers. Based on this creative leap, the analyst was able to recommend that the store write to birdseed buyers and make them a money-off offer on top-of-the-line kitchens. The result was that more of the birdseed buyers bought kitchens sooner and spent more when they did.

The next benefit of creative thinking over mere deduction is that it looks forward rather than merely backward. One of many overused phrases in business is the expression "Driving by looking in the rear-view mirror." An occasional glance in the mirror is of course an essential part of safe driving. However, while I can find no academic source for this assertion, it seems reasonable to suggest that looking at the road ahead correlates strongly with success in the field of safe driving.

I currently help manage the advertising for Britain's biggest supermarket chain. The company recently experienced a reversal of fortune when its profits collapsed and its stock fell dramatically. The reasons for this were manifold and purely coincidental with me starting to work for them. The main cause of the company's fall from grace was a poor decision in its store planning a few years earlier. It was justly proud of its loyalty card, which tracks every purchase made by 70% of its customers. The data is so rich that an apocryphal story has it that the store is able to identify that a customer is pregnant before she knows herself. Analysis of these data showed a continued customer preference for large, out of town stores.

Unfortunately, this backward-looking behavioral data was not predictive of a seismic shift in the way people shop for groceries in the UK. Over the next few years, customer behaviors polarized. Online shopping became the way people buy large, bulky dry goods. Smaller town center stores meanwhile grew in popularity as customers got into the habit of buying their fresh produce and prepared meals more or less daily on their way home from work. Soon, the financial press was full of artfully composed photographs of my client's deserted out-of-town superstores. The rest is history.

Meanwhile, the highly creative CEO of one of the UK's smaller supermarket brands was reaping the rewards of having purchased the town center sites previously eschewed by his largest competitor. Soon his company was the fastest-growing supermarket chain in Britain, and he was lauded on the front pages of every business magazine. It was not so much that he had taken a gamble (the sites were going ridiculously cheap, so the stakes were not that great). It was that he had not become a prisoner on the deductive analysis of retrospective behavioral data. Instead, he had observed an emerging trend and asked himself "What if?"

The third benefit of creative thinking in business is the unfair advantage it can give firms in the creation of differentiated products and services. "Differentiate or die" is a frequently quoted business adage. In an age of bewildering plenty, the truism about the better mousetrap still holds true when it comes to the design of products and, increasingly, of services too. Especially now that expert product reviews are merely a few clicks away.

In designing these better mousetraps, creative thinking is arguably more important than ever. Take the example of cars, a consumer durable I have spent much of my life advertising. Years ago, it was very easy to distinguish one make from another. Now their designs are all modeled using the same software, which operate using the same formula for optimizing aerodynamics, interior space, and so on. It is therefore inevitable that even cars from different manufacturers will tend to look the same.

Likewise, computer-aided flexible manufacturing has compressed product life cycles. The length of time for which a car's features will remain unique has reduced dramatically. Just look at the speed with which the features of a new top-of-the-line Lexus or Mercedes-Benz appear in mass-market cars from Ford and GM. It used to take decades. Now the time is measured in years, or less. Creative thinking can enable businesses to create more lasting competitive advantage than mere product optimization alone can achieve. Consider Toyota's lateral shift to hybrid drive, for instance, or Tesla's radical move into full electric vehicles.

There is a fascinating debate in business circles over the competing strategies propounded by W. Chan Kim and Renée Mauborgne (2005) in their book *Blue Ocean Strategy* and by Patrick Barwise and Sean Meehan (2004) in their book *Simply Better*. The former argued that differentiation is best achieved through dramatic, disruptive, and creative reframings of entire markets. A classic example here is, of course, Apple. The latter make the case that successful differentiation is simply the result of meeting the needs of the existing category user more effectively. Arguably the revival of the Ford Motor Company under Alan Mulally is a good example of this approach.

In my experience, both strategies have their merits, and both strategies require creative thinking, not just the former. Although it is easy to see that disruptive Blue Ocean thinking demands a creative mindset, so too does a Simply Better approach. The reason is that to meet the needs of users requires more than simply excellent research and analysis. It demands the ability to empathize, to think oneself into the shoes of another person. This in itself is a creative act, and one that few businesspeople force themselves to perform nearly often enough.

Much of my work in advertising involves the creation of differentiation where there is none. In the words of the Pointy-Haired Boss in a classic Dilbert cartoon, "Our product is no better and no cheaper than the competition. That only leaves fraud, which I'd like you to refer to as Marketing." It is a cynical and not entirely accurate point of view of contemporary business practice. However, it conveniently brings me to the fourth reason why I believe creativity is important in business: It helps you tell compelling stories that capture the imagination of the people you would like to choose your product.

Ever since that marketing guru Aristotle first codified the principles of rhetoric, it has been an accepted truth that decisions are influenced as much by emotion as by logic. Indeed, the theory of cognitive dissonance suggests that logic is often a mere afterthought deployed to rationalize a decision that we have already taken emotionally.

In advertising, the campaigns that win creative awards have also been shown to be the most effective in generating demand for a client's product, or in maintaining its price premium. There is a reason for this. In his book *Thinking, Fast and Slow*, the Nobel-winning psychologist Daniel Kahneman (2011) described the two kinds of thinking processes that humans have evolved to use in our waking lives. System One thinking is always on. While using System One, the brain requires little energy. So it's the system we use most of the time. It's a more or less autonomous process, well suited for boring tasks like driving along an empty freeway. By contrast, System Two thinking happens when the brain is fully engaged on a demanding mental task, like driving a race car. It demands a lot of energy, which is why most of us try to avoid it as much as possible.

Neuroscientists make a strong argument that "creative" advertising is more effective because it plants stronger memory structures in our brains while we are thinking in low-engagement System One mode (Heath, 2012). Such advertising tells a captivating story, amuses us, or moves us. It does not rely solely on rational persuasion, if at all. The memory structures that this kind of advertising implants are triggered the next time we are out shopping, resulting in the advertised brand appearing in our mental short-list of options to choose. Advertising strategists call this *mental availability*.

So creativity is of prime importance in marketing and advertising. However, I have left what I believe is creativity's principal contribution to commercial success until last, and that is the importance of imagination in the origination and communication of visionary corporate goals. In their book *Built to Last*, Stanford academics Jim Collins and Jerry Porras (1994) show how companies that have a clear and compelling vision at their heart have consistently delivered higher and longer-lasting shareholder value than their less visionary peers.

There are two main reasons for this. The first is that, as we have seen, truly creative thinking is as much a guide for the future as much as it is a rallying cry for the present. Steve Jobs's mission of making "tools for creative people" allowed his business to expand beyond the world of computing into entertainment and communication. However, at the same time it imposed clear limits on the behavior of the Apple brand—with the result that I doubt we will see Apple making control systems for nuclear power plants at any point in the future. (Although nothing is impossible.)

The second reason why visionary companies tend to be "built to last" is that the ability to create a compelling vision strongly correlates with the quality most management theorists characterize as "leadership" (see also Royston and Reiter-Palmon, this volume). To compel people to invest their physical and emotional energy toward a collective objective requires an inspiring vision, and to lay out an inspiring vision is in itself a creative act. Such a vision may nod to the past, but it expresses an aspiration to shape the future. And only the creative imagination lets us see what might be, rather than merely what is.

Encouraging Creativity in the Workplace

So far, I have described the five reasons why I believe creativity is essential to the success of any modern commercial organization. Now I would like to touch on the four practices that I have found most effective in inculcating creative thinking in businesses. Most of these practices are teachable. For this reason, the following section leads naturally to a discussion of the role of educators in establishing the habits of creative thinking that their students may find useful in any future commercial career.

First, it is essential to realize that creativity is as hard a form of work as management accounting or process engineering. It requires discipline and application. It is not an easy way out for people who find physics difficult. My friend and academic creativity expert Jonathan Plucker says it best when he defines creativity as "the production of a perceptible product that is novel and useful" (Plucker, Beghetto & Dow, 2004, p. 90; see also Dow, this volume). There are a lot of tough-minded words in that one simple phrase; *product* and *useful* being two that especially stand out. Note the absence of words like *beautiful* or *inspiring*. Creative artifacts may have these attributes, but utility is Plucker's core evaluative criterion.

So creativity is a tough-minded business. And the people who do it best are often pretty tough-minded too. Creative people, as often noted by Plucker, do not have to have "long hair and dance around meadows wearing crystals." They can be jocks with engineering degrees who do not hang around art galleries much and have little tolerance for experimental jazz. As you will learn elsewhere in this book, the originator of much modern thinking on creativity was a man named E. Paul Torrance. According to his biographer, he was first inspired to study creativity when he served on the staff of the U.S. military's survival school (Millar, 1995).

He was impressed by how fighter pilots—jocks with buzz cuts and thousand-yard stares—became remarkably creative when abandoned in the middle of the woods. Even though this was at the start of their course and they had received minimal survival training, they invented novel ways to filter water, catch food, shelter themselves from the weather, and so on. Torrance's fighter pilots came from a military culture not renowned for its liberality of thought. Intellectually, they had "hard" engineering backgrounds. Yet they showed an impressive ability to make original, useful things.

Thinking creatively is hard work. And perhaps the hardest work occurs at the start of the creative journey. Which brings me to my second success factor for creative thinking in business: the practice of clearly defining at the outset the problem that creativity is being asked to solve.

In my own field of advertising, the creative process begins with some highly rational, deductive, and often binary thinking. Is the market for the product growing, static, or shrinking? Will the most advantage be gained by growing the market, or by stealing a bigger share of that market? Are we addressing people who are in the market for the product now, or those who may have a need for the product only at some future point?

By doing this hard work upfront, advertising strategists try to define as single-mindedly as possible what will make the creative product "useful." This helps the rest of the creative team work out exactly where to focus their limited time. Interestingly, my engineer friends tell me they go through a similar process at the start of a project. They break the challenge down into a series of discrete problems that need to be solved in order achieve the entire end result. A good example of this approach is the so-called "Five Whys?" technique developed by Toyota. First, the general problem is observed. This is achieved by having a junior engineer stand and watch the problematic part of the process for several days, presumably in some sort of Zen trance. Then the rest of the engineering team asks itself "Why is this happening?" five times until the root cause is defined. This is the problem that the team then attacks using creative thinking.

My third observation about the practices that encourage creativity is potentially a rather controversial one. For decades, businesses have relied on the ritual of the "brainstorm" to generate avenues of approach to solving problems. The brainstorm, and its grown-up sibling, the "workshop," can be successful in developing a broad range of creative ideas in a limited time. However, it is my view that they are by no means a creative panacea, and on more than one occasion I have seen them do more creative harm than creative good.

Brainstorming—the act of gathering a group of people to attack a problem through the spontaneous generation of ideas—was popularized by advertising man James Webb Young (1965) in his book *A Technique for Producing Ideas*. In the right circumstances, group idea-generation sessions can be very fruitful. However, in many businesses, those circumstances can prove elusive. A large number of us are natural self-editors when it comes to exposing early, ill-formed thoughts in public. This is especially true when there are people senior to us in the room. In some cultures, someone who spontaneously voices their ideas can be seen as pushy, or worse.

Furthermore, there is the simple biological fact that some people's creativity is more fertile early in the morning, while others are more creatively fluent in the evening. The expectation that everyone in a group can be on peak creative form at the same time of day is naive at best. Then there is the sad truth that many workshops take place not to generate ideas at all, but to build consensus around a course of action already decided on by management. Rather than opening up thinking, this kind of workshop is used to close it down. This is an especially pernicious perversion of the creative process, as it can render colleagues cynical about the very idea of free creative thinking for the remainder of their tenure in the firm.

A good leader will come to understand the thinking styles of his or her colleagues and adapt their process of collective idea-generation accordingly. Some contributors to the process will be more than happy to broadcast their first thoughts. Others will prefer to share their ideas more anonymously through a sticky note exercise. Still others will want to think about the problem overnight and respond with their ideas in a more considered way, maybe in the form of a prose argument or a diagram.

If workshops do not always encourage creative thinking, what else can a business do to increase the creativity of its people? The first and most helpful course of action may be to relocate the bathrooms. Let me explain.

A while ago, my agency inhabited a building that was spread across two floors. Specifically the first floor and the fifth floor. As well as the sheer inefficiency of the arrangement (not helped by a very unreliable elevator), the quality of our work suffered. The kind of chance meetings that naturally occur between people from different departments ceased to happen. Cultural synapses ceased to function.

When we moved to an office where we were all located together on one big floor, our creative work noticeably improved. It became natural for people from different departments to say hello as they made their way to the kitchen, or, yes, the bathroom. On the way back, you would often find that you'd had an idea to share with the person you'd encountered earlier.

I have a friend who works at Google's office in London. He invited me there for lunch a few months ago. After a delicious meal in one of the several Google restaurants in the building, I offered to pay. He laughed. "If you work here, you don't need to pay. It's all free!" he boasted. Perhaps Google has realized that such generosity turns its staffers into lifers. Although maybe there is another reason for the policy: My friend says that rather than rushing out to grab a sandwich and returning to their desks for a solitary lunch, Google people sit down to lunch together. Conversation flows. Chance encounters happen.

I have always been fascinated by the Manhattan Project, the crash program of scientific development that resulted in the world's first atomic bombs. In particular, I was curious the way its leading scientist, Robert Oppenheimer, had been able to get such a diverse group of specialists to crack such a complicated theoretical and engineering problem in such a short amount of time. My curiosity took me to Los Alamos, NM, one cold day in November. It was here that the bombs were designed and assembled. On the drive up to the desolate mesa on which the town sits, one of the principal reasons started to become clear to me. To maintain security, Oppenheimer and his military counterpart General Leslie Groves had insisted on a remote location for the project. This had the effect of concentrating all of the scientists in one place, miles from the nearest city.

Contemporary accounts of Los Alamos are not flattering to the place. It was cold and rainy. The accommodation was basic, to say the least. People ate together in one large mess hall. It was like a college, but a college on steroids. There was nowhere else to go. Los Alamos became a creative pressure cooker. Its inhabitants hated it. But the environment brought them together into a kind of critical mass. Add the initiator of a clearly defined set of problems to solve, and a self-sustaining chain reaction of creativity occurred.

Preparing Students for Creativity in Business

So far, we have discussed the five reasons why I believe creative thinking is central to the success of businesses. I have also offered four observations on how businesses can encourage the practice of creativity amongst their employees. Now I would like to consider, albeit briefly, the role of educators in preparing their students for careers in a commercial world that places increasing value on an individual's ability to create, in Plucker et al.'s (2004) words, products that are novel and useful in a specific context.

This is dangerous ground for me, as I am not an educator. Both my parents were teachers, and they were always critical of those outside the profession who felt compelled to tell them what they should be doing, based on only the slenderest evidence, or often none at all. So I will do my best to tiptoe through this minefield and ask for forgiveness in advance in case my clumsiness touches off any unintended explosions.

My first request to educators, and perhaps more importantly to administrators and legislators, is to recognize that there is an economic imperative behind teaching creativity as much as there is a philosophical and humanitarian one. Nations are as reliant on the ability of their citizens to create new forms of value as businesses are on the creative skills of their employees. This is something the Chinese government has realized. Long derided as unimaginative and as obsessed with narrow factual learning as Dickens's Thomas Gradgrind, Chinese educators are now being encouraged to embrace the teaching of creativity and critical thinking. So much so that creative education is a key pillar of China's 2010 educational 10-year plan.

As I was growing up, the emphasis of my schooling was on rational thinking and deductive logic. I am grateful for this: This education stretched my inherited allocation of intelligence to the point where I can just about keep up with some of my brighter colleagues. So I was fascinated to read about the Torrance kids, a cohort of school-leavers followed over many years by E. Paul Torrance (he of survival school fame). Drawing on evidence from this famous longitudinal study, researchers have concluded that the measured creativity of a school student is a more accurate predictor of future career success than his or her measured intelligence (Millar, 2002; Plucker, 1999). Perhaps those who are responsible for the design of school and college curricula should be more familiar with Torrance and this classic study.

My next request of educators is to familiarize themselves with some of the proven techniques for inculcating the habits of creative thought that are covered elsewhere in this book. However, I do have a concern about these techniques. They sometimes appear to encourage a position of "That's enough about history or physics. Now we're going to learn about creativity." By teaching creativity as a separate topic, educators may be at risk of encouraging their students to see creative thinking as a specialty, rather than as something that should be inherent in their approach to all academic subjects. An oft-repeated mantra of educators of my parents' generation was that "all teachers, irrespective of their subject, should be teachers of math and English." The same could and should be said of creative thinking.

My final suggestion to educators, and their students, is to teach broadly and to encourage curiosity in a broad range of subjects, not all of them traditionally considered worthy of classroom time. Because new ideas often result from the fusion of previously unrelated concepts, creativity surely favors the well-stocked mind. The most creative people I have known are also the broadest in their range of interests and passions. I am often reminded of Steve Jobs's famous 2005 Stanford University commencement address, when he said that one of his most important educational experiences was a course he audited in calligraphy and typography. It was this that critically influenced his insistence that the interface of Apple computers should always be aesthetically elegant and beautifully simple.

Conclusion

In this short chapter, I have attempted to provide arguments for the importance of creative thinking in business. I have also made some observations on the practices that encourage creativity to thrive or perish within organizations. I have also overstepped my competence in making a few suggestions for educators based on my experience as a businessperson. In closing, I would just like to say how much I envy you the chance to learn more about the theory and practice of creativity and to convey that knowledge to the next generation of business leaders—which is why I cannot wait to read the other chapters of this book.

Recommended Readings

Amabile, T., & Kramer, S. (2011). *The progress principle: Using small wins to ignite joy, engagement and creativity at work*. Boston, MA: Harvard Business Review Press.

Bennis, W., & Biederman, P. W. (1998). *Organizing genius: The secrets of creative collaboration*. Reading, MA: Addison-Wesley.

Catmull, E. (2014). *Creativity, Inc.: Overcoming the unseen forces that stand in the way of true inspiration*. New York, NY: Random House.

Kay, J. (2011). *Obliquity: Why our goals are best achieved indirectly*. London, England: Profile Books.

Hegarty, J. (2014). *Hegarty on creativity: There are no rules*. London, England: Thames & Hudson.

Trott, D. (2014). *Predatory thinking*. London, England: Pan Macmillan.

References

Barwise, P., & Meehan, S. (2004). *Simply better: Winning and keeping customers by delivering what matters most.* Boston, MA: Harvard Business School Press.

Collins, J. C., & Porras, J. I. (1994). *Built to last: Successful habits of visionary companies.* New York, NY: Harper Business.

Heath, R. (2012). *Seducing the subconscious: The psychology of emotional influence in advertising.* Malden, MA: Wiley-Blackwell.

Kahneman, D. (2011). *Thinking, fast and slow.* New York, NY: Farrar, Straus and Giroux.

Kim, W. C., & Mauborgne, R. (2005). *Blue ocean strategy: How to create uncontested market space and make the competition irrelevant.* Boston, MA: Harvard Business School Press.

Millar, G. W. (1995). *E. Paul Torrance—The creativity man: An authorized biography.* Norwood, NJ: Ablex Publishing.

Millar, G. W. (2002). *The Torrance kids at mid-life: Selected case studies of creative behavior.* Westport, CT: Ablex Publishing.

Plucker, J. A. (1999). Is the proof in the pudding? Reanalyses of Torrance's (1958 to present) longitudinal study data. *Creativity Research Journal, 12,* 103–114.

Plucker, J. A., Beghetto, R. A., & Dow, G. T. (2004). Why isn't creativity more important to educational psychologists? Potentials, pitfalls, and future directions in creativity research. *Educational Psychologist, 39,* 83–96.

Young, J. W. (1965). *A technique for producing ideas.* Chicago, IL: Advertising Publications.

CHAPTER 13

Leadership and Creativity

What Leaders Can Do to Facilitate Creativity in Organizations

Ryan P. Royston and Roni Reiter-Palmon

Key Take-Aways

This chapter reviews what leaders can do to promote individual and team creativity in order to provide efficient and innovative solutions to problems. Many challenges arise when leading creative teams. Creative teams are often made up of individuals with a wide range of experiences, backgrounds, and opinions and may have vastly different views on how to approach a problem. Leaders serve many critical functions in promoting creativity in teams, including:

- Playing a critical part of helping teams capitalize on diverse perspectives when they effectively manage team interactions.
- Facilitating creativity when they encourage information sharing, create an environment of psychological safety and trust where team members feel safe in providing ideas and solutions, provide support for creativity, and encourage interaction, collaboration, and participation.
- Influencing team creativity by managing the relationship between their team and the environment outside of the team by ensuring adequate resources and collaboration with outside sources.

- Strengthening individual and team creativity by serving as champions of innovation and actively advocating resources to support innovative ideas.

Although leading individuals and teams for creativity poses many challenges, today's organizational leaders are also a critical element influencing and promoting creative and innovative outcomes.

Leadership and Creativity

Organizations often face complex problems where simple or routine solutions will not work. Instead, these problems require creative or innovative ideas or solutions. The 21st century has seen a dramatic increase in global expansion and competition, economic fluctuations, and increasingly complex use of technology. These changes have forced organizations to adapt to new environments, anticipate changes in consumer demands, and better predict future challenges. Creativity and innovation are also critical to success in most other organizations including nonprofits, educational institutions, and social service agencies. For instance, creativity may be required in order to best use limited space on a college campus or in adapting public health educational materials for use in other countries. These challenges require organizations to innovate and be creative (Ford & Gioia, 1995; Shalley, Zhou, & Oldham, 2004; West, Hirst, Richter, & Shipton, 2004).

Most often, these obstacles and challenges are too complicated to be solved by a single individual, or even a team of individuals with similar expertise and backgrounds. Thus, teams that are more diverse in their backgrounds and experience are better able to overcome challenges (Kozlowski & Bell, 2008). Teams are increasingly used by leaders to solve problems and overcome challenges faced by the organization because teams allow diverse perspectives, increased knowledge, and expertise (Harvey, 2014; Kozlowski & Bell, 2008; Mesmer-Magnus & DeChurch, 2009). However, these teams face many challenges to being creative, which is why the leader's role is critical to the team's success. Leaders ensure creativity in teams by establishing an environment where individuals feel safe contributing their ideas and solutions, promoting an environment conducive to creativity and innovation, facilitating effective communication and collaboration, and managing conflict that might arise between individuals involved in the creative process. Further, leaders manage interactions between the team and the external environment by ensuring teams have sufficient resources, providing access to additional sources of information, protecting teams from negative organizational influences, and championing innovative initiatives.

Managing Team Interactions

Ensuring a team is composed of diverse individuals is one important way in which leaders can increase creativity in team settings. However, while teams made up of individuals with diverse backgrounds, experiences, and perspectives tend to show enhanced creativity and innovation, these differences also provide many challenges in how team members communicate and approach problems (Ilgen, Hollenbeck, Johnson, & Jundt, 2005). Leaders play a critical role in helping teams utilize the benefits of diversity, effectively promote task conflict, and alleviate instances of relational conflict.

Helping the Team Take Advantage of Diversity

When discussing diversity, it is important to differentiate between demographic diversity and functional diversity. Demographic diversity refers to differences among individuals such as ethnic identity, race, gender, age, or nationality. Functional diversity refers to differences such as job-related skills, ability, and knowledge, which are more relevant to performance (Milliken, Bartel, & Kurtzberg, 2003).

Research on demographic diversity in teams suggests that it does not influence creativity and innovation (Hülsheger, Anderson, & Salgado, 2009; Paletz, Peng, Erez, & Maslach, 2004). However, functional diversity has been shown to influence team creativity. Past research has shown a positive relationship between functional diversity and team creativity (Hülsheger et al., 2009). Teams made up of individuals with a variety of backgrounds, skills, and experiences tend to show higher levels of performance than teams that are made up of individuals who share similar experience and knowledge (Fay, Borrill, Amir, Haward, & West, 2006; Keller, 2001). Further, teams composed of individuals that possess different perspectives, knowledge, abilities, and experiences can share their different perspectives with others, thereby allowing the team to conceptualize and evaluate the problem from multiple viewpoints and develop a more comprehensive and creative solution to the problem at hand (Cronin & Weingart, 2007; McLeod, Lobel, & Cox, 1996).

Leaders can influence the level of functional diversity in team problem-solving efforts by choosing individuals who demonstrate a wide range of knowledge, expertise, and skills. However, selecting a functionally diverse team is the easy part. The challenge for leaders is to make sure that the team effectively utilizes the experience and knowledge possessed by the team. Leaders can influence the association between functional diversity and team creativity by promoting an environment where information can be freely exchanged, viewpoints can be discussed, and differing opinions and viewpoints are valued by the leader and the team. Mitchell et al. (2015) found that leader inclusiveness, or when leaders encourage and value differing points of view, increased team performance in functionally diverse teams because it facilitates a sense of shared team identity. Additionally, it diminished some of the negative effects of perceived individual differences in statuses. When leaders create an environment of open sharing of experience and perspectives, teams are better able to take advantage of the knowledge, skills, and expertise shared among team members.

Encouraging Receptivity of Ideas and Perspectives

Similarly, leaders play a critical role in making sure team members are open and receptive to ideas and perspectives offered by other members of the team. Hoever, van Knippenberg, van Ginkel, and Barkema (2012) found that one way leaders can facilitate a climate of receptivity, thereby increasing team creativity, is to encourage perspective taking, in which team members try to understand where others are coming from when they make suggestions. When teams were encouraged to consider the thoughts and motives of other team members, they tended to show increased creativity relative to homogeneous teams; conversely, when there was no such encouragement from the leader, diverse teams showed the same level of creativity as homogeneous teams (Hoever et al., 2012). However, perspective taking may not naturally occur in diverse teams, thus leaders are in a unique position to facilitate perspective taking by ensuring that team members are respectful of others' ideas and remain receptive of shared perspectives. Not only does this action lead to more creative outcomes in teams, but consideration of others' viewpoints can reduce team conflict, which can be harmful to creativity.

Effectively Managing Conflict

Conflict is frequently observed in teams and in organizations when individuals of differing views must work together to achieve a goal. Team conflict can be viewed in two ways—either as relationship-oriented or task-oriented conflict (Jehn, Greer, Levine, & Szulanski, 2008). Task-oriented conflict refers to when individuals disagree on the problem or challenge and often has a positive relationship with creativity (Yong, Sauer, & Mannix, 2014). In contrast, relational-oriented conflict refers to disagreements among a team based on personal beliefs, preferences, or other characteristics and often hampers creativity (Jehn, 1995; Jehn & Mannix, 2001).

When teams experience relational conflict, creativity and innovation suffer because of team members feeling that contributions will be overly criticized by others, a lack of trust among others, negative competitiveness, and a loss of commitment to team goals (Jehn et al., 2008). Team members perceiving relational conflict often feel the team environment is neither safe to share their own ideas and perspectives, nor safe to provide constructive criticism or feedback to others' ideas, both of which are critically important to increasing creativity. If ideas will be met with criticism or ridicule, individuals often resist sharing ideas or cooperating with one another, particularly among team members who might already be susceptible to feelings of anxiety or fear of undue criticism (Chen, 2006; Desivilya, Somech, & Lidgoster, 2010). Further, perceived relational conflict generally leads team members to feel negative emotions such as anxiety, stress, fear, and frustration, thus limiting their creative potential and progress on team goals (Chen, 2006). When team members perceive high relational conflict, they are also less likely to engage in positive conflict management tactics, such as attempting to see one another's perspectives, gaining a shared understanding of differences, or attempting to work out a solution that fulfills all team members' needs (Desivilya et al., 2010).

Task conflict occurs when team members can question and discuss differing approaches to solving a problem and incorporate these differing viewpoints into the most appropriate and comprehensive solution (Kurtzberg & Amabile, 2001). Thus, task conflict may be beneficial in early stages of problem solving as it allows more aspects of the problem to be considered, and any differences in perspective can be discussed to make sure the team is approaching the problem using the best strategy (Kurtzberg & Amabile, 2001; Mannix & Neale, 2005). Additionally, when teams experience some task conflict, it serves to increase critical thinking about the problem and ensures a complete solution is developed (Jehn, 1995). Further, a meta-analysis of the relationship between task conflict, relational conflict, and team performance showed that task conflict appears to be more strongly tied to performance in teams that experience less relational conflict (de Wit, Greer, & Jehn, 2012).

Some aspects of the team climate play a critical role in determining whether task conflict will help or hinder creativity. For instance, task conflict that occurs in a climate of participative safety, where individuals feel comfortable sharing ideas and providing open evaluation of others' ideas, often shows a positive relationship with team creativity (Fairchild & Hunter, 2014). Further, task conflict facilitates creativity when it occurs in a collaborative manner and the conflict focuses on the task at hand, instead of when aimed at individuals (DeChurch, Mesmer-Magnus, & Doty, 2013). Focus on the task prevents task conflict from turning into relational conflict. However, it should be noted that too much task conflict may lose its benefits to teams. Farh, Lee, and Farh (2010) found that task conflict had a curvilinear relationship with team creativity, meaning that moderate levels of task conflict were most strongly related to team creativity, while low levels and high levels of task conflict did not show as strong of a relationship with team creativity.

There are a number of ways in which leaders can promote appropriate task conflict while also reducing relational conflict. Teams that are made up of diverse individuals may have very different views on how to approach a problem and how they share information, thus leaders are in a critical position to monitor and facilitate appropriate communication (Fairchild & Hunter, 2014). Furthermore, creative individuals are often independent, competitive, and critical, making it more likely that these teams may see higher levels of conflict due to personality differences (Feist, 1998; Silvia, Kaufman, Reiter-Palmon, & Wigert, 2011). Leaders are responsible for creating an environment conducive to task conflict to promote idea generation and evaluation, while ensuring that relational conflict does not detract from the creative process. By creating an environment of safety, individuals know they can trust their leader and each other with their ideas and perspectives.

Furthermore, leaders are often looked to as a role model on appropriately handling conflict (Fairchild & Hunter, 2014). Leaders therefore can influence team conflict by setting expectations for appropriate interactions and ways to handle conflicts that arise between group members (Salas, Cooke, & Rosen, 2008). Lee, Lin, Huan, Huang, and Teng (2015) found that task interdependence tends to reduce relational conflict. Task interdependence requires individuals to collaborate to complete a task or reach a goal and leaders play a vital role in facilitating the team in working together to reach a goal. Additionally, leaders must ensure that there are appropriate levels of task conflict, as too high of levels are detrimental. This requires leaders to monitor communication and facilitate understanding of where each team member is coming from when making suggestions.

Support for Creativity and Creating a Climate for Creativity

Support for creativity and innovation is another critical way in which leaders can facilitate creativity. When employees feel that leaders support creativity, they are more likely to communicate openly and suggest new ideas, thus leading to greater creativity in groups (Scott & Bruce, 1994). Support for innovation has been shown to be one of the strongest predictors of creativity and innovation (Hülsheger et al., 2009) and has been shown to be a vital component to developing a climate for creativity (Amabile & Grykiewicz, 1989; Hunter, Bedell, & Mumford, 2007; Mathisen & Einarsen, 2004). When group members do not feel social support or encouragement from their leaders, they are less likely to take part in creative endeavors (Scott & Bruce, 1994). Leaders can provide the necessary support for creativity and innovation in several ways. Research has shown that transformational leadership, in which leaders concentrate on providing intellectual stimulation, individualized concern, and inspirational motivation to followers, creates a climate supportive of creativity and innovation (Chen, Farh, Campbell-Bush, Wu, & Wu, 2013; Elkins & Keller, 2003; Hirst, van Dick, & van Knippenberg, 2009). Leaders can demonstrate these transformational leader behaviors by responding to concerns and challenges in a positive and encouraging manner, thus motivating team members to engage in similar behaviors in their interactions with each other (Edmondson, 1999; Nijstad, Berger-Selman, & De Dreu, 2014). Transformational leaders also provide recognition for efforts, offer emotional support, appropriately monitor individual progress, include others in decision-making processes, and remain open and accessible to followers, thus facilitating creativity (Carmeli, Reiter-Palmon, & Ziv, 2010; Cheung & Wong, 2011; Denti & Hemlin, 2013).

Providing Feedback

Creative individuals can be sensitive to criticism, particularly when criticism appears in the early stages of idea generation (Gallucci, Middleton, & Kline, 2000). Thus, when leaders or other team members provide negative feedback early in the creative problem solving process, it may actually be detrimental to creative performance (Mumford, Longergan, & Scott, 2002). However, this does not mean that leaders need to refrain from criticism. It is important that constructive criticism is provided, and that employees understand that the goal is to improve the idea and facilitate creativity, not avoid new ideas. In addition to feeling support from the leader, team members must feel support for creativity among their team members (Chen et al., 2013). Leaders therefore have the responsibility to not only ensure that their own interactions with the team support creativity, but also that the team members support each other in being creative.

One way that leaders can also provide support to individuals is by monitoring their progress and providing support and feedback. Monitoring may take the form of providing feedback and evaluating a team's progress and outcomes. Research suggests that monitoring becomes more important as teams move from initial idea development and into implementation (Mumford et al., 2002). However, too much monitoring of subordinates hampers creativity (Choi et al., 2009; Shalley & Gilson, 2004; Zhou, 2003). Amabile, Schatzel, Moneta, and Kramer (2004) found that negative monitoring, such as too close of monitoring, was related to perceptions of less leader support.

Leader social skills also play an important role in how to deliver feedback and monitor, as well as how subordinates receive it. Leaders often have more experience than the teams they lead and can provide valuable feedback, but must be seen as attentive to team needs, open, and accessible in order for teams to accept feedback (Carmeli et al., 2010).

Promoting Collaboration

Leaders also create a climate that is conducive to creativity by facilitating effective collaboration between team members. Collaboration increases as team members are encouraged to participate in each phase of the problem-solving process. Collaboration is an important component to creativity because creative tasks are often complex, ambiguous, and require team members to be highly adaptive to changes in the team and the task (Burke et al., 2006; Janssens & Brett, 2006). Additionally, knowledge sharing among team members facilitates greater collaboration, but team members must feel that the environment is conducive to sharing their ideas without criticism and that their contributions will be valued by the leader and other team members. Team members may also be concerned about being negatively evaluated by either their leader or others in the team, which may decrease their participation and contribution of ideas (Reiter-Palmon, Wigert, & de Vreede, 2011). Team members may be hesitant to share ideas if they feel competitive with other individuals in the group or feel there is a risk that others on the team may steal their ideas and present them as their own (Kahai, Sosik, & Avolio, 2003). Similarly, information sharing as part of the collaborative process can be quickly halted if one team member dominates the discussion, thus preventing others from participating or contributing their ideas and perspectives. Leaders can encourage collaboration and information sharing by creating an environment where team members are willing to share ideas and knowledge, feel safe in contributing without negative consequences, feel that their ideas and perspectives will be valued, and feel empowered to participate in the problem-solving process. Further, leaders can ensure that all team members can participate in the discussion and that one member is not overly dominating or that other members avoid participating.

An important aspect of creating a climate for creativity is encouraging participation, which refers to how much effort each team member puts forth to complete a task (Kahai et al., 2003). Participation is vital to problem solving in creative teams because each team member possesses skills and knowledge that is necessary to appropriately and efficiently solve the problem. Thus, increased participation is related to team cooperation as ideas and contributions can be put forth and elaborated upon by others, thus integrating one another's knowledge and increasing the likelihood of problem solving (Hansen, Mors, & Løvås, 2005; Mathieu, Maynard, Rapp, & Gilson, 2008; Nijhof & Kommers, 1985). Work on organizational social networks has also shown that high levels of participation, information sharing, and turn-taking among team members bolsters outcomes and productivity in teams (Curhan & Pentland, 2007; Orbach, Demko, Doyle, Waber, & Pentland, 2015). Further, participation is necessary in order to turn ideas into products and results (De Dreu, Carsten, & West, 2001). Teams with high levels of participation assimilate knowledge and create a common core, thus increasing the team's ability to solve problems (Hansen et al., 2005). Leaders can encourage participation in teams by modeling open communication, providing recognition to individuals for their contributions, and ensuring that the team environment is conducive to idea sharing. Leaders should also monitor team communication to ensure that no one member dominates the conversation. Further, the leader may have to monitor communication to ensure team members are supportive of one another and encourage reticent team members to participate when needed (Farris, 1972; Paulus, Larey, & Dzindolet, 2001).

Trust and psychological safety are critical considerations in creating a climate of creativity (Barczak, Lassk, & Mulki, 2010; Carmeli, Sheaffer, Binyamin, Reiter-Palmon, & Shimoni, 2014; Kessel, Kratzer, & Shultz, 2012). Trust refers to each individual's perception that the team can accomplish goals, that the team is competent, and that team actions will not harm the individual (Ilgen et al., 2005). Psychological safety refers to a shared belief among all team members that the environment is safe for interpersonal risk-taking and a feeling of confidence that individuals will not be embarrassed, rejected, or punished for contributing their ideas (Edmondson, 1999).

Psychological safety ensures a sense of shared respect and trust among team members, thus encouraging information sharing, collaboration, and critical analysis of a problem because each team member feels his or her views and perspectives will be valued by others (Carmeli et al., 2014; Edmondson, 1999; Kessel et al., 2012). Psychological safety is also an important influence on whether teams will benefit from task conflict, while also reducing the risk of negative relational conflict (Bradley, Postlethwaite, Klotz, Hamdani, & Brown, 2012). Leaders who develop a sense of trust and safety in teams early on in team formation tend to see lower levels of negative conflict over the course of the team's lifespan. On the other hand, when leaders neglect to create an environment of psychological safety, team members withhold information and tend to interpret the actions of others in a negative way, leading to conflict and consequently, lower levels of creativity (Curşeu & Schruijer, 2010; Nicholson & West, 1988; West & Richter, 2008).

Another issue with lack of trust among team members or of trust in the leader is that negative experiences are often more powerful and long-lasting than positive experiences (Choi et al., 2009). It has been suggested that when individuals have a negative interaction with their leader, this single event can cancel out many of the past positive interactions an individual may have had with that leader (Baumeister, Bratslavsky, Finkenauer, & Vohs, 2001). In the same way, when individuals experience one incident in which the leader may not seem supportive, they may discount other instances in which the leader provided positive support. Thus, it is critical that leaders be perceptive of how they deliver feedback to individuals or teams.

Leaders can create a sense of psychological safety and trust among team members by promoting open communication where followers perceive it is safe to propose new ideas (Baer & Frese, 2003). Leaders also serve as a source of information for the team in how they should communicate (Salas et al., 2008). Therefore, leaders are in a critical position to role model information sharing, providing appropriate criticism, and ensuring contributions are welcomed and valued from each member. Leaders therefore are also responsible for ensuring that team members appropriately understand others' contributions and reach a shared understanding of the problem in an effort to work collaboratively (Reiter-Palmon, de Vreede, & de Vreede, 2013). When team member interactions become tense, leaders should facilitate positive resolutions to disagreements to ensure that relational conflict does not manifest (Reiter-Palmon et al., 2013).

Team members tend to be highly cognizant of how their leader responds to negative events, which forms their perceptions of the psychological safety climate (Salas et al., 2008). When leaders are regarded as fair, open, honest, caring, and trustworthy, this sets a positive reference for team member interactions and encourages information sharing, thus enhancing creativity in individuals (Ma, Cheng, Ribbens, & Zhou, 2013). Further, when leaders allow employees room to make mistakes, perceptions of psychological safety are increased, which then leads to higher levels of creativity (Hirak, Peng, Carmeli, & Schaubroeck, 2012). Several leadership styles may also promote feelings of psychological safety, and consequently, increase creativity and innovation in individuals and teams. For instance, transformational leaders focus on empowering individuals and ensuring their personal growth, which leads to higher levels of trust with the leader and perceived support (Carmeli et al., 2014). The positive feelings resulting from perceived leader support and psychological safety promote problem-solving capacity (Nijstad et al., 2014). Servant leadership, referring to leaders who put the needs of followers first, similarly builds a feeling of group safety and community where individuals can share information and perspectives, thus bolstering team creativity (Schaubroeck, Lam, & Peng, 2011). Likewise, ethical leaders create an environment of trust and cooperation, which facilitates information sharing and increases creativity (Avey, Wernsing, & Palanski, 2012; Boies, Fiset, & Gill, 2015; Carmeli et al., 2014).

Managing the Outside Environment

In addition to managing team social interactions and creating a team climate conducive to creativity, leaders are responsible for facilitating connections between their followers and information, which may be in the form of other teams, the organization, or even resources outside of the organization (Mumford et al., 2002). Leaders thus function in a boundary-spanning role in which they serve as a link for the team to access outside sources of information (Reiter-Palmon et al., 2013). Teams do not exist in a vacuum and having access to outside sources of information can greatly bolster creativity when communication with these sources is effective. It has been suggested that communication within an organization and the amount of information shared may be one of the best predictors of innovation over time (Monge, Cozzens, & Contractor, 1992). Having strong communication channels with outside contacts allows teams access to even more knowledge and viewpoints that might not be available within the team (Han, Han, & Brass, 2014). Leaders can manage the communication between teams and outside sources by establishing relationships with other organizational leaders. By establishing connections with others within the organization, leaders can ensure that team innovation is consistent with organizational needs, priorities, and initiatives (Venkataramani, Richter, & Clarke, 2014). Just as important as establishing communication channels with sources in the greater organization is ensuring that the team is protected from unwanted or negative organizational influence or distractions (Morgeson, DeRue, & Karam, 2010; Mumford, 2000). Thus, leaders serve as a shield so that the team is able to work independently and without negative distraction from outside demands.

In addition to organizational relationships, leaders should develop relationships with those outside of the organization. For instance, in meeting consumer demands, it is critical to understand the targeted consumer and current market that can be accomplished by establishing working relationships with those who have the necessary information. Communication with competitors, suppliers, consumers, and collaborators allows a greater understanding of how the team and organization operate within the wider environment (Mathieu, Marks, & Zaccaro, 2001; Scott & Bruce, 1994). Troy, Szymanski, and Varadarajan (2001) found that open communication and availability of market information are critical for effective idea generation. Thus, leaders can then provide teams with valuable information that was not easily accessible and more effectively facilitate new product idea generation.

Another way in which leaders can support their team is through being an "innovation champion." These individuals are oftentimes leaders who can effectively advocate the importance of an innovative idea and gather support for its pursuit. Consequently, an innovation champion can gain support for innovation by negotiating for the necessary materials or resources for the team to accomplish its goals. In order for leaders to effectively advocate the needs of their teams, they must be effective and compelling communicators with the ability to promote the importance of their team's work through negotiation and persuasion (Howell & Boies, 2004; Markham & Aiman-Smith, 2001; Mumford et al., 2002). Additionally, innovation champions who are outside of the team are also necessary. When innovation champions exist outside the team, they serve as an additional advocate to advance creative pursuits and ventures throughout the organization.

In conclusion, this chapter reviewed how leaders can promote creativity in individuals and teams in order to come to efficient and innovative solutions to problems. There are many challenges with leading creative teams, especially as creative teams are often made up of individuals with a wide range of experiences, backgrounds, and opinions and may have vastly different views on how to approach a problem. However, leaders can turn these challenges into opportunities to capitalize on the diverse perspectives in the way they manage team interactions. Leaders facilitate creativity when they encourage information sharing, create an environment of psychological safety and trust where team members feel safe in providing ideas and solutions, provide support, and encourage interaction, collaboration, and participation. Leaders also influence team creativity in the way they manage the relationship between teams and the environment outside of the team by ensuring adequate resources and collaboration with outside sources. Leaders can also bolster creativity in individuals and teams by serving as champions of innovation. Although leading individuals and teams for creativity poses many challenges, today's organizational leaders are also in a critical position to influence and promote creative outcomes and innovation.

Recommended Readings

Burke, C. S., Stagl, K. C., Klein, C., Goodwin, G. F., Salas, E., & Halpin, S. M. (2006). What type of leadership behaviors are functional in teams? A meta-analysis. *The Leadership Quarterly, 17,* 288–307.

Elkins, T., & Keller, R. T. (2003). Leadership in research and development organizations: A literature review and conceptual framework. *The Leadership Quarterly, 14,* 587–606. doi:10.1016/S1048-9843(03)00053-5

Mumford, M. D. (2000). Managing creative people: Strategies and tactics for innovation. *Human Resource Management Review, 10,* 313–351. doi:10.1016/S1053-4822(99)00043-1

Reiter-Palmon, R., de Vreede, T., & de Vreede, G. J. (2013). Leading creative interdisciplinary teams: Challenges and solutions. In S. Hemlin, C. M. Allwood, B. R. Martin, & M. D. Mumford (Eds.), *Creativity and leadership in science, technology and innovation* (pp. 240–267). New York, NY: Routledge.

West, M. A., Hirst, G., Richter, A., & Shipton, H. (2004). Twelve steps to heaven: Successfully managing change through developing innovative teams. *European Journal of Work and Organizational Psychology, 13,* 269–299. doi:10.1080/13594320444000092

References

Amabile, T. M., & Gryskiewicz, N. D. (1989). The Creative Environment Scales: Work environment inventory. *Creativity Research Journal, 2,* 231–253. doi:10.1080/10400418909534321

Amabile, T. M., Schatzel, E. A., Moneta, G. B., & Kramer, S. J. (2004). Leader behaviors and the work environment for creativity: Perceived leader support. *The Leadership Quarterly, 15,* 5–32.

Avey, J. B., Wernsing, T. S., & Palanski, M. E. (2012). Exploring the process of ethical leadership: The mediating role of employee voice and psychological ownership. *Journal of Business Ethics, 107*(1), 21–34. doi:10.1007/s10551-012-1298-2

Baer, M., & Frese, M. (2003). Innovation is not enough: Climates for initiative and psychological safety, process innovations, and firm performance. *Journal of Organizational Behavior, 24*(1), 45–68. doi:10.1002/job.179

Barczak, G., Lassk, F., & Mulki, J. (2010). Antecedents of team creativity: An examination of team emotional intelligence, team trust and collaborative culture. *Creativity and Innovation Management, 19,* 332–345. doi:10.1111/j.1467-8691.2010.00574.x

Baumeister, R., Bratslavsky, E., Finkenauer, C., & Vohs, K. (2001). Bad is stronger than good. *Review of General Psychology, 5,* 323–370.

Boies, K., Fiset, J., & Gill, H. (2015). Communication and trust are key: Unlocking the relationship between leadership and team performance and creativity. *The Leadership Quarterly.* Advance online publication. doi:10.1016/j.leaqua.2015.07.007

Bradley, B. H., Postlethwaite, B. E., Klotz, A. C., Hamdani, M. R., & Brown, K. G. (2012). Reaping the benefits of task conflict in teams: The critical role of team psychological safety climate. *Journal of Applied Psychology, 97,* 151–158. doi:10.1037/a0024200

Burke, C. S., Stagl, K. C., Klein, C., Goodwin, G. F., Salas, E., & Halpin, S. M. (2006). What type of leadership behaviors are functional in teams? A meta-analysis. *The Leadership Quarterly, 17,* 288–307.

Carmeli, A. E., Reiter-Palmon, R., & Ziv, E. (2010). Inclusive leadership and employee involvement in creative tasks in the workplace: The mediating role of psychological safety. *Creativity Research Journal, 22,* 250–260.

Carmeli, A., Sheaffer, Z., Binyamin, G., Reiter-Palmon, R., & Shimoni, T. (2014). Transformational leadership and creative problem-solving: The mediating role of psychological safety and reflexivity. *The Journal of Creative Behavior, 48,* 115–135. doi:10.1002/jocb.43

Chen, M. (2006). Understanding the benefits and detriments of conflict on team creativity process. *Creativity and Innovation Management, 15,* 105–116. doi:10.1111/j.1467-8691.2006.00373.x

Chen, G., Farh, J., Campbell-Bush, E. M., Wu, Z., & Wu, X. (2013). Teams as innovative systems: Multilevel motivational antecedents of innovation in R&D teams. *Journal of Applied Psychology, 98,* 1018–1027. doi:10.1037/a0032663

Cheung, M. Y., & Wong, C. (2011). Transformational leadership, leader support, and employee creativity. *Leadership & Organization Development Journal, 32,* 656–672. doi:10.1108/01437731111169988

Choi, J. N., Anderson, T. A., & Veillette, A. (2009). Contextual inhibitors of employee creativity in organizations: The insulating role of creative ability. *Group & Organization Management, 34,* 330–357. doi:10.1177/1059601108329811

Cronin, M. A., & Weingart, L. R. (2007). Representational gaps, information processing, and conflict in functionally diverse teams. *The Academy of Management Review, 32,* 761–773. doi:10.2307/20159333

Curhan, J. R., & Pentland, A. (2007). Thin slices of negotiation: Predicting outcomes from conversational dynamics within the first 5 minutes. *Journal of Applied Psychology, 92,* 802–811. doi:10.1037/0021-9010.92.3.802

Curşeu, P. L., & Schruijer, S. L. (2010). Does conflict shatter trust or does trust obliterate conflict? Revisiting the relationships between team diversity, conflict, and trust. *Group Dynamics: Theory, Research, and Practice, 14*(1), 66–79. doi:10.1037/a0017104

De Dreu, C. W., Carsten, K. W., & West, M. A. (2001). Minority dissent and team innovation: The importance of participation in decision making. *Journal of Applied Psychology, 86,* 1191–1201. doi:10.1037/0021-9010.86.6.1191

de Wit, F. C., Greer, L. L., & Jehn, K. A. (2012). The paradox of intragroup conflict: A meta-analysis. *Journal of Applied Psychology, 97,* 360–390. doi: 10.1037/a0024844

DeChurch, L. A., Mesmer-Magnus, J. R., & Doty, D. (2013). Moving beyond relationship and task conflict: Toward a process-state perspective. *Journal of Applied Psychology, 98,* 559–578. doi:10.1037/a0032896

Denti, L., & Hemlin, S. (2013). What connects leadership and creativity? The mechanisms through which leaders may influence follower and team creativity. In S. Hemlin, C. M. Allwood, B. M. Martin, & M. D. Mumford (Eds.), *Creativity and leadership in science, technology and innovation* (pp. 58–80). New York, NY: Routledge

Desivilya, H. S., Somech, A., & Lidgoster, H. (2010). Innovation and conflict management in work teams: The effects of team identification and task and relationship conflict. *Negotiation and Conflict Management Research, 3*(1), 28–48. doi:10.1111/j.1750-4716.2009.00048.x

Edmondson, A. (1999). Psychological safety and learning behavior in work teams. *Administrative Science Quarterly, 44,* 350–383. doi:10.2307/2666999

Elkins, T., & Keller, R. T. (2003). Leadership in research and development organizations: A literature review and conceptual framework. *The Leadership Quarterly, 14,* 587–606. doi:10.1016/S1048-9843(03)00053-5

Fairchild, J., & Hunter, S. T. (2014). 'We've got creative differences': The effects of task conflict and participative safety on team creative performance. *The Journal of Creative Behavior, 48,* 64–87. doi:10.1002/jocb.41

Farh, J., Lee, C., & Farh, C. C. (2010). Task conflict and team creativity: A question of how much and when. *Journal of Applied Psychology, 95,* 1173–1180. doi:10.1037/a0020015

Farris, G. F. (1972). The effect of individual roles on performance in innovative groups. *R&D Management, 3,* 23–28.

Fay, D., Borrill, C., Amir, Z., Haward, R., & West, M. A. (2006). Getting the most out of multidisciplinary teams: A multi-sample study of team innovation in health care. *Journal of Occupational and Organizational Psychology,* *79,* 553–567.

Feist, G. J. (1998). A meta-analysis of personality in scientific and artistic creativity. *Personality & Social Psychology Review, 2,* 290–309.

Ford, C. M., & Gioia, D. A. (1995). *Creative action in organizations: Ivory tower visions & real world voices.* Thousand Oaks, CA: Sage.

Gallucci, N. T., Middleton, G., & Kline, A. (2000). Perfectionism and creative strivings. *The Journal of Creative Behavior, 34,* 135–141.

Han, J., Han, J., & Brass, D. J. (2014). Human capital diversity in the creation of social capital for team creativity. *Journal of Organizational Behavior, 35,* 54–71. doi:10.1002/job.1853

Hansen, M. T., Mors, M. L., & Løvås, B. (2005). Knowledge sharing in organizations: Multiple networks, multiple phases. *Academy of Management Journal, 48,* 776–793. doi:10.5465/AMJ.2005.18803922

Harvey, S. (2014). Creative synthesis: Exploring the process of extraordinary group creativity. *The Academy of Management Review, 39,* 324–343. doi:10.5465/amr.2012.0224

Hirak, R., Peng, A. C., Carmeli, A., & Schaubroeck, J. M. (2012). Linking leader inclusiveness to work unit performance: The importance of psychological safety and learning from failures. *The Leadership Quarterly, 23,* 107–117. doi:10.1016/j.leaqua.2011.11.009

Hirst, G., van Dick, R., & van Knippenberg, D. (2009). A social identity perspective on leadership and employee creativity. *Journal of Organizational Behavior, 30,* 963–982. doi:10.1002/job.600

Hoever, I. J., van Knippenberg, D., van Ginkel, W. P., & Barkema, H. G. (2012). Fostering team creativity: Perspective taking as key to unlocking diversity's potential. *Journal of Applied Psychology, 97,* 982–996. doi:10.1037/a0029159

Howell, J. M., & Boies, K. (2004). Champions of technological innovation: The influence of contextual knowledge, role orientation, idea generation, and idea promotion on champion emergence. *The Leadership Quarterly, 15,* 123–143. doi:10.1016/j.leaqua.2003.12.008

Hülsheger, U. R., Anderson, N., & Salgado, J. F. (2009). Team-level predictors of innovation at work: A comprehensive meta-analysis spanning three decades of research. *Journal of Applied Psychology, 94,* 1128–1145. doi:10.1037/a0015978

Hunter, S. T., Bedell, K. E., & Mumford, M. D. (2007). Climate for creativity: A quantitative review. *Creativity Research Journal, 19,* 69–90. doi:10.1080/10400410709336883

Ilgen, D. R., Hollenbeck, J. R., Johnson, M., & Jundt, D. (2005). Teams in organizations: From input-process-output models to IMOI models.

Annual Review of Psychology, 56, 517–543. doi:10.1146/annurev.psych. 56.091103.070250

Janssens, M., & Brett, J. M. (2006). Cultural intelligence in global teams a fusion model of collaboration. *Group & Organization Management, 31,* 124–153.

Jehn, K. A. (1995). A multimethod examination of the benefits and detriments of intragroup conflict. *Administrative Science Quarterly, 40,* 256–282. doi: 10.2307/2393638

Jehn, K. A., Greer, L., Levine, S., & Szulanski, G. (2008). The effects of conflict types, dimensions, and emergent states on group outcomes. *Group Decision and Negotiation, 17,* 465–495. doi:10.1007/s10726-008-9107-0

Jehn, K. A., & Mannix, E. A. (2001). The dynamic nature of conflict: A longitudinal study of intragroup conflict and group performance. *Academy of Management Journal, 44,* 238–251. doi:10.2307/3069453

Kahai, S. S., Sosik, J. J., & Avolio, B. J. (2003). Effects of leadership style, anonymity, and rewards on creativity-relevant processes and outcomes in an electronic meeting system context. *The Leadership Quarterly, 14,* 499–524. doi:10.1016/S1048-9843(03)00049-3

Keller, R. T. (2001). Cross-functional project groups in research and new product development: Diversity, communications, job stress, and outcomes. *Academy of Management Journal, 44,* 547–559. doi:10.2307/3069369

Kessel, M., Kratzer, J., & Schultz, C. (2012). Psychological safety, knowledge sharing, and creative performance in healthcare teams. *Creativity and Innovation Management, 21,* 147–157. doi:10.1111/j.1467-8691.2012.00 635.x

Kozlowski, S. J., & Bell, B. S. (2008). Team learning, development, and adaptation. In V. I. Sessa, M. London, V. I. Sessa, & M. London (Eds.), *Work group learning: Understanding, improving and assessing how groups learn in organizations* (pp. 15–44). New York, NY: Lawrence Erlbaum.

Kurtzberg, T. R., & Amabile, T. M. (2001). From Guilford to creative synergy: Opening the black box of team-level creativity. *Creativity Research Journal, 13,* 285–294.

Lee, C., Lin, Y., Huan, H., Huang, W., & Teng, H. (2015). The effects of task interdependence, team cooperation, and team conflict on job performance. *Social Behavior and Personality, 43,* 529–536. doi:10.2224/sbp. 2015.43.4.529

Ma, Y., Cheng, W., Ribbens, B. A., & Zhou, J. (2013). Linking ethical leadership to employee creativity: Knowledge sharing and self efficacy as mediators. *Social Behavior and Personality, 41,* 1409–1419. doi:10.2224/ sbp.2013.41.9.1409

Mannix, E., & Neale, M. A. (2005). What differences make a difference? The promise and reality of diverse teams in organizations. *Psychological Science in the Public Interest, 6*(2), 31–55. doi:10.1111/j.1529-1006.2005.00022.x

Markham, S. K., & Aiman-Smith, L. (2001). Product champions: Truths, myths and management. *Research-Technology Management, 44*(3), 44–50.

Mathieu, J. E., Marks, M. A., & Zaccaro, S. J. (2001). Multi-team systems. *International Handbook of Work and Organizational Psychology, 2,* 289–313.

Mathieu, J., Maynard, M. T., Rapp, T., & Gilson, L. (2008). Team effectiveness 1997–2007: A review of recent advancements and a glimpse into the future. *Journal of Management, 34,* 410–476. doi:10.1177/0149206308316061

Mathisen, G. E., & Einarsen, S. (2004). A review of instruments assessing creative and innovative environments within organizations. *Creativity Research Journal, 16,* 119–140. doi:10.1207/s15326934crj1601_12

McLeod, P. L., Lobel, S. A., & Cox, T. H. (1996). Ethnic diversity and creativity in small groups. *Small Group Research, 27,* 248–264. doi:10.1177/1046496496272003

Mesmer-Magnus, J. R., & DeChurch, L. A. (2009). Information sharing and team performance: A meta-analysis. *Journal of Applied Psychology, 94,* 535–546. doi:10.1037/a0013773

Milliken, F. J., Bartel, C. A., & Kurtzberg, T. R. (2003). Diversity and creativity in work groups: A dynamic perspective on the affective and cognitive processes that link diversity and performance. In P. B. Paulus & B. A. Nijstad (Eds.), *Group creativity: Innovation through collaboration* (pp. 32–62). New York, NY: Oxford University Press.

Mitchell, R., Boyle, B., Parker, V., Giles, M., Chiang, V., & Joyce, P. (2015). Managing inclusiveness and diversity in teams: How leader inclusiveness affects performance through status and team identity. *Human Resource Management, 54,* 217–239. doi:10.1002/hrm.21658

Monge, P. R., Cozzens, M. D., & Contractor, N. S. (1992). Communication and motivational predictors of the dynamics of organizational innovation. *Organization Science, 3,* 250–274. doi:10.1287/orsc.3.2.250

Morgeson, F. P., DeRue, D. S., & Karam, E. P. (2010). Leadership in teams: A functional approach to understanding leadership structures and processes. *Journal of Management, 36*(1), 5–39. doi:10.1177/0149206309347376

Mumford, M. D. (2000). Managing creative people: Strategies and tactics for innovation. *Human Resource Management Review, 10,* 313–351. doi:10.1016/S1053-4822(99)00043-1

Mumford, M. D., Lonergan, D. C., & Scott, G. (2002). Evaluating creative ideas: Processes, standards, and context. *Inquiry: Critical Thinking Across the Disciplines, 22,* 21–30.

Nicholson, N., & West, M. A. (1988). *Managerial job change: Men and women in transition*. New York, NY: Cambridge University Press. doi:10.1017/CBO9780511522116

Nijhof, W., & Kommers, P. (1985). An analysis of cooperation in relation to cognitive controversy. In R. Slavin, S. Sharan, S. Kagan, R. Hertz-Lazarowitz, C. Webb, & R. Schmuck (Eds.), *Learning to cooperate, cooperating to learn* (pp. 125–145). New York, NY: Springer USA.

Nijstad, B. A., Berger-Selman, F., & De Dreu, C. W. (2014). Innovation in top management teams: Minority dissent, transformational leadership, and radical innovations. *European Journal of Work and Organizational Psychology, 23*, 310–322. doi:10.1080/1359432X.2012.734038

Orbach, M., Demko, M., Doyle, J., Waber, B. N., & Pentland, A. (2015). Sensing informal networks in organizations. *American Behavioral Scientist, 59*, 508–524. doi:10.1177/0002764214556810

Paletz, S., Peng, K., Erez, M., & Maslach, C. (2004). Ethnic composition and its differential impact on group processes in diverse teams. *Small Group Research, 35*, 128–157.

Paulus, P. B., Larey, T. S., & Dzindolet, M. T. (2001). Creativity in groups and teams. In M. E. Turner (Eds.), *Groups at work: Theory and research* (pp. 319–338). Mahwah, NJ: Lawrence Erlbaum.

Reiter-Palmon, R., de Vreede, T., & de Vreede, G. J. (2013). Leading creative interdisciplinary teams: Challenges and solutions. In S. Hemlin, C. M. Allwood, B. R. Martin, & M. D. Mumford (Eds.), *Creativity and leadership in science, technology and innovation* (pp. 240–267). New York, NY: Routledge.

Reiter-Palmon, R., Wigert, B., & de Vreede, T. (2011). Team creativity and innovation: The effect of team composition, social processes and cognition. In D. M. Michael (Ed.), *Handbook of organizational creativity* (pp. 295–326). San Diego, CA: Academic Press.

Salas, E., Cooke, N. J., & Rosen, M. A. (2008). On teams, teamwork, and team performance: Discoveries and developments. *Human Factors, 50*, 540–547. doi:10.1518/001872008X288457

Schaubroeck, J., Lam, S. K., & Peng, A. C. (2011). Cognition-based and affect-based trust as mediators of leader behavior influences on team performance. *Journal of Applied Psychology, 96*, 863–871. doi:10.1037/a0022625

Scott, S. G., & Bruce, R. A. (1994). Determinants of innovative behavior: A path model of individual innovation in the workplace. *Academy of Management Journal, 37*, 580–607. doi:10.2307/256701

Shalley, C. E., & Gilson, L. L. (2004). What leaders need to know: A review of social and contextual factors that can foster or hinder creativity. *The Leadership Quarterly, 15,* 33–53. doi:10.1016/j.leaqua.2003.12.004

Shalley, C. E., Zhou, J., & Oldham, G. R. (2004). The effects of personal and contextual characteristics on creativity: Where should we go from here? *Journal of Management, 30,* 933–958. doi:10.1016/j.jm.2004.06.007

Silvia, P. J., Kaufman, J. C., Reiter-Palmon, R., & Wigert, B. (2011). Cantankerous creativity: Honesty-humility, agreeableness, and the HEXACO structure of creative achievement. *Personality and Individual Differences, 51,* 687–689. doi:10.1016/j.paid.2011.06.011

Troy, L. C., Szymanski, D. M., & Varadarajan, P. R. (2001). Generating new product ideas: An initial investigation of the role of market information and organizational characteristics. *Journal of the Academy of Marketing Science, 29,* 89–101. doi:10.1177/0092070301291006

Venkataramani, V., Richter, A. W., & Clarke, R. (2014). Creative benefits from well-connected leaders: Leader social network ties as facilitators of employee radical creativity. *Journal of Applied Psychology, 99,* 966–975. doi:10.1037/a0037088

West, M. A., Hirst, G., Richter, A., & Shipton, H. (2004). Twelve steps to heaven: Successfully managing change through developing innovative teams. *European Journal of Work and Organizational Psychology, 13,* 269–299. doi:10.1080/13594320444000092

West, M. A., & Richter, A. (2008). Climates and cultures for innovation and creativity at work. In J. Zhou & C. E. Shalley (Eds.), *Handbook of organizational creativity* (pp. 211–236). New York, NY: Lawrence Erlbaum.

Yong, K., Sauer, S. J., & Mannix, E. A. (2014). Conflict and creativity in interdisciplinary teams. *Small Group Research, 45,* 266–289. doi:10.1177/1046496414530789

Zhou, J. (2003). When the presence of creative coworkers is related to creativity: Role of supervisor close monitoring, developmental feedback, and creative personality. *Journal of Applied Psychology, 88,* 413–422. doi:10.1037/0021-9010.88.3.413

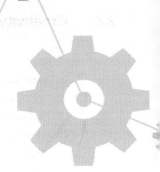

Creativity and Conformity

A Paradoxical Relationship

Ronald A. Beghetto

Key Take-Aways

- Creativity is somewhat paradoxical.
- One way to think about creativity is a blend between originality and conformity to task constraints.
- The level of originality and conformity to task constraints necessary for creativity varies depending on the specific context.

How might we think about the relationship between creativity and conformity? A common way is to view them as opposites. Conformity refers to thinking and acting in expected, accepted, and conventional ways. Few things could seem further from creativity. Indeed, creativity is often associated with "thinking outside the box" and new ways of thought and action. In fact, if you were to perform a quick Internet search on the terms *creativity* and *conformity*, you likely would find commentaries that describe the perils of conformity and how it can stifle or even kill creativity. Although the idea that conformity can stifle creativity seems clear, the actual relationship between creativity and conformity is not as straightforward as it may initially seem. In fact, conformity and creativity have a closer relationship than most people realize.

How might two seemingly opposing concepts be related? Creativity researchers have noted that many creative breakthroughs have come from the combination of opposites. Rothenberg (1996) called this "Janusian thinking" after the Roman god Janus, who simultaneously gazes in opposing directions (e.g., past and future). An example is Einstein's revolutionary ideas about gravity. Specifically, Einstein recognized that a person falling is simultaneously experiencing the opposing states of being at rest and in motion, which resulted in "a new conception of gravity in the general theory of relativity" (Rothenberg, 2014, p. 37).

A fascinating result of blending opposites is that it can lead to outcomes that have emergent properties. Emergent properties represent new features that are not true of the initial concepts that have been combined (Sawyer, 2012). An example is the concept of "frenemy," which combines the opposites of friend and enemy. A frenemy has properties that are different from both friends and enemies. It thereby represents a new and meaningful category that we can use to describe the relationships we have with certain people in our lives who are neither friends nor enemies. As these examples illustrate, creativity can emerge from the combination of seemingly opposing elements. The purpose of this Hot Topic is to explore the paradoxical relationship between creativity and conformity by explaining how creativity can emerge from the combination of originality and conformity.

Originality and Conformity

It is true that a simple act of conformity (e.g., complying with existing rules, expectations, and standards) can hardly be called creative. New products, ideas, and behaviors must demonstrate some level of originality to be deemed creative (Plucker, Beghetto, & Dow, 2004; Runco, 2003). Indeed, that is why we have patent laws. It is also true, however, that an act of originality is not necessarily creative. Writing a love sonnet about the beauty of gravity instead of solving a problem on a physics exam is original, but not creative in the context of the physics exam. Creativity is more than originality (Feist, 1998; Runco, 2003). Creativity requires that original expression is also meaningful in the context of the particular task, problem, or situation (Beghetto, 2013; Dow, this volume; Kaufman & Beghetto, 2009; Plucker et al. 2004). In this way, creativity can be thought of as a blend of originality and conformity. At first blush, this may seem impossible or at least incorrect.

How might creativity result from the blending of conformity and originality? The idea of creativity requiring originality is rather straightforward. In fact, creativity and originality are often viewed as synonyms. Creativity researchers, however, tend to differentiate between originality and creativity. As alluded to earlier, creativity scholars view originality as a necessary but insufficient aspect of creativity. One way to think of creativity is constrained originality. This means that originality is constrained by the need to meet task constraints, to be meaningful, and to be useful. Put simply, an original solution to a complex problem would be meaningless if it was impossible to carry out. There are always constraints placed on creativity (Sternberg & Kaufman, 2010). As such, creativity requires a certain level of conformity to the constraints of a situation, problem, or context. A poem, no matter how original, must meet the conventions of Haiku poetry to be considered a creative Haiku poem. A new approach to solving a math problem must be mathematically accurate in order to be considered a creative solution to the problem. A wildly original idea for fixing a leaky roof (e.g., cover the leak with peanut butter) cannot be considered creative if it is ultimately useless in the long run.

In this way, the assertion that creativity is a blend of originality and conformity is not as puzzling as it may first seem. In fact, this assertion aligns quite nicely with the definition that creativity researchers generally agree on: *Creativity is the combination of originality, novelty, or newness and usefulness, meaningfulness, value, or meeting task constraints as defined within a particular context* (Beghetto, 2013; Plucker et al., 2004). As this definition suggests, creativity requires that original expressions of thought and action conform to some criteria—be it usefulness, meaningfulness, value, or meets tasks constraints—in order for it to be considered creative. In can therefore be said that creativity requires conformity to help ensure that the new and original idea, behavior, or action is meaningful for the task at hand. This is not to say that all forms of creative expression require the same level of conformity.

A painting you make for yourself need not conform to the aesthetic standards of a professional artist to be considered creative. You can still considerer your painting creative as long as it conforms to your own subjective sense of beauty (see Beghetto & Kaufman, 2007). For others to consider it creative, however, it must conform to the standards set by your audience (Glăveanu, 2013; Kaufman & Beghetto, 2009). In this way, creativity can be thought of as a blending of conformity and originality as determined by the particular situation or context—including your own subjective experience. This more nuanced view of creativity moves us away from pitting creativity and conformity as opposites and, instead, allows us to think about the various ways that conformity and originality can come together as a creative outcome. One way to do this is to think about conformity and originality along a continuum (see Figure HT6.1).

As illustrated in Figure HT6.1, on one end of the continuum is conformity, and on the other end is originality. Toward the middle is a blend of conformity and originality. The shaded grey area can be thought of as the region in which conformity and originality combine in the form of creativity. In some cases, there is a bit more conformity blended with a bit less originality (e.g., developing a novel approach to solving a mathematical problem). In other cases, there might be more originality blended with conformity (e.g., coming up with an interpretive dance to convey emotion). Still in other cases, there may be somewhat equal blends of originality and conformity (e.g., a short story published in a popular science fiction magazine). In all such cases, however, there is a blending of originality and conformity as determined by the various conditions of the situation or task.

Context Matters

The various conditions under which creativity can emerge from originality and conformity underscore the importance of context (Kaufman & Beghetto, 2013; Plucker et al., 2004). In schools, for instance, creative behaviors can easily be labeled "misbehaviors." Indeed, researchers have noted that teachers often view creativity as a desired trait in theory, but not in practice. As Runco (2007) explained, "no doubt [teachers] do respect creativity, in the abstract, but not when faced with a classroom with 30 energetic children!" (p. 178). Other researchers have highlighted how teachers tend to view creative students in a negative light (Scott, 1999; Westby & Dawson, 1995). One way of interpreting this situation would be to assume that teachers hold a negative view of creative expression in their classroom. An alternative interpretation would be that its not that teachers dislike creativity in their classroom, but rather they do not like it when students are unable to know when and when not to be creative (Kaufman, Beghetto, & Watson, 2015). In other words, teachers likely want their students to learn how to strike a balance between originality and conformity so as to develop real-world creativity, rather than demonstrate originality

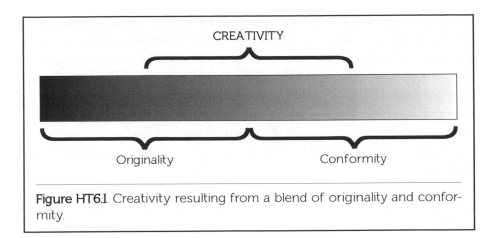

CREATIVITY

Originality   Conformity

Figure HT6.1 Creativity resulting from a blend of originality and conformity.

for originality's sake, which often results in unnecessary disruptions and can actually stifle creativity.

An example may help clarify. Consider a student who chooses to write poems about the beauty of science in her "observation log" instead of adhering to her teacher's instructions to record and scientifically interpret observational data. Even if her poetry might otherwise be considered creative in another context (e.g., language arts class), it is understandable how a teacher might be frustrated with a student who fails to meet the task constraints of the science assignment. The issue here is not that the student is misbehaving. Rather, the problem is that the student's creativity is misplaced. If, for instance, the student was redirected to share her poetry in her language arts class, then that would be the appropriate time and place for that form of creative expression. Moreover, the teacher might also encourage the student to demonstrate her creativity in science by providing novel and scientifically justified interpretations of the observational data collected. If the student is able to learn the appropriate time and place for creative expression, then most teachers would likely welcome student creativity.

Accomplished creators therefore know how to "read the situation" and determine when it is appropriate and feasible to express their creativity. This knowledge is called *creative metacognition* and has been defined as a "combination of creative self-knowledge (knowing one's own creative strengths and limitations, both within a domain and as a general trait) and contextual knowledge (knowing when, where, how, and why to be creative)" (Kaufman & Beghetto, 2013, p. 160). Developing the requisite self-knowledge and contextual knowledge for high levels of creative accomplishment takes time. Researchers (e.g., Ericsson, 1996) estimate an average of 10 years (or 10,000 hours) of deliberate practice to develop the knowledge necessary for creative achievement. Put simply, accomplished creators have developed the knowledge and experience necessary to determine whether they are capable of being creative and whether it makes sense to try to be creative in a particular situation.

As mentioned, knowing how to strike the right balance between originality and conformity will vary across particular domains (e.g., poetry, science, mathematics, digital arts) and subdomains (e.g., sonnet, Haiku, free verse poetry, slam poetry). The balance will also vary by level of creative accomplishment. Creative thoughts and actions that are focused more on subjective experiences (and not evaluated by others) may require both lower levels of originality and lower levels of conformity than those that are being evaluated or judged by experts (see discussion of 4-C model of creativity in Beghetto & Kaufman, this volume). Other factors, including everything from temporary personal factors (e.g., your mood) to more stable and global factors (e.g., cultural norms and historical time periods) can also play a role in influencing your ability to strike the right balance between originality and conformity. The key take-away is that there are no easy or fixed recipes for creativity. The level of originality and conformity necessary for creative expression will vary depending on the particular task and sociocultural and historical context—and creators may not know the proper balance until they are within those particular contexts.

Creativity In and Outside the Box

In closing, it may be worthwhile to return to the slogan "think outside the box" and briefly discuss why it is somewhat problematic when it comes to understanding creativity in practice. The problem with this slogan is that it refers only to the originality necessary for creativity and abandons the requirement of conforming to situational or task constraints. A more accurate slogan might therefore be: "Think originally inside the box" (Beghetto, 2016). The criteria of meaningfulness, value, and usefulness represent the constraints of the box. Working originally within such constraints is the hallmark of creative thought and action. Unless you are able to conform to those constraints, your efforts will not be considered creative. Creativity therefore has an evaluative or verification component (Wallas, 1926). Creativity is not simply about imagining new alternatives—those alternatives must be put into action and tested against real-world constraints. In some cases, these tests can be thought experiments (e.g., tested against the constraints of logic); in other cases they will be tested in the material world (e.g., can I actually sit on this new type of chair?).

Thinking originally inside the box does not preclude building a new box. Creative breakthroughs often result from recognizing that former constraints are no longer viable in light of new ideas (e.g., Einstein's theory of relativity). In such cases, new boxes (i.e., new criteria) are established. Creativity that results in the development of a new box, however, still emerges from conforming to the criteria of value, meaningfulness, usefulness, or beauty (e.g., it is more meaningful to view some phenomenon from a new theory than the previously held theory; a new style of painting is recognized as having aesthetic value by art critics and fellow painters).

In sum, the slogan "think outside the box" encourages people to avoid conformity and, instead, focus on originality. This slogan is not completely empty. Given that most people are risk averse (Mumford, Blair, Dailey, Leritz, & Osburn, 2006), being able to take the risks necessary to generate new thoughts and actions is something many of us can improve upon. Moreover, there really is no such thing as a completely constraint-free situation. As such, our efforts to be original will always be constrained by some set of factors. The key issue here is learning how to strike the right balance.

It is true that too much conformity can suppress creativity and, in many situations, we probably tend to underestimate the amount of freedom we have available to put our own unique twist on routine ways of thinking and acting. At the same time, too much originality can overshadow creativity and, somewhat ironically, result in conforming to the status quo by default. This can happen when we ignore real-world constraints, and thereby people fail to see the relevance of our ideas or our ideas lack feasibility for the particular circumstances. Fortunately, once we are able to recognize that creativity can result from an appropriate blend of originality and conformity, we will be in a better position to work toward establishing that blend and not give up so quickly when we face setbacks. In some cases, this will require working harder to make sure our ideas and actions conform to existing task constraints. In other cases, it will require being willing to take the risks necessary to try out new ways of thinking and acting.

Recommended Readings

Baer, J. (in press). Creativity doesn't develop in a vacuum. *New Directions for Child and Adolescent Development.*

Beghetto, R. A. (2013). *Killing ideas softly? The promise and perils of creativity in the classroom.* Charlotte, NC: Information Age.

Beghetto, R. A. (2016). Creative learning: A fresh look. *Journal of Cognitive Education and Psychology, 15,* 6–23.

Beghetto, R. A. (2016). *Big wins, small steps: How to lead for and with creativity.* Thousand Oaks, CA: Corwin.

Beghetto, R. A., & Kaufman, J. C. (2014). Classroom contexts for creativity. *High Ability Studies, 25,* 53–69.

Beghetto, R. A., Kaufman, J. C., & Baer, J. (2014). *Teaching for creativity in the Common Core*. New York, NY: Teachers College Press.

Kaufman, J. C., & Beghetto, R. A. (2013). In praise of Clark Kent: Creative metacognition and the importance of teaching kids when (not) to be creative. *Roeper Review, 35,* 155–165.

Plucker, J. A., Beghetto, R. A., & Dow, G. (2004). Why isn't creativity more important to educational psychologists? Potential, pitfalls, and future directions in creativity research. *Educational Psychologist, 39,* 83–96.

Sternberg, R. J., & Kaufman, J. C. (2010). Constraints on creativity: Obvious and not so obvious. In J. C. Kaufman & R. J. Sternberg (Eds.), *The Cambridge handbook of creativity* (pp. 467–482). New York, NY: Cambridge University Press.

References

Beghetto, R. A. (2013). *Killing ideas softly? The promise and perils of creativity in the classroom*. Charlotte, NC: Information Age.

Beghetto, R. A. (2016). *Small steps, big wins: A creative approach to instructional leadership*. Thousand Oaks, CA: Corwin.

Beghetto, R. A., & Kaufman, J. C. (2007). Toward a broader conception of creativity: A case for "mini-c" creativity. *Psychology of Aesthetics, Creativity, and the Arts, 1,* 73–79.

Ericsson, K. A. (Ed.). (1996). *The road to expert performance: Empirical evidence from the arts and sciences, sports, and games*. Mahwah, NJ: Erlbaum.

Feist, G. J. (1998). A meta-analysis of personality in scientific and artistic creativity. *Personality and Social Psychology Review, 2,* 290–309.

Glăveanu, V. P. (2013). Rewriting the language of creativity: The Five A's framework. *Review of General Psychology, 17,* 69.

Kaufman, J. C., & Beghetto, R. A. (2009). Beyond big and little: The Four C model of creativity. *Review of General Psychology, 13,* 1–12.

Kaufman, J. C., & Beghetto, R. A. (2013). In praise of Clark Kent: Creative metacognition and the importance of teaching kids when (not) to be creative. *Roeper Review, 35,* 155–165.

Kaufman, J. C., Beghetto, R. A., & Watson, C. (2015). Creative metacognition and self-ratings of creative performance: A 4-C perspective. *Learning and Individual Differences, 23,* 53–69. doi:10.1016/j.lindif.2015.05.004

Mumford, M. D., Blair, C., Dailey, L., Leritz, L. E., & Osburn, H. K. (2006). Errors in creative thought? Cognitive biases in a complex processing activity. *Journal of Creative Behavior, 40,* 75–109.

Plucker, J. A., Beghetto, R. A., & Dow, G. (2004). Why isn't creativity more important to educational psychologists? Potential, pitfalls, and future directions in creativity research. *Educational Psychologist, 39*, 83–96.

Rothenberg, A. (1996). The Janusian process in scientific creativity. *Creativity Research Journal, 9*, 207–231.

Rothenberg, A. (2014). *Flight from wonder: An investigation of scientific creativity.* New York, NY: Oxford University Press.

Runco, M. A. (2003). Creativity, cognition, and their educational implications. In J. C. Houtz (Ed.), *The educational psychology of creativity* (pp. 25–56). Cresskill, NJ: Hampton Press.

Runco, M. A. (2007). *Creativity theories and themes: Research, development, and practice.* Burlington, MA: Elsevier Academic Press.

Sawyer, R. K. (2012). *Explaining creativity: The science of human innovation* (2nd ed.). New York, NY: Oxford University Press.

Scott, C. L. (1999). Teachers' biases toward creative children. *Creativity Research Journal, 12*, 321–337.

Sternberg, R. J., & Kaufman, J. C. (2010). Constraints on creativity: Obvious and not so obvious. In J. C. Kaufman & R. J. Sternberg (Eds.), *The Cambridge handbook of creativity* (pp. 467–482). New York, NY: Cambridge University Press.

Wallas, G. (1926). *The art of thought.* New York, NY: Harcourt, Brace & World.

Westby, E. L., & Dawson, V. L. (1995). Creativity: Asset or burden in the classroom? *Creativity Research Journal, 8*, 1–10.

CHAPTER 14

Technology and Creativity

Timothy J. Magner

Key Take-Aways

- We cannot prepare for technological transition to end, but rather must prepare ourselves and our students to adapt to the constant pace of transformation.
- In educational technology, one must strive to design the "right environment to support the required activity," with *right* and *required* as defined by student needs and curricular demands.
- The purposes and expectations that drive the design of learning environments and tool selection have the potential to both enhance and limit student creativity.
- Students should be enabled to create both *with* and *through* technology as part of their academic experience.
- Being both intentional and transparent about the integration of technology is essential not only for student creativity, but also to foster in them the skills and desire to become the custodians and facilitators of the next generation of creativity as well.

Overview

As one begins to explore the intersections of technology and creativity in an educational context, there are several ideas that are worth considering and that will be explored here. First, in Exponential Convergence, we will discuss the implications of the rapid and seemingly relentless pace of technological change. In Splashing or Swimming, we will look at the types of fundamental considerations that should inform the choice of classroom technology. The section Creation or Consumption will look at the philosophical questions prompted by open-ended technological tools. Building on these thoughts, we next look at the varying outcomes that emerge as we enable and encourage students to Create With or Create Through Technology. And finally, we discuss the importance of choice and thoughtful decision making in selecting technologies and technology-mediated experiences in The Value of Intentionality.

Exponential Convergence

Chances are that while you are reading this there is, somewhere close to you, a cell phone. And further, chances are that it is a *smartphone*, a device that in addition to allowing you to accomplish two-way voice communication, the textbook definition of *phone*, also functions as a small computer. Beyond storing your contacts and allowing you to compose notes, this small computer probably also allows you to text, take and share photographs and short videos, manage your calendar, make a video call, deposit a check, surf the Internet, play games, check the weather, play music, listen to the radio, read the news, read a book, watch movies or even watch live TV, and this is just the start. All in the palm of your hand.

It wasn't always this way. Until the mid-1990s, most of these activities required a separate device to accomplish each task. Individuals had, if they were wealthy enough, a telephone for voice communication; a radio for listening to live music and talk; a television for watching TV; a VCR or DVD player for watching a movie; a stereo, CD player, or MP3 player for listening to recorded music; a camera for taking pictures; a computer for writing and connecting to the Internet; and a video game console for playing games. Over the past 20 years, each of these discrete devices have converged, first to the personal computer and then to the cell phone.

What spurred this convergence is the unprecedented increase in computing power and paradoxical decrease in price of these converged devices, brilliantly predicted and nicely encapsulated in something know as Moore's Law.

Gordon Moore was the cofounder of technology firm and computer chip maker Intel. In 1965, Moore predicted that because of the ability to increase the number of integrated circuits on a single chip, computational power would double every year. Over time this number has been adjusted to about every 18 months, and even today, Intel still achieves doubling about every 2 and a half years (Clark, 2015). At the same time, the cost of these devices has generally fallen by about 50% in the same period. So computers are becoming twice as fast and half as expensive about every 18 to 24 months. That means, for young adults in their early 20s, there were between 6 and 7 generations of computers developed while they were in elementary and secondary school and another two while they were undergraduates. Conservatively then, computers are 2^8 or 256 times more powerful today than they were when those students began kindergarten.

But what is important to realize is that this doubling has been going on since at least 1965. So today, computers are something on the order of 2^{33} or roughly 8,589,934,592 times more powerful than they were in 1965. The phone in your pocket is literally millions of times more powerful than the capsules that the astronauts took to the moon in the late 1960s and early 1970s. And further,

> in 1997, an IBM supercomputer named Deep Blue became the first program to beat a reigning world [chess] champion in a match under standard time controls. Since then, data processors have only gotten smarter. The standard iPhone is now capable of the feat that Deep Blue performed less than two decades ago (Kaplan, 2015, para. 16)

While the density of transistors is reaching a physical limitation and thus beginning to slow the pace of compounded doubling, computing capacity still continues to increase today (Simonite, 2016). The cell phone in your pocket, the one that is millions of times more powerful than its predecessors will itself be eclipsed by the next version that will be significantly more powerful, as will the version after that. What all of this highlights is that technology is advancing both rapidly and exponentially. This expansion means that these machines will be able to do more, and do it faster and likely cheaper than last year's model, but not as much, as fast, or as inexpensively as next year's.

As educators we must recognize that we are in the midst of this rapid transition and must not work to prepare for it to finish, but rather prepare ourselves and especially our students to adapt to this constant pace of transformation. We cannot chase the technology, we must teach our students to create and be creative within this changing context.

Splashing or Swimming

As Loveless (2002) wrote, "the designs of new communications technologies for creative interactions are presenting challenges to expectations of traditional classroom settings in terms of spaces, time, portability, connectivity and flexibility for individuals and communities" (p. 4). As educators looking to utilize technology to support creativity, how does one respond to those challenges listed above?

In the early days of computing in education, advocates would often argue that a computer was, "a tool, like a pencil," to indicate both the functional nature of the device, as well as its potential as a creative outlet. Like a pencil, which can be used for both writing and drawing, a computer can be used for a variety of activities. However, this articulation misses both the immersive potential that technology can provide, as well as the criticality of the environmental dependencies essential for technology to achieve that potential. A better metaphor for technology, rather than as a tool, one might argue, is that technology is an environment like a swimming pool.

Like swimming pools, technology at scale is a significant investment and requires constant care and attention with software and hardware upgrades, virus checking, and the like. Similarly spanning the range from the inflatable kiddie pool to the Olympic-sized competition pool, to the outdoor water park variety, technologies come in different shapes, sizes, and capacities and are best suited for different functions at different times and with different expectations about inputs and outcomes. For example, although the water necessary to fill the average backyard pool makes that spot a pleasing diversion on a summer afternoon, putting that same amount of water into an Olympic-sized venue would make it entirely unusable for its intended purpose. And finally, while it is possible to use a pool without knowing how to swim, and to operate one without supervision, neither is recommended both for safety reasons, and because the full potential of the experience is limited when the users are not sufficiently trained in the skills that allow maximum utility and maximum enjoyment. So too is this the case with technology in education. Without sufficient facility with the software, whether through training, tinkering, or experience, the full potential of the device is unrealized. Teachers, in this metaphor, are both the swim coach, teaching new strokes and encouraging greater productivity, and the lifeguards, ensuring that those pursuing either play or purposeful activities remain safe and behave accordingly.

But just as the empty swimming pools of Southern California became the ersatz skateparks and proving grounds of the early 1970s skateboard pioneers, sometimes individuals will find a creative outlet, or explore creative expression with the technology in ways that are orthogonal to, or at least unintended by the original inventors.

As educators looking to support creativity with technology, it is important to understand the kinds of experiences one is attempting to foster. Are you expecting splashing or swimming? Are you looking to go wading or to have your charges swim the 400-meter individual medley or perform a reverse 3 1/2 somersault with 1/2 twist? If you bring your toddler to the deep end, or your high schooler to the wading pool, you will need to provide different types of supervision and should expect different results. This is not to say that toddlers need only stay in shallow water or that high schoolers cannot find joy or creative expression within a seemingly limited environment, but that the expectations for support and for outcomes should be calibrated with the extent of the environment involved. And, more importantly, the kind of technology environment should be thoughtfully curated based on the kinds of experiences desired and the range of outcomes expected. To paraphrase the builder's motto, "the right tool for the right job," in educational technology one should strive for the "right environment to support the required activity," with *right* and *required* as defined by the student needs and curricular demands.

Creation or Consumption

In 2004, Apple introduced GarageBand, a digital music application. The application included a range of digital imitations of real-life instruments such as an electric piano, guitars, drums, horns, and strings (Future Music, 2011). In addition to the individual instruments, GarageBand also included a series of audio effects and short loops of digital instrument sounds. Since its inception, the software application has been expanded with increasingly sophisticated features and upgraded to enable both the import of existing music files as well as the export of tracks compiled in GarageBand. The software facilitates the creation of *songs* through the arrangement of either new note combinations played by the user or through compilations of the existing music loops either by themselves or in conjunction with note combinations played by the user. These two types of note sequencing options raise a fundamental question: Is stringing together a series of prerecorded tracks *creative* or is it simply repackaging or *consuming* the *creative* work of another? Similar questions have been raised about other types of applications such as image editors like Adobe's Photoshop and the myriad new cell phone apps that allow for the editing, morphing, and otherwise transmogrification of photos.

One of the affordances of digital technology is the inherent capacity for the recombination and repurposing of digital files. All digital artifacts, whether documents, images, sound files, videos, web pages, or programs themselves, are editable, whether innately by simple copying or through labored reverse engineering. This mutability has been the source of a great deal of controversy with regard to copyright and intellectual property as original creators and developers from Apple to the artist Prince work diligently to either prevent or at least collect royalty payments from the makers of derivative works. On the flip side, this mutability has also been embraced as an inherent *right* of all technology users having spawned the *free software* movement, which argues that,

> users have the freedom to run, copy, distribute, study, change and improve the software. Thus, "free software" is a matter of liberty, not price. To understand the concept, you should think of "free" as in "free speech," not as in "free beer" (Free Software Foundation, 2015c, para. 1)

This approach, embodied in models such as Wikipedia (Wikimedia Foundation Inc., 2015), Copy Left (Free Software Foundation, 2015b), Creative Commons (2015), and some types of open source software projects (Free Software Foundation, 2015a), emphasize the ability for content consumers to edit, update, republish, and repackage content for the good of the user community, although most often without the ability to generate revenue from the derivative work.

However, as Mitchell, Inouye, and Blumenthal (2003) wrote for the National Research Council, "the more software tools emphasize ease of use or familiar metaphors, the more they must depend on restrictive assumptions in order to do so" (p. 3). Do these digital tools that facilitate, and one would argue promote, editorial derivation actually encourage true creativity or just give the veneer of creativity to simplistic recombinations of actual creative work?

The use of Plucker, Beghetto, and Dow's (2004) definition of creativity as "the interplay between ability and process by which an individual or group produces an outcome or product that is both novel and useful as defined within some social context" (p. 156) is particularly instructive here.

With regard to the "interplay between ability and process," because the software application provides even novice users with significant capabilities, the notion of ability is now twofold: one ability in the content area itself (music, visual art, programming, etc.) and one ability to manipulate the software application. As users become more facile with the operational aspects of the software, they may or may not come to a greater appreciation for, greater understanding of, or greater skill with the underlying theoretical frameworks of the content areas themselves. The migration from the opportunity to easily combine the loops of digital music provided by the application, to the skillful linking of these samples, for example, may evidence an increase in the user's understanding of the application, but may not have any bearing on the user's actual *musical* creativity. On the other hand, this increased facility might also inspire the user to explore music theory directly through other digital and analog means, but the understanding is not necessarily innate within the software application itself. As Loveless (2007) noted, "there is always the danger that descriptions of creativity be reduced to just having ideas, recording, mimicking and showing—remaining in the initial stages and processes without the opportunity or desire to take these further" (p. 14).

Similarly, with regard to *novelty* and *usefulness*, one can argue whether the recombination of provided samples, or the transmogrification of an existing image is truly *novel*. The website OBAMA-ME, for example, which allows users to create a posterized version of themselves in the style of the now-famous campaign poster from President Barack Obama's 2008 campaign, is an example of technology's capacity to enable even those with limited or no ability to *create* a *novel* work. In further amplification of these issues, the poster, which was vaunted as innovative at the time, was later surrounded by controversy because the poster artist lied about which image he had used and the Associated Press photographer who took the original picture the poster is derived from sued for copyright infringement (Katz, 2012). In a counter example, a young mother who took a grainy video of her son dancing to the Prince song "Let's Go Crazy" and posted it on the video sharing website YouTube was successful in having the copyright challenge by Prince's record label Universal Music Publishing Group overturned under the guise of the copyright law's Fair Use provisions (Electronic Frontier Foundation, 2015). Whether this video is novel or perhaps just a *novelty*, the level of ability required to create it was minimal and the process to capture and post and promote the video has been streamlined by both technological innovation and companies such as YouTube owner Google, whose goal is to facilitate this kind of information sharing.

However, technology can also facilitate the creation of truly novel, and in some cases, truly unprecedented constructions. The undulating glass and steel roof of the Robert and Arlene Kogod Courtyard at the Smithsonian Donald W. Reynolds Center for American Art and Portraiture, for example, has a surface area of 37,500 square feet, weighs some 900 tons, and is comprised of 864 individual panes of glass, no two of which are alike. The roof's complexity is such that it was essentially impossible to create and implement such a structure without the use of computer technology. Here is an installation that is both novel in design and construction, and because it provides a roof over an interior courtyard, is also undisputedly useful.

But perhaps the most critical element of Plucker et al.'s (2004) definition for our purposes is the phrase "as defined within some social context." As they noted,

> the recognition that creativity varies as a function of the social context in which it is situated is an acknowledgment that what is viewed as creative within one social context will not necessarily be seen as creative in another social context. (Plucker et al., 2004, p. 158)

As educators then, the *social context* in which we facilitate our students' creativity is a determining factor in how we both enable and evaluate their creative endeavors. As with the swimming pool analogy above, the purpose and expectations of the environment we create and the tools we choose provide both a potentially expansive and limiting context in which our students operate. As Loveless (2007) wrote, "our knowledge of creativity emerges as we think at the edges of our practice, and figure out how to use tools and media in distinctive ways to express our imagination and capabilities" (p. 14). This builds on the National Research Council's statement that,

> such tools not only must be available, but they also must be objects of critical reflection; they must be open to adjustment and tweaking, they must support unintended and subversive uses—not just anticipated ones—and they must not be too resistant to being torn apart and reconceived. (Mitchell et al., 2003, p. 3)

We must be ever mindful, then, of the interplay between the elements of creativity in the ways we foster and evaluate student creative expression.

Loveless (2002) identified a number of ways educators can be mindful of the need for creativity in constructing lessons and creating learning environments, including:

- awareness of the ways in which creativity is related to knowledge across the curriculum;
- opportunities for exploration and play with materials, information, and ideas;
- opportunities to take risks and make mistakes in a nonthreatening atmosphere;
- opportunities for reflection, resourcefulness, and resilience;
- flexibility in time and space for the different stages of creative activity;

- sensitivity to the values of education that underpin individual and local interest, commitment, potential, and quality of life; and
- teaching strategies that acknowledge "teaching for creativity" as well as "teaching creatively."

As educators, the creativity we seek to foster must be that of our students, and the contexts we create, the tools we select, and the environments we establish must all be in that service. But it is incumbent on us as learning professionals to also view the contextualization, selection, and environmental establishment as our creative landscape and thus be conscious of and reflect on our own digressive, innovative, and creative potential to harness the available resources to develop novel environments, unique tasks, and additional creative outlets that continue to push our students and ourselves toward that creative horizon.

Create With or Create Through

Loveless (2002) identified a range of activities and processes that teachers and students have undertaken that support creativity and also take advantage of affordances of digital technologies:

- **developing ideas:** supporting imaginative conjecture, exploration, and representation of ideas;
- **making connections:** supporting, challenging, informing, and developing ideas by making connections with information, people, projects, and resources;
- **creating and making:** engaging in making meanings though fashioning processes of capture, manipulation, and transformation of media;
- **collaboration:** working with others in immediate and dynamic ways to collaborate on outcomes and construct shared knowledge; and
- **communication and evaluation:** publishing and communicating outcomes for evaluation and critique from a range of audiences.

Similarly, Fisher, Higgins, and Loveless (2006) have gone further, creating clusters of purposeful activities that utilize digital technologies in a learning context (Table 14.1).

Mitchell et al. (2003) have also developed a model of interdependent interaction between scientific, cultural, and business practices that places information technology at the center as a facilitator and "glue" between and among

Table 14.1

Clusters of Purposeful Activity With Digital Technologies

Knowledge Building	• adapting and developing ideas • modelling • representing understanding in multimodal and dynamic ways
Distributed cognition	• accessing resources • finding things out • writing, composing, and presenting with mediating artefacts and tools
Community and communication	• exchanging and sharing communication • extending the context of activity • extending the participating community at local and global levels
Engagement	• exploring and playing • acknowledging risk and uncertainty • working with different dimensions of interactivity • responding to immediacy

Note. From *Teachers Learning With Digital Technologies: A Review of Research and Projects* (p. 3) by T. Fisher, C. Higgins, & A. Loveless, 2006, Bristol, England: Futurelab. Copyright 2006 by Futurelab. Reprinted with permission.

those domains (Figure 14.1). Although created in a commercial business context, for purposes of this discussion, we are including teaching as the "business practice" facilitated by technology.

Mitchell et al. (2003) went further and overlayed the creative dimension on the same domains (Figure 14.2), recognizing that there is a domain of technological creativity that at once informs and facilitates the development of creative expression within its own domain as well as being informed by and an enabler and facilitator of creative expression between and among the other domains as well. As Mitchell et al. (2003) noted,

> These various interrelationships suggest the importance not only of specialized loci of creativity, such as highly focused research laboratories and individual artist's studios, but also of creativity clusters—complexes of interconnected activity, encompassing multiple domains, which provide opportunities and incentives for productive cross-fertilization. (p. 23)

What Loveless (2002) and Fisher et al. (2006) demonstrated with their compilations is a range of activities that individuals pursue using technology as the tool of creative expression, such as writing, editing pictures, composing music, discovering new information, exploring other cultures via video, or even interactive discussions with users around the globe. In these cases, we posit,

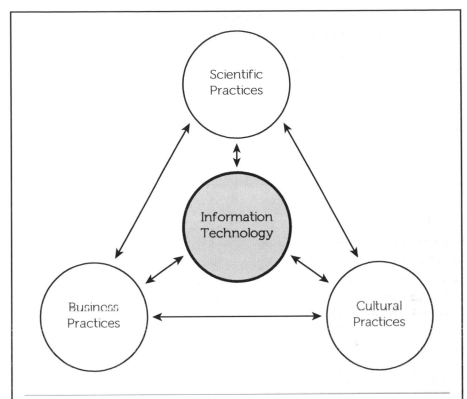

Figure 14.1. Information technology as glue. From *Beyond Productivity: Information Technology, Innovation, and Creativity* (p. 25), by W. J. Mitchell, A. S. Inouye, & M. S. Blumenthal, 2003, Washington, DC: National Academies Press. Copyright 2003 National Academies Press. Reprinted with permission.

individuals are creating *through* the technology. It is the affordances of the technology that support the means of expression.

This is the realm in which most educators will interact with students in a technology context. Software and hardware are made available for use within a classroom context, but can be utilized in a variety of combinations, as outlined by Loveless (2002) and Fisher et al. (2006). When creating *through* technology, students are provided with a range of tools and environments that allow them to develop output products that may or may not be digital in final form. For example, students might produce an essay, spreadsheet, or picture that is output in hard copy, or they might produce a database or video that remains digital. As described above, the combination of tools selected and the type of environment structured play a significant role in helping to facilitate the nature and extent of student creative expression.

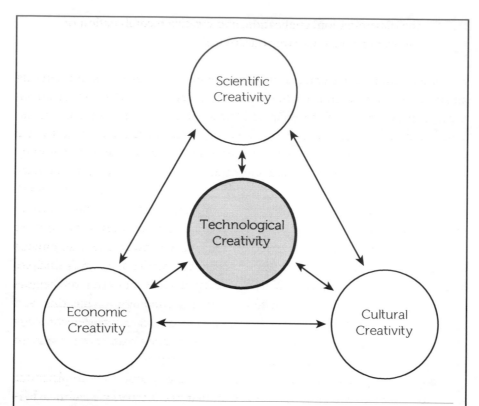

Figure 14.2. Domains of creative activity. From *Beyond Productivity: Information Technology, Innovation, and Creativity* (p. 22), by W. J. Mitchell, A. S. Inouye, & M. S. Blumenthal, 2003, Washington, DC: National Academies Press. Copyright 2003 National Academies Press. Reprinted with permission.

There is also another means of creative expression supported by technology. This means is no less important and, one might argue, is even more critical to the future creative expression than creating through technology, and that is the creativity and innovation expressed *with* the technology itself. This creativity takes place in activities such as computer hardware design, software programming, app development, video game development, and other innovations in the creation of the new tools, environments, and systems that are available to support the creativity of others. As Mitchell et al. (2003) noted,

> information technology is, by its very nature, a powerful amplifier of creative practices. Because software can readily be copied and disseminated, and because there can be an unlimited number of simultaneous users, software supports

the dissemination, application, and creative recombination of innovations on a massive scale. (p. 26)

Programming tools and software development platforms are proliferating and become more readily available even for primary students. Whether through open source languages such as php and Python or the growing number of free-ware computer based tools such as Alice (http://www.alice.org), Hackety Hack (http://hackety.com), Arduino (http://arduino.cc), as well as programming apps such as Scratch (https://scratch.mit.edu) and Tynker (https://www.tynker.com) and game design apps such as Hopscotch (http://gethopscotch.com), Kodu (http://www.kodugamelab.com), and Gamestar Mechanic (https://gamestarmechanic.com), to name but a few, the opportunities to bring these tools into classrooms or school-based contexts are increasing. They also provide a platform for students to explore important mathematics and logic principles and to see alternative means of creative expression. Especially given the heightened recognition of the importance of science, technology, engineering, and mathematics fields, embracing the opportunities for creating *with* technology as part of each student's academic experience may open pathways for student creativity outside of traditional school-based constructs.

In addition, given the juxtaposition of technology tools as both platforms and outlets for creative expression, it is vital that as educators we embrace language and perspective that value the *creativity* inherent in programmed code or the function and interface of a computer application, as well as in the arts. As Sir Ken Robinson (2006) observed in a TED Talk, "Many highly talented, brilliant, creative people think they're not—because the thing they were good at at school wasn't valued, or was actually stigmatized." At the same time, technology may enable more students to be creative in the arts and facilitate their artistic creativity as never before.

The Value of Intentionality

Technological innovation has always been a source of both excitement and fear. As author Arthur C. Clarke (1973) famously opined, "any sufficiently advanced technology is indistinguishable from magic" (p. 2), while at the same time, General Omar Bradley observed that "if we continue to develop our technology without wisdom or prudence, our servant may prove to be our executioner" (Clark & Lilley, 1989, p. 4). As we discussed in the opening section, with the pace of innovation both unrelenting and rapidly increasing, with technology tools ever more sophisticated, we are for perhaps the first time in history in a situation where children and adults are learning both the capabilities and limits of advanced technology at the same time. Teachers of students as young as primary school are now faced with students who are more familiar with and more facile with technology tools than they are. Whether smartphones, tablets, or other mobile devices, many students have on-demand access to technology at home or in their backpack as sophisticated as, and in many cases more sophisticated than, what is available at school.

This proliferation has also created a cultural and behavioral disconnect as social conventions, mores, and manners are trampled when technologies intrude unimpeded into our living, learning, and working spaces. The cliché of the teen or tween with his or her face buried in a phone at the dinner table, or the young couple who text each other across the room, or the documented preference of students for digital rather than face-to-face interaction (Peacock & Sanghani, 2014), all highlight the ways in which technology is changing the social dynamic. The fact that an increasing number of adults could also be caught doing any of the aforementioned demonstrates the extent to which all generations are impacted by this cultural juggernaut. As writer Stuart Brand (1987) noted, "Once a new technology rolls over you, if you're not part of the steamroller, you're part of the road" (p. 9).

Although as citizens we must make our own choices with regard to how quickly and completely we allow technology to infuse our lifestyle, as educators we have an important obligation to be caretakers of the learning space and the creative environments we establish for our students. Teachers have always been gatekeepers, using professional judgment and a keen understanding of the needs of their students to moderate the introduction of concepts, information, and experiences. The introduction of technology should be no different.

Unfortunately, however, technology integration is often done by acquisition rather than design. New hardware is purchased because funds are available, because it is *time* or to demonstrate to the community that the school or district is *modern*, *21st century*, or *progressive*. As often as not, because the implementations are device centric, not student or learning centric, their success varies widely across classrooms, schools, and districts.

For example, the much vaunted 1-to-1 initiatives that began first with desktops, moved to laptops, and are now focused on tablets and pads, are often driven by the noble desire to ensure that all students have access to a computing device and have the added benefit that the standardization of student access to the same device should make device management and curricular design easier and more effective. However, by focusing on the device (i.e., one [desktop, laptop, tablet, etc.] per student) rather than on the specific learning objectives to be achieved or experiences to be enjoyed, all too often the device selected may not meet the full range of needs. A tablet may be an excellent choice for web browsing or remote data collection, but it may prove underpowered for a database application or an awkward form factor to compose a long essay. It is also increasingly true that many adults, and even many students, actually possess multiple devices—a cell phone, a tablet, a laptop, and a desktop—each designed and equipped to accomplish different tasks in different contexts. On-demand access to the appropriate tool, then, is the desired paradigm, rather than lock-step standardization. Having a variety of form factors available for use in different contexts, however, requires flexibility and planning, but may in fact be more effective in the long run because educators can select the tools that meet their objectives rather than trying to force their objectives to conform to a specific form factor.

As educators we have both the responsibility and the opportunity to be intentional in our selection of and use of technology. By basing our choices on the needs of our students, the kinds of experiences we wish to provide, and the outcomes we wish to foster, we not only engage in a thoughtful process of selection, but we also provide both an example of and a context for our students to frame their own interactions with technology. For example, the act of determining that pencil and paper for drawing or glue and scissors for cutting and pasting are preferable to doing those tasks on a digital tablet in a certain instance may ensure that important learning elements are preserved or that students have essential experiences.

Using collaborative dialogue with both colleagues and students, as well as a structured process to make thoughtful and intentional decisions about when, where, and how to use technology in a particular lesson, curriculum unit, or educational experience allows for a thorough discussion of what the essential learning experiences and expected student outcomes are and how they can be aligned with the specific affordances of a particular technology. For example, using one of Loveless's (2002) activities from above, "exploration and representation of ideas" could be done using Internet searches; finding a range of global sources including online text, images, and video; collecting them into a digital dropbox; then sorting and arranging them in a graphic organizer; and finally compiling them into a documentary feature with live video, presentation slides, and voiceovers, all scripted using a word processor. Or the same activity could be accomplished with students sitting in small groups discussing a topic orally, coming to consensus, and creating a poster with markers and paper to share their findings with the class. Either approach could be educationally valuable, each one has its critical elements and dependencies, and it is up to the educator to determine which type of experience is desired and thus which type of technology is most appropriate to achieve that end.

As our society becomes more immersed in technology, it is perhaps even more important that schools create environments in which the use of technology is defined and intentional. For example, the *flipped classroom* concept posits the notion that technology can be best used to distribute information such as reading assignments and even classroom lectures to students outside of school through presentations, podcasts, videos, websites, and online simulations that are accessed at home or during other nonclass time, freeing classroom time for discussion, hands-on projects, and other collaborative exploration (FLIP Learning, 2014). One possible implication of this approach is that schools could become a lower tech environment that emphasizes collaborative hands-on construction and creative exploration built upon knowledge and concepts that students acquired through technology-delivered resources at their higher tech home.

If we seek to provide social contexts for students individually and in groups to "produce an outcome or product that is both novel and useful" (Plucker & Beghetto, 2004, p. 156), then we must create environments where they have the tools and resources, but most importantly the time, guidance, and freedom to explore, innovate, and experiment. Technology can provide all of those things, but the intentional absence of technology can provide them as well. As educators, by being both intentional and transparent about our integration of technology, we can foster not only the creative output of our students, but foster in them the skills and desire to become the custodians and facilitators of the next generation of creativity as well.

Recommended Reading

Bergmann, J., & Sams, A. (2012). *Flip your classroom: Reach every student in every class every day.* Arlington, VA: International Society for Technology in Education.

Frazel, M. (2010). *Digital storytelling guide for educators.* Arlington, VA: International Society for Technology in Education.

Oppenheimer, T. (2004). *The flickering mind: Saving education from the false promise of technology.* New York, NY: Random House.

Robinson, K. (2001). *Out of our minds: Learning to be creative.* Chichester, England: Capstone.

Sheninger, E. C. (2014). *Digital leadership: Changing paradigms for changing times.* Thousand Oaks, CA: Corwin.

References

Brand, S. (1987). *The media lab: Inventing the future at M.I.T.* New York, NY: Penguin.

Clark, A. A., & Lilley, J. F. (1989). *Defense technology.* New York, NY: Praeger.

Clark, D. (2015). Intel rechisels the tablet on Moore's Law. *Wall Street Journal.* Retrieved from http://blogs.wsj.com/digits/2015/07/16/intel-rechisels-the-tablet-on-moores-law

Clarke, A. C. (1973). *Profiles of the future: An inquiry into the limits of the possible.* New York, NY: Holt, Rinehart and Winston.

Creative Commons. (2015). *About the licenses.* Retrieved from https://creative-commons.org/licenses

Electronic Frontier Foundation. (2015). *Lenz v. Universal.* Retrieved from https://www.eff.org/cases/lenz-v-universal

Fisher, T., Higgins, C., & Loveless, A. (2006). *Teachers learning with digital technologies: A review of research and projects.* Bristol, England: Futurelab.

FLIP Learning. (2014). *Definition of flipped learning.* Retrieved from http://www.flippedlearning.org/definition

Free Software Foundation. (2015a). *Categories of free and nonfree software.* Retrieved from http://www.gnu.org/philosophy/categories.html

Free Software Foundation. (2015b). *What is copyleft?* Retrieved from http://www.gnu.org/copyleft/copyleft.html

Free Software Foundation. (2015c). *What is free software?* Retrieved from http://www.gnu.org/philosophy/free-sw.html

Future Music. (2011). A brief history of GarageBand. *Music Radar.* Retrieved from http://www.musicradar.com/tuition/tech/a-brief-history-of-garage-band-400471

Kaplan, S. (2015). Chess player accused of cheating with hidden camera and Morse code messages. *The Washington Post.* Retrieved from https://www.washingtonpost.com/news/morning-mix/wp/2015/09/09/chess-player-accused-of-cheating-with-hidden-camera-and-morse-code-messages

Katz, B. (2012). Artist admits lying over Obama poster image. *Reuters.com.* Retrieved from http://www.reuters.com/article/obama-poster-crime-idU SL2E8DOC8I20120224

Loveless, A. (2002). *Literature review in creativity, new technologies and learning.* Bristol, England: Futurelab.

Loveless, A. (2007). *Creativity, technology and learning: A review of recent literature.* Bristol, England: Futurelab.

Mitchell, W. J., Inouye A. S., & Blumenthal, M. S. (2003). *Beyond productivity: Information technology, innovation, and creativity.* Washington, DC: National Academies Press.

Peacock , L., & Sanghani, R. (2014, April 29). Teenagers 'more confident talking to each other via smartphones than face-to-face'—study. *The Telegraph.* Retrieved from http://www.telegraph.co.uk/women/mother-tongue/10793984/Teenagers-more-confident-talking-to-each-other-via-smartphones-than-face-to-face-study.html

Plucker, J. A., & Beghetto, R. A. (2004). Why creativity is domain general, why it looks domain specific and why the distinction does not matter. In R. J. Sternberg, E. L. Grigorenko, & J. L. Singer (Eds.), *Creativity: From potential to realization* (pp. 153–168). Washington, DC: American Psychological Association.

Plucker, J. A., Beghetto, R. A., & Dow, G. T. (2004). Why isn't creativity more important to educational psychologists? Potentials, pitfalls, and future directions in creativity research. *Educational Psychologist, 39,* 83–96.

Robinson, K. (2006). *Do schools kill creativity?* Presentation at TED2006 conference, Monterey, CA. Retrieved from https://www.ted.com/talks/ken_robinson_says_schools_kill_creativity

Simonite, T. (2016). Intel puts the brakes on Moore's Law. *MIT Technology Review.* Retrieved from http://www.technologyreview.com/s/601102/intel-puts-the-brakes-on-moores-law

Wikimedia Foundation Inc. (2015). *Wikipedia: Five pillars.* Retrieved from https://en.wikipedia.org/wiki/Wikipedia:Five_pillars

Creative Leisure

C. Boyd Hegarty

Key Take-Aways

- Considering how creativity and leisure overlap may help us to better recognize creativity for creativity's sake and how self-expression plays a role in everyday creativity.
- The social context by which a perceptible product is both novel and useful within creative leisure hinges upon the self as the judge.
- Creative leisure may represent a peak experience in both leisure and creativity.
- It is imperative that creativity be understood more as a means of self-expression rather than only as a way to innovate or cope with reality.

An older Chinese man hops along a path in a Shanghai park mimicking the movements of a frog; his self-designed exercise routine. Another person builds a sand castle on the beach on the Gulf Coast of Florida, spending hours to sculpt each detail, only for it to be washed away to sea as the tide comes in. A group of friends on Facebook comment on a user's status, responding with wild ideas for his request for help in deciding on a username for his new e-mail address. A mother improvises an off-the-cuff story to her children at bedtime, complete with original music and silly voices. These are acts of *creative leisure*. These experiences are perhaps those in which creativity is most meaningful in our everyday lives. Research and theoretical writing that consider both creativity and leisure literature, however, are just beginning to emerge, despite this naturally important confluence.

People who study creativity have certainly mentioned aspects of leisure, especially during discussions of everyday creativity (Richards, 2007), personal creativity (Runco, 1996), self-actualized creativity (Maslow, 1959), self-expression (Henderson, 2004), intrinsic motivation (Amabile, 1996), flow (Csikszentmihalyi, 1996), and enjoyment (Csikszentmihalyi, 1996; Henderson, 2004). We also have seen creativity in leisure activities in relation to successful aging (Fisher & Specht, 1999).

The relationship between creativity and leisure overlaps in significant and important ways. This relationship is particularly important because current leisure thinking may be able to transform how we define everyday creativity. For example, we may better recognize creativity for creativity's sake and how self-expression plays a role in everyday creativity.

Defining Leisure and Creativity

The concept of leisure is usually defined in three ways: as time, as recreation (a specific act), or as a psychological state (Russell, 2004). I adopt the latter of these definitions. More specifically, peak leisure experience, as defined by Neulinger (1974), is one in which the participant has a high sense of perceived freedom and intrinsic motivation. Plucker, Beghetto, and Dow (2004) stated that creativity "is the interaction among aptitude, process, and environment by which an individual or group produces a perceptible product that is both novel and useful as defined within a social context" (p. 90). Anchoring the definition of creativity that Plucker et al. (2004) proposed are the commonly referred aspects of *novelty* and *utility*. These terms are the cornerstones of most definitions of creativity. Utility requires that a product or outcome be usefully applied to a context.

Self-Actualized Creativity

Maslow's (1959, 1963) conceptualization of creativity seemingly differs from that of Plucker et al. (2004) in that it is dependent upon a personal trait: self-actualization. Davis (1998) also based much of his argument toward the importance of creativity via the notion that creativity and self-actualization are the same. On one hand, this works in contrast to the definition put forth by Plucker et al. (2004). Perhaps one may extract pieces of self-actualized creativity that can be nested within their definition. The measurement of this type of creativity may extend beyond a tangible product viewed within a social context to that which is perhaps more implicit. Self-actualized creativity is done for the sake of being creative, regardless of the domain, and many times regardless of the product (Maslow, 1959). Self-actualized creativity thus has a product that is less tangible, despite that it may produce and often does produce a tangible product.

The key production of self-actualized creativity may be self-expression and even happiness. Creative leisure is housed within these two definitions of creativity. A critical piece that merges the definitions is that the social context by which a perceptible product is both novel and useful must hinge upon the self as judge. An act of creative leisure may be deemed creative by a social group, another person, or a field or entire domain, but if it is not considered creative by the creator, it is not creative leisure. Creative leisure is tied directly to the judgment of the individual. In addition, although self-actualized creativity represents an aspect of creative leisure, it does not represent the whole construct.

A small body of research indicates that when both creativity and leisure occur together, peak experience and subjective well-being may be associated (Csikszentmihalyi, 1975, 1990; Maslow, 1959, 1963). Beyond this, self-expression emerges when creativity is done for its own sake (Fisher & Specht, 1999; Henderson, 2004); thus, it is possible that creativity in one's leisure is not only important, but that self-expression is an important aspect of that behavior.

Nash (1953) wrote that

> in considering the power that lies in each man, recreation is the name given to those activities which furnish man an outlet for creativity, when work ceases to be challenging and stimulating. Leisure time should provide an opportunity for a basic human need—creative experience. (p. 166)

This statement beckoned the field of leisure research to investigate the importance of creativity in leisure, but sadly, this call was hardly advanced. I argue that leisure is that which defines our humanity, and through leisure is how we as humans fully express ourselves. When one merges creativity and leisure, one moves toward evaluating how an individual experiences self-expression, happiness, and joy. Further, when merging creativity and leisure, or *creative leisure*, this could perhaps represent a peak experience in both leisure and creativity. One experiences a high sense of freedom, intrinsic motivation, and reward, one expresses the self to the self, and this is done for the sake of doing it.

Creativity and Self-Expression

The notion of creativity as self-expression is not often discussed in current literature. Self-expression itself is lacking in the subject indices of both the *Handbook of Creativity* (Sternberg, 1999) and the *Encyclopedia of Creativity* (Runco & Pritzker, 1999), texts generally thought to be standard references in creativity theory and research. When self-expression is acknowledged, it is done so as a part of a larger whole of creativity and rarely as a central component of the creative experience. However, Runco (2007) did touch on self-expression in more recent writing and proposed that individual self-expression may be related to ego strength. This idea should be explored as it relates to creative leisure.

Henderson (2004) has posed the seldom-asked question of how enjoyment plays a role in the creative process. Using qualitative methods, the researcher studied the creativity and emotion of seven adult participants. The intent was to investigate the affective nature of creativity of inventors within the framework of Russ's (1993) five affective dimensions. Four new categories emerged from the interviews including *affective pleasure in self-expression*. An inventor reported, "The expression of something is very important to me. And doing it clearly and efficiently and beautifully . . . . If truth be told, if I could make a living at writing, I might rather do it than engineering" (Henderson, 2004, p. 308).

Although this initial research on self-expression suggests its importance in creativity, it has yet to be determined if self-expression is a worthy piece of the definition of creativity. Even more importantly, how self-expression relates to Plucker et al.'s (2004) definition of creativity, because of its relevance in the field, is necessary.

Leisure and Self-Expression

In the context of leisure, self-expression has also received little attention. Tinsley and Kass (1978) identified self-expression as one of eight types of leisure. Stebbins (2001) also discussed self-expression when researching serious leisure and casual leisure. Dumazedier (1967) proposed five functions of leisure satisfactions: relaxation, diversion, knowledge, social participation, and creativity. In addition, although self-expression and creativity have been touched upon in leisure, this area has yet to be adequately explored and certainly not fully explored via the currently proposed definition of creative leisure.

Creativity, Leisure, and Finding Flow

Csikszentmihalyi's (1975, 1990, 1996) concept of flow, on the other hand, addresses both leisure and creativity. Flow occurs when challenge is in balance with one's skill level when engaged in a given activity (Csikszentmihalyi, 1975, 1997). Flow occurs typically when the activity is autotelic, or done for its own sake. The notion of an activity being done for its own sake relates directly to Neulinger's (1974) concept of perceived freedom and intrinsic motivation. One might conclude that if something is done for the sake of doing it, paramount to a tangible outcome, then perceived freedom and intrinsic motivation would be high, as it is in creative leisure.

Csikszentmihalyi (1996) has applied flow to such pastimes as rock climbing and painting (Csikszentmihalyi, 1975, 1990), and how creative people experience flow (Csikszentmihalyi, 1996). However, this research has not explicitly addressed the crossover between leisure and creativity for everyday persons. The focus has generally either been on leisure alone or on eminent creative persons. Ironically, this has emphasized the product associated with creativity as it relates to flow rather than the intrinsic outcomes. In this regard, flow is a means by which creativity occurs rather than an outcome of seeking creativity. Flow certainly looks to be a factor of creative leisure; however, creative leisure may also occur as more of a mindset (such as self-actualization), and not be necessarily domain specific or even domain dependent. It also may occur for individuals in short vignettes that do not require deep concentration and long blocks of time to achieve.

Creativity, Leisure, and Aging

Creativity has been examined in the aging population. In their qualitative analysis of creativity and aging, Fisher and Specht (1999) investigated aspects of creativity and aging through the interviews of 36 older adult participants in a fine arts exhibition. The data suggest the process is what allows a person to fulfill creative expression. Further, Lemons (2005) juxtaposed improvisation and creativity with adults and identified seven categories consistent across fields in which improvisation was utilized, including honest emotional expression, self-actualization, and joy. This research points toward the value of intrinsic outcomes, and moves beyond previous research focused on both domain-specific creativity and production with older adults.

Simonton (1991) researched creativity as it relates to the life span of aging adults and in doing so discovered a number of key issues. He noted that studies show poetic creativity peaks in the 20s and 30s, whereas scholarship may peak in the 50s. Simonton's research showed that although these ideas may have some merit, a few other key phenomena occur. First, creativity does peak early, but this peak tends to be based less on age and more on stage of career. People tend to peak early in their careers; however, when relating quality of creativity versus quantity, this relationship does not change throughout time. Although output across individuals tends to decrease, and degree of quality decreases, the ratio of number of creative outputs to quality remains relatively equal. This dynamic means that while the quantity decreases, the ability to create does not diminish with age. One may also choose a career shift to maximize one's creativity.

At retirement, many experience a revival. In this instance, people tend to remain focused on quality and motivated to leave a lasting impression or swan song. Simonton (1991) described how empirical research reveals that individuals experience a renaissance of creativity in their lives, typically after their late 60s. Importantly, the scales of creativity and change over age are not deterministic—an individual has the control to determine levels of creativity. A person in his or her 60s may be producing more quantity and quality of creative outputs than a person in his or her late 20s.

> The important implication . . . is that the career trajectory reflects not the inexorable progression of an aging process tied extrinsically to chronological age, but rather entails the intrinsic working out of a person's creative potential by successive acts of self-actualization. (Simonton, 1991, p. 99)

Although limited in scope, this research has looked at creativity for creativity's sake for older adults as it relates to well-being. One might conclude that we devalue the production of older adults. However, as Simonton and others have shown, older adults can be highly productive in their creativity. Perhaps collective American thinking of young and middle-aged adults is that these groups should be focused on bread-winning, building up the 401k, childraising in a traditional sense, and so forth. Leisure is viewed more as a way to reinvigorate oneself for work rather than a deeply meaningful expression of the self, and creativity is relegated to either a function of socially valued innovation or reduced to little-c creativity (inherently devalued in its name alone).

Youth and Creative Leisure

It is no secret that creativity research has primarily focused on youth (and to a lesser degree, business), particularly in traditional educational settings. This makes sense for many reasons, but perhaps does not cover all of the key areas where children are actualizing creativity. While play research considers just that, there are areas such as youth recreational programming (both formal and informal) that are largely untouched. For example, the summer camp industry is just getting around to empirically considering the impact of its work on creativity in children, despite decades of largely colloquial assumptions of the important impacts camps have in influencing children's creativity. Despite the glut of youth-focused creativity research and theory, there are yet more studies and consideration to be done.

Work and Creative Leisure

Runco (2005) proposed that individuals are less likely to actualize creativity in their job the further they are in their careers because the risks become too great for them to do so. A person may have too much on the line between a high salary and years of investment in a career to risk a creative idea or act that may fail. Some may seek creativity away from their work, while others may toil until retirement to discover creativity as they decompress from an increasingly restrictive career. Still, others may not be able to find a creative outlet because it is too daunting.

The peak of creativity after retirement, therefore, may be associated with persons having more time to develop their leisure lives and seek creativity. Another reason may be that one's job itself and all of the social constraints associated with it reduce a person's ability to have a sense of freedom away from his or her work. This is the "What would people at work think if they saw this?" type of fear. As persons become more entrenched in their careers, risk becomes too great, and perception of freedom to create subsides. These individuals may forget or lose motivation to be creative.

All of these aspects of creative leisure are ripe for research—especially as more than 70 million Americans will be over the age of 65 years old in the United States in the next 22 years. Further, if these baby boomers continue to work after age 65, will they have access to this resurgence of creativity? Generally, it is increasingly more important to investigate how life stage and age relate to creative leisure. Meanwhile, China is now the Earth's largest country, with the fastest growing older adult population on the planet. The relevancy for a focus on meaning of creative leisure for all ages is increasingly globally relevant.

Freedom and Constraints

Perhaps one of the greatest aspects of creative leisure is that it is accessible to just about anyone; one just needs the willingness and desire to express oneself to oneself. Recently at a conference, I was asked how constraints (seemingly the antithesis of freedom) may hinder creative leisure. For example, what if a person does not have the money to sign up for local pottery class? First, there are always barriers in life—they may be health-related, financial, and geographic. Creativity, however, is not limited to the chosen few. Thus, it is the job of the researchers (across disciplines), professionals (e.g., camp directors, teachers, parks and recreation leaders, recreational therapists), individuals (across the life span), and institutions to promote creative leisure as a means of expression despite constraints, and perhaps as a means by which to mediate constraints.

Individuals may have the sense of freedom to allow themselves to seek creativity, but when seeking it, certain constraints such as rules or a budget may actually enhance this experience. For example, a woman signs up for a collage class with the desire to actualize more creativity, but upon taking the class becomes self-conscious about her ability among the other students and thus not able to stretch her creative wings. One day, she is the only student that shows up for class and the instructor decides to change the rules. She must use all of the materials available to her in this class to design a collage. This woman has a peak creative experience, a sense of joy, and high-perceived freedom and intrinsic motivation; yet, there were constraints to her activity. Sometimes our constraints allow us to be creative. It, ironically, may release us from being overwhelmed by too much freedom.

Future Research

As Roberta Milgram (personal communication, January 23, 2008) has suggested, the areas of creativity and leisure have a vast amount of crossover that has yet to be explored. Research in this area is contingent, however, on the adoption and value of leisure by researchers. Ruth Russell wrote in a personal communication (September 13, 2007):

> The more I reflect on leisure's significance, the more convinced I become that leisure is likely the most vital force in our personal lives, as well as the lives of our communities, nations, and world. Because leisure is individual and collective, vital to survival and frivolous, historical and contemporary, and good and bad, it deserves full measure of our taking it quite seriously.

Richards (2007) stated, "We use our everyday creativity throughout our lives, at work and leisure" (p. 4). Therefore, it is clearly imperative that creativity be understood more as a means of self-expression and fulfillment that makes us human rather than as merely a way to innovate or cope with reality. That which encompasses more than utility and novelty, then, is creative leisure.

Our creative leisure is a means by which we express our personal thoughts, feelings, and needs of our existence. Leisure alone and creativity alone do not implicate this powerful nature. Thus, a greater understanding of how persons actualize creativity is required. How do freedom and constraints factor in the experience? Are there certain activities or domains by which some are more likely to experience creative leisure? Are some people more likely to seek creative leisure, and why? Can creative leisure be quantified? Is creative leisure related to subject well-being and happiness? What is the meaning and reality of creative leisure across the globe and within cultures and subcultures? Do some have more access to creative leisure than others? By asking these questions, we can enhance our understanding of creative leisure and further develop this important, yet to be explored, concept.

My Own Creative Leisure

I personally discovered my own creative leisure as a counselor at a summer camp in the 1990s. For me it was allowing myself to look and feel silly and try new things I had never done, freeing myself by letting go of inhibitions and fear. One of my favorite experiences was writing and performing an operetta at an evening campfire for more than 200 children. This might not be creative leisure for all people, but it was for me and I still try to go back to camp every few years to run a campfire filled with singing and creatively improvised storytelling. This type of experience is vital to me, and I believe a similar type of very personal creative leisure experience can be important for most individuals. In our current paradigm, where economics, and work, and keeping up with the Joneses, seems to be what Americans value the most, I argue that our creative leisure is the force that frees us of this paradigm, and strikes at the heart of our existence, if only in slight moments of escape. This force is vital to our lives and in the defining of our humanity; certainly investigating this aspect of human behavior is critical.

Recommended Readings

Hegarty, C. B. (2009). The value and meaning of creative leisure. *Psychology of Aesthetics, Creativity, and the Arts, 3*, 10–13. doi: 10.1037/a0014879

Hegarty, C. B., & Plucker, J. A. (2012). Creative leisure and self-expression. *The International Journal of Creativity & Problem Solving, 22*, 63–78.

Maslow, A. H. (1959). Creativity in self-actualizing people. In H. H. Anderson (Ed.), *Creativity and its cultivation* (pp. 83–95). New York, NY: Harper & Brothers.

References

Amabile, T. M. (1996). *Creativity in context*. Boulder, CO: Westview Press.

Csikszentmihalyi, M. (1975). *Beyond boredom and anxiety*. San Francisco, CA: Jossey-Bass.

Csikszentmihalyi, M. (1990). *Flow: The psychology of optimal experience*. New York, NY: Harper & Row.

Csikszentmihalyi, M. (1996). *Creativity: Flow and the psychology of discovery and invention*. New York, NY: HarperCollins.

Csikszentmihalyi, M. (1997). *Finding flow*. New York, NY: Basic Books.

Davis, G. (1998). *Creativity is forever* (4th ed.). Dubuque, IA: Kendall/Hunt.

Dumazedier, J. (1967). *Toward a society of leisure*. New York, NY: Free Press.

Fisher, B. J., & Specht, D. K. (1999). Successful aging and creativity in later life. *Journal of Aging Studies, 13*, 457–473.

Henderson, S. J. (2004). Product inventors and creativity: The finer dimensions of enjoyment. *Creativity Research Journal, 16*, 293–312.

Lemons, G. (2005). When the horse drinks: Enhancing everyday creativity using elements of improvisation. *Creativity Research Journal, 17*, 25–36.

Maslow, A. H. (1959). Creativity in self-actualizing people. In H. H. Anderson (Ed.), *Creativity and its cultivation* (pp. 83–95). New York, NY: Harper & Brothers.

Maslow, A. H. (1963). The creative attitude. *The Structurist, 3*, 4–10.

Nash, J. B. (1953). *Philosophy of leisure and recreation*. St. Louis, MO: C. V. Mosby.

Neulinger, J. (1974). *The psychology of leisure: Research approaches to the study of leisure*. Springfield, IL: Charles C. Thomas.

Plucker, J. A., Beghetto, R. A., & Dow, G. T. (2004). Why isn't creativity more important to educational psychologists? Potentials, pitfalls, and future directions in creativity research. *Educational Psychologist, 39*, 83–96.

Richards, R. (2007). Everyday creativity: Our hidden potential. In R. Richards (Ed.), *Everyday creativity* (pp. 25–53). Washington, DC: American Psychological Association.

Runco, M. A. (1996). Personal creativity: Definition and developmental issues. *New Directions for Child Development, 72*, 3–30.

Runco, M. A. (2005). Motivation, competence, and creativity. In A. J. Elliot & C. S. Dweck (Eds.), *Handbook of competence and motivation* (pp. 609–623). New York, NY: Guilford Press.

Runco, M. A. (2007). To understand is to create: An epistemological perspective on human nature and personal creativity. In R. Richards (Ed.), *Everyday creativity* (pp. 91–107). Washington, DC: American Psychological Association.

Runco, M. A., & Pritzker, S. R. (1999). *Encyclopedia of creativity*. San Diego, CA: Academic Press.

Russ, S. W. (1993). *Affect and creativity: The role of affect and play in the creative process*. Hillsdale, NJ: Lawrence Erlbaum.

Russell, R. V. (2004). *Pastimes: The context of contemporary leisure* (3rd ed.). Champaign, IL: Sagamore.

Simonton, D. K. (1991). Creative productivity through the adult years. In H. R. Moody (Ed.), *Aging: Concepts and controversies* (pp. 95–100). Thousand Oaks, CA: Pine Forge Press.

Stebbins, R. A. (2001). The costs and benefits of hedonism: Some consequences of taking casual leisure seriously. *Leisure Studies, 20,* 305–309.

Sternberg, R. J. (1999). *Handbook of creativity.* Cambridge, England: Cambridge University Press.

Tinsley, H. E. A., & Kass, R. A. (1978). Leisure activities and need satisfaction: A replication and extension. *Journal of Leisure Research, 10,* 191–202.

About the Editor

Jonathan Plucker, Ph.D., is the Julian C. Stanley Endowed Professor of Talent Development at Johns Hopkins University, where he works in the School of Education and Center for Talented Youth. Previously, he was Raymond Neag Endowed Professor of Education at the University of Connecticut and Professor of Educational Psychology and Cognitive Science at Indiana University, where he was the founding director of the Center for Evaluation and Education Policy. He graduated with a B.S. in chemistry education and M.A. in educational psychology from the University of Connecticut, then after briefly teaching at an elementary school in New York, received his Ph.D. in educational psychology from the University of Virginia. His research examines creativity, education policy, and talent development, with more than 300 publications to his credit. His books include *Critical Issues and Practices in Gifted Education* with Carolyn Callahan (Prufrock Press), *Intelligence 101* with Amber Esping (Springer), *Essentials of Creativity Assessment* with James Kaufman and John Baer (Wiley), and *Excellence Gaps in Education: Expanding Opportunities for Talented Students* with Scott Peters (Harvard Education Press). Professor Plucker has worked on projects involving educators, schools, and students in all 50 states and several other countries. He is a Fellow of the American Psychological Association and American Association for the Advancement of Science and recipient of the 2001 Daniel E. Berlyne Award for research by a junior scholar and 2012 Rudolf Arnheim Award for Outstanding Achievement in Psychology and the Arts from APA and the 2007 E. Paul Torrance Award for creativity research and 2013 Distinguished Scholar Award from the National Association for Gifted Children.

About the Authors

Ronald A. Beghetto serves as professor of educational psychology in the Neag School of Education at the University of Connecticut. His research focuses on promoting creativity in everyday teaching, learning, and leadership practices. A central theme of his work is helping students and educators reclaim creativity in schools and classrooms. His work also highlights how making slight changes to existing teaching, learning, and leadership practices can result in new ways of thinking and acting. Dr. Beghetto is a Fellow of the American Psychological Association and serves as the Editor of the *Journal of Creative Behavior*.

David H. Cropley is associate professor of engineering innovation at the University of South Australia. Dr. Cropley is author of four books, including *Creativity in Engineering: Novel Solutions to Complex Problems* (Academic Press, 2015) and *The Psychology of Innovation in Organizations* (Cambridge University Press, 2015). His research interests include the measurement of product creativity, the assessment of the innovation capacity of organizations, and creativity in the context of crime and terrorism.

Richard N. Dino is associate professor of management department at the University of Connecticut School of Business and Director of the University's Innovation Quest Program. He served as the Founding Executive Director of Connecticut Center for Entrepreneurship and Innovation (CCEI), launched the CCEI's Innovation Accelerator, was codirector of the Innovation Research Experience for Undergraduates (iREU) Program in the Chemical and Biomolecular Engineering Department in the UConn School of Engineering, where he also was co-director of the Entrepreneurial Senior Design Program. He has extensive experience as an entrepreneur and worked for a number of global enterprises.

Gayle T. Dow is an associate professor of psychology and Director of the Creativity Research Lab at Christopher Newport University. She received her Ph.D. from Indiana University in Educational Psychology and currently teaches courses in psychology, gifted education, and creative thinking. She has authored several articles and book chapters on methods to foster critical and creative thinking, which have appeared in *Creativity Research Journal*, the *Journal of Educational Psychology*, *Educational Psychologist*, and *Virginia Journal of Educators*.

Amber Esping is an associate professor of educational psychology at Texas Christian University (TCU) in Fort Worth. Her scholarship focuses on the history of (1) intelligence theory and testing and (2) existential psychology applied to academic contexts. She is coauthor (with Jonathan Plucker) of *Intelligence 101*, and author of a forthcoming book, *The Well-Lit Room*.

Gregory J. Feist currently is professor of psychology in personality psychology at San Jose State University and director of the M.A. Program in Research and Experimental Psychology. He is widely published in the psychology of creativity and psychology of science. He received his Ph.D. in 1991 from the University of California at Berkeley. He is coauthor of the introductory text *Psychology: Perspectives and Connections* (McGraw-Hill).

Richard Florida is Director of Cities at the Martin Prosperity Institute at the University of Toronto's Rotman School of Management. He is also global research professor at New York University, and senior editor for *The Atlantic*, where he cofounded and serves as Editor-at-Large for *CityLab*. He is the author of *The Rise of the Creative Class*.

Amy K. Graefe's interest in creativity grew from her 23 years as a gifted education coordinator in Greeley, CO, with experience at all levels K–12. Her research interests include creativity in the content areas, the impact of Advanced Placement courses on Latina high school students, and the perceptions of gifted high school students on self-determination and empowerment. She is also an adjunct professor at the University of Northern Colorado in gifted and talented education.

Magdalena G. Grohman's research background is in creative thinking, problem solving, and education. She is an associate director of the Center for Values in Medicine, Science and Technology, University of Texas at Dallas. Since 2007, Dr. Grohman has been leading Summer Seminars on creative thinking for teachers at the Dallas Museum of Art. In the fall of 2010, together with the DMA's Center for Creative Connections staff and visiting artists, she started *Think Creatively!* workshops for the Dallas Museum of Art visitors. She received her M.A. and Ph.D. in psychology from Jagiellonian University in Krakow, Poland.

C. Boyd Hegarty received his Ph.D. from Indiana University and has taught and done research in higher education for more than 10 years. His scholarly pursuits included creative leisure, creativity and summer camps, and gender inclusion. He is currently working as an independent consultant and researcher.

James C. Kaufman is a professor of educational psychology at the Neag School of Education at the University of Connecticut. He is the author/editor of more than 35 books, including *Creativity 101* (2nd ed., 2016), *Cambridge Handbook of Creativity* (2010), and *Teaching for Creativity in the Common Core Classroom* (2014). A former president of American Psychological Association's (APA's) Division 10, he has won NAGC's Torrance Award, APA's Berlyne and Farnsworth Awards, and Mensa's research award.

Alexis W. Lee is a first-year graduate student in the Clinical Psychology Ph.D. program at Case Western Reserve University. After graduating from Hamilton College, she worked as a research associate at Haskins Laboratories. She works with Dr. Sandra Russ to understand how pretend play is linked to creativity and emotional well-being. She is interested in how anxiety and poor coping skills can be alleviated through play to help children regulate their emotions more effectively.

Richard Madden is Strategy Partner at Bartle Bogle Hegarty London, one of the world's most awarded advertising agencies. A graduate of Oxford University, he has worked in the communications industry for more than 25 years, first as a copywriter and then as a strategist. His clients include banks, retailers, and automakers. While not planning communications strategies, Richard writes and lectures on the link between creativity and advertising effectiveness, a subject he is especially passionate about.

Timothy J. Magner's 25-year career in educational technology includes serving as director of the U.S. Department of Education's Office of Educational Technology, Executive Director for the Partnership for 21st Century Skills, Executive Director of K12 Education for Microsoft, the director of the Schools Interoperability Framework, as well as a classroom teacher and district technology leader. He earned his B.A. from William & Mary, his M.Ed. from Harvard University, and his Ed.D. from Pepperdine University.

David Neustadter is Senior Vice President of Production for New Line Cinema. He has executive produced several hit movies, including *The Conjuring*, *Annabelle*, *We're the Millers*, and *A Nightmare on Elm Street*. Neustadter began his career at New Line in 2003 as a development intern. In 2011, Neustadter was selected by *The Hollywood Reporter* for its "Next Gen" list of studio executives 35 and under. He is a graduate of Indiana University.

Stuart N. Omdal was an elementary teacher for 15 years and now is in his 22nd year as a professor of gifted education at the University of Northern Colorado, where he is the director of Summer Enrichment Programs and of the Center for the Education & Study of Gifted, Talented, Creative Learners at UNC. His professional interests include creativity in education, twice-exceptionality, and underachievement of students from nondominant cultural and language groups.

Meihua Qian is an assistant professor of educational psychology at Clemson University and has been studying creativity for more than 10 years in both the United States and China. She received her Ph.D. in educational psychology and inquiry methodology from Indiana University.

Roni Reiter-Palmon is the Varner Professor of Industrial/Organizational (I/O) Psychology and the director of the I/O Psychology Graduate Program at the University of Nebraska at Omaha. She received her Ph.D. in I/O Psychology from George Mason University. Her research focuses on creativity and innovation in the workplace, development of leadership and creative problem solving skills, and leading creative individuals. She is the editor of *Psychology of Creativity, Aesthetics and the Arts*, and serves on the editorial boards of several business, organizational behavior, leadership, and psychology journals.

Ryan P. Royston is a Ph.D. student at the University of Nebraska at Omaha. His research interests and current projects include creative mindsets and creative performance, emerging leadership, and leader and follower identity integration. He is also an associate with the Center for Applied Psychological Services, the organizational consulting arm of the I/O Psychology program at the University of Nebraska at Omaha.

Mark A. Runco has studied creativity and innovation for 35 years. He is professor at the University of Georgia, as well as Distinguished Research Fellow at the American Institute for Behavioral Research and Technology. His Ph.D. is in cognitive psychology from the Claremont Graduate School. He is founding editor of the *Creativity Research Journal* and coeditor of the *Encyclopedia of Creativity* (1999, 2011). His textbook *Creativity: Research, Development, and Practice* (Academic Press, 2010, 2014) has been translated into eight languages.

Sandra W. Russ, a clinical child psychologist, is Distinguished University Professor of Psychology at Case Western Reserve University and holds the Louis D. Beaumont University Professor chair. Her research program has focused on relationships among pretend play, creativity, and adaptive functioning in children. She is author of *Affect and Creativity: The Role of Affect and Play in the Creative Process* (Lawrence Erlbaum, 1993), *Play in Child Development and Psychotherapy: Toward Empirically Supported Practice* (Lawrence Erlbaum, 2004), and *Pretend Play in Childhood: Foundation of Adult Creativity* (APA, 2014).

Dean Keith Simonton is Distinguished Professor of Psychology at the University of California, Davis. His honors include the William James Book Award, the Sir Francis Galton Award for Outstanding Contributions to the Study of Creativity, the Rudolf Arnheim Award for Outstanding Contributions to Psychology and the Arts, the George A. Miller Outstanding Article Award, the Theoretical Innovation Prize in Personality and Social Psychology, the E. Paul Torrance Award for Creativity, and three Mensa Awards for Excellence in Research.

Cynthia Sifonis was trained in the Creative Cognition approach to examining creativity at Texas A&M University. She has since used those skills to examine how viewing examples constrains creativity and how conceptual distance affects the creativity of ideas generated through analogy. She shares her love of creativity by teaching creativity in the classroom, running creativity-enhancing analogy workshops for local automobile manufacturers, and participating in events such as the "Einstein Moments" booth at the Electric Forest Festival.

Heather T. Snyder is professor of psychology at Edinboro University of Pennsylvania where she has taught since 2002. Her research focuses on creativity in college students, including creativity measurement, factors associated with creative performance, creative self-perceptions, creative teaching, and teaching creativity. Snyder leads a Creativity Research Group with undergraduate student research assistants. She is currently the treasurer for APA Division 10: Society for the Psychology of Aesthetics, Creativity and the Arts.

Thomas B. Ward is professor of psychology at the University of Alabama. He has conducted externally funded research and published extensively on the nature of concepts, including how they are acquired, structured, combined, and used in creative and noncreative endeavors. He also served as editor of the *Journal of Creative Behavior* from 1999 to 2013. His most recent line of research examines creativity and problem solving in virtual environments.

Index